Fodor's 89
London

Fodor's Travel Publications, Inc.
New York and London

ISBN 0–679–01670–8

Fodor's London

Editor: Richard Moore
Assistant Editors: Caz Philcox, Judy Tither
Area Editor: Christopher Pick
Editorial Contributors: Jamie Ambrose, Sheila Brownlee, Patrick Conner, Avril Cridlan, John Elsom, John Lahr, Mark Lewes, Ann Saunders, Hicky Taylor
Art Director: Fabrizio La Rocca
Cartographer: David Lindroth
Illustrator: Karl Tanner
Cover Photograph: Stroheim/West Light

Design: Vignelli Associates

Special Sales

Fodor's Travel Publications are available at special discounts for bulk purchases (100 copies or more) for sales promotions or premiums. Special editions, including personalized covers, excerpts of existing guides, and corporate imprints, can be created in large quantities for special needs. For more information write to Special Marketing, Fodor's Travel Publications, 201 East 50th Street, New York, NY 10022. Enquiries from the United Kingdom should be sent to Merchandise Division, Random House UK Ltd, 30–32 Bedford Square, London WC1B 3SG.

MANUFACTURED IN THE UNITED STATES OF AMERICA

10 9 8 7 6 5 4 3 2 1

Contents

Maps

Foreword

This is an exciting time for Fodor's, as it begins a three-year program to rewrite, reformat, and redesign all 140 of its guides. Here are just a few of the exciting new features:

★ Brand-new computer-generated maps locating all the top attractions, hotels, restaurants, and shops

★ A unique system of numbers and legends to help readers move effortlessly between text and maps

★ A new star rating system for hotels and restaurants

★ Restaurant reviews by major food critics around the world

★ Stamped, self-addressed postcards, bound into every guide, give readers an opportunity to help evaluate hotels and restaurants

★ Complete page redesign for instant retrieval of information

★ ITINERARIES—The experts help you decide where to go and how to organize your time

★ FODOR'S CHOICE—Our favorite museums, beaches, cafés, romantic hideaways, festivals, and more

★ HIGHLIGHTS '89—An insider's look at the most important developments in tourism during the past year

★ TIME OUT—The best and most convenient lunch stops along the shopping and exploring routes

★ A 10-page Traveler's Menu and Phrase Guide in all major foreign guides

★ Exclusive background essays create a powerful portrait of each destination

★ A minijournal for travelers to keep track of their own itineraries and addresses

While every care has been taken to assure the accuracy of the information in this guide, the passage of time will always bring change, and consequently, the publisher cannot accept responsibility for errors that may occur.

All prices and opening times quoted here are based on information available to us at press time. Hours and admission fees may change, however, and the prudent traveler will avoid inconvenience by calling ahead.

Fodor's wants to hear about your travel experiences, both pleasant and unpleasant. When a hotel or restaurant fails to live up to its billing, let us know and we will investigate the complaint and revise our entries where the facts warrant it.

Send your letters to the editors of Fodor's Travel Publications, 201 E. 50th Street, New York, NY 10022. European readers may prefer to write to Fodor's Travel Publications, 30–32 Bedford Square, London, WC1B 3SG, England.

Highlights '89 and Fodor's Choice

Highlights '89

A few statistics to start with. The London Tourist Board celebrated its 25th birthday in 1988 and they marked the event by recording the changes in the capital and its visitors since 1963. In 1963, 1.6 million visitors came to London and spent about £9 million (people didn't keep track then of the cash flow as they do now!). In 1987, nine million visitors came from overseas and spent £3,650 million. Currently over 200,000 Londoners earn their living from tourism.

If you are wondering what the best thing to see in London is, here is how other visitors rate the available attractions. The top ten are the Tower of London 72%, the British Museum 51%, the National Gallery 49%, Madame Tussaud's 47%, the Tate Gallery 35%, the Victoria and Albert Museum 30%, the Trocadero 28%, the Science Museum 22%, the Natural History Museum 22%, and the Zoo 18%.

And while the visitors are discovering these attractions, how did they rate the Londoners they met? Eighty two percent of overseas visitors found them friendly (slightly less than in previous years), and only 3% found Londoners positively unfriendly.

After some years when, touristically speaking, the capital city was in the doldrums, with few new facilities for the ever-increasing crowds of visitors, London is now sprucing up its image. New museums and specialty shopping areas are opening and existing institutions are modernizing and improving their image. Londoners and visitors alike continue to await signs of improvement in transportation, however, long one of London's weakest spots, although even here there are one or two pieces of encouraging news to report.

Much of the good news is taking place in Docklands, the area east of Tower Bridge, on each side of the river. Due to open in 1989 is the new **Design Museum,** which promises some exciting ways of displaying good consumer design. The Museum is part of the **Butler's Wharf** development, which, when it is finished in about 1990, will have specialty shops and restaurants designed to rival Covent Garden, the trend-setting newcomer of the early 1980s. On the north bank of the river, **Tobacco Dock** is another large-scale shopping development designed to entice tourists away from the traditional haunts further west. The Docklands Light Railway, which started running in fall 1987, is already proving a fun way of exploring Docklands and of reaching Greenwich rapidly. We can expect many more tourist developments down the Thames during the next few years.

The south bank of the river, for years a run-down area with little of interest to the visitor, is looking increasingly lively—and so for this edition of the guide we have introduced a new exploration route. This passes **Hay's Galleria,** the new shopping area west of Tower Bridge; established sights such as *H.M.S. Belfast,* **Southwark Cathedral,** and the **Shakespeare Globe Museum;** the new **Museum of the Moving Image,** the latest of the attractions in the South Bank Arts Complex; and the **Museum**

of Garden History, one of the many specialist museums flourishing in London. In addition to the inherent interest of all these places, the walk offers fine prospects across the river in St. Paul's Cathedral and the Palace of Westminster.

New attractions opening in late 1988 and during 1989 are: **Royal Britain,** which re-creates the story of England's royal families from the earliest days to the present; the delightful small **Fan Museum** in Greenwich; and the **Bank of England Museum** in the City. Other established museums undertaking a major renovation of their collections include the **Imperial War Museum** and the **Victoria & Albert Museum.**

At the same time, we are sad to report that more and more of London's major national museums are starting to charge visitors for admission. Both the **Imperial War Museum** and the **Science Museum** have announced that charges will be levied during 1989; the **Natural History Museum** and the **National Maritime Museum** already charge for entry, while the **Victoria & Albert Museum** askes for a "voluntary contribution."

Traveling about London is becoming increasingly frustrating. After several years of decline, partly linked with deliberately low fares (now abandoned) on buses and underground trains, traffic levels are rising, leading to traffic jams, and slow journeys by bus and taxi. The underground, too, is ever more crowded, and London Regional Transport's management seems unable, or unwilling, to improve train frequencies and traveling conditions—despite the bad publicity they received during the public enquiry into the disastrous fire in fall 1987 at King's Cross station in which 31 people lost their lives. One problem is that L.R.T. receives far less subsidy from public funds than almost any other major rapid transportation system in the western world.

One piece of good news on the transport front is the opening of the Thames Line's high-speed riverbus service along the river, with regular services throughout the day between Chelsea and east of Tower Bridge; there is a promise to extend the service to Greenwich during 1989.

With one exception, there have been no new hotels built in London since 1976. However, over 26 luxury hotels have recently been extensively refurbished. This trend is likely to continue, for the cost of land for redevelopment in central London makes building hotels an unviable project. The old Piccadilly, now the **Meridien Piccadilly,** was totally remodeled at a cost of around £16 million, and reopened in 1986. The classic **Dorchester** will be closed throughout 1989 for a radical facelift. The **London Hilton** has recently been renovated, and the **Charing Cross Hotel** is in the process of updating as we go to press. The **Goring** is reaching the end of an expensive redecorating scheme, which has resulted in some very lavish bedrooms and a repelling pink foyer.

The great hotel news, though, is that within the next few years the derelict St. George's Hospital at Hyde Park Corner, across from Apsley House and the gardens of Buckingham Palace, is to be turned into the exclusive **St. George's Hotel** at a reputed cost of £100 million. In this way London is guarding its atmospheric hostelries, and avoiding the faceless international design that afflicts so many city hotels.

Visitors who in the past have found London's **pub opening times** bewilderingly frustrating can now take heart. In July '88 the laws were revised, and now pubs can open from 11 AM to 11 PM on weekdays, thus doing away with the afternoon closure.

The distant past has been to the forefront of people's minds in London in the last few months. Construction work in the capital still turns up fascinating archaeological finds, and in '88 two major discoveries were made, one from Roman times, the other medieval. Historians have always known that Roman Londinium must have had a **Circus**—all provincial cities did—but they never managed to pinpoint its position. Digging at Guildhall Yard, right in the heart of London's most historic area, revealed substantial traces of part of the foundations for a Circus, as well as other Roman buildings. As a result, archaeologists have had to readjust their ideas about the layout of Londinium.

Nearer our own time, the foundation of a palace, **The Rosary Palace,** belonging to Edward II, and built in 1325, has come to view on the South Bank, during work on the construction of Hays Wharf. Digging nearby also revealed the site of Sir John Fastolf's house. He was the model for Shakespeare's Falstaff.

On a final historical note, 1988 marked the 400th anniversary of the Defeat of the Spanish Armada, and the foiling by Elizabeth I's fleet—considerably aided by the weather—of the invasion attempt. The year was marked with pageants, exhibitions, and firework displays. With a history like hers, London always finds something to celebrate.

Fodor's Choice

While no two people ever agree on what makes a perfect vacation, it's always fun to find out what others think. Here are a few choice ideas to enhance your visit to London. For more details on them, refer to the appropriate sections of this guidebook.

Views

From Waterloo Bridge at dusk, across to St. Paul's

The city seen from Parliament Hill Fields on a bright day

Down the Mall to Buckingham Palace, from underneath Admiralty Arch

The towers of Whitehall seen from the bridge over the lake in St. James's Park

Greenwich Royal Naval Hospital, viewed from Island Gardens, across the Thames

The Houses of Parliament, floodlit, seen across the river from St. Thomas's Hospital

Walks

Across Kensington Gardens, Hyde Park, and St. James's Park—from Kensington Palace to the Horse Guards

Along the South Bank of the Thames, from Lambeth Palace to Blackfriars Bridge

An upriver walk from Chiswick Mall to Hammersmith Bridge

Across Hampstead Heath, from Hampstead Village to Kenwood

Gardens

Queen Mary's Rose Garden, Regent's Park, in early summer

The Little Cloisters of Westminster Abbey

The formal gardens of the Dutch House, at Kew

The Knot Garden at Hampton Court, plus the spring tulips in the main gardens there

The Chelsea Flower Show, Royal Hospital Chelsea, in May

Monuments

The Albert Memorial, Kensington Gardens

The Charlie Chaplin statue in Leicester Square

The Elgin Marbles in the British Museum

The monument to the Great Fire of London

The statue of Winston Churchill in Parliament Square

Museums

The Wallace Collection, Manchester Square

Sir John Soane's Museum, Lincoln's Inn Fields

The Clore Galleries (Turner Collection) at the Tate

The Linley Sambourne House, Stafford Terrace

The British Museum, with plenty of time on your hands

Times to Treasure

Tea at the Hyde Park Hotel

The last night of the Proms in September

The Oxford and Cambridge Boat Race from the towpath, end of March

Speakers' Corner, Hyde Park, on a Sunday morning

The State Opening of Parliament

Shopping

Saturday in the Portobello Road Market

The January sale at Harrods

Wandering round the Covent Garden area

Looking for presents in the General Trading Store on Sloane Street

Secondhand book trawling on Charing Cross Road

Hotels

The Berkeley (*Very Expensive*)

Blakes (*Very Expensive*)

Brown's (*Very Expensive*)

Eleven Cadogan Gardens (*Expensive*)

Number Sixteen (*Expensive*)

The Portobello (*Moderate*)

Prince (*Moderate*)

The Vicarage (*Inexpensive*)

Restaurants

Le Gavroche (*Very Expensive*)

The Meridien Oak Room (*Expensive*)

The Greenhouse (*Expensive*)

Chiang Mai (*Moderate*)

Joe Allen's (*Moderate*)

St. Quentin (*Moderate*)

Geale's (*Inexpensive*)

Pubs

The Cheshire Cheese

The Dove, Hammersmith (by the river)

The Lamb

The Lamb and Flag

The Prospect of Whitby (by the river)

Central London

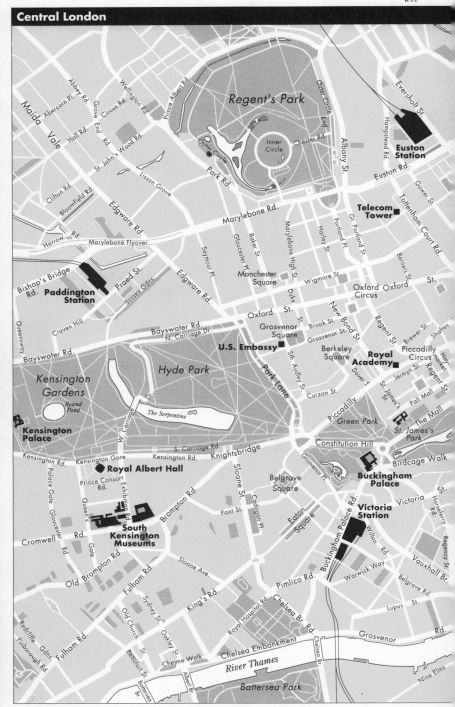

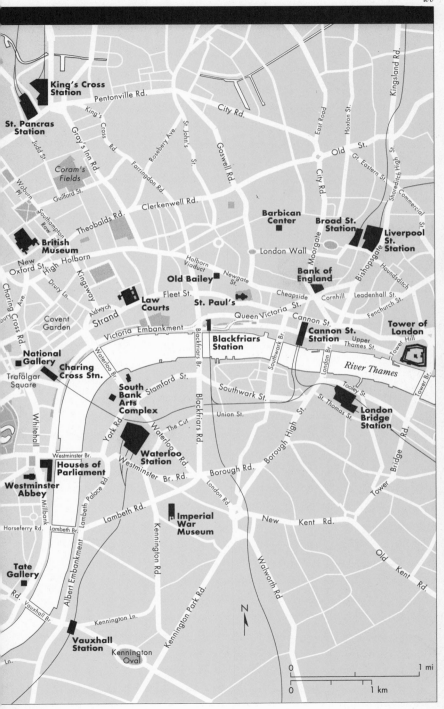

World Time Zones

MONDAY
SUNDAY

+12 +13   -9

International Date Line

-10

-11

-11   -10

+11

+12

-7

-8   -7

-5   -4

-7

-8   -6

-5

-6

-4   -3

-5

-4

-3

-3

+11   +12   -11   -10   -9   -8   -7   -6   -5   -4   -3   -2

Numbers below vertical bands relate each zone to Greenwich Mean Time (0 hrs.).
Local times frequently differ from these general indications,
as indicated by light-face numbers on map.

Auckland, **1**	Denver, **8**	New York City, **16**	Rio de Janeiro, **23**
Honolulu, **2**	Chicago, **9**	Washington, DC, **17**	Buenos Aires, **24**
Anchorage, **3**	Dallas, **10**	Miami, **18**	Reykjavik, **25**
Vancouver, **4**	New Orleans, **11**	Bogotá, **19**	Dublin, **26**
San Francisco, **5**	Mexico City, **12**	Lima, **20**	London (Greenwich), **27**
Los Angeles, **6**	Toronto, **13**	Santiago, **21**	Lisbon, **28**
Edmonton, **7**	Ottawa, **14**	Caracas, **22**	Algiers, **29**
	Montreal, **15**		Paris, **30**
			Zürich, **31**

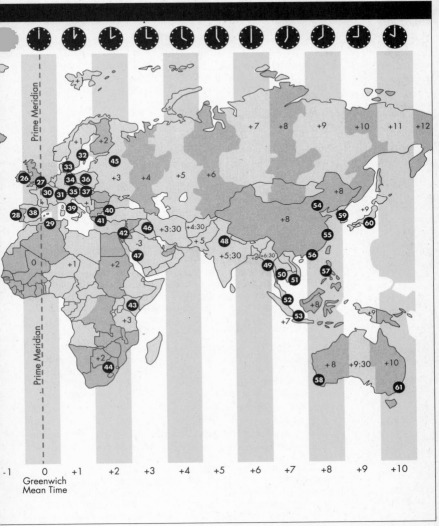

Stockholm, **32**	Rome, **39**	Mecca, **47**	Hong Kong, **56**
Copenhagen, **33**	Istanbul, **40**	Delhi, **48**	Manila, **57**
Berlin, **34**	Athens, **41**	Rangoon, **49**	Perth, **58**
Vienna, **35**	Jerusalem, **42**	Bangkok, **50**	Seoul, **59**
Warsaw, **36**	Nairobi, **43**	Saigon, **51**	Tokyo, **60**
Budapest, **37**	Johannesburg, **44**	Singapore, **52**	Sydney, **61**
Madrid, **38**	Moscow, **45**	Djakarta, **53**	
	Baghdad, **46**	Beijing, **54**	
		Shanghai, **55**	

Introduction

by John Lahr

*Mr. Lahr has
written* Notes on
a Cowardly Lion,
*the life of his
father, Bert
Lahr, and* Prick
Up Your Ears,
*the biography of
Joe Orton, the
English
playwright,
which is now a
successful film.
He has lived in
London for 17
years.*

I live at the top of an Edwardian house that looks south from Hampstead down over all of central London. At night, when the wind blows and the clouds roll past the dormer window, it feels like being on the prow of a ship. London is blinking in front of me. I can see St. Paul's Cathedral and, panning over church steeples and the treetops, the Telecom Tower, Big Ben, and the spires of Westminster.

The metropolis is only 15 minutes away; but on my balcony I can hear the owl hooting in the garden and I can see the poplars bend in the chill breeze. I have lived in this house for a decade now. My son was born downstairs in the bedroom. My wife and I have grown into middle age here. The vista has been the background for all these changes: at once unvarying and always surprising. I find this comforting. I never expected to be an expatriate.

The London sky has been a continuing astonishment to me. It seems so close. It makes me feel rooted to the earth. In Manhattan, where I'm from, I had to stick my head out of the window and gaze up 12 stories to see if the sun was shining. The plants in the courtyard were green all year round since plastic knows no season. "You've got to come and see my house. It's just like New York," said a friend, recently transplanted to California. "I've got trees in my garden that *die!*"

After a while, the natural world becomes a memory to the New Yorker. Bustling from one controlled environment to another, air-conditioned in summer and central-heated in winter, the four seasons to a New Yorker are more apt to suggest a restaurant than the rhythms of life. Inevitably, like any species adapting to a harsh and unpromising environment, the New Yorker evolves a tough carapace to survive.

But London, like the soft light that defines it, is a gentler world, built to a more human scale. Londoners are suspicious of high-rise buildings, which at first surprised me. But now I know why. They want that connection to the earth and the solace of making their patch beautiful. My patch is a terrace of houses set off from Englands Lane, a busy thoroughfare that looks surprisingly as it did at the turn of the century. A canopy of trees lines the private road which at night is lit by electrified Victorian street lamps.

We don't own a garden, but all the houses have them. I've played croquet and soccer, picked plums and chased cats in the green expanses behind the houses. I see now what I didn't see at first, that the London garden is a symbol of British civility: it slows the Londoner down, forcing him to attend to the glory of the world and not just his own glory. When I look at the lane, I'm reminded that New York is for work and London is for living.

The New Yorker scrambles to survive in spite of the city, which exists as a kind of obstacle course to be negotiated each day. London is a sprawl of overlapping villages which seems to have evolved for the benefit of its citizens rather than big business or developers. Even if private space is small and at a premium, public space is capacious and well-planned.

I've always loved London's parks and spent a lot of time in them. My courting days in the early '60s were spent in St. James's Park, feeding ducks from the bridge that crosses the bird sanctuary pond and explaining to Anthea why I couldn't marry her. I fortunately lost the argument, but not my affection for the place. The night I finally asked for her hand, I didn't get it. I found myself on the street at midnight but, without luggage, no hotel would take me. So I slept in a deck chair by St. James's Park bandstand. Police, looking very tall from where I sat, moved me on in the middle of the night. It began to rain. I ended the evening curled around the toilet bowl in the last stall of the Hilton's men's room.

I waited in the park the next morning for the right hour to return. I sat next to a natty Jewish man who confided he was a fence for stolen goods. I told him my story. He advised me to put a handkerchief in the breast pocket of my three-piece suit. He offered me a piquant bit of advice. "Remember," he said, "Look British, think Yiddish."

My son Christopher now comes to the park with his grandmother to tempt the gulls from the very spot where we debated our future, and I'm still trying to put names to all the species of fowl that are just birds to me. I still bring visitors to the park to look at the bird sanctuary and the odd spectacle of Whitehall's roofs lit up like exotic minarets.

The parks supply the city with an element of calm and care. Londoners seem to take them for granted; but, coming from a society where every pleasure must be bought, the parks seem to me munificent. Hampstead Heath is both my sport and my refuge.

I moved to London to convalesce from ambition. In New York, I was working but not living; in London, there is much more time to work and to play.

The Heath keeps me playful. Chris and I have bushwacked through thickets in long games of hide-and-seek, gone blackberrying, jumped off bales of summer hay, tried vainly to get kites to fly, sprinted through innumerable games of soccer. We hold Chris's birthday on the Heath, a football match with 20 kids, three referees, one yellow card, and popcorn. Sometimes we stop to watch other people play. Once we saw the Orange People, the followers of Bhagwan Shree Rajneesh, in a terrific game. I remember one *sannyasin* yelling to his teammate, "Get stuck in *Pradhartha!*" And another time, after I'd retrieved a ball, the player said: "Thanks, Dad." I needed to sit down after that.

The run-up to Christmas in London is particularly enjoyable. Pumpkins have in the past few years become easily available, and so Halloween is another ritual occasion to infect the English with some American pleasures. The carving of the pumpkin, the baked seeds, even pumpkin soup delight our London friends; but they flunk the notion of trick-or-treat. The sight of troops of children waiting outside their doors for treats of candy doesn't capture the British sense of fun.

So we put jack-o'-lanterns on the garden wall, ghoulish masks in the trees, let the kids pelt each other with socks filled with flour and serve up jacket potatoes and coconut ice, a Yorkshire delicacy for "mischief night," the antecedent to America's Halloween.

Once, waiting to buy a pumpkin, an English lady accidentally stepped on my foot and apologized. "Sorry," she said, "there's a limit to space." English life is about limits—of class, of wealth, of power, of sex, of space. And this sense of boundaries feeds the pleasure the Londoner takes in his festivals, especially Christmas. I spend a lot of time attending pantomimes around Christmas. As one glimpse of a pantomime dame will show, pantomime is about teasing boundaries: for two hours the world is turned upside down. Then, the habitual irony with which the British display their skepticism about the future is replaced by the brazenness of carnival. Last winter, on my way through Covent Garden, I stopped to watch a punk, street-theater version of *Cinderella*, where a bored prince was musing in song about the excitement of other local nobility:

Prince Andrew is a photographer,
Prince Andrew drives a helicopter,
Prince Andrew won the Falklands War.

Part of the ritual of my Christmas is the Lisson Grove Market. I miss the sludge of New York street talk, but the London vendors have a jaunty patter all their own. "Never mind £35. Never mind £22. I'll make you the envy of everybody here for £10," says my favorite spieler, a Cockney selling cut-rate Christmas presents from the back of his van. "Let's see those hands. . . . Too late, too late, will be the cry, the fellah with the bargains has passed you by."

Crowds press near the truck as he asks them to hold their £10 notes over their heads. The theatrical touch whips up excitement in the market. His riff is always the same: "To see who's kidding and who's bidding, to separate the needy from the greedy. . . . If I went much lower, I'd be in Tottenham bloody underground." He holds up the china tea set and the Kitchen Devil knives, joking as he hands them down to the punters while his sidekick collects the cash. "We take any money here," he says, "except matrimony."

Markets make shopping a social event, part of the routine of daily London life that brings its communities closer together. In America, the shopping mall and supermarket have helped to strip the cities of local life and contributed to a sense of isolation. London's markets are crucial to its social fabric. Culture is like an ember—it dies on its own and grows in contact with others. At Queen's Crescent, the local market that I reach through a passageway with the graffiti STOP THE WAR, PLEASE, one lady serenaded the line at the "stolen goods stall" with a music hall turn:

How could Red Riding Hood
Have been so very good
And still keep the wolf from the door?

While getting my five pounds of chicken wings, I heard two old dears summarize the rueful tentativeness that characterizes the British and the hard life so many have endured. "At least," said one, "there's light at the end of the tunnel." Her friend shook her head: "The light at the end of the tunnel may be an oncoming train." American optimism is based on myths of abundance; and British skepticism on myths of scarcity.

The London markets offer a happy, modest sense of wellbeing. And if locals don't have much money these days to spend on food they dispense their wit and wisdom generously. "The English don't like friction," said an Irishman, arguing with the flower seller at Queen's Crescent. "Look at their desserts. Suet. Custard. They slide right off the plate."

Often on Saturday afternoon, I work my way down Haverstock Hill, browsing in the bookshops on the way to Camden Market, and hit Inverness Street before the fish shops have rolled down their iron gratings and washed away the pungent aroma of squid and sea bass.

Camden Market, with its spill-over from Dingwalls, tends to be trendier and the gossip more worldly. I heard one harassed filmmaker complaining to Alan Bennett, who moved unnoticed through the crowd: "I've gone from production to retrospective without distribution."

Joe Orton used to move anonymously through Chapel Market in Islington listening to conversations; and I often think of Orton when I take Christwice a week to Anna Scher's extraordinary children's theater, where kids from the age of six learn to express themselves through theater games and improvisation. The streets are meaner here than in Hampstead, the faces more tightly drawn. There's tension in the air, which is why Orton liked it: a world in all its vulgar imperfection. The locals have found wisdom even in this. Watching me replace a mottled melon on her stall, the fruit seller sweetly pointed out: "Things taste better if they've got spots."

Community, my wife is apt to remind me, quoting Dietrich Bonhöffer, "is a place where the connections in our hearts make themselves known in the bonds between people and where the tugging and pulling of these bonds keep opening our hearts." London's greatest gift to me has been in fostering this sense of community, and the opening up of my heart to a notion of individuality more profound than the American's threadbare "destiny of me." In our area of Camden, we know probably 150 people within 15 minutes of our house. Over a period of time, the lives of the people become the fabric of our lives, and ours of theirs.

Like all American overachievers, I was raised with an ambition to be a big fish; but London has taught me the truth of R.H. Tawney's dictum: "Freedom for the pike is death to the minnow." Londoners often discount their city as old, boring, and in decline. "Why do you want to live here?" I'm frequently asked. To them the idea of New York, and the entrepreneurial dynamism it symbolizes, is thrilling. But they mistake panic for energy. A city of aliens, New York reflects the metabolism of the uprooted in search of a destiny.

For all its problems, London is a more benign and progressive place. A society, like a child, cannot grow well with constant anxiety. The achievements of the health service, comprehensive education, and the welfare system reduce in London life the corrosive insecurity that keeps America producing but also keeps it from maturing. In London, I may earn 20 times less than I could in America but the quality of life is 20 times better.

"A person of faith is bound to be a person on the way, a visitor, the eternal sojourner on earth," said one of the ministers at Disciples House, a Christian fellowship where we worship. He was quoting a former dean of Harvard's Divinity School, and the words seemed to speak to the predicament of the expatriate. "His road is permanently venture, it is created under his own feet."

My road, which at first was just a path to my writing desk, now takes me farther afield; to Education Authority meetings about multi-ethnic education and integration of children with special needs into mainstream schools; to Haverstock School where for nine years each Monday evening I've played basketball for the Haverstock Hawks (an ageing jock with a good jump shot but no speed and only a few more years of glory before hanging up my Converse All-Stars); to the Swiss Cottage community center where my wife works. To get to the community center, I walk along Eton Avenue, gazing into the bedsitters with luggage piled on top of dressing tables, reminding me of flight. But the network of our associations roots us to London life in a way that the restless momentum of New York would never allow.

Nothing changes without being unbalanced; and moving to London has provided us with a saner, more moral climate in which to grow as a family. Even with the theater, which I write about for *New Society*, London has provided a kind of continuity I could never find in New York.

I've grown up around theater. It's my heritage; and, to a lesser extent, my living. In New York, theater is dying; but, even in difficult times, London theater is part of the city's notion of civilized life. The stage is still the place where the culture debates itself; where, in Peter Brook's words, we pass the current of civilization to each other. In London, the playwright continues to be the subject of front-page news; and plays get debated in editorials and even in Parliament.

I like the West End. I like its noisy congestion; the salt beef at the Nosh Bar near the Windmill; the smell of duck from Chinatown restaurants. I like walking through Covent Garden at night, when darkness somewhat mutes its renovation and the buskers serenade you with music hall tunes. On the cobbled streets near Drury Lane, a busker gave me a memorable rendition of *I Painted Her:*

Up the middle
And down the back
In every hole
And every crack

Drury Lane is London's oldest theater, the first to be allowed to open after Cromwell's Commonwealth. These streets, which are filled for me with the history of Garrick and Dr. Johnson, also carry sublime memories of Dame Edna, throwing gladioli at the Drury Lane audience and confiding ever so nicely with her music hall panache:

I've felt a strong sensation
Like a supernatural force.
Would I be mistaken or have we had
A kind of intercourse?

Sometimes, on my way to the National Theatre, I go via the Embankment walkway just to listen to the saxophonist wail Dave Brubeck riffs at the passersby. I look forward to these outings at the National and plan for them. Whatever the quality of the play, the walk back over Waterloo Bridge is too spectacular to hurry. The bridge was the first sight I showed

Christopher as a baby when I took him downtown; and usually the first place I bring visitors. "Oh, wow!" I heard one daft American student say, as she swivelled her head from Parliament to the Savoy to the illuminated cupola of St. Paul's. "Just like L.A."

The Thames flows slowly, almost apologetically, through London, carrying with it the dust of centuries. Boats pitch and roll on their moorings; flags snap in the breeze. The scene epitomizes London's combination of action and detachment. The spotlit buildings announce London's power and wealth; but the river promises movement and change. The sight always exhilarates me. I feel far away from the world I first bustled in, but not lonely. Exile, they say, is being separated from your gods. In London, I've found new ones. Due north from the bridge, only a bus ride away, is my balcony, and my sleeping family, and my patch. Home.

1 Planning Your Trip

Before You Go

Government Tourist Offices

Contact the **British Tourist Authority** (BTA) for free information.

In the U.S. 40 W. 57th St., New York, NY 10019, tel. 212/581–4700; John Hancock Center, Suite 3320, 875 N. Michigan Ave., Chicago, IL 60611, tel. 312/787–0490; World Trade Center, 350 S. Figueroa St., Suite 450, Los Angeles, CA 90017, tel. 213/628 –3525; 2305 Cedar Springs Rd., Suite 210, Dallas, TX 75201, tel. 214/720–4040; 2580 Cumberland Pkwy., Suite 470, Atlanta, GA 30339, tel. 404/432–9635.

In Canada. 94 Cumberland St., Suite 600, Toronto, Ontario M5R 3N3, tel. 416/925–6326.

In the U.K. Victoria Station Forecourt, London SW1V 1JT, tel. 01/730–3488.

Tour Groups

Care to sip sherry in the House of Lords, catch hit shows before they cross the Atlantic, or just hop aboard a whistle-stop tour of London's most famous highlights? Then you might want to consider a package tour. Creative itineraries abound, offering access to places you might not be able to get to on your own as well as to the more traditional spots. They also tend to save you some money on airfare and hotels. If group travel is not your cup of tea, look into independent tours, perhaps less intimidating here than in other areas of the world, thanks in part to the absence of a language barrier.

When considering a tour, be sure to find out exactly what expenses are included (particularly tips, taxes, side-trips, additional meals, and entertainment); government ratings of all hotels on the itinerary and the facilities they offer; cancellation policies for both you and for the tour operator; and, if you are traveling alone, what the single supplement is. Most tour operators request that bookings be made through a travel agent—there is no additional charge for doing so. Listed below is a sampling of operators and packages to give you an idea of what is available. Contact your travel agent or the British Tourist Authority for additional resources.

General-Interest Tours **American Express Vacations** (Box 5014, Atlanta, GA 30302, tel. 800/241–1700 or in Georgia, tel. 800/282–0800) is a veritable supermarket of tours—you name it, they've either got it packaged or will customize a package for you.
Maupintour (Box 807, Lawrence, KA 66044, tel. 913/843–1211 or 800/255–4266) offers "London and the Edinburgh Festival," and other packages.
All of the nearly two dozen different tours offered by **Cosmos/Globus Gateway** (150 S. Los Robles Ave., Pasadena, CA 91101, tel. 818/449–0919 or 800/556–5454) take in London's sights along with the rest of the country. **Cosmos/Globus Gateway** (95–25 Queen's Blvd., Rego Park, NY 11375, tel. 718/268–1700) is the more budget-minded of the affiliated companies.
Trafalgar Tours (21 E. 26th St., New York, NY 10010, tel. 212/689–8977 or 800/854–0103) has a "London Theatre Week" with sightseeing and two shows, and a "Garden Tour of Great Brit-

ain" taking in the Glasgow Garden Festival and the Chelsea Flower Show. Trafalgar, which typically serves a clientele aged 45+, also features "Cost Saver" holidays that use tourist class rather than first class hotels to knock a sizeable amount off the trip's tab.

The British Connection (2490 Black Rock Tpke., Suite 240, Fairfield, CT 06430, tel. 203/661–7742 or 800/654–2171) serves up out-of-the-ordinary theater, shopping, and Chelsea Flower Show tours.

Special-Interest Tours
Culture: *Polly Stewart Fritch* (1 Scott La., Greenwich, CT 06830, tel. 203/661–7742) offers "cultural–culinary" tours with cooking demonstrations and behind-the-scenes visits to unique markets. Thanks to some well-placed friends, Fritch's tour also features such extras as an insider's tour of Parliament with time to sip sherry in a private room in the House of Lords.

Stately Homes: *Olson-Travelworld Ltd* (5855 Green Valley Circle, Culver City, CA 90230, tel. 213/670–7100 or 800/421–2255) highlights Britain's regal showplaces in "Stately Homes, Gardens, and Castles."

Christmas: *Olson's* also offers a deluxe holiday package featuring the season's traditional pantomime performances and other special entertainment and cuisine.

Barge Cruising: Drift along the Thames to Oxford and Windsor with *Floating Through Europe* (271 Madison Ave., New York, NY 10016, tel. 212/685–5600).

Sports: *Travel Concepts* (373 Commonwealth Ave., Suite 601, Boston, MA 02115–1815, tel. 617/266–8450) has packages that include a trip to the British Open Golf Tournament and the Royal Regatta at Henley-upon-Thames (an hour outside London).

Singles and Young Couples: *Trafalgar Tours* offers "Club 21–35,"—faster paced tours for travelers unafraid of a little physical activity whether it's bike riding or discoing the night away.

Music: *Dailey-Thorp Travel* (315 W. 57th St., New York, NY 10019, tel. 212/307–1555) offers deluxe opera and music tours such as the "English Festivals Revisited" including concerts and operas in Brighton and Bath as well as London. Itineraries vary according to available performances.

Package Deals for Independent Travelers

British Airways (tel. 800/AIRWAYS) has packages designed for the traveler who doesn't like group travel: you choose the length of stay and pick from hotel and car rental options. Theater packages are also available. **Globus Gateway** *(see* General-Interest Tours) gives you "A Week in London" with a half-day's sightseeing, tickets to a show, and other perks. A one-week or two-week London and Paris package is also available. **American Express** *(see* General-Interest Tours) has four-day and eight-day packages. "The Londoner" from **TWA Getaway Vacations** (tel. 800/GETAWAY) gives you eight days to knock about, theater tickets, and a half-day of sightseeing. **Pan Am Holidays'** "London Center Stage" adds a second night of theater tickets and some additional sightseeing for a bit more money. **CIE Tours** (122 E. 42nd St., New York, NY 10168, tel. 212/972–5735) combines a London city package with self-drive tours of the surrounding country-side.

When to Go

The heaviest tourist season in Britain runs from mid-April to mid-October, with a small peak around Christmas—though the tide never really ebbs away. The spring is the time to see the countryside and the London gardens at their freshest; early summer to catch the roses and full garden splendor; the fall for near ideal exploring conditions. The British take their vacations mainly in July and August, and the resorts are crowded. London in summer, however, though full of visitors, is also full of interesting things to see and do, while the parks and surrounding countryside are perfect for relaxing. The winter can be rather dismal, frequently wet, and usually cold, but all the theaters, concerts, and exhibitions are going full speed.

In the main, the climate is mild, though the weather is changeable and unpredictable, often from hour to hour. London has summer temperatures that can easily be in the mid-80s, and sometimes high humidity too. You should remember that few London buildings have air conditioning, and dress accordingly. The average annual rainfall in London is 23 inches, but who trusts averages?

Average Daily	**Jan.**	43F	6C	**May**	62F	17C	**Sept.**	65F	19C
Maximum and		36	2		47	8		52	11
Minimum	**Feb.**	44F	7C	**June**	69F	20C	**Oct.**	58F	14C
Temperatures		36	2		53	12		46	8
	Mar.	50F	10C	**July**	71F	22C	**Nov.**	50F	10C
		38	3		56	14		42	5
	Apr.	56F	13C	**Aug.**	71F	21C	**Dec.**	45F	7C
		42	6		56	13		38	4

Festivals and Seasonal Events

Top seasonal events in and around London include the Chelsea Flower Show in May, the Queen's official birthday parade in June, Derby Day at Epsom Racecourse in June, Wimbledon Lawn Tennis Championships and Henley Regatta in June, and the City of London Festival in July. Tickets for the prestigious sporting events must be obtained months in advance—check first to see if your travel agent can procure tickets. There is a complete list of ticket agencies in *Britain Events*, free from the British Tourist Authority.

Jan. 4–15: London International Boat Show, the largest boat show in Europe. Earl's Court Exhibition Centre, Warwick Rd., London SW5 9TA, tel. 0932/54511.
Feb. 9–12: Crufts Dog Show, more than 100 pedigree breeds compete to be Top Dog. Earl's Court Exhibition Centre, Warwick Rd., London SW5 9TA, tel. 01/493–6651.
Mar. through Dec: Shakespeare Season, featuring the famous Royal Shakespeare Company at the Memorial Theatre. Stratford-upon-Avon, Warwickshire, CV37 6BB, box office tel. 0789/295623.
Mar. 7–Apr. 2: Daily Mail Ideal Home Exhibition, consumer show of new products and ideas for the home. Earl's Court Exhibition Centre, Warwick Rd., London SW5 9TA, tel. 01/ 222–9341.

Mar. 14–25 and mid-Sept: Chelsea Antiques Fair, a twice-yearly fair with wide range of pre-1830 pieces for sale. Old Town Hall, King's Rd., Chelsea, SW3 4PW, tel. 044-47-2514.

Mar. 24–27: Devizes to Westminster International Canoe Race, a 125-mile race along the Kennet and Avon Canal and the Thames. No tickets required. For information tel. 0344/483232.

During Apr.: Camden Festival features opera, jazz, film, dance, exhibits, and children's events. Held throughout the Borough of Camden. For information tel. 01/388–1394.

Mid-Apr: London Marathon, a New York-style marathon through London's streets. Information from Box 262, Richmond, Surrey TW10 5JB, tel. 01/948–7935.

Late Apr: International Contemporary Art Fair, at which galleries from the world over exhibit and sell their artists' works. Alexandra Park, Wood Green, London N22, tel. 01/486–1951.

Mid-May: Royal Windsor Horse Show, a major show-jumping event attended by some members of the Royal Family. Show Box Office, 14 Brooksby Walk, Homerton, London E9 6DA, tel. 01/533–3332.

Late May: The Chelsea Flower Show, Britain's major flower show, covers 22 acres. Royal Hospital Rd., Chelsea, SW3, tel. 01/834–4333.

Late May–early June: Beating Retreat by the Guards Massed Bands, when more than 500 musicians parade at Horse Guards, Whitehall. Tickets from Premier Box Office, The Ticket Centre, 1b Bridge St., London SW1 2JR, tel. 01/839–6815.

Early June: Derby Day, a famous horse-racing event is held at Epsom Racecourse in Surrey. Information from United Racecourses Ltd., Racecourse Paddock, Epsom, Surrey KT18 5NJ, tel. 037/27–26311.

Early to mid-June: The Grosvenor House Antiques Fair is one of the most prestigious antiques fairs in Britain. Grosvenor House Hotel, Park La. London W1A 3AA, tel. 0799-26699.

Mid-June: Trooping the Colour, Queen Elizabeth's colorful official birthday parade is held at Horse Guards, Whitehall. Write for tickets early in the year to The Brigade Major, HQ Household Division, Horse Guards, Whitehall, London SW1A 2AX.

Late June–early July: Wimbledon Lawn Tennis Championships, held at the All England Lawn Tennis and Croquet Club in Wimbledon. Write early for tickets for Center and Number One courts; tickets for outside courts available daily at the gate. Church Rd., Wimbledon, London SW19 5AE, tel. 01/946–2244.

Late June–early July: Henley Royal Regatta, an international rowing event and top social occasion, at Henley-on-Thames, Oxfordshire. For information tel. 0491/572153.

July–Sept: Henry Wood Promenade Concerts, a marvelous series of concerts at the Royal Albert Hall and other venues. Box Office, Royal Albert Hall, Kensington Gore, SW7 2AP, tel. 01/589–8212.

July: City of London Festival is an arts festival held throughout The City. For information tel. 01/377–0540.

Mid-to late July: The Royal Tournament features military displays and pageantry by the Royal Navy, the Royal Marines, the Army, and the Royal Air Force. Earl's Court Exhibition Center, Warwick Rd., London SW5 9TA, tel. 01/930–4288.

Mid-Sept: Chelsea Antiques Fair *(see* Mar. 14–25 above).

Early Oct: The Horse of the Year Show has the world's top show jumpers at the Wembley Arena. Show Box Office, 14 Brooksby Walk, Homerton, London E9 6DA, tel. 01/533–3332.

Early Nov: London to Brighton Veteran Car Run, run from Hyde Park in London to Brighton in East Sussex. No tickets required. For information tel. 01/235–8601.

Mid-Nov: Lord Mayor's Procession and Show. At the Lord Mayor's inauguration, a procession takes place from the Guildhall in the City to the Royal Courts of Justice. No tickets required. For information tel. 01/606–3030.

Mid-Dec: Olympia International Show Jumping Championships, international equestrian competition at Olympia. Hammersmith Rd., London W14 8YT, tel. 01/385–1200.

What to Pack

Pack light because porters and baggage trolleys are scarce and luggage restrictions on international flights are tight. Airlines allow two pieces of check-in luggage and one carry-on piece, per passenger. Each piece of check-in luggage cannot exceed 62 inches (length + width + height) or weigh more than 70 pounds. The carry-on luggage cannot exceed 45 inches (length + width + height) and must fit under the seat or in the overhead luggage compartment. Within Europe, airlines allow two pieces of check-in luggage totaling 44 pounds. The restrictions for carry-on luggage are the same as for international flights.

London can be cool, damp, and overcast, but long days of warm sunshine aren't unknown. You'll need a heavy coat for winters and a light-weight coat or warm jacket for summer. There's no time of year when a raincoat or an umbrella won't come in handy. As in any American city, jackets and ties are appropriate for expensive restaurants and nightspots, casual clothes are fine elsewhere. Jeans are as popular in Great Britain as they are at home and are perfectly acceptable for sightseeing and informal dining. Tweeds and non-matching jackets are popular here with men. For women, ordinary street dress is acceptable everywhere.

You'll need an electrical adapter for your hair-dryer and small appliances. The voltage is 220, with 50 cycles. If you plan to stay in budget hotels, take your own soap. Many do not provide soap and some give guests only one tiny bar per room.

Taking Money Abroad

Traveler's checks and major U.S. credit cards—particularly Visa—are accepted in London. You'll need cash for some of the smaller restaurants and shops. Although you won't get as good an exchange rate at home as abroad, it's wise to change some money into pound sterling before you go, to avoid long lines at airport currency exchange booths. Most U.S. banks will change your money into pound sterling. If your local bank can't provide this service, you can exchange money through Deak International. To find the office nearest you, contact Deak at 630 Fifth Ave., New York, NY 10011, tel. 212/635–0515.

For safety and convenience, it's always best to take traveler's checks. The most recognized traveler's checks are **American Express, Barclay's, Thomas Cook,** and those issued through major commercial banks such as **Citibank** and **Bank of America.**

Some banks will issue the checks free to established customers, but most charge a 1% commission fee. Buy part of the traveler's checks in small denominations to cash toward the end of your trip. This will save your having to cash a large check and ending up with more foreign money than you need. You can also buy traveler's checks in pound sterling, a good idea if the dollar is falling and you want to lock in the current rate. Remember to take the addresses of offices where you can get refunds for lost or stolen traveler's checks.

Banks and bank-operated currency exchange booths in airports and railway stations are the best places to change money. Hotels and privately run exchange firms will give you a significantly lower rate of exchange.

Getting Money from Home

There are at least three ways to get money from home: (1) Have it sent through a large commercial bank with a branch in London. The only drawback is that you must have an account with the bank; if not, you'll have to go through your own bank and the process will be slower and more expensive. (2) Have it sent through American Express. If you are a cardholder, you can cash a personal check or a counter check at an American Express office for up to $1,000; $200 will be in cash and $800 in traveler's checks. There is a 1% commission on traveler's checks. American Express has a new service that will be available in most major cities worldwide by January 1989, called American Express MoneyGram. Through this service, you can receive up to $5,000 cash. For the American Express MoneyGram location nearest your home and to find out where the service is available overseas, call 800/543–4080. You do not have to be a cardholder to use this service. (3) Have it sent through Western Union. The U.S. number is 800/988–4726. If you have a MasterCard or Visa, you can have money sent for any amount up to your credit limit. If not, have someone take cash or a certified cashier's check to a Western Union office. The money will be delivered in two business days to a bank in London. Fees vary with the amount of money sent. For $1,000 the fee is $67; for $500, $57.

British Currency

The units of currency in Great Britain are the pound sterling and the pence (p). There are bills of 50, 20, 10, and 5 pounds. Coins are £1, and 50, 20, 10, 5, 2, and 1p. At press time (mid-February) the exchange rate was about .57 to the U.S. dollar, and .44 to the Canadian dollar.

What It Will Cost

London *can* be an expensive city to visit, but, with care, you need not find it so. The main problem, as we go to press, is the relative value of the dollar against the pound, which forces a certain wariness on the visitor. You should keep an eagle eye open for the fluctuations in the exchange rates, and shop around before changing traveler's checks.

The main item on your budget will be your hotel. London hotels are expensive relative to other European countries, and the service that they offer is not always commensurate with the amount they charge. The better-value hotels often lie outside the central area of the city, which means adding transport costs to the hotel rate, and so reducing the benefit.

The situation with restaurants is very different. London is bursting with eating places of every price and cuisine; finding somewhere to match both your palate and your pocketbook will be no problem at all. (For price ranges for hotels and restaurants *see* Lodging and Dining chapters.)

Getting about town isn't expensive. The Underground and bus systems run on a simple area system, with plenty of special tickets on offer for visitors. The cost will depend on the length of your stay and the amount of use you want to make of the facilities—the more you use the travel cards, the greater the savings. *(See* Getting Around in Essential Information.)

Sample Costs A cinema seat in the West End will cost £3.50–£4.50 (cheaper on Mondays and matinees); a theater seat from £5 to about £20; admission fee to a museum or gallery around £2 (though many are free); coffee around 50p; a pint of light (lager) beer in a pub £1.10; whiskey, gin, vodka, etc. by the glass in a pub £1 and up (the measure is smaller than in the United States); house wine by the glass in a pub around £1, in a restaurant £1.50; a Coke around 50p; a ham sandwich from a sandwich shop in the West End £1; a one-mile taxi ride £2.50; an average tube or bus ride 50p, a longer one 80p.

Passports and Visas

American All U.S. citizens require a passport to enter Great Britain. Applications for a new passport must be made in person; renewals can be obtained in person or by mail (*see* below). First-time applicants should apply well in advance of their departure date to one of the 13 U.S. Passport Agency offices. In addition, local county courthouses, many state and probate courts, and some post offices accept passport applications. Necessary documents include: (a) a completed passport application (Form DSP–11); (b) proof of citizenship (birth certificate with raised seal or naturalization papers); (c) proof of identity (driver's license, employee ID card, or any other document with your photograph and signature); (d) two recent, identical, two-inch square photographs (black and white or color); (e) $42 application fee for a 10-year passport (those under 18 pay $27 for a five-year passport). Passports are mailed to you in about 10 working days.

To renew your passport by mail, you'll need completed Form DSP–82, two recent, identical passport photographs, and a check or money order for $35.

A visa is not required for a U.S. citizen to enter Great Britain for stays of up to six months.

Canadian All Canadians must have a valid passport to enter Great Britain. Send completed application (available at any post office or passport office) to the Bureau of Passports, Complexe Guy Favreau, 200 Dorchester West, Montreal, Quebec H2Z 1X4. Include $25, two photographs, a guarantor, and proof of Canadian citizenship. Applications can be made in person at the regional passport offices in Edmonton, Halifax, Montreal, Toronto, Vancouver, or Winnipeg. Passports are valid for five years and are non-renewable.

Visas are not required for Canadian citizens traveling to Great Britain.

Customs and Duties

On Arrival There are two levels of duty-free allowance for travelers entering Great Britain: one for goods bought outside the EEC or in a duty-free shop in the EEC; and the other, for goods bought in the EEC.

In the first category, you may import duty-free: 200 cigarettes or 100 cigarillos or 50 cigars or 250 grams of tobacco (these allowances are doubled if you live outside Europe); two liters of table wine and, in addition, (a) one liter of alcohol over 22% by volume (most spirits), (b) two liters of alcohol under 22% by volume (fortified or sparkling wine), or (c) two more liters of table wine; 50 grams of perfume; ¼ liter of toilet water; and other goods up to a value of £32.

In the second category, you may import duty-free: 300 cigarettes or 150 cigarillos or 75 cigars or 400 grams of tobacco; five liters of table wine and, in addition, (a) 1½ liters of alcohol over 22% volume (most spirits), (b) three liters of alcohol under 22% volume (fortified or sparkling wine), or (c) three more liters of table wine; 75 grams of perfume; 375 ml of toilet water; and other goods to the value of £250. No animals or pets of any kind can be brought into the United Kingdom without a lengthy quarantine. *The penalties are severe and strictly enforced.*

Similarly, fresh meats, plants and vegetables, controlled drugs, and firearms and ammunition may not be brought into Great Britain. There are no restrictions on the import or export of British and foreign currencies.

You will face no customs formalities if you enter Scotland or Wales from any other part of the United Kingdom, though anyone coming from Northern Ireland should expect a security check.

On Departure **U.S. residents** bringing any foreign-made equipment from home, such as cameras, should carry the original receipt or register it with U.S. Customs before leaving home (Form 4457), otherwise they may end up paying duty upon return. U.S. residents may bring home duty-free up to $400 worth of foreign goods, as long as they have been out of the country for at least 48 hours. Each member of the family is entitled to the same exemption, regardless of age, and exemptions can be pooled. For the next $1,000 worth of goods, a flat 10% rate is assessed; above $1,400, duties vary with the merchandise. Included for travelers 21 or older are one liter of alcohol, 100 cigars (non-Cuban), and 200 cigarettes. Only one bottle of perfume trademarked in the United States may be brought in. However, there is no duty on antiques or art over 100 years old. Anything exceeding these limits will be taxed at the port of entry, and may be taxed additionally in the traveler's home state. Gifts valued under $50 may be mailed to friends or relatives at home duty-free, but not more than one package per day to any one addressee and not to include perfumes costing more than $5, tobacco, or liquor.

Canadian residents have a $300 exemption and may also bring in duty free up to 50 cigars, 200 cigarettes, two pounds of tobacco, and 40 ounces of liquor, provided these are declared in writing to customs on arrival and accompany the traveler in hand or checked-through baggage. Personal gifts should be mailed as "Unsolicited Gift—Value under $40." Request the Canadian Customs brochure, "I Declare" for further details.

Traveling with Film

If your camera is new, shoot and develop a few rolls before leaving home. Pack some lens tissue and an extra battery for your built-in light meter. Invest about $10 in a skylight filter for your lens. It will protect the lens and also reduce haze.

Film doesn't like hot weather. If you're driving in summer, don't store film in the glove compartment or on the shelf under the rear window. Put it behind the front seat on the floor, on the side opposite the exhaust pipe.

On a plane trip, never pack unprocessed film in check-in luggage; if your bags get X-rayed, you can say goodbye to your pictures. Always carry undeveloped film with you through security and ask to have it inspected by hand. (It helps to isolate your film in a plastic bag, ready for quick inspection.) Inspectors at American airports are required by law to honor requests for hand inspection; abroad, you'll have to depend on the kindness of strangers.

The old airport scanning machines—still in use in some Third World countries—use heavy doses of radiation that can turn a family portrait into an early morning fog. The newer models—used in all U.S. airports—are safe for anything from five to 500 scans, depending on the speed of your film. The effects are cumulative; you can put the same roll of film through several scans without worry. After five scans, though, you're asking for trouble.

If your film gets fogged and you want an explanation, send it to the National Association of Photographic Manufacturers, 600 Mamaroneck Ave., Harrison, NY 10528. They will try to determine what went wrong. The service is free.

Staying Healthy

There are no serious health risks associated with travel to London. If you have a health problem that might require purchasing prescription drugs while in Great Britain, have your doctor write a prescription using the drug's generic name. Brand names vary widely from country to country. To avoid problems clearing customs, diabetics carrying needles and syringes should have a letter from their physician confirming their need for insulin injections.

The International Association for Medical Assistance to Travelers (IAMAT) is a worldwide association offering a list of approved doctors whose training meets very high standards. For a list of British physicians and clinics that are part of this network, contact IAMAT, 736 Center St., Lewiston, NY 14092, tel. 716/754–4883. **In Canada:** 188 Nicklin Rd., Guelph, Ont. NIH 7L5. **In Europe:** Gotthardstrasse 17, 6300 Zug, Switzerland. Membership is free.

Shots and Medications. Inoculations are not needed for Great Britain.

Insurance

Travelers may seek insurance coverage in three areas: health and accident, lost luggage, and trip cancellation. Your first step is to review your existing health and home-owner policies; some health insurance plans cover health expenses incurred while traveling, some major medical plans cover emergency transportation, and some home-owner policies cover the theft of luggage.

Health and Accident Several companies offer coverage designed to supplement existing health insurance for travelers:

Carefree Travel Insurance (Box 310, 120 Mineola Blvd., Mineola, NY 11501, tel. 516/294–0220 or 800/645–2424) provides coverage for medical evacuation. It also offers 24-hour medical advice by phone.

Health Care Abroad, International Underwriters Group (243 Church St. West, Vienna, VA 22180, tel. 703/281–9500 or 800/237–6615) offers comprehensive medical coverage, including emergency evacuation, for trips of 10–90 days.

International SOS Insurance (Box 11568, Philadelphia, PA 19116, tel. 215/244–1500 or 800/523–8930) does not offer medical insurance but provides medical evacuation services to its clients, who are often international corporations.

Travel Guard International, underwritten by Cygna (1100 Centerpoint Dr., Stevens Point, WI 54481, tel. 715/345–0505 or 800/782–5151) offers medical insurance, with coverage for emergency evacuation when Travel Guard's representatives in the United States say it is necessary.

Lost Luggage Lost luggage is usually covered as part of a comprehensive travel insurance package that includes personal accident, trip cancellation, and sometimes default and bankruptcy insurance. Several companies offer comprehensive policies:

Access America Inc., a subsidiary of Blue Cross-Blue Shield (Box 807, New York, NY 10163, tel. 800/851–2800).

Near, Inc. (1900 N. MacArthur Blvd., Suite 210, Oklahoma City, OK 73127, tel. 800/654–6700).

Travel Guard International *(See* Health and Accident Insurance above.)

Trip Cancellation Flight insurance is often included in the price of a ticket when paid for with American Express, Visa, and other major credit and charge cards. It is usually included in combination travel insurance packages available from most tour operators, travel agents, and insurance agents.

Renting and Leasing Cars

Renting If you're flying into London and planning to spend some time there, save money by arranging to pick up your car in the city the day you arrive; otherwise, arrange to pick up and return your car at the airport. You'll have to weigh the added expense of renting a car from a major company with an airport office against the savings on renting a car from a budget company with offices in town. You could waste precious hours trying to locate the budget company in return for only small financial savings. If you're arriving and departing from different airports, look for a one-way car rental with no return fees. If you're traveling to more than one country, make sure your rental contract permits you to take the car across borders and that the insurance policy covers you in every country you visit. Be prepared to pay more for a car with an automatic transmission. Since they are not as readily available as those with manual transmissions, reserve them in advance. Rental rates vary widely, depending on size and model, number of days you use the car, insurance coverage, and whether special drop-off fees are imposed. In most cases, rates quoted include unlimited free mileage and standard liability protection. Not included are Collision Damage Waiver (CDW), which eliminates your deductible payment should you have an accident, personal accident insurance, gasoline, and European Value Added Taxes (VAT). The VAT in Great Britain is 15%.

Driver's licenses issued in the United States and Canada are valid in Great Britain. You might also take out an International Driving Permit before you leave, to smooth out difficulties if you have an accident or as an additional piece of identification. Permits are available for a small fee through local offices of the **American Automobile Association** (AAA) and the **Canadian Automobile Association** (CAA), or from their main offices: AAA, 8111 Gatehouse Rd., Falls Church, VA 22047, tel. 703/ AAA–6000; CAA, 2 Carlton St., Toronto, Ont. M5B 1K4, tel. 416/964–3170.

It's best to arrange a car rental before you leave. You won't save money by waiting until you arrive in London, and you may find that the type of car you want is not available at the last minute. Rental companies usually charge according to the exchange rate of the dollar at the time the car is returned or when the credit card payment is processed. Three companies with special programs to help you hedge against the falling dollar by guaranteeing advertised rates if you pay in advance are: **Budget Rent-a-Car,** 3350 Boyington St. Carrollton, TX 75006, tel. 800/527–0700; **Connex Travel International,** 983 Main St. Peekskill, NY 10566, tel. 800/333–3949; and **Cortell International,** 770 Lexington Ave., New York, NY 10021, tel. 800/223–6626, in New York 800/442–4481. Other budget rental companies serving London include: **Europe by Car,** One Rockefeller Plaza, New York, NY 10020, tel. 800/223–1516, in California 800/252–9401; **Foremost Euro-Car,** 5430 Van Nuys Blvd., Van Nuys, CA 91404, tel. 800/423–3111; and **Kemwel,** 106 Calvert St., Harrison, NY 10528, tel. 800/678–0678. Other companies include **Avis,** tel. 800/331–1212; **Hertz,** tel. 800/223–6472, in New York 800/522–5568; and **National** or **Europcar,** tel. 800/Car-Rent.

Leasing For trips of 21 days or more, you may save money by leasing a car. With the leasing arrangement, you are technically buying a car and then selling it back to the manufacturer after you've used it. You receive a factory-new car, tax free, with international registration and extensive insurance coverage. Rates vary with the make and model of car and length of time used.

Before you go, compare long-term rental rates with leasing rates. Remember to add taxes and insurance costs to the car rentals, something you don't have to worry about with leasing. Companies that offer leasing arrangements include **Europe by Car** and **Kemwel,** both listed above.

Rail Passes

If you plan on doing a lot of traveling while in Great Britain, you might consider purchasing a *BritRail Pass*, which gives unlimited travel over the entire British Rail network.

A variety of passes are offered. The adult first-class pass costs $230 for seven days, $350 for 14 days, $440 for 21 days, and $520 for one month. The adult second-class pass costs $166 for seven days, $249 for 14 days, $319 for 21 days, and $369 for one month. Senior citizens can obtain a *Senior Citizen Pass*, which entitles the bearer to unlimited first-class travel. It costs $195 for seven days, $295 for 14 days, $375 for 21 days, and $445 for one month. Young people (aged 16–25) can purchase the *Brit-Rail Youthpass*, which allows for unlimited second-class travel. It costs $139 for seven days, $209 for 14 days, $269 for 21 days, and $309 for one month.

You *must* purchase the *BritRail Pass* before you leave home. It is available from most travel agents throughout the world, or from one of these BritRail Travel International offices: 630 Third Ave., New York, NY 10017, tel. 212/599–5400; Cedar Maple Plaza, 2305 Cedar Springs, Dallas, TX 75201, tel. 214/748–0860; 333 N. Michigan Ave., Chicago, IL 60601, tel. 312/263–1910; 800 S. Hope St., Suite 603, Los Angeles, CA 90017, tel. 213/624–8787; 94 Cumberland St., Toronto, Ont. M8V 3S4, tel. 416/929–3333; 409 Granville St., Vancouver, B.C. V6C 1T2, tel. 604/683–6896.

Student and Youth Travel

The **International Student Identity Card** entitles students to youth rail passes, special fares on local transportation, Intra-European Student Charter flights, and discounts at museums, theaters, sports events, and many other attractions. If purchased in the **United States,** the $10 cost of the ISIC also includes $2,000 in emergency medical insurance, plus $100 a day for up to 60 days of hospital coverage. Apply to the Council on International Educational Exchange (CIEE), 205 E. 42nd St., New York, NY 10017, tel. 212/661–1414. **In Canada,** the ISIC is available from the Association of Student Councils, 187 College St., Toronto, Ont. M5T 1P7.

The **Youth International Educational Exchange Card** (YIEE), issued by the Federation of International Youth Travel Organizations (FIYTO), 81 Islands Brugge, DK-2300 Copenhagen S, Denmark, provides similar services to nonstudents under the age of 26. **In the United States,** the card costs $10 and is available from CIEE (address above) or from ISE, Europa House, 802 W. Oregon St., Urbana, IL 61801, tel. 217/344–5863. **In Canada,** the YIEE is available from the Canadian Hostelling Association (CHA), 333 River Rd., Vanier, Ottawa, Ont. K1L 8H9, tel. 613/476–3844.

An **International Youth Hostel Federation** (IYHF) membership card is the key to inexpensive dormitory-style accommodations at thousands of youth hostels around the world. Hostels provide separate sleeping quarters for men and women at rates ranging from $7 to $15 a night per person and are situated in a variety of buildings, including converted farmhouses, villas, and restored castles, as well as specially constructed modern buildings. IYHF membership costs $20 a year and is available in the United States through American Youth Hostels, Box 37613, Washington, DC 20013, tel. 202/783–6161. AYH also publishes an extensive directory of youth hostels around the world.

Economical **bicycle tours** for small groups of adventurous, energetic students are another popular AYH student travel service. The AYH 16-day tour of England for $1,300 (from New York) is a typical offering. For information on these and other AYH services and publications, contact the address above.

Council Travel, a CIEE subsidiary, is the foremost U.S. student travel agency, specializing in low-cost charters and serving as the exclusive U.S. agent for many student airfare bargains and student tours. CIEE's 80-page *Student Travel Catalog* and "Council Charter" brochure are available free from any Council Travel office in the United States (enclose $1 postage if ordering by mail). In addition to CIEE headquarters at 205 E. 42nd Street and branch office at 35 W. 8th Street in New York City, there are Council Travel offices in Berkeley, La Jolla, Long Beach, Los Angeles, San Diego, and San Francisco, CA; Chicago, IL; Amherst, Boston, and Cambridge, MA; Portland, OR; Providence, RI; Austin and Dallas, TX; and Seattle, WA.

The **Educational Travel Center,** another student travel specialist worth contacting for information on student tours, bargain fares, and bookings, may be reached at 438 N. Frances Street, Madison, WI 55703, tel. 608/256–5551.

Students who would like to work abroad should contact **CIEE's Work Abroad Department** (205 E. 42nd St., New York, NY 10017). The council arranges various types of paid and voluntary work experiences overseas for up to six months. CIEE also sponsors study programs in Europe, Latin America, and Asia, and publishes many books of interest to the student traveler: These include *Work, Study, Travel Abroad: The Whole World Handbook* ($8.95 plus $1 postage); *Work Your Way Around the World* ($10.95 plus $1 postage); and *Volunteer! The Comprehensive Guide to Voluntary Service in the U.S. and Abroad* ($5.50 plus $1 postage).

The Information Center at the **Institute of International Education** has reference books, foreign university catalogs, study-abroad brochures, and other materials, which may be consulted by students and nonstudents alike, free of charge. The Information Center, 809 UN Plaza, New York, NY 10017, tel. 212/984–5413), is open from 10 AM to 4 PM, Mon.–Fri., and until 7 PM Wed. evenings. It is not open on weekends or holidays.

IIE administers a variety of grant and study programs offered by U.S. and foreign organizations, and publishes a well-known annual series of study-abroad guides, including *Academic Year Abroad, Vacation Study Abroad,* and *Study in the United Kingdom and Ireland.* The institute also publishes *Teaching Abroad,* a book of employment and study opportunities overseas for U.S. teachers. For a current list of IIE publications with prices and ordering information, write to Publications Service, Institute of International Education, 809 UN Plaza, New York, NY 10017. Books must be purchased by mail or in person; telephone orders are not accepted.

General information on IIE programs and services is available from its regional offices in Atlanta, Chicago, Denver, Houston, San Francisco, and Washington (DC).

Traveling with Children

Publications *Children's Guide to London* by Christopher Pick (Cadogan Books, 16 Lower Marsh, London SE1 7RJ; $8.50).

A Capital Guide for Kids: A London Guide for Parents with Small Children by Vanessa Miles (Allison & Busby, 6a Noel St., London W1V 3RB; £1.95).

Kids' London by Elizabeth Holt and Molly Perham (St. Martin's Press, 175 Fifth Ave., New York, NY 10010).

"Children's London," a booklet free from the London Visitor and Convention Bureau (Tourist Information Centre, Victoria Station Forecourt, London SW1V 1JT, tel. 01/730–3488).

Family Travel Times, an 8 to 12-page newsletter published 10 times a year by **TWYCH** (Travel with Your Children), 80 Eighth Ave., New York, NY 10011, tel. 212/206–0688. Subscription includes access to back issues and twice-weekly opportunities to call in for specific advice.

Family Travel Organizations **American Institute for Foreign Study** (AIFS), 102 Greenwich Ave., Greenwich, CT 06830, tel. 203/869–9090, offers a family vacation program in London and England specifically designed for parents and children.

Families Welcome! (1416 Second Ave., New York, NY 10021, tel. 212/861–2500 or 800/472–8999) is a travel agency that arranges tours to London as well as Europe brimming with family-oriented choices and activities. The London package can include a free second room for children at the Regent Crest Hotel.

Hotels **Novotel London** allows up to two children to stay free in their parents' room. **Trusthouse Forte Hotels** have special Babycare Kits and children's menus; children under five are free and ages six to 13 in parents' room enjoy reduced rates. **Basil Street Hotel** (Basil St., Knightsbridge, London SW3 1AH, tel. 01/581–3311) is notably friendly and offers moderately priced two-room suites connected by a bath. (Keep in mind that in Great Britain, hotels will often allow only three people in a room.)

Getting There On international flights, children under two not occupying a seat pay 10% of an adult fare. Various discounts apply to children aged two to 12. Reserve a seat behind the bulkhead of the plane, which offers more leg room and can usually fit a bassinet (supplied by the airline). At the same time, inquire about special children's meals or snacks, offered by most airlines. (See TWYCH's "Airline Guide," in the Feb. 1988 issue of *Family Travel Times*, for a rundown on services for children offered by 46 airlines.) Ask airlines in advance if you can bring aboard your child's car seat. For the booklet, "Child/Infant Safety Seats Acceptable for Use in Aircraft," write Community and Consumer Liaison Division, APA–400 Federal Aviation Administration, Washington, DC 20591, tel. 202/267–3479.

Baby-sitting Services First check with the hotel desk for recommended child-care arrangements. Local agencies: **Babyminders** and **Childminders**

(67a Marylebone High St., London W1 3AH, tel. 01/935–3515); **Babysitters Unlimited** (313 Brompton Rd., London SW3 2DY, tel. 01/730–7777); **Universal Aunts** (250 King's Rd., London SW3 5UE, tel. 01/730–9834).

Pen Pals For names of children in London to whom your children can write before your trip, send a self-addressed, stamped envelope to: **International Friendship League** (55 Mt. Vernon St., Boston, MA 02108, tel. 617/523–4273); **Student Letter Exchange** (308 Second St. NW, Austin, MN 55912).

Miscellaneous For information and advice when in London call **Kidsline**, tel. 01/222–8070; and **Children's London**, tel. 01/246–8007. Also, several London parks offer One O'clock Clubs for children under five; for information call the **Greater London Council**, tel. 01/633–3679.

Hints for Disabled Travelers

The Information Center for Individuals with Disabilities (20 Park Plaza, Room 330, Boston, MA 02116, tel. 617/727–5540) offers useful problem-solving assistance, including lists of travel agents that specialize in tours for the disabled.

Moss Rehabilitation Hospital Travel Information Service (12th St. and Taber Rd., Philadelphia, PA 19141, tel. 215/329–5715) provides information on tourist sights, transportation, and accommodations in destinations around the world. The fee is $5 for each destination. Allow one month for delivery.

Mobility International (Box 3551, Eugene, OR 97403, tel. 503/343–1284) has information on accommodations, organized study, etc. around the world.

The Society for the Advancement of Travel for the Handicapped (26 Court St., Brooklyn, NY 11242, tel. 718/858–5483) offers access information. Annual membership costs $40, or $25 for senior travelers and students. Send $1 and a stamped, self-addressed envelope.

The Itinerary (Box 1084, Bayonne, NJ 07002, tel. 201/858–3400) is a bimonthly travel magazine for the disabled.

Access to the World: A Travel Guide for the Handicapped by Louise Weiss is useful but out of date. Available from Facts on File (460 Park Ave. South, New York, NY 10016, tel. 212/683–2244).

Hints for Older Travelers

The American Association of Retired Persons (AARP, 1909 K St. NW, Washington, DC 20049, tel. 202/662–4850) has two programs for independent travelers: (1) *The Purchase Privilege Program,* which offers discounts on hotels, airfare, car rentals, and sightseeing; and (2) the *AARP Motoring Plan,* which offers emergency aid and trip routing information for an annual fee of $29.95 per couple. The AARP also arranges group tours, including apartment living in Europe, through two companies: **Olson-Travelworld** (5855 Green Valley Circle, Culver City, CA 90230, tel. 800/227–7737) and **RFD, Inc.** (4401 W. 110th St., Overland Park, KS 66211, tel. 800/448–7010). AARP members must be 50 or older. Annual dues are $5 per person or per couple.

When using an AARP or other identification card, ask for a reduced hotel rate at the time you make your reservation, not when you check out. At restaurants, show your card to the maitre d' before you're seated, since discounts may be limited to certain set menus, days, or hours. When renting a car, remember that economy cars, priced at promotional rates, may cost less than cars that are available with your ID card.

Elderhostel (80 Boylston St., Suite 400, Boston, MA 02116, tel. 617/426–7788) is an innovative 13-year-old program for people 60 and older. Participants live in dorms on some 1,200 campuses around the world. Mornings are devoted to lectures and seminars; afternoons, to sightseeing and field trips. The all-inclusive fee for 2–3 week trips, including room, board, tuition, and round-trip transportation, is $1,700–$3,200.

Travel Industry and Disabled Exchange (TIDE, 5435 Donna Ave., Tarzana, CA 91356, tel. 818/343–6339) is an industry-based organization with a $15 per person annual membership fee. Members receive a quarterly newsletter and information on travel agencies and tours.

National Council of Senior Citizens (925 15th St. NW, Washington, DC 20005, tel. 202/347–8800) is a nonprofit advocacy group with some 4,000 local clubs across the country. Annual membership is $10 per person or $14 per couple. Members receive a monthly newspaper with travel information and an ID card for reduced-rate hotels and car rentals.

Mature Outlook (Box 1205, Glenview, IL 60025, tel. 800/336–6330), a subsidiary of Sears Roebuck & Co., is a travel club for people over 50, with hotel and motel discounts, and a bimonthly newsletter. Annual membership is $7.50 per couple. Instant membership is available at participating Holiday Inns.

Travel Tips for Senior Citizens (U.S. Dept. of State Publication 8970, revised Sept. 1987) is available for $1 from the Superintendent of Documents, U.S. Government Printing Office, Washington, DC 20402.

Getting to London

Since the air routes between North America and London are heavily traveled, the passenger has many airlines and fares to choose from. But fares change with stunning rapidity, so consult your travel agent on which bargains are currently available.

From North America by Plane

Be certain to distinguish among (a) nonstop flights—no changes, no stops; (b) direct flights—no changes but one or more stops; and (c) connecting flights—two or more planes, two or more stops.

The Airlines The U.S. airlines that serve London are **Delta,** tel. 800/241–4141; **TWA,** tel. 800/892–4141; **Pan Am,** tel. 800/221–1111; **American Airlines,** which also serves Manchester, England, tel. 800/433–7300; and **Northwest Airlines,** which also serves Glasgow, Scotland, tel. 800/447–4747.

Flying Time to London From New York: six and a half hours. From Chicago: seven and a half hours. From Los Angeles: 10 hours.

Discount Flights The major airlines offer a range of tickets that can increase the price of any given seat by more than 300%, depending on the day of purchase. As a rule, the further in advance you buy the ticket, the less expensive it is and the greater the penalty (up to 100%) for canceling. Check with airlines for details.

The best buy is not necessarily an APEX (advance purchase) ticket on one of the major airlines. APEX tickets carry certain restrictions: they must be bought in advance (usually 21 days), they restrict your travel, usually with a minimum stay of seven days and a maximum of 90, and they also penalize you for changes—voluntary or not—in your travel plans. But, if you can work around these drawbacks (and most can), they are among the best-value fares available.

Charter flights offer the lowest fares but often depart only on certain days, and seldom on time. Though you may be able to arrive at one city and return from another, you may lose all or most of your money if you cancel your ticket. Travel agents can make bookings, though they won't encourage you, since commissions are lower than on scheduled flights. Checks should, as a rule, be made out to the bank and put in a specific escrow account for your flight. To make sure your payment stays in this account until your departure, don't use credit cards as a method of payment. Don't sign up for a charter flight unless you've checked with a travel agency about the reputation of the packager. It's particularly important to know the packager's policy concerning refunds should a flight be canceled. One of the most popular charter operators is **Council Charter** (tel. 800/223-7402) a division of **CIEE** (Council on International Educational Exchange). Other companies advertise in Sunday travel sections of daily newspapers.

Somewhat more expensive—but up to 50% below the cost of APEX fares—are tickets purchased through companies known as consolidators that buy blocks of tickets on scheduled airlines and sell them at wholesale prices. Here again, you may lose all or most of your money if you change plans, but at least you will be on a regularly scheduled flight with less risk of cancellation than a charter. Once you've made your reservation, call the airline to make sure you're confirmed. Among the best known consolidators are **UniTravel** (tel. 800/325-2222) and **Access International** (250 W. 57th St., Suite 511, New York, NY 10107, tel. 212/333-7280). Others advertise in the Sunday travel section of the daily newspapers as well.

A third option is to join a travel club that offers special discounts to its members. Three such organizations are **Moments Notice** (40 E. 49th St., New York, NY 10017, tel. 212/486-0503); **Discount Travel International** (114 Forrest Ave., Narberth, PA 19072, tel. 215/668-2182); and **Worldwide Discount Travel Club** (1674 Meridian Ave., Miami Beach, FL 33139, tel. 305/534-2082). These cut-rate tickets should be compared with APEX tickets on the major airlines.

Enjoying the Flight. If you're lucky enough to be able to sleep on a plane, it makes sense to fly at night. Many experienced travelers, however, prefer to take a morning flight to Europe and arrive in the evening, just in time for a good night's sleep. Since the air on a plane is dry, it helps, while flying, to drink a lot of non-alcoholic liquids; drinking alcohol contributes to jet lag. Feet swell at high altitudes, so it's a good idea to remove your shoes while in flight. Sleepers usually prefer window seats to curl up against; those who like to move about the cabin ask for aisle seats. Bulkhead seats (adjacent to the Exit signs) have more leg room, but seat trays are attached to the arms of your seat rather than to the back of the seat in front.

Smoking. If smoking bothers you, ask for a seat far away from the smoking section. If you are on a U.S. airline and the attendant tells you there are no nonsmoking seats, insist on one: FCC regulations require domestic airlines to find seats for all nonsmokers.

Luggage   **Regulations.** Airlines allow two pieces of check-in luggage and one carry-on piece, per passenger, on international flights from North America. Each piece of check-in luggage cannot exceed 62 inches (length + width + height), or weigh more than 70 pounds. The carry-on luggage cannot exceed 45 inches (length + width + height), and must fit under the seat or in the overhead luggage compartment. On flights within Europe, you are allowed to check a total of 44 pounds, regardless of luggage size. Requirements for carry-on luggage are the same as for trans-Atlantic flights.

Insurance. On international flights, airlines are responsible for lost or damaged property up to $9.07 per pound (or $20 per kilo) for checked baggage, and up to $400 per passenger for unchecked baggage. If you're carrying any valuables, either take them with you on the airplane or purchase additional lost-luggage insurance. Not all airlines sell you this added insurance. Those that do will sell it to you at the counter when you check in, but you have to ask for it. Others will refer you to the insurance booths located throughout airports. These are operated by **Tele-Trip** (tel. 800/228–9792), a subsidiary of Mutual of Omaha. They will insure your luggage for up to 180 days. The insurance is for checked luggage only, and for a minimum valuation of $500 to a maximum of $3,000. Rates vary with number of days. For $500 for 180 days, the rate is $100; for $3,000, $380. **Travelers' Insurance Co.** (1 Tower Sq., Hartford, CT 06183) will insure checked or hand baggage for $500 to $2,000 valuation per person, for up to 180 days. Rates for one to five days for $500 valuation are $10; for 180 days, $85. Itemize the contents of each bag in case you need to file a claim.

Labeling luggage. Be certain to put your home address on each piece of luggage, including hand baggage. If your lost luggage is recovered, the airline must deliver it to your home, at no charge to you.

2 Portraits of London

London at a Glance:
A Chronology

This date table parallels events in London's history with events in the world at large, especially in the Americas, to give a sense of perspective to the chronology of London. The dates of British kings and queens are those of their reigns, not of their lives.

London

c 400 BC Early Iron Age hamlet built at Heathrow (now London airport)

54 BC Julius Caesar arrives with short-lived expedition

AD 43 Romans invade Britain, led by the Emperor Claudius

60 Boudicca, queen of Iceni, razes the first Roman Londinium to the ground

c 100 The Romans make Londinium center of their British activities, though not the capital

410 Romans withdraw from Britain

856 Alfred the Great (871–99), King of the West Saxons, "restored London and made it habitable"

1040 Edward the Confessor moves his court to Westminster and begins the reconstruction of the Abbey and its monastic buildings

1066 William the Conqueror (1066–87), Duke of Normandy, wins the battle of Hastings

1067 William grants London a charter confirming its rights and privileges

1078 The Tower of London begins with the building of the White Tower

1097 Westminster Hall completed under William II, Rufus (1087–1100)

1123 St. Bartholomew's Hospital founded by Rahere

1132 Charter of Liberties granted by Henry I (1100–35), giving London the right to choose its own sheriffs

1136 Fire destroys London Bridge (new one built 1176–1209)

1185 Knights Templar build the New Temple by the Thames

1191 First Mayor of London elected

1265 First parliament held in Westminster Abbey Chapter House

1314 Old St. Paul's completed

1327 Incorporation of first Trade Guilds (which govern the City for centuries)

The World

329 BC	Alexander the Great reaches India (dies 323)
47–45 BC	Civil War in Italy, Julius Caesar is victor
c AD 30	Jesus crucified in Jerusalem
70	St. Paul's missionary journeys
105	Paper first used in China
410	The Visigoths overrun Italy and destroy Rome
476	Last Roman emperor of the West dethroned
c 600	Mayan civilization at its height in Yucatan Peninsula
610	The Byzantine Empire founded
622	Mohammed's life's work begins; 632 he dies and Arab conquests start
800	Charlemagne crowned Holy Roman Emperor in Rome

c 1000	Vikings arrive in America (via Greenland)
c 1050	Printing in China from moveable type

1096	First European Crusade to the Holy Land

1154	Chartres Cathedral begun

1161	Chinese use gunpowder in warfare
1170	Fall of the Toltecs in Central Mexico

1206	The Mongols under Genghis Khan start the conquest of Asia
1275	Marco Polo reaches China
1309	Papacy moves from Rome to Avignon
1320s	Early stirrings of the Renaissance in Italy (Dante, etc.)
1337	Hundred Years War begins between France and England

London

1348–58 The Black Death in London; one third of the population dies

1382 The Peasants' Revolt destroys part of the city

1411 The Guildhall (already centuries on the same site) rebuilt

1476 William Caxton (1422–91) introduces printing to England in Westminster

c 1483 London's population estimated at around 75,000

1515 Henry VII's tomb in the Abbey created

1529 Hampton Court given by Cardinal Wolsey to Henry VIII; it becomes a favorite royal residence

1568 Royal Exchange founded

1588 Preparations at Tilbury to repel the Spanish invasion; the Armada defeated in the Channel

1599 Shakespeare's Globe Theatre built on the South Bank

1603 Population of London over 200,000

1605 Unsuccessful Gunpowder Plot to blow up the Houses of Parliament

1619–22 Banqueting House built

1640s New fortifications for the defense of the capital built at the start of the Civil War between the Crown and Parliament forces

1649 Charles I (1625–49) beheaded outside the Banqueting House on Whitehall

1658 Oliver Cromwell (Lord Protector) dies

1660 Charles II (1649–85) restored to the throne (the Restoration) after exile in Europe

1665 The Great Plague; deaths probably reach 100,000 (official figure for one week alone was 8,297)

1666 The Great Fire burns for three days; 89 churches, 13,200 houses destroyed over an area of 400 streets

1675 Sir Christopher Wren (1632–1723) begins work on the new St. Paul's

1682–92 Main work on the Royal Hospital Chelsea

1688 William III (1689–1702) transfers from Whitehall Palace to Kensington Palace

1694 The Bank of England founded

1698 Whitehall Palace destroyed by fire

1732 Number 10 Downing Street becomes the Prime Minister's official residence

1739–53 Mansion House built

1755 Trooping the Colour first performed for George II

The World

1348	Europe ravaged by the Black Death (originating in Asia)
1368	Ming Dynasty established in China
1380	Tamerlane (Timur the Lame) begins his conquests in Central Asia

1445	Gutenberg prints the first book in Europe
1453	Fall of Constantinople to the Turks
1492	Columbus sails to the Caribbean and "discovers" the New World; the Moors finally expelled from Spain
1493	Treaty of Tordesillas divides the New World between Spain and Portugal

c 1500	The Italian Renaissance in full flower
1520	Slave trade from Africa to the New World begins
1521	Martin Luther denounced; the Portestant Reformation begins
1532	Inca Empire destroyed by Pizarro
1571	The Spanish conquer the Philippines

1602	Dutch East India Company founded
1607	First permanent English settlement in America at Jamestown, Virginia
1608	Quebec founded by the French
1620	The *Mayflower* arrives off New England
1625	New Amsterdam founded by Dutch colonists
1632	The Taj Mahal built at Agra in India
1645	Tasman, a Dutch mariner, circumnavigates Australia and discovers New Zealand
1656	St. Peter's in Rome finished
1664	The British seize New Amsterdam and rename it New York

1684	La Salle travels up the Mississippi and annexes Louisiana for France
1690	Calcutta founded by the English

1703	Foundation of St. Petersburg, capital of the Russian Empire
1759–60	The British win New France—Quebec 1759, Montreal 1760
1775–76	The American Revolution and the Declaration of Independence
1789	Start of the French Revolution (fall of Bastille)

London

1762 George III (1760–1820) makes Buckingham Palace the royal residence

1773 Stock Exchange founded in Threadneedle Street

1792 Bank of England built

1801 Population just under 1,000,000 (first census)

1802 First gaslights on the London streets

1805 Spectacular funeral of Horatio Nelson (1758–1805), who was killed at the battle of Trafalgar

1812 Regent's Park laid out

1817 First Waterloo Bridge built

1827 Marble Arch erected; in 1851 moved to the northeast corner of Hyde Park

1829–41 Trafalgar Square laid out

1834 The Houses of Parliament gutted by fire; 1840–52 the winning design built

1835 Madame Tussaud settles in Baker Street

1836 London's first railway begins operation, London Bridge to Deptford

1837 Victoria (1819–1901) comes to the throne

1838 National Gallery opens in Trafalgar Square

1845 British Museum completed

1851 The Great Exhibition, Prince Albert's brainchild, held in the Crystal Palace, Hyde Park

1863 Arrival of the Underground (the Tube), first train on the Metropolitan Line

1869 Albert Embankment completed, first stage in containing the Thames floodwaters

1870 The Albert Hall opens

1878 First electric lights on the London streets

1894 Tower Bridge constructed

1897 Queen Victoria celebrates her Diamond Jubilee

1901 Victoria dies, marking the end of an era; London's population reaches around 4,500,000

1914–18 World War I—London bombed (1915) by German Zeppelins; (355 incendiaries, 567 explosives; 670 killed, 1,962 injured)

1926 General Strike; London is partly paralyzed

1935 London County Council establishes a Green Belt to preserve the city's outer open spaces

1939–45 World War II—air raids, between Sept. '40 and July '41 45,000–50,000 bombs (including incendiaries) are dropped on London; '44 Flying Bomb (Doodlebug) raids; '45 V2 raids; during the latter two series of raids 8,938 killed, 24,504 injured. Total casualties for the whole war, about 30,000 killed, more than 50,000 injured

The World

1798–1812	The Napoleonic Wars, spreading French domination across Europe and into Russia
1803	The United States is nearly doubled in size by the Louisiana Purchase
1807	The Slave Trade abolished in the British Empire
1815	Napoleon returns from exile in Elba, loses the Battle of Waterloo, and is again exiled, to St. Helena in the south Atlantic
1819	The United States buys Florida from Spain
1823	Promulgation of the Monroe Doctrine
1840	Britain introduces the first postage stamp
1846	Beginning of the Mexican War
1848	Marx and Engels publish the *Communist Manifesto*
1857	The Indian Mutiny
1861–65	The American Civil War
1867	Establishment of the Dominion of Canada
1869	Suez Canal completed; first U.S. transcontinental railroad opened
1870	Franco-Prussian War
1880s	The European powers (Germany, Belgium, Britain) seize control of most of middle Africa
1898	The Spanish-American War
1899	The Boer War begins in southern Africa
1900	The Boxer Rebellion breaks out in China
1914	The opening of the Panama Canal
1914–18	World War I; in 1917 the United States enters the war
1917	A Jewish home in Palestine promised by the Balfour Declaration
1920	The League of Nations founded in Geneva
1922	Mussolini comes to power in Italy
1929	World Depression brought on by the stock market crash
1933	President Roosevelt introduces the New Deal; Hitler becomes German Chancellor, marking the beginning of the Nazi era
1937	War begins between Japan and China

London

1946 Heathrow Airport opens

1951 The Festival of Britain spurs postwar uplift

1953 Coronation of Queen Elizabeth II (born 1926)

1956 Clean Air Act abolishes open fires and makes London's mists and fogs a romantic memory

1965 Sir Winston Churchill's funeral, a great public pageant; the Post Office Tower—now the Telecom Tower—one of Britain's tallest buildings, opens

1973 New Stock Exchange opens

1974 Covent Garden fruit and vegetable market moves across the Thames, the original area is remodeled

1976 National Theatre opens on the South Bank

1977 Queen Elizabeth celebrates her Silver Jubilee

1980 The siege of the Iranian Embassy establishes the expertise of Britain's anti-terrorist forces

1981 National Westminster Tower, Britain's tallest building, opens in the City; Prince Charles marries Lady Diana Spencer in St. Paul's Cathedral

1982 The Barbican Centre opens

1983 The first woman Lord Mayor takes office

1984 The Thames Barrier, designed to prevent flooding in central London, is inaugurated

1986 The Greater London Council is abolished; London's population now stands at approximately 6,696,000

The World

1939–45 World War II; in 1941 the United States enters the war after Pearl Harbor; 1944 the Allies land in Normandy; 1945 defeat of Germany, the atom bomb is dropped on Japan

1945 The United Nations opens in New York

1946–49 Civil War in China

1947 India and Pakistan gain independence

1948 The State of Israel is established

1950 Beginning of the Korean War

1953 Death of Stalin

1956 The Suez crisis, France and Britain invade the Suez Canal zone; Russia stamps out the Hungarian Revolt

1957 Foundation of the European Economic Community (EEC) by the Treaty of Rome

1961 Berlin Wall constructed

1962 Cuban missile crisis

1963 President Kennedy assassinated

1966 Cultural Revolution in China

1969 First man lands on the moon

1973 United States abandons the Vietnam War; Britain joins the EEC

1974 President Nixon resigns

1979–84 Wastage among World leaders; 1979 Shah of Iran falls; 1980 Yugoslavia's Marshall Tito dies; 1981 President Sadat of Egypt is assassinated; 1982 President Brezhnev of the U.S.S.R. dies; 1984 Indira Ghandi of India assassinated

1982 The Falklands War between Argentina and Britain

1985 Mikhail Gorbachev comes to power in the Soviet Union

1986 The Chernobyl reactor disaster in the Soviet Union

Wren and the Great Fire of London

by Ann Saunders

Author of Art and Architecture of London, *Dr. Saunders lectures to visiting American students on London history and costume. She is a leading figure in the London Topographical Society.*

Since England as a whole is so rich in medieval churches, the perceptive visitor to the City of London may wonder why there are none around. Except for five on the northern edge of the City, there seems to be nothing earlier than the late 17th century. The answer lies in the four terrible days and nights, between September 2 and 5, 1666, when fire destroyed five-sixths of the mainly timber-built, medieval city. Those four days did three to four times as much damage as did Hitler's bombs and rockets in the six years of World War II. This was how it happened.

On the night of Saturday, September 2, 1666, the king's own baker, Master Robert Farynor, put out the oven fire in his bakehouse in Pudding Lane near the north end of London Bridge and went to bed. He was quite certain that he had extinguished his stove, but in the small hours of the morning his manservant was awakened by smoke and, realizing that the house was on fire, roused the household whose members crept to safety across the roof to the house next door, with the exception of a maid who, scared of heights, died in the flames.

For the next four days, the fire raged. A steady wind blew from the northeast, the Essex side, of the city, driving the flames through the narrow streets of timber-framed houses. The flames were carried toward Thames Street, the riverside area, where stocks of oil, coal, hay, timber, and hemp lay piled on the quayside; the fire could not have been given a surer foothold. At first, the severity of the danger was not realized; Samuel Pepys, civil servant and diarist, roused by his servant who was working late, looked out of the window "but being unused to such fires as followed, I thought it far enough off, and so went to bed again and to sleep." At about the same time, some wary citizens had called the Lord Mayor, Sir Thomas Bludworth, from his bed. He dismissed the danger. "Pish! a woman might piss it out," he was reported as having said; and the opportunity to control the fire was lost. Before morning, St. Magnus Church was destroyed and the Thames water house on the north end of the bridge, which could throw a jet of water over the steeple of the church, was gone, too. People began, desperately, to evacuate their goods; some threw their treasures into the Thames in the hope that they might be washed back on a later tide. Samuel Pepys dug a hole in his back garden to bury state papers—his home served as the Admiralty's office—and his much valued Parmesan cheese.

The fire began to work its way into the heart of the City; it destroyed the Royal Exchange, took the medieval Guildhall, whose oak timbers were so stout that for hours they glowed "in a bright, shining coale, as it had been a palace of gold or a great building of burnished brass." At last the fire reached St. Paul's Cathedral, crowning the western hill of the City. The old cathedral had been one of the great wonders of medieval Europe. The City booksellers, convinced that the sanctity of the cathedral and the thickness of its stone walls would be proof even against this fire, had filled the crypt with their books. Their faith was ill-founded for the flames took hold of St. Paul's and gutted it. The lead of the roof flowed in volcanic torrents down Ludgate Hill.

The king, Charles II, and his brother, the duke of York, alerted by Pepys, organized fire-fighting teams from among the panic-stricken citizens; houses were blown up to create firebreaks, thatched roofs torn down to prevent sparks from igniting them. But it was not till Wednesday night that the wind dropped, and a light fall of rain, early on Thursday morning, made it possible to gain some sort of control over the disaster. In those four days, the fire had swept from close to the eastern boundary of the City, near to London Tower, as far westward as Fleet Street, to within a hundred yards of the Temple church. Some 400 streets containing 13,200 houses were wiped out; London lost St. Paul's Cathedral, 87 churches, the Guildhall, the Royal Exchange, the Custom House, the Leadenhall, and 44 City Company Halls. All that remained was a paring around the northeastern and northern edges. Five medieval churches remained unscathed, as did St. Bartholomew-the-Great further north. Samuel Pepys' house was safe, too.

The person who best kept his head was the king himself. On September 13, he issued a proclamation declaring that London would be rebuilt of stouter, less combustible materials, that the streets must be wider, that a proper survey should be made so that no man should lose what was rightly his, that he himself would be responsible for the rebuilding of the Custom House, and that those who rebuilt in an approved manner would be rebated the hearth tax (domestic rates) for seven years. Others reacted to the king's lead with equal speed and efficiency; within a week of the fire's ending, the king received a plan from a young mathematician, Dr. Christopher Wren of Oxford University, demonstrating how the city might be newly laid out in an ideal, geometric manner. Within the following week, four more such plans reached the monarch. Charles, who had spent his years of exile during the Civil War as a poor relation at the magnificent court of Louis XIV, wanted to seize this chance to emulate France. But he was a realistic man. A commission was set up—six men, three chosen by the king and three by the city, two of whom had already put forward plans of their own. Wren was one of the king's team. Commendably prompt, the Commission announced their finding on October 24. London must be rebuilt on the old street plan, with such road widenings and improvements as could be made without causing too much disturbance. Speed in rebuilding and the restoration of trade were imperative.

It is fashionable to lament the rejection of Wren's plan as London's great lost opportunity. I myself doubt this. A great city evolves gradually; its streets and buildings represent the needs, concerns, ambitions, and dreams of its citizens. Overall plannings or redevelopments, whether they be the product of one man's vision or a committee's consensus, are apt to disregard the human needs of those who are going to live there. London may well have been wise to retain its medieval street plan.

In this emergency, 17th-century society—the king, the City authorities, Parliament—moved with a speed almost unbelievable in the 20th century. By February 1667, a series of bills had been drafted, debated, and passed to become the Fire Acts. They laid down that houses of standard types were to be built of non-combustible materials with flat, uniform frontages. The picturesque timber-framed, lathe-and-plaster dwellings, one floor jutting out above another, possibly with a thatched roof as crown, were banished from the City. A special Fire Court was set up to resolve disputes about land and tenure, the judges and lawyers volunteering to work without fees in this unparalleled emergency; it sat for six years and gave judgment in some 1,500 cases which, considering that 13,200 houses had been destroyed, many of them held in multiple tenancies, suggests that most parties exercised common sense and restraint in building claims. When all was settled, the City authorities, by way of thanks and recognition of services, commissioned full-length portraits of the 22 judges, which are still in the possession of the Guildhall.

The homeless citizens were instructed to pay half a mark (37½p) for a hastily sworn-in surveyor to stake out the limits of their former houses so that the land could be cleared and rebuilding begin. The great shortages were of money, men, and materials. But a tax to be levied on coal entering the Port of London was authorized to pay for the reconstruction of St. Paul's, the churches, and public buildings; the City authorities and the Livery Companies dug into their resources and, in days when prudent people kept a good part of their substance in gold pieces in a money-chest under their own roofs, neighbor lent to neighbor and the great rebuilding began. The new houses were built from London's own earth; the clay of the Thames basin, once fired, made excellent bricks. The Guild laws, restricting labor to local residents, were relaxed so that help could come in from all over the country. By 1671, within five years, more than 7,000 houses—95% of what was to be rebuilt—were completed or well under way; the new Custom House was finished, and the Royal Exchange enlarged and reopened. In that year, Lord Mayor's Day was once again celebrated with ceremony and pageantry.

The coal tax came in slowly at first and this, coupled with lack of stone, meant that the cathedral and city churches remained unbuilt, though sites were cleared and men worshipped in temporary "tabernacles." Eighty-seven churches had been destroyed, 51 were rebuilt, many parishes being amalgamated. For all of these, Wren provided the designs, though inevitably the detailed working-out was undertaken by other hands, and site supervision was necessarily the responsibility of others. Fourteen churches were begun in 1670; between the mid-1670s and the early 1680s, there were some 30 under construction. By 1685, the main structures of most were completed; towers and spires were added or finished in the early 1700s, after half a generation's breathing space. In creating these churches, Wren—the son of a dean, the nephew of a bishop—had to decide what an Anglican church should look like. The great medieval Catholic tradition of church building had fallen into abeyance with the Reformation; then, the emphasis had been on the altar, and an impenetrable screen often separated the priest from his flock. Now, communion was to be celebrated in the sight of all, since all would participate, and a greater importance would be given to the sermon, which would have to be audible—in short, the need was for a church for *congregational* worship. Wren advanced no single solution but, in almost all his churches, he placed the emphasis on the body of the nave and brought the chancel well within the church.

Wren was, in most cases, working on cramped and irregularly shaped sites and, at the beginning, it was still uncertain how large and how steady an income would be produced by the coal tax. The exteriors of Wren's churches are very plain; sometimes, in London's busy streets, it is possible to walk past and, unless you are observant, to miss the entrance—St. Peter, Cornhill, is a good example. But one feature stands out, even today: to each church, Wren gave a distinctive tower, spire, or steeple, and by them you can still pilot your way around the City's streets. Inside the church the provision of fittings was the responsibility of the parish and so, from examining the altar, the pulpit, the organ, the font, and the woodwork in general, we can deduce a good deal about the wealth and taste of each 17th-century parish.

Of those 51 churches, time, chance, the developer, and wartime damage have taken their toll. Between 1781 and 1939, 19 of Wren's churches were destroyed; another seven were lost to the bombs and were not restored after the war. Of those that remain, most are in excellent condition, well looked-after, and well-loved. Some remain as parish churches; others, owing to dwindling congregations, have become Guild churches with special weekday responsibilities toward London's daytime, working population, or toward particular religious or social needs. Many of them depend upon voluntary help with supervision, and so are not open all the time. But they are still there, playing their part in the religious, social, and ceremonial life of the City.

All the time that he was planning or supervising the City churches, Wren was thinking about St. Paul's. Even before the fire, he had been called in by the Dean and Chapter to advise on how the cathedral should be restored after the damage and decay of the Civil War and the Commonwealth years. After the disaster, when it proved impossible to improvise a temporary church because of the calcined condition of the remaining fabric, Dean Sancroft, later Archbishop of Canterbury, wrote to Wren, "You are so absolutely and indispensably necessary to us that we can do nothing, resolve on nothing, without you." After several rejected plans, Wren undertook the Great Model, which can still be seen in the crypt of St. Paul's. It is over 18 feet long, cost over £500 to make—a first-class house on a main street could then be had for £400. It was to be a single-story building in the shape of a Greek cross with arms of equal length, with a giant portico, and a dome 120 feet wide—eight feet wider than the present dome and only 17 feet smaller than St. Peter's in Rome. But the design was too revolutionary, too great a departure from the traditional Latin cross of the old cathedral, and the clergy rejected it. Their reaction was not all prejudice; there was a practical need to choose a building that could be completed a part at a time. Wren resolved to "make no more models, or publickly to expose his Drawings" but, patient as always, produced a compromise design, Latin cross in shape with a cupola surmounted with a spire. Nine years of deliberation and argument had slipped by since the fire; it was time for work to begin. The king gave his Warrant to this hybrid plan in May 1675, authorizing Wren, whom he had knighted two years before and who had been Surveyor-General since 1669, to make "variations, rather ornamental than essential, as from time to time he should see proper." Wren took advantage of this liberty to return much closer to his preferred design, and to give us the masterpiece which is St. Paul's.

When the site was cleared and they began to set out the foundations, Wren told a workman to find a sizable piece of stone to use as a marker. The man brought, at random and by chance, a piece of an old gravestone with one word upon it: RESURGAM —the Latin for "I shall rise again." Everyone took this to be a good omen. And rise the cathedral did—520 feet long and 365 feet in height, from the crown of the lantern over the dome to the ground—and all in a comparatively short space of time, the first service being held in the choir on December 2, 1697. Even so, there were criticisms and disagreements: at one stage, hoping to speed matters, Parliament tried to hold back half of each of Wren's annual payments of £200 until the work was completed. There were also agitations for the dome to be clad in copper rather than in somber and dignified lead. Despite everything, Wren and his team of craftsmen and skilled laborers worked on steadily. His son, the younger Christopher, placed the last stone on the lantern late in October 1708, watched by old Edward Strong the mason, whose brother Thomas had laid the foundation stone in June 1675. It had taken 120 years and 13 architects to build St. Peter's in Rome; St. Paul's was the work of one man, completed in half a lifetime.

Wren lies buried in the crypt, with the proudest epitaph that any architect could ever have: *Lector, si monumentum requiris, circumspice*—Reader, if you seek his monument, look around you.

The London Art Scene

by Patrick Conner

The author of
several books on
art, Dr. Conner is
also a fine art
dealer in London,
specializing in the
Far East.
Formerly, he was
Keeper of Fine
Art at the Royal
Pavilion in
Brighton.

London is a picture hunter's paradise. Apart from the public galleries, there are hundreds of commercial art galleries offering pictures and prints of every kind, and at every price, from Old Masters to modern apprentices.

But commercial art galleries can be off-putting places, especially in the fashionable West End. They do not exactly beckon to the casual passerby. The window display consists of perhaps a single picture, or none; in an austere front room sits a forbiddingly well-bred receptionist. Is this a club for members only? Is formal dress required? Is there a password? No, no, and no. A commercial art gallery is a shop, after all. Anyone can browse; no one need buy; no one need pay for admission (in contrast to many "public" galleries, where entrance charges are becoming increasingly common). And many of these galleries present a program of changing exhibitions, which once again are free.

Art galleries fall into two categories: those that deal with the work of living artists, and those that deal with the work of dead ones. The first kind generally operates by taking a percentage of the artist's sales, while the second kind buys and sells old (or oldish) pictures just as an antique shop buys and sells its objects. London has plenty of both kinds, but it is the second variety, dealing in earlier pictures, that has won the city its reputation as the center of the world art trade.

Especially good value, perhaps, are English watercolors. In other forms of visual art the British (it must be admitted) may sometimes have lagged behind their European neighbors, but they developed the subtle art of watercolor to an unrivaled degree, especially at the end of the 18th century and in the earlier part of the 19th. Why this happened isn't clear—possibly there is something in the British climate that favors the watery medium; whatever the reason, the collector has a wide choice. Watercolors by such leading masters as Turner, Cotman, or Girtin call for a long purse, but London's galleries contain many excellent works by lesser names. You can still buy a respectable 19th-century watercolor for two or three hundred pounds, or a lively pencil sketch for a good deal less.

The two most fruitful districts for the picture hunter are situated on either side of Piccadilly. To the north is the Bond Street area, including the smaller streets on each side (and Sotheby's in the middle); and to the south is the district of St. James's, extending from King Street (home of Christie's) to the western part of Jermyn Street, to which it is linked north-south by Bury Street and Duke Street. These two districts are scarcely a stone's throw apart, and yet each has its own distinct atmosphere.

In Bond Street the flavor is an international one, of haute couture, gilt furniture, silver ornaments, and other conspicuous symbols of wealth. This does not mean, however, that there is nothing for the less affluent collector. For example, the venerable firm of Agnew's (43 Old Bond St.), of which some member of the Agnew family has been a partner or director since 1817, offers not only old masters in the million-pound category, but also 19th-century drawings from a couple of hundred pounds. Once a year, generally in the spring, Agnew's mounts an exhibition of English watercolors to which its loyal clients (often of modest means) make an annual pilgrimage, returning home with a small but pleasing trophy.

Proceeding northward one might visit Leger Galleries (13 Old Bond St.) for high-quality English pictures, and Colnaghi next door (#14) for European works of art of all kinds. After Old Bond Street has become New Bond Street, turn left into Grafton Street for something rather different: The Portal Gallery, at #16a, presents the work of naive painters—the gallery claims "the finest collection of self-taught British Fantasy Artists this side of the Bosphorus."

In Clifford Street, the next right turning off New Bond Street, are other specialized galleries. The Maas Gallery (#15a), which deals in Victorian paintings and prints, was founded by Jeremy Maas in 1960, when Victoriana was still regarded by many people as a joke in bad taste. By contrast Leinster Fine Art (#3, fourth floor) promotes modern German Expressionist art; the entrance is in Old Burlington Street. Returning to New Bond Street and still walking north, we reach the Fine Art Society (148 New Bond St.), next to the august premises of Wildenstein. Despite its name, the Fine Art Society is a commercial art gallery, and a very stimulating one at that, which stages exhibitions of British painting within the period 1850–1950, and is particularly strong in Scottish artists. Almost opposite at #33 is the old, established firm of Arthur Ackermann & Son, noted for its sporting scenes.

The St. James's gallery district has perhaps a more traditional, discreet, and gentlemanly air than the flashier Bond Street nearby. Here, among the established shops selling handmade shoes or badger-hair shaving brushes, are two dozen picture galleries, whose small size hardly suggests the large stock of paintings that occupy the racks in the basement. Bury Street is a good hunting ground for early English watercolors, which may be found (at prices ranging from two figures to six) at the galleries of ex-Guards officer Bill Thomson (1 Bury St.), Martyn Gregory (#34), and Morton Morris (#32); Martyn Gregory also specializes in pictures related to the China Trade. Parallel to Bury Street runs Duke Street, home of several old master galleries; at its foot are the turreted premises of Spink and Son, renowned for oriental art among much else. In Ryder Street, which links Bury Street to Duke Street, former doctor Chris Beetles (#10) holds a large stock of works by late Victorian watercolorists and illustrators; at #5, Peter Nahum—who has been described as a "flamboyant fuse-wire haired, Victorian art whizz"—offers "master drawings" and high-quality paintings of the 19th century.

The London print-dealing world is in a state of flux. Numerous galleries have sprung up and disappeared in the last few years. Of the more settled businesses, Agnew's and Colnaghi's in Old Bond Street can be relied upon to provide old master prints, as can Christopher Mendez (58 Jermyn St.). Garton and Cooke (39–42 New Bond St.) stocks British prints of the period 1850–1950, mostly in the range £200–£4,000. For sporting prints try Ackermann (33 New Bond St.), or the small but expanding Burlington Gallery nearby (10 Burlington Gdns). The Witch Ball (2 Cecil Ct., off Charing Cross Rd.) specializes in prints relating to theater and ballet. Old prints are also sold in many antique shops and antiquarian bookshops. But the collector should be wary of decorative flower prints, for example, presented in heavily marbled mounts and mock-antique maple frames; the buyer may well be paying more for the packaging than for the print itself.

For 20th-century limited-edition prints one may visit the William Weston Gallery (7 Royal Arcade, Albermarle St.), or the Redfern Gallery (20 Cork St.). Cork Street runs parallel to New Bond Street and is almost entirely composed of up-market dealers in modern pictures. Prices at these two galleries start at about £300; at the Redfern one may find lithographs by Chagall or Henry Moore for under £1,000, while etchings by Whistler or Miro start at £1,500 or so. Post-1880 prints with a French emphasis are supplied by Editions Graphiques (3 Clifford St.).

This brief survey has done no justice to the many other hunting grounds in London. The collector who seeks modern paintings at moderate prices should try the galleries grouped around Portobello Road and Westbourne Grove. The Motcomb Street district, to the south side of Knightsbridge, offers a series of galleries largely devoted to decorative paintings of the 19th and 20th centuries—note the Victorian paintings at Christopher Wood (15 Motcomb St.), and the "orientalist" pictures of the Arab world at the Mathaf Gallery (#24). There are further clusters of galleries in Fulham, Chelsea, Pimlico, Belgravia, Covent Garden, Hampstead . . .

A fuller guide to London's art dealers can be found in the monthly pocket-size publication *Galleries*, which you can pick up free from most leading West End galleries. This includes an index of dealers listed according to their specialties ("African Art," "Animals," and so on), as well as useful local maps showing the distribution of many, although not all, of the galleries in each area. *Galleries* also gives a preview of the month's picture auctions.

There are four major auction houses in London—all of them proud of their long traditions and enveloped in mystique. They are Christie's (8 King St.) in St. James's; Sotheby's (34–35 New Bond St.), with an unimposing entrance that's easy to miss—look for the 3,000-year-old Egyptian sculpture of a lioness-headed goddess in the gable above the doorway; Phillips (7 Blenheim St.) just off New Bond Street; and Bonham's (Montpelier St.), a mile or so to the west of the other three, but conveniently close to Harrods.

All four can claim to have been established (on different premises) since the 18th century. Christie's was founded in 1766 by James Christie, the son of a Scottish feather-bed beater, who rose to win many friends in high places, and was described by ladies as irresistible. Sotheby's was founded by a bookseller who held his first auction in 1745. For many years Sotheby's was concerned only with books, and the firm did not handle pictures or furniture until the 20th century. Bonham's opened its doors in 1793; and in 1796 Harry Phillips, who had served hitherto as James Christie's chief clerk, resigned to found the firm that still carries his name. Phillips got off to a flying start by selling the pictures that had been owned by Queen Marie Antoinette before she lost her head. In later life Harry Phillips put up for sale some of Queen Victoria's royal cast-offs, at the only public auction ever held in Buckingham Palace.

Sotheby's is the largest of the auction houses, having overtaken Christie's in the early 1950s. Phillips and Bonham's are a good deal smaller, although Phillips put on a spurt in the 1970s. Bonham's hopes to gain from the refurbishment of its premises undertaken in 1987–88; among its attractions are sales devoted to particular themes, such as "Dogs in Art," held in February to coincide with Crufts' Dog Show, and "Marine Pictures" in August at the time of the Cowes Regatta. Almost anything can be sold at auction. One of Bonham's more intriguing sales included the series of telegrams, sent in 1910, that enabled the murderer Dr. Crippen to be brought to justice.

In addition to the big four, there are dozens of smaller auction houses in London, some specializing in a single commodity such as stamps, or coins, or carpets; others dealing with general antiques—the latter often operated by estate agents. Well worth noting is Christie's secondary auction house, known as Christie's South Kensington, (85 Old Brompton Rd.) near South Kensington Underground station. Large quantities of pictures and antiques, usually within the £50-£1,000 range, are sold here—oil paintings on most Tuesdays, and drawings and watercolors on most Wednesdays.

London auctions are still dominated by dealers rather than private buyers. Moreover, the dealers all seem to know one another, and thus create a sense of conspiracy from which the visitor may feel excluded. But don't be intimidated by this, nor by the apparent self-assurance of the auction staff (Christie's and Sotheby's still echo to the nasal vowels of the English upper-class accent). The private individual's bid is as good as anyone else's. And the actual process of bidding is straightforward enough, despite the myths. ("Remember not to scratch your nose during the bidding," newcomers may still be told, "or you'll come away with a bill for half a million pounds.") In practice no such accident will happen; the auctioneer must be sure that you are actually bidding (rather than sneezing, yawning, or groaning), and in cases of doubt he or she will enquire "Are you bidding, Sir (or Madam)?" In any case, you don't have to attend the sale in person; bids can be left at the auction house, or sent by mail or telephone.

And of course, looking is free. Before each sale the pictures or objects are usually on view for at least a day or two. If you don't want to buy the published catalogue (which can be expensive), you can refer to "desk" catalogues in the auction room. The catalogues in the principal auction rooms include estimates of what each lot will realize, but don't place too much faith in these, as the actual sums achieved often vary a good deal.

Auctions are perhaps less colorful affairs than they once were. Gone are the days when Bill Brooks of Christie's South Kensington would threaten to turn the fire extinguishers onto his audience if they didn't bid more briskly. Also on the way out is the questionable, if time-honored, auctioneer's practice of inventing non-existent buyers ("sold to Carruthers") to disguise the fact that the lot had not reached its minimum reserve price, and thus had not really been sold at all. One Phillips auctioneer, who happened to be fond of cricket, often used the names of Australian cricketers in this way: "sold to Lillee."

Three words of caution to the intending buyer at auction. (1) Don't forget that the successful bidder must pay a 10% "buyer's premium" in addition to the hammer price (the percentage may be a little different in certain auctions), and also Value Added Tax on that premium (VAT is not charged on the "hammer price" itself). (2) Satisfy yourself about the picture before you buy because it will be difficult to obtain a refund. (3) Don't assume that auction prices are necessarily lower than dealers' prices. Many dealers hold a stock of pictures that have accumulated over a considerable period, and whose prices have often not kept up with those achieved at auction. A not untypical recent case is that of the Bury Street dealer who had an Edward Lear watercolor for sale at £3,000. For two years he displayed it on his walls, or took it to antiques fairs, without finding a buyer. Then it was noticed by a representative of Christie's who was looking for dealers' stock to fill out an auction sale of watercolors. The dealer handed over the picture, which was duly auctioned—and fetched £4,500.

London's Theaters

by *John Elsom*

President of the International Association of Theater Critics, John Elsom is also a professor at the City University, London.

London is famous for its theaters and there are a lot of them, more than in Paris, New York, or Moscow. They are comparatively easy to find, which is helpful for the visitor, and they come in all shapes and sizes, from stately opera houses and national theaters to tiny "black box" studios. There are historic theaters, and ones that opened last week, and ones maybe that should not have opened at all. I have to admit that, having been a theater critic in London for 20 years, I still sometimes feel like a child let loose in a sweetshop. What did I do right, God, that I should be so lucky?

But there is one embarrassing problem. When friends come to London for a few days, they often ask me what shows they should see, and this is rarely an easy question to answer. It is not just a matter of remembering what productions are actually playing in some 60 theaters during the days in question, but of guessing at their tastes. If I recommend a boring play to somebody whom I suspect of being a rather boring person, then I quickly discover that he or she is not boring at all, but sharp, sophisticated, and very indignant; the opposite, of course, can also happen. Due to some quirk of temperament—although there may be a loftier explanation—I never feel satisfied with the safe choices, the ones that any travel company would recommend.

Most people, for example, like musicals; and over the past 10 years, London has taken over from New York as the world's center for spectacular musicals. The Broadway hits, *Cats*, *Les Misérables*, and *The Phantom of the Opera*, all originated in London (where they are still playing), as did *Evita*, *Starlight Express*, and *Jesus Christ, Superstar!*. As if in some trans-Atlantic pact, many current London musical hits, *Kiss Me; Kate!*, *Follies*, and *42nd Street*, came from Broadway. At one time it was said that British theater could not produce musicals. It had neither the talent nor the resources. All that has changed.

There are other obvious recommendations. Shakespeare is alive and well and usually playing in one of our two national companies: the Royal Shakespeare Company and the National Theatre. For opera and ballet lovers, and for those who enjoy grand settings, there is the Royal Opera House, Covent Garden, or its often more adventurous rival, the English National Opera at the Coliseum. For tired businessmen, there are glamor revues in Soho; for families, there are West End comedies and whodunits; and for those who like to contribute to *The Guinness Book of World Records*, Agatha Christie's *The Mousetrap* has been playing continuously in London since 1952, the longest unbroken run of any play anywhere in the world.

But no self-respecting critic would ever recommend *The Mousetrap*, not even to an enemy—suggestions like that can be left to the London Tourist Board. This is not just intellectual snobbery. Plays by Christie and Noël Coward, not to mention Shakespeare, Shaw, Wilde, and Maugham, are performed all over the world. To millions of people, they represent the international face of British theater—slick, efficient, and often profound entertainment. But there is a private face as well, more anxious, cautious, and human, and when friends visit London, I want to introduce them to the distinctive quality of our theaters rather than to the postcard images.

When I try to explain, however, what is so special about them, I start stammeringly to use phrases like "living history" and "a sense of continuity." The theater in London has evolved over three centuries, and at no time has the weight of the past squeezed the life from the present. Nor have traditions been ignored to pursue the latest fashion. Even in Sir Henry Irving's day (the late 19th century), or David Garrick's (the mid-18th century), a delicate balance was maintained between the old, the new, and the futuristic.

In practical terms, this means that British actors are usually trained to speak Shakespeare as well as Samuel Beckett, that our directors have a strong grounding in classical theater, and that our writers use skills in phraseology and dramatic construction that owe a considerable debt to the past. Christopher Hampton and Tom Stoppard can write epigrams to match those of Oscar Wilde. But nowhere is this blend of past and present more vividly illustrated than in the architecture and geography of London's theaterland.

London is often described as a collection of villages, built at different times and reflecting the priorities of the ages that brought them into being. The same might be said of its theaters. The theaters on the South Bank, for example, near Waterloo Station, were all built or renovated during the 1960s and 1970s, at a time when civic and national idealism conspired to provide culture for the people. The National Theatre, one example of this altruism, is a bold concrete construction, with defiant flytowers, likened by one of its less enthusiastic supporters to a bunker, presumably with hidden guns either trained upon or defending the Houses of Parliament across the river.

The Barbican, near St. Paul's, is another example of post-war reconstruction, which now provides a London home for the Royal Shakespeare Company. A forbidding and sometimes confusing mass of apartments and tower blocks, the Barbican is the largest arts center in Europe, with two theaters, an art gallery, a concert hall, a cinema, a library, and the Guildhall School of Music and Drama. However formidable the Barbican and the National Theatre may seem from a distance, their foyers and auditoriums are spacious and welcoming, with bookshops, cafés, and restaurants, and spaces for small musical ensembles and poetry readings. No commercial impresario could afford to be so lavish with space, or would want to pay the heating bills. These were theaters designed for an age of public subsidy, and their programs reflect this high-mindedness.

The West End theaters, on the other hand, were mainly built at the turn of the century, for openly commercial reasons, as part of an attempt to turn Piccadilly and Shaftesbury Avenue into a dignified playground for the newly rich Victorian and Edwardian middle classes. Piccadilly has since become the center for the British entertainment industry, which now embraces much more than the theater itself to include films, records, videos, television, and fashion as well. In the dozens of restaurants around Shaftesbury Avenue, half of British show business seems to take its lunch; the air is full of stage gossip and the smells of exotic cooking. The other half dines in Covent Garden to meet journalists from Fleet Street.

Piccadilly Circus itself is a poor reflection of what it once was, when the neon lights first lit up the exuberant facades of its Victorian mansion blocks. Nowadays, afflicted by schemes for its improvement, it feels unloved and unfinished. But there are gems, among them the delightful Criterion Theatre, first built in 1873 and rebuilt in 1884, and recently restored to its original soft, muted colors, painted ceilings, and eccentric tiling. It was the first British theater to be placed below street level. The lessons learned from the failures in its air-conditioning system were later applied to ventilating the Underground.

Since Piccadilly Circus itself was developed in 1885, the Criterion Theatre is one of its original buildings, clearly expressing a Victorian middle-class wish for intimate, comfortable theaters, far removed from the big, vulgar music halls (vaudeville theaters). Since it was intended for that purpose, the stage and the auditorium are most suited to comfortable plays, comedies, and dramas with small casts and no complicated scenery.

Fanning out from Piccadilly Circus are three famous theater streets: Haymarket, Coventry Street (leading to Leicester Square), and Shaftesbury Avenue. Leicester Square now has only one-and-a half theaters: the modern Prince of Wales Theatre designed to house musicals and spectacular revues, and the little Artaud Theatre, in a room above a pub. The other Leicester Square theaters have been transformed into cinemas and nightclubs, but in the Square itself, there is a half-price ticket booth offering cheap seats for many productions on the day of the performance only.

In 1721, a summer theater opened on Haymarket, known as the Little Theatre in the Hay. It had to battle against government restrictions, but it eventually received a royal patent to become the Theatre Royal, Haymarket. The existing theater, which opened in 1821, is notable, apart from its classical columns and portico, for being the first theater anywhere to have what is now known as a "picture frame" stage. In the 1880s it became famous for elegant drawing room plays ("society drama"), and some of that high style has persisted today.

On the other side of the road there is another historic theater, Her Majesty's, built in 1896–97 by the actor-manager, Sir Herbert Beerbohm Tree. As an actor, Tree is best remembered as Svengali in *Trilby*, while as a director, he was noted for his scenic effects—real rabbits hopping around an ethereal glade in *A Midsummer Night's Dream*. He would thoroughly have approved of the current production at Her Majesty's, *The Phantom of the Opera*. He would have wanted to play both the Phantom and the falling chandelier. It is a very appropriate musical for this theater, with its gilt and marbled-plaster auditorium in a style derived, as Tree proudly but inaccurately boasted, from the court of the French Sun King himself, Louis XIV.

Shaftesbury Avenue was built in the 1890s and early 1900s to be a show business boulevard. The Edwardian theaters line up, side by side, sumptuously dressed like *demi-mondaines* and as virtuous: the Apollo, the Lyric, the Queen's, the Globe, and, at Cambridge Circus, where the avenue intersects with Charing Cross Road, the massive Palace Theatre, a center for musicals.

These were the theaters which, in the inter-war years, saw the triumphs of Noël Coward and John Gielgud, the young Laurence Olivier and Gertie Lawrence; and they survived the war to everybody's surprise with their pride merely ruffled. Only the deplorable modern facade to the Queen's Theatre shows what damage might have been done.

These are theaters primarily designed for civilized, social gatherings, intimate but not too small, elaborate but not grandiose. Partly because of such theaters, Britain has developed a tradition of intelligent, middlebrow comedy writing, of which Coward and Somerset Maugham were exponents in the 1930s, just as Alan Ayckbourn, Simon Gray, Michael Frayn, Peter Shaffer, and Tom Stoppard are today. As if to suggest that such witty sophistication is skin deep, Soho lurks beyond the Shaftesbury Avenue stage doors, a maze of narrow streets and alleys, where London swung in the 1960s.

Many felt that Soho swung too far in the wrong direction and it certainly acquired a sleazy reputation. But the area has once more become a cosmopolitan center for the entertainment industry. There are jazz clubs (including Ronnie Scott's) and the London headquarters of film, record, and television companies. There are several theaters too, including the London Palladium, the last and most prestigious vaudeville house in London, the Prince Edward (a modern theater for musicals), the Piccadilly, and what was once known as the Windmill Theatre—named after the Moulin Rouge, which used to offer London versions of the opulent sex revues of Paris.

The old Windmill, apart from offering statuesque nudes and drafty fan dancers, had a remarkable reputation for discovering comics, who had to be funny to raise a smile from the dirty raincoat brigade. Peter Sellers was just one of the comics who served their apprenticeships at the Windmill. Now, Raymond's Revuebar has taken over from the Windmill as a glamor theater and has a little studio attached, the Boulevard, where today's comics try out their acts.

Shaftesbury Avenue crosses over Charing Cross Road and continues up toward Holborn, ending in the large punctuation point of Shaftesbury Theatre. But on the other side of Cambridge Circus, the character of theaterland changes. The bustle and raffishness of Soho has gone, and the feeling is of being in an Edwardian amusement arcade. There are Edwardian theaters in Charing Cross Road itself and in St. Martin's Lane, but this is, in fact, an older district of London, more Regency and early Victorian than Edwardian, the district of which the West End was originally deemed to be "west."

This is Covent Garden, where Eliza Doolittle once sold flowers in a supposedly incurable Cockney accent, before (in Shaw's *Pygmalion* and *My Fair Lady)* Professor Higgins redeemed her from the gutter. The old market has been similarly transformed into a smart and cheerful piazza, with bright, trendy shops and some lively street theater, including on occasions the best rap dancing in town. The British Theatre Museum now occupies one former warehouse in the market, both appropriate and a little superfluous, for the whole area is steeped in British theatrical history.

Backing the marketplace on one side is the Royal Opera House, built in six months, from December 1857 to May 1858, which achieved a small miracle of clear design, elegant elaboration, and spaciousness. In another street near the piazza is the Theatre Royal, Drury Lane, completed in 1812, the finest example of Georgian classical theater architecture in Britain. These two theaters, both built on sites occupied by theaters since the early 18th century, were for a hundred years in deadly rivalry. They were the Patent Houses, the only ones allowed to perform straight, non-musical plays. Until their exclusive rights were revoked in 1843, the various actor-managers that ran them, and many of the writers who created the successes that they staged, waged endless struggles for supremacy.

But the history of Covent Garden does not end with the patent houses, for in a side street near Drury Lane is the old Lyceum Theatre (now a dance hall), where Sir Henry Irving strutted the boards in the last decades of the 1800s and terrified audiences in *The Bells*. Irving, the most eminent British actor since Garrick a hundred years before, and the first to be knighted, did much to restore and popularize the plays of Shakespeare. In his Beefsteak Club, in rooms above his theater, he entertained members of the Royal Family.

To the south of Covent Garden, in the Strand, is the Savoy Theatre. Built by the impresario D'Oyly Carte in 1881, it immediately became the home of the Savoyard operas by Gilbert and Sullivan. The Savoy was the first public building in the world to be lit entirely by electric light made possible "by the incandescent lamps of Mr. J.W. Swan of Newcastle-upon-Tyne," much to the annoyance of Irving who preferred the grainy, foggy texture of gas lamps.

In 1905, the Aldwych and the Strand Theatres opened as part of a development scheme housing the Waldorf Hotel. The Aldwych was famous in the 1930s for its farces, written by Ben Travers for a redoubtable comedy team; but it became even better known in the 1960s as the temporary London home of the Royal Shakespeare Company. Another Covent Garden theater, formerly the New and now the Albery (to the west of the area on St. Martin's Lane), housed the Old Vic company during the latter years of World War II. Those seasons are still remembered as providing the most exciting classical productions ever seen in Britain, one answer to the "doodlebugs"—the rocket bombs fired against London.

All these theaters (and there are many more) are within easy walking distance of each other. Despite its diversity, the heart of London's theaterland is remarkably compact. But if you talk to ardent drama students, or to high-minded enthusiasts with no professional ambitions at all, they might tell you about the theater without even mentioning the West End. This is because, for the past 50 years, the most exciting productions in town have started in theaters away from the center. Before 1939, the Old Vic near Waterloo Station provided the best productions of Shakespeare, usually staged with very little money; while Sadlers Wells in Islington (which was a sister theater to the Old Vic) pioneered British opera and ballet.

During the 1950s, the revival of post-war British theater was spearheaded by two companies led by two charismatic directors, George Devine and Joan Littlewood. The Royal Court in Sloane Square was taken over in 1955 by the English Stage

Company, with Devine as its artistic director and with the declared policy of encouraging new playwrights. The results were immediate and dramatic. John Osborne's *Look Back in Anger* in 1956 caught the post-war mood of iconoclasm and doubt; and in the wake of that success came other young dramatists, including Arnold Wesker, Edward Bond, and Howard Brenton. Devine died in 1966, but the tradition that he established has continued, and the Royal Court is still the leading avant-garde theater in London, rivaled only perhaps by other West London theaters, Riverside Studios in Hammersmith, and the Bush Theatre in Shepherds Bush.

Littlewood was less of an intellectual. She wanted to create a working class theater movement, left-wing and serious in intent, but popular in means. She harnessed the old techniques of music hall and pantomime to themes that ranged from nuclear disarmament to the history of the First World War (in *Oh, What a Lovely War!*, 1963). Although she has long retired, the Theatre Workshop in Stratford, East London, has become a model for other theaters and their directors, not only in Britain.

There was, in fact, a remarkable group of directors, writers, and actors in Britain during the 1950s and 1960s, who collectively transformed the theater. One of their main targets was the commercialism and, as they saw it, the complacency of the West End; values they sought to challenge. The success of this post-war theater movement can be illustrated most obviously by the establishment of the two national companies. There had been sturdy demands for a national theater for more than a hundred years: In the 1960s, Britain established two, both working in old theaters (the Aldwych and the Old Vic) until new ones could be built for them. They developed different reputations. The National Theatre, led by Olivier, was considered to be an "actors' theater," with the performances of Olivier himself leading the way. The Royal Shakespeare Company was a "directors' theater," where the emphasis among the actors was on teamwork. The National Theatre tackled a wider range of drama, world classics, and major new plays as well as revivals of famous British plays. The Royal Shakespeare Company, led by Peter Hall, had as its house dramatist Shakespeare; and, in Stratford-upon-Avon, its main theater was committed to the work of the Elizabethan and Jacobean playwrights. In London, and in its various studios, it could, and did, introduce new and European plays into its repertoire. Its company style evolved during the 1980s toward major musicals *(Les Misérables)* and such epics as its dramatization of Charles Dickens's *Nicholas Nickleby*.

The differences between the two companies became blurred when Hall succeeded Olivier at the National Theatre in 1973, and was followed at the Royal Shakespeare Company by Trevor Nunn. The national companies also expanded with time; currently the RSC runs five theaters, three in Stratford and two at the Barbican, with additional RSC productions playing in the West End. The NT has its three contrasting theaters on the South Bank, the Olivier, the Lyttelton, and the Cottesloe, and also regularly transfers productions to the West End.

There were, however, other results from the post-war British theater revival, such as the establishment of suburban and regional repertory theaters, of which the Lyric, Hammersmith, and Greenwich theaters in South London are the best examples. Another effect, dating from the late 1960s and early 1970s, was the growth of fringe theater clubs, which now can be found all round London. The standards are variable, but they can be very high, particularly at the Donmar Theatre in Covent Garden, the Bush, and the Hampstead Theatre in Swiss Cottage.

And so, to return to the original questions: What shows should visitors see in London? What are the leading theaters? I usually try to suggest a package, which includes one West End comedy, one major new play, one musical, a classical production at one of the national companies, and some talent-spotting, checking the listings in *Time Out* (the weekly "What's On" magazine) to find out what is playing in the fringe theaters or at the Royal Court. Within each of these choices, I recommend mainly on the quality of the production, but also try to bear in mind the nature of the theater, particularly its history and architecture.

Having thus solemnly deliberated, and presented a well-balanced program, I can sit back, confident that most of my friends will ignore it anyway and see *Cats*, *The Mousetrap*, and the Tower of London, before flopping with exhaustion on the floor of Harrods Food Hall. Never mind. I tried.

3 Essential Information

Arriving and Departing

By Train   London is served by no fewer than 15 railway stations, so be absolutely certain of the station for your departure or arrival. All have Underground stations either in the train station or within a few minutes' walk from it, and most are served by several bus routes. British Rail controls all major rail services. The principal routes that connect London to other major towns and cities are on an InterCity network; unlike its European counterparts, British Rail makes no extra charge for the use of this express service network.

Seats cannot be reserved by phone. You should apply in person to any British Rail Travel Centre or directly to the station from which you depart. Below is a list of the major London rail stations and the areas they serve.

Charing Cross (tel. 01/928–5100) serves southeast England, including Canterbury, Margate, Dover/Folkestone.
Euston/St. Pancras (tel. 01/387–7070) serves East Anglia, Essex, the northeast, the northwest, and northern Wales, including Coventry, Stratford-upon-Avon, Birmingham, Manchester, Liverpool, Windermere, Glasgow, and Inverness.
King's Cross (tel. 01/278–2477) serves the east Midlands, the northeast including York, Leeds, Newcastle, and north and east Scotland including Edinburgh, and Aberdeen.
Liverpool Street (tel. 01/928–5100) serves Essex and East Anglia.
Paddington (tel. 01/262–6767) serves south Midlands, west and south Wales, and the west country, including Reading, Bath, Bristol, Oxford, Cardiff, Swansea, Exeter, Plymouth, and Penzance.
Victoria (tel. 01/928–5100) serves southern England, including Gatwick Airport, Brighton, Dover/Folkestone (from May), and the south coast.
Waterloo (tel. 01/928–5100) serves southwestern United Kingdom, including Salisbury, Bournemouth, Portsmouth, Southampton, and the isles of Wight, Jersey, and Guernsey.

Fares. There is a wide, bewildering range of "savers" and other ticket bargains. Unfortunately, ticket clerks cannot always be relied on to know which type best suits your needs, so be sure to ask at the information office first. **Cheap Day Returns** are best if you're returning to London the same day, and many family and other discount railcards are available. You can hear a recorded summary of timetable and fare information to many InterCity destinations by dialing the appropriate "dial and listen" numbers listed under British Rail in the telephone book.

By Bus   "Bus" in Britain generally refers to part of the local transport system; "coach," meanwhile, is more similar to a Greyhound and is used for longer, cross-country trips.

The **National Express** coach service has routes to over 1,000 major towns and cities in the United Kingdom. It's considerably cheaper than the train, although the trips will usually take longer. National Express offers two types of service: an ordinary service that makes frequent stops for refreshment breaks, and a *Rapide* service, which has hostess and refreshment facilities on board. Day returns are available on both, but booking is advised on the *Rapide* service. National Express coaches leave Victoria Coach Station (Buckingham Palace Rd.)

at regular intervals, depending on destination. For travel information, dial 01/730–0202.

In addition to National Express, **Greenline** operates bus services within a 30–40 mile radius of London. A *Golden Rover* ticket, which allows unlimited travel, is available. Contact Greenline for more information, tel. 01/668–7261.

By Car London radiates with approach routes; the major ones are designated as either "motorways" (six-lane major highways; look for an "M" followed by a number), or "A" roads (the letter "A" followed by a number); the latter may be either "dual carriageways" (four lanes) or two-lane highways. The speed limit on motorways and dual carriageways is 70 mph, and on all other roads it is 60 mph.

Because of their greater number of lanes, motorways are usually a faster option for getting in or out of town than A roads, and many motorways merge back into A roads some distance out of London. That said, during peak hours on weekdays you can get caught in the commuter crush, and easily spend half an hour or more stuck in traffic jams; stay tuned to radio stations for regular traffic updates.

The recently completed M25 encircles Greater London—ideal if you're staying in the suburbs and want a quick getaway, or wish to connect with one of its many junctions.

From Downtown to the Airports **Heathrow.** The Piccadilly Line serves Heathrow (all terminals) with a direct Underground link. Trains run every four to eight minutes; journey time is roughly 40 minutes; price is £1.70 one way. LRT's *Airbus* service also runs to Heathrow; two routes stop at many central locations, including most major hotels. The A1 leaves every 20 minutes from Victoria Station, 6:40 AM–9:30 P.M. daily; journey time is about an hour. The A2 leaves Euston Station every 20 minutes, 6:20 AM–9:30 PM daily; journey time is about an hour and 20 minutes. Price for each route is £3 single.

An alternative to the Airbus, serving Gatwick and Luton as well as Heathrow, is the *Flightline Coach* which leaves from Victoria Coach Station. Coach 767 departs every 20 minutes, 6:40 AM–12:40 PM, then every half hour until 9:05 PM. Journey time is approximately 45 minutes.

By car, the most direct route from Central London is via the M4. By taxi, the fare from downtown should be around £18; the journey time will depend on the traffic.

Gatwick. Fast non-stop trains leave Victoria Station every 15 minutes, 5:30 AM–10 PM; journey time is approximately 30 minutes. Price is £5, single. Some airlines have offices at Victoria, so it is possible to check your luggage before you arrive at the airport. Regular bus services are provided by *Greenline Coaches* (tel. 01/668–7261), including the Flightline 777 which leaves Victoria Coach Station every 30 minutes. Journey time: about 70 minutes.

By car, take the A23 and then the M23 from central London.

Important Addresses and Numbers

Tourist Information The main **London Tourist Information Centre** at Victoria Station Forecourt provides details about London and the rest of Britain, including general information; tickets for tube and bus; theater, concert, and tour bookings; accommodations; etc. Open April–October daily 9–8:30; rest of the year, Monday–Saturday 9–7, Sunday 9–5.

Other information centers are located in *Harrods* (Brompton Rd., SW3) and *Selfridges* (Oxford St., W1) and are open store hours only; also at *Heathrow Airport* (Terminals 1, 2, and 3).

The **British Travel Centre** (12 Regent St., W1, tel. 01/730–3400) provides details about travel, accommodations, and bookings for the whole of Britain. Open weekdays 9–6:30 and weekends 10–4.

The **Clerkenwell Heritage Centre**, 33 St. John's Sq., EC1, tel. 01/250–1039. Open weekdays 10–6.

Embassies and Consulates   **American Embassy**, 24 Grosvenor Sq., W1A, 1AE, tel. 01/499–9000. Located inside the embassy is the American Aid Society, a charity set up to help Americans in distress. Dial the embassy number and ask for extension 570 or 571.

Canadian High Commission, Canada House, Trafalgar Sq., London SW1Y 5BJ, tel. 01/629–9492.

Emergencies   For police, fire brigade, or ambulance, dial 999.

The following hospitals have 24-hour emergency rooms: **Guys**, St. Thomas St., SE1, tel. 01/407–7600; **Royal Free**, Pond St., Hampstead, NW3, tel. 01/794–0500; **St. Bartholomew's**, West Smithfields, EC1, tel. 01/600–9000; **St. Thomas's**, Lambeth Palace Rd., SE1, tel. 01/928–9292; **University College**, Gower St., W1, tel. 01/387–9300; **Westminster**, Dean Ryle St., Horseferry Rd., SW1, tel. 01/828–9811.

Pharmacies   Chemists (drugstores) with late opening hours include **Bliss Chemist**, 50–56 Willesden Lane, NW6, tel. 01/624–8000, open daily 9 AM–2 AM, also the branch at 5 Marble Arch, W1, tel. 01/723–6116, open daily 9 AM–midnight; **Boots**, 439 Oxford St., W1, tel. 01/409–2857, open Thursday 8:30–7; and **Underwoods**, 114 Queensway, W2, tel. 01/229–4819, open Monday–Saturday 9 AM–10 PM, Sunday 10–10.

Travel Agencies   **American Express**, 6 Haymarket, SW1, tel. 01/930–4411, and at 89 Mount St., W1, tel. 01/499–4436; **Hogg Robinson Travel/Diners Club**, 176 Tottenham Court Rd., W1, tel. 01/580–0437; **Thomas Cook**, 45 Berkeley St., Piccadilly W1, tel. 01/499–4000.

Credit Cards   Should your credit cards be lost or stolen, here are some numbers to dial for assistance: **Access (MasterCard)**, tel. 0702/352255; **American Express**, tel. 0273/696933 for credit cards, tel. 0273/693555 for traveler's checks; **Barclaycard (Visa)**, tel. 0604/21288; **Diners Club**, tel. 0252/516261.

Staying in Touch

Telephones   There are three types of phones, two which accept coins and one which accepts phone cards. The older pay-on-answer phone accepts only 10p coins. To operate: Lift the receiver and you will hear the dial tone—a continuous purring or high-pitched hum. Dial the number and wait for your party to answer, at which time the ringing tone will change to a series of rapid "pips"—the pay tone. Press a 10p coin into the slot and wait until the coin drops before talking. Insert additional coins each time the pay tone sounds. If you hear a repeated single tone after dialing, the line is busy; a continuous tone means the line is unobtainable.

The newer, coin-operated phones are of the push-button variety; some take all coins, others all but the 20p piece. Insert the coins *before* dialing (minimum charge is 10p). There are no pips, and the indicator panel shows you how much money is left; add more whenever you like. If there is no answer, replace the receiver and your money will be returned.

Cardphones operate with special cards that you can buy from post offices or newsagents displaying the green and white phone card sign. They are ideal for longer calls, are composed of units of 10p, and come in values of £1, £2, £4, £10, and £20. To use, lift the receiver, then insert your card and dial your number. An indicator panel shows the number of units used. At the end of your call the card will be returned.

For long distance calls within Britain, dial the area code (which begins with a zero), followed by the number. The area code for London is 01, but do not use it unless dialing a London number from outside the capital.

All calls are charged according to the time of day. Peak rate (most expensive) runs 9 AM–1 PM weekdays; standard rate is 8 AM–9 AM and 1 PM–6 PM weekdays; cheap rate is 6 PM–8 AM weekdays and all day on weekends.

International Calls. These are usually cheaper when made weekdays between 8 PM and 8 AM, and at any time on weekends. For direct dialing, dial 010, then the country code, area code, and number. For the international operator, credit card, or collect calls, dial 155. For directory enquiries (information) in most countries, dial 153. Bear in mind that hotels usually levy a hefty surcharge on calls made from hotel rooms; better to use the pay phones located in most hotel foyers.

Operators and Information. To call the operator, dial 100; directory enquiries (information) for London numbers only, 142; information for the rest of Britain, 192. No charge is made for any of the above.

Mail The **London Chief Post Office** (King Edward St., EC1, tel. 01/239–5047) is open weekdays 8–7, Saturday 9 AM–12:30 PM, except on public holidays. The **Trafalgar Square Post Office** (24–28 William IV St., WC2, tel. 01/930–1178) is open Monday–Saturday 8 AM–8 PM, and on Sunday and bank holidays 10–5; however, these hours may soon be subject to change. Most other post offices are open weekdays 9–5:30, and on Saturday 9–12:30 or 1. Stamps may be bought from main or sub-post offices (the latter are located in shops), or from stamp machines located outside post offices. Mailboxes are known as post or letter boxes and are painted bright red; large tubular ones are set on the edge of sidewalks, while smaller boxes are set into post office walls.

Postal Rates. At press time, spring 1988, postal rates are as follows: airmail letters up to 10 grams to the United States and Canada, 31p; postcards and air letters, 26p. Letters and postcards to EEC countries go for 18p, and to the rest of Europe for 22p. Letters within the United Kingdom are 18p for first class, 13p for second class. Always check rates in advance, however, as they are subject to change.

Receiving Mail. If you're uncertain where you'll be staying, you can have mail sent to you c/o Poste Restante to the **London Chief Post Office,** King Edward Street, EC1. The service is free and may be used for three months. Alternatively, **Ameri-**

can Express (6 Haymarket, SW1, tel. 01/930–4411, or any other branch) will accept letters free of charge on behalf of its customers; non-customers pay 60p.

Getting Around

By Underground   Known colloquially as "the tube," London's extensive Underground system is by far the most widely used form of city transport. Trains run both beneath and above ground out into the suburbs, and all stations are clearly marked with the London Underground circular symbol. (A "subway" sign refers to an under-the-street crossing.) Trains are all one class; smoking is *not* allowed on board or in the stations.

There are nine basic lines—all named—plus the East London line, which runs from Shoreditch and Whitechapel across the Thames and south to New Cross. The Central, District, Northern, Metropolitan, and Piccadilly lines all have branches, so be sure to note which branch is needed for your particular destination. Electronic platform signs tell you the final stop and route of the next train, and some signs also indicate how many minutes you'll have to wait for the train to arrive.

From Monday to Saturday, trains begin running just after 5 AM; the last services leave central London between midnight and 12:30 AM. On Sundays, trains start two hours later and finish about an hour earlier. Frequency of trains depends on the route and the time of day, but normally you should not have to wait more than 10 minutes in central areas.

A pocket map of the entire tube network is available free from most Underground ticket counters. There should also be a large map on the wall of each platform—though often these are defaced beyond recognition.

Fares. For both buses and tube fares, London is divided into five concentric zones; the fare goes up the further afield you travel. Ask at Underground ticket counters for the London Regional Transport booklet "Tickets," which gives details of all the various ticket options and bargains for the tube; after some experimenting, you'll soon know which ticket best serves your particular needs. Till then, here is a brief summary of the major ticket categories.

Singles and Returns. For one journey between any two stations, you can buy an ordinary single for travel anytime on the day of issue; if you're coming back on the same route the same day, then an ordinary return costs twice the single fare. Singles vary in price from 40p (50p in the central zone) to £1.70—not a good option for the sightseer who wants to make several journeys.

Cheap Day Return. Issued Monday–Friday after 9:30 AM and anytime on weekends. Basically good for a return journey from a station inside the zones to one outside—such as from Bond Street to Hampton Court.

One Day Off-Peak Travelcards. Allows unrestricted travel on both bus and tube; valid Monday–Friday after 9:30 AM, weekends, and all public holidays. Price £2.

One Day Capitalcard. Works the same way as a One Day Travelcard, but allows use of British Rail service within Greater London as well. Price £2.60. Both Travelcards and Capitalcards may be purchased for weekly or monthly use, as well as for one day; a photograph is required, and prices vary according to the number of zones traveled.

London Underground

UNDERGROUND

Key to lines

Bakerloo		East London
Central		Jubilee
Circle		Metropolitan
District		Northern

Piccadilly	
Victoria	
British Rail	
Docklands Light Railway	

○ Interchange stations

✤ Connections with British Rail

⧗ Connections within walking distance

✳ Closed Sundays

✱ Closed Saturdays and Sundays

▲ Served by Piccadilly line early mornings and late evenings Mondays to Saturdays and all day Sundays

† See poster maps at Underground stations for opening and closing times of these stations

Visitor's Travelcard. May be bought in the United States and Canada as well as in London, for one, three, four, and seven days. The three- and four-day passes cannot be purchased in London. Apply to travel agents or to BritRail Travel International.

For more information, there are LRT Travel Information Centres at the following tube stations: **Oxford Circus,** open Monday –Saturday 8:30–6 and Thursday until 9:30; **Piccadilly Circus,** open Monday–Sunday 8:30–9:30; **Victoria,** upstairs open Monday–Sunday 8:30–9:30; **St. James's Park,** open Monday–Friday 8:30–6; and **Heathrow,** open daily. For information on all London bus and tube times, fares, etc., dial 01/222–1234; the line is operated 24 hours.

By Bus London's bus system now consists of the bright red double- and single-deckers, plus, in the outer zones, other buses of various colors. Destinations are displayed on the front and back, with the bus number on the front, back, and side. By no means do all buses run the full length of their route at all times, so always check the termination point before boarding, preferably with the conductor or driver. Many buses are still operated with a conductor whom you pay after finding a seat, but there is now a move to "one-man" buses, in which you pay the driver upon boarding.

Buses stop only at clearly indicated stops. Main stops—at which the bus *should* stop automatically—have a plain white background with a red LRT symbol on it. There are also request stops with red signs, a white symbol, and the word "Request" added; at these you must hail the bus to make it stop. Smoking is not allowed on the lower deck of a double-decker, and is discouraged on the top deck, except at the back. Although you can see much of the town from a bus, *don't* take one if you want to get anywhere in a hurry; traffic often slows travel to a crawl, and during peak times you may find yourself waiting 20 minutes for a bus and then not being able to get on it once it arrives. If you do go by bus, ask at a Travel Information Centre for a free London Wide Bus Map.

Fares. Single fares start at 35p for short distances (50p in the central zone). As previously mentioned, Travelcards are good for both tube and bus; there are also a number of bus passes available for daily, weekly, and monthly use, and prices vary according to zones.

By Taxi Those big, black taxicabs are as much a part of the London streetscape as the red double-decker buses, yet some now come in a variety of colors and carry advertising on their sides. Hotels and main tourist areas have taxi ranks (just take the first at the top of the "queue"), but you can also flag one down from the roadside. If the taxi flag is up or the yellow "for hire" sign is lit on the top, then the taxi is available for passengers. Many cab drivers often cruise at night with their "for hire" signs unlit; this is to enable them to choose their passengers and avoid those they think might cause trouble. If you see an unlit, passengerless cab, hail it: you just might be lucky.

Fares. Fares start at 80p when the flag falls and increase by units of 20p per 495 yards or 60 seconds. After six miles the rate changes to 20p per 330 yards (or one minute). A 40p surcharge is added on weekday nights 8–midnight and Saturday up to 8 PM. The surcharge rises to 60p on Saturday nights, Sundays, and public holidays—except over Christmas and New Year's Eve when it rises even higher to £2.

By Car The best advice about driving in London is: don't. Because the capital grew up as a series of villages, there never was a central plan for London's streets, and the result is a winding mass of chaos, aided and abetted by a passion for one-way systems.

If you must risk life and limb, however, the speed limit is 30 mph in the royal parks as well as it (theoretically) is in all streets—unless you see the large 40 mph signs (and small repeater signs attached to lamp posts) found only in the suburbs.

Other basic rules: Pedestrians have total right-of-way on "zebra" crossings—those black and white stripes that stretch across the road between two beacons. The beacons have orange flashing lights on top, and the crossing itself has zig-zag markings on both sides. It is illegal to park within the zig-zag area, or to pass another vehicle at a zebra crossing. On other crossings pedestrians must yield to traffic, but they do have right of way over traffic turning left at controlled crossings—if they have the nerve.

Traffic lights sometimes have arrow-style lights directing left or right turns; it is therefore important not to get into the turn lane if you mean to go straight ahead, so try to catch a glimpse of the road markings in time. The use of horns is prohibited between 11:30 PM and 7 AM.

You can park at night in 30 mph zones, provided you are within 25 yards of a lit street lamp, but not within 15 yards of a road junction. To park on a bus route, side (parking) lights must be shown, but you'll probably be fined for obstruction. During the day—and probably at all times—it is safest to believe that you can park nowhere except at a meter or a garage; otherwise, you run the risk of a £12 fine, a tow-away cost of £57, or a wheel clamp, which clamps a wheel immovably and costs £37 to get released. Note that it is now illegal to park on the sidewalk in London.

London Districts Greater London is divided into 32 boroughs—33, when you consider the City of London, which has all the powers of a London borough. More useful for finding your way around, however, are the subdivisions of London into various postal districts. Throughout the guide we've listed the full postal code for places you're likely to be contacting by mail, although you'll find the first half of the code more important. The first one or two letters give the location: N=north, NW=northwest, etc. Don't expect the numbering to be logical, however. You won't, for example, find W2 next to W3.

Guided Tours

Orientation Tours **London Regional Transport**'s official guided sightseeing tours
By Bus (tel. 01/222–1234) offer passengers a good introduction to the city from double-decker buses (seating capacity 64–72). Tours run daily every half hour 10–5, from Marble Arch (top of Park Lane near Speakers' Corner), Victoria Station, and Piccadilly Circus (Haymarket). The route covers roughly 18–20 miles and lasts 1½ hours; no stops are included. Tickets may be bought from the driver, or in advance from the London Tourist Information Centre at Victoria. Other agencies offering half- and full-day bus tours include **Evan Evans** (tel. 01/930–2377),

London Postal Districts

Frames Rickards (tel. 01/837–3111), and **Travellers Check-In** (tel. 01/580–8284). These tours have a smaller seating capacity of approximately 53 passengers, and include stops at places of special interest, such as St. Paul's Cathedral and Westminster Abbey. Prices and pick-up points vary according to the sights visited, but many pick-up points are at major hotels.

By River From April to October boats cruise up and down the Thames, offering a different view of the London skyline. Most leave from Westminster Pier (tel. 01/930–4097), Charing Cross Pier (Victoria Embankment, tel. 01/839–3312), and Tower Pier (tel. 01/488–0344). Downstream routes go to the Tower of London, Greenwich, and Thames Barrier; upstream destinations include Kew, Richmond, and Hampton Court. Most of the launches seat between 100 and 250 passengers, have a public address system, and provide a running commentary on passing points of interest. Depending upon destination, river trips may last from one to four hours. For more information, call **Catamaran Cruises**, tel. 01/839–2349, or **Travel Cruises**, tel. 01/928–9009.

By Canal During summer, narrow boats and barges cruise London's two canals, the Grand Union and Regent's Canal; most vessels (seats about 62) operate on the latter, which runs between Little Venice in the west (nearest tube Warwick Ave. on the Bakerloo Line) and Camden Lock (about 200 yards north of Camden Town tube station). **Jason's Canal Cruises** (tel. 01/286–3428) operates one-way and round-trip narrow boat cruises on this route. During April, May, and September, there are two cruises per day; from June to August there are four. Trips last 1½ hours and cost £2.95 for adults, £1.50 for children and senior citizens.

Canal Cruises (tel. 01/485–4433) also offers cruises from March to October on the *Jenny Wren* (£2.10 adults, £1.10 children and senior citizens), and all year on the floating restaurant *My Fair Lady* (Tues.–Sat. dinner £16.95, Sun. lunch £12.75).

By Plane If land and water aren't enough, you may choose to see London by airship. The *Skyship 600* (tel. 01/995–7811) provides aerial tours of the city from a blimp during the summer months. Seating capacity is limited to 12, and the price is enormous: £125–£150 per person.

Walking Tours One of the best ways to get to know London is on foot, and there are many guided walking tours from which to choose. **London Walks** (tel. 01/882–2763), **Cockney Walks** (tel. 01/504–9159), **Streets of London** (tel. 01/882–3414), and **Discovering London** (tel. 0277/213704) are just a few of the better known firms, but your best bet is to peruse a variety of leaflets at the London Tourist Information Centre at Victoria Station. Length of walks vary (usually 1–3 hours), and you can generally find one to suit even the most specific of interests—Shakespeare's London, say, or a Jack the Ripper tour. Prices range around £2.25 for adults.

If you'd rather explore on your own, then the City of London Corporation has laid out a **Heritage Walk** which leads through Bank, Leadenhall, and Monument; follow the trail by the directional stars set into the sidewalks. A map of this walk may be found in *A Visitor's Guide to the City of London*, available from the City Information Centre across from St. Paul's Cathedral. Another option is to follow the **Silver Jubilee Walkway**, created in 1977 in honor of the 25th anniversary of the reign of the present Queen. The entire route covers 10 miles and is marked by a series of silver crowns set into the sidewalks; Parliament Square makes a good starting point. Several books are available from the British Travel Centre (12 Regent St., W1) which also list a number of different walks to follow.

Excursions **LRT, Evan Evans, Frames Rickards,** and **Travellers Check-In** (*see* Orientation Tours) all offer day excursions (some combine bus and boat) to places of interest within easy reach of London, such as Windsor, Hampton Court, Oxford, Stratford, and Bath. Prices vary and may include lunch and admission or admission only.

Personal Guides **Prestige Tours** (tel. 01/584–3118) operates a fleet of normal London taxis, each driven by a qualified guide. Tours are available all year, and a day's advance booking is usually enough to arrange an expert tour of the capital. There are three basic tours: full-day (around six hours) for £130; half-day (three hours) for £80; and the two-hour "Easy Rider" for £55. Alternatively, you can arrange an out-of-town trip such as Stratford combined with Oxford. Rates may seem high, but are for up to four people.

Other personal guides operate their own service. **Heritage Services Jaguar Tour,** for instance, offers customized tours guided by the owner, Lord Dillon, who takes customers wherever they want, for however long they want, in his Jaguar. The price per hour is £20 in London, an extra £5 is added for out of the city destinations. The Jaguar carries three passengers. For more information, tel. 01/994–9174 or 01/994–4319. Details of similar private operators may be found in brochures at the London Tourist Information Centre in Victoria Station or at the British Travel Centre.

Opening and Closing Times

Banks Normally open Monday–Friday 9:30–3:30, some branches do provide services on Saturday. Banks at major airports and train stations also have extended hours.

Museums Most museums are open Monday–Saturday 10–5 or 10–6, and Sunday 2–5 or 2–6, including most bank holidays, but are closed on public holidays such as Good Friday. Check individual listings for definite opening hours.

Pubs At present, pubs and bars have strict licensing hours. Since mid-1988 most pubs are open Monday–Saturday 11 AM–11 PM; Sunday 12–3, and 7–10 or 10:30.

Shops Usual business hours are Monday–Saturday 9–5:30 or 9–6. Some shops have late opening hours on Wednesday or Thursday until 7 or 7:30 PM, and in spite of the laws, many are open on Sunday.

Tipping

Many restaurants and large hotels (particularly those belonging to chains) will automatically add a 10% to a 15% service charge to your bill, so always check in advance before you hand out any extra money. If a service charge has been added, you are not expected to tip any member of the staff—unless you would like to because of exceptional service. If you are dissatisfied with any service, however, refuse to pay the service charge, stating your reasons for doing so; you will legally be in the right.

Do not tip cinema or theater ushers, elevator operators, or bar staff in pubs—although you may buy them a drink if you're feeling generous. You do not have to tip washroom attendants, either, although many do display a saucer and you may leave 5p or 10p if you like.

The following may be used as guides for other tipping situations:
Restaurants: 10%–15% of the check for full meals if service is not already included; nothing if you're just having coffee or tea. **Taxis:** 10%, depending upon size of fare. **Porters:** 50p per bag. **Doormen:** 50p for hailing taxis, 50p for carrying bags to check-in desk. **Bellhops:** £1 for carrying bags to rooms, £1 for room service. **Hairdressers:** 10%–15% of the bill.

Sports

London is not a sporting place. That said, there are a few events sports fans will want to try to see.

Two annual events that are fun for spectators to watch are the Boat Race, the rowing race between Oxford and Cambridge universities, and the London Marathon. The Boat Race, held on a Saturday in late March or early April, starts at Putney and finishes at Mortlake, which is a good place to stand and watch. The crowd is good-humored, and there's generally lots of space to see what's happening. The marathon, held on a Sunday in late April and modeled on the New York Marathon, is a similarly happy occasion, with families and friends turning out in force to cheer on the thousands of participants. The race starts on Blackheath, at the top end of Greenwich Park (*see* Greenwich), and finishes at the south end of Westminster Bridge.

Tennis Tickets for the Wimbledon tennis championship are costly, hard to obtain, and sold months in advance. However, you can gain entrance by arriving early in the day and standing in line; this is especially recommended during the first week of the championship fortnight, when it is not difficult to get in and plenty of top stars can be seen playing on the outer courts, where there are no reserved seats and the atmosphere is pleasantly informal.

Cricket If you have mastered the arcane complexities of cricket, make for either the Lord's ground (just north of Regent's Park) or the Oval ground, south of the river. There are matches here most summer weekends and often during the week as well.

Soccer Wembley Stadium (*see* Off the Beaten Track) is the scene of the Cup Final, played each May at the conclusion of the soccer season, and it is also the venue of other major soccer and rugby matches. Soccer clubs in London include Arsenal and Tottenham Hotspur, in north London; West Ham United in east London; Crystal Palace and Wimbledon in south London; and Chelsea, Fulham, and Queen's Park Rangers on the western edge of central London. Soccer matches are often the scene of, at best, exuberant partisanship and, at worst, aggressive violence; if you want to attend a match, telephone the club in advance to find out how to reach the stand (in England, spectators sit in a building called the "stand"; if you stand up to watch a match, you do so on the terraces)—or better still, go with someone who knows his or her way around locally. The home of rugby football is at Twickenham, in west London.

Golf There are many fine golf courses in the outer suburbs of London, where the built-up area gradually merges into the countryside.

Hotel Fitness Centers **The Peak Health Club at the Hyatt Carlton Tower** (2 Cadogan Pl., London SW1, tel. 01/235–5411) offers the most complete hotel fitness facilities in central London, with Nautilus-type stations, Lifecycles, rowing machines, treadmills, aerobics classes, and even a sauna equipped with TV. Tennis is available across the street in Cadogan Gardens.

The Meridien Le Piccadilly Hotel (Piccadilly, London W1, tel. 01/427–8114) houses the elegant, turn-of-the-century Champney's Club, with free weights, Universal stations, treadmills, exercycles, and a small pool. Aerobics, yoga, and body-shaping classes round out the program.

The Olympian Health Club in the St. James Court Hotel (Buckingham Gate, London SW, tel. 01/834–6655) is brand new, and offers treadmills, a rowing machine, electronically monitored cycles, 14 Universal stations, plus yoga and aerobics.

Jogging Centrally located **Green Park** and **St. James's Park** are adequate for short runs, except on summer afternoons when the many lawn chairs make the going too crowded. Far better is bucolic **Hyde Park** which, with adjoining **Kensington Gardens**, measures four miles around. Run on asphalt trails among formal rose gardens and ballfields. A 2½ mile loop can be made by starting at either Hyde Park Corner or Marble Arch, and turning at the Serpentine. **Regent's Park** is convenient to much of north London and a loop of the perimeter measures about 2½ miles. For longer runs, try **Hampstead Heath,** Hampstead tube stop, or the wilder **Richmond Park,** housing deer and other animals (stick to the lightly-traveled roads), via the Richmond tube stop.

4 Exploring London

Orientation

Traditionally, London has been divided between the City to the east, where its banking and commercial interests lie, and Westminster to the west, the seat of the royal court and of government. That distinction remains today, as our two most substantial exploring sections—the **City**, and **Westminster and Royal London**—demonstrate. The City route has a distinctly financial orientation, while the Westminster exploration roves through history, passing royal palaces, past and present, and surveying the government area around Parliament Square.

London expanded outward from Westminster during the 17th century, the rate of development steadily increasing as the decades passed. Elegant town houses were built for the nobility first in St. James's and Mayfair, and later in Chelsea, Knightsbridge, and Kensington. These remain pleasant, if very pricey, residential neighborhoods, as well as being busy, elegant shopping areas, as our three walks around them will show.

London also enjoys unique "lungs," a great swathe of greenery across the city center, thanks to its past kings and queens, who reserved large areas for their own hunting and relaxation. The inevitable passage of time opened them up to the public. The largest of these "royal parks"—no longer monarchical possessions, but administered by a government department—are described in the section on **Hyde Park and Kensington Gardens.**

In the 19th century, London spread by leaps and bounds, especially following the construction of the railways, which made commuting to and from the center easy. Our section on **Regent's Park and Hampstead** covers an interesting area of the city; one of the latest royal parks; some typical suburbia in Camden Town; and Hampstead village, as fashionable now as it was as an 18th-century health resort.

The river Thames was for centuries London's most important highway, and in the last few years it has been enjoying something of a renaissance. The sections on **Greenwich** and the **Thames Upstream** investigate some of the interesting attractions to be found away from the center, though still on the river, while the **South Bank** takes you along the river's south side, traditionally less fashionable than the north side, but with just as varied and distinguished a history and as vibrant a contemporary life.

Numbers in the margins correspond with points of interest on the maps.

Westminster and Royal London

The sites covered in this chapter—Trafalgar Square, Buckingham Palace, the Houses of Parliament, and Westminster Abbey
—form what some Londoners know, only slightly facetiously,
as the Golden Triangle. You won't find much gold here; like
Dick Whittington—a legendary Lord Mayor who rose from
rags to riches—you'll be disappointed if you arrive hoping to
find the streets paved with it, but you will find almost all of
London's major tourist attractions within and along the sides
of the triangle. All the sights here could easily be seen in a day,
though it would be an exhausting one. But you could also devote
a month or more to exploring the area and still feel that you
were only scratching the surface, such is the variety and richness of this deeply historic and fascinating part of London.

London is unique among the great cities in Europe in having
not one but two centers, the City and Westminster. The City,
where the Romans settled, is the older. Westminster, at not
much more than 1,000 years old, is a real youngster by comparison. The two areas had parallel, though quite separate, developments from the time that the 11th-century king, Edward
the Confessor, moved his court away from the cramped quarters of the City to Westminster, a couple of miles or so upstream, and in the process, built a great abbey church, or minster, there. The City was thus freed to continue and develop as
the commercial center of London, while Westminster became
the seat of government and the royal residence. These roles
have in the main continued uninterrupted to the present day.
The name Westminster itself underlines this separation, as it
means exactly what it says—the "west" minster, or church to
the west of the City.

Our description of Westminster takes you from Trafalgar
Square to Buckingham Palace, and then to Parliament Square,
though there's no reason why you can't go in the opposite,
clockwise, direction. Trafalgar Square is the point in London to
and from which all distances in the rest of Britain are officially
measured, making it the geographical—if not the psycho-
logical—center of the capital.

Trafalgar Square and the National Gallery

Trafalgar Square, probably the most famous of London's
squares, stands on the site of what was originally the Royal
Mews, or stables, of the nearby Palace of Whitehall. The mews
were established in the 14th century by Edward I—not to be
confused with the much earlier Edward the Confessor who
built Westminster Abbey and had no number. (Kings and
queens of England only begin to be numbered from William the
Conqueror, William I, in 1066.) The poet Chaucer was for a
time Clerk of these Mews. The square as it is today dates from
about 1830 when the central portion was leveled, the National
Gallery begun, and the statue of Lord Nelson, victor of the battle of Trafalgar in 1805, was erected. At the same time, the
❶ square's name was changed. **Nelson's Column,** a statue 185 feet
up in the air on the summit of a massive gray column, is certainly the most famous in London, and the most dominant landmark
in the square. Four huge lions, designed by the Victorian painter Edwin Landseer, guard the base of the column, which in
turn is decorated by four massive bronze panels cast from the

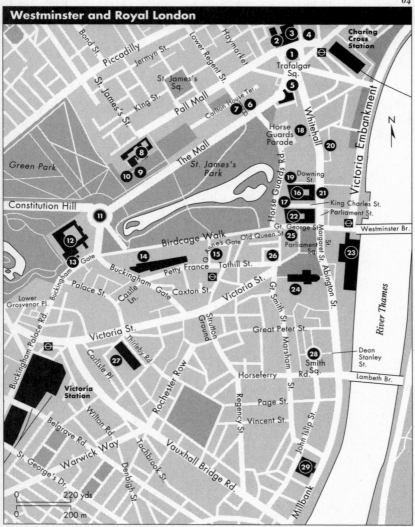

Westminster and Royal London

Charing Cross Station

Trafalgar Sq.

Nelson's Column

Whitehall

Victoria Embankment

Horse Guards Parade

St. James's Park

The Mall

Green Park

Constitution Hill

Birdcage Walk

Buckingham Gate

Palace St.

Victoria St.

Victoria Station

River Thames

Westminster Br.

Lambeth Br.

Vauxhall Bridge Rd.

Millbank

Admiralty Arch, **5**
Banqueting House, **20**
Buckingham Palace, **12**
Cabinet War Rooms, **17**
Cenotaph, **21**
Central Hall, **26**
Clarence House, **9**
Duke of York Steps, **7**

Foreign Office, **16**
Home Office, **22**
Horse Guards Parade, **18**
Houses of Parliament, **23**
ICA, **6**
Lancaster House, **10**
National Gallery, **2**
National Portrait Gallery, **3**

Nelson's Column, **1**
Number 10 Downing Street, **19**
Queen Anne's Gate, **15**
Queen's Gallery, **13**
Queen Victoria Memorial, **11**
St. James's Palace, **8**

St. John's, **28**
St. Margaret's, **25**
St. Martin-in-the-Fields, **4**
Tate Gallery, **29**
Wellington Barracks, **14**
Westminster Abbey, **24**
Westminster Cathedral, **27**

French guns captured at the Napoleonic naval battles of St. Vincent, Aboukir Bay, Copenhagen, and Trafalgar itself. Each panel depicts a scene from the battle in which the guns were captured. On either side of Nelson's column is a large fountain. The originals were installed when the square was laid out, but were replaced after World War II. They are the focus of many annual celebrations, particularly New Year's Eve, when great crowds see the New Year in. The square has also been the favorite site for political rallies and marches, when politicians of all persuasions address the assembled supporters. Less controversial gatherings take place at Christmas, when a huge fir tree is set up in the square forming a natural focus for carolers and other Yuletime revelers. A gift from Norway, the tree is that country's way of saying thank you to the people of Britain for their assistance in World War II.

② The north side of Trafalgar Square is formed by the long, low facade of the **National Gallery,** one of the world's great art collections. The Gallery was founded in 1824, when George IV encouraged the government to buy up the paintings of a recently deceased art lover of Russian extraction called John Angerstein. The collection was housed in Angerstein's mansion on Pall Mall until its present home was built in 1832–38. From this nucleus the National Gallery grew rapidly, until by 1900 it had become one of the world's foremost collections. Today, practically every artist of significance, from the 14th to the 19th century, is represented here.

As you can't see everything in one visit, study the plans prominently displayed as you go in, pick up a free floor plan, and choose those painters or periods that interest you most. In contrast to most other leading London museums, the National Gallery has the advantage of being easy to negotiate. The one problem is that rooms are often closed for redecoration or for rehanging pictures, so detours may be necessary. When rooms are closed, important pictures often are rehung in the Lower Ground Floor.

As we do not have space to give a rundown on the vast number of pictures and periods covered by the collection, we have chosen 10 of our favorite pictures to act as key points for your exploration. They are arranged by the number of the rooms in which they normally hang.

Ucello (1397–1475), *St. George and the Dragon.* An early Italian fairytale illustration, with a nightmarish dragon, a coolly elegant princess, and St. George in shining armor on a prancing toy horse. Room 2.
Leonardo da Vinci (1452–1519), *Virgin of the Rocks.* A hauntingly graceful Madonna, sitting in a jagged dream landscape. Room 8.
Rubens (1577–1640), *Samson and Delilah.* A dramatic, very sexy version of Samson's visit to the barber. Room 20.
Rogier van der Weyden (1399–1467), *St. Ivo.* An uncannily modern face, which may be of St. Ivo, patron saint of lawyers, or of an unknown man, reading a letter. Room 25.
Caravaggio (1571–1610), *The Supper at Emmaus.* Christ blessing bread after his resurrection, so dramatically posed and lit that you are drawn into the room with him. Room 29.
Constable (1776–1837), *The Haywain.* One of the greatest pictures ever painted of a peaceful English country scene. Room 35.

Turner (1775–1851), *The Fighting Téméraire.* In the same room is this evocative canvas of an old French wooden battleship being towed into a luminous sunset to be broken up for scrap. Room 35.

Gainsborough (1727–88), *Mr. and Mrs. Andrews.* A husband and wife on their Suffolk estate—a quintessentially English countryside scene of the 18th century. Room 39.

Ingres (1780–1867), *Portrait of Madame Moitessier.* A superbly opulent portrait by a French master who catches the face exactly, and paints the rich fabric of the madame's dress with brilliant brush strokes. Room 43.

Monet (1840–1926), *The Waterlily Pond.* One of the many paintings by Monet of his garden in Giverny, with the pond a pool of flickering color. Room 46.

Our list leaves out El Greco, Veronese, Titian, Michelangelo, Rembrandt, and dozens of others, from whose paintings you will want to select your own list of favorites.

The National Gallery is in the middle of a building program, which is greatly extending its exhibition space. One extension was finished in 1975, and another one on a site beside the present galleries is expected to open in 1991. *Trafalgar Sq., tel. 01/ 839–3321; 01/839–3526 (recorded information). Admission free. Open Mon.–Sat. 10–6, Sun. 2–6; July–Sept., Wed. until 8; closed Good Fri., May Day.*

Time Out The **National Gallery Restaurant** is a serviceable place for a cup of coffee or a snack lunch. Fuel food. Be prepared for crowds at peak times.

Outside the Gallery, on the grass slopes in front, stand two small statues. One is James II, a brother of Charles II, who tried unsuccessfully to return Britain to Catholicism. He is wearing Roman garb, as was popular in official portraits and statues of the times. The sculptor was Grinling Gibbons, whose work crops up often in London. He was a brilliant Dutch artist who flourished at the end of the 17th century, and was Master Carver in Wood to the Crown. At the other end of the facade is George Washington, in a replica of the famous statue by Houdon in Richmond, Virginia, presented to Britain by the Commonwealth of Virginia in 1921.

❸ Just around the corner is the **National Portrait Gallery,** a collection of famous British faces down the ages. While many of the pictures are not masterpieces, the gallery has a distinctly idiosyncratic and engaging personality, and a uniformity of theme that many other collections lack. The Gallery isn't limited to painted portraits; there are busts, photographs, even cartoons. In recent years, the people who work on the displays have shown a real theatrical flair, and many rooms have the effect of stage sets, with drapes, furniture, and other props to set the particular periods. It helps to visit with a knowledgeable Brit, or pick up explanatory material in the gallery's shop. *2 St. Martin's Pl., tel. 01/930–1552. Admission free. Open Mon.– Fri. 10–5, Sat. 10–6, Sun. 2–6. Closed Good Fri.*

❹ To the east of the National Gallery is the beautiful church of **St. Martin-in-the-Fields**—not that there are any fields in evidence today. It was built in 1724 and remains among the most distinctive and dignified of London's 18th-century churches, not least for its elegant spire. The church, dedicated to St. Martin of Tours, the patron saint of the poor, still actively carries on its traditional role of caring for the destitute. Its name is also associated with the Academy of St. Martin-in-the-Fields, which was founded here. This small orchestra rose rapidly to fame in the 1950s for its performances of Baroque music, and clinched its international reputation by providing the music for the Oscar-studded movie, *Amadeus*. The church is still used for concerts and recitals, and a candle-lit performance here can be a memorable experience. The interior is a bit fusty these days, unlike other churches of the period that have been restored to their original glory. There is a small, semi-permanent crafts market in the courtyard behind the church. At the **London Brass Rubbing Centre** in the crypt of St. Martin's, you can make your own copies from replica tomb brasses, some from churches throughout Britain. Wax, paper, and instructions are provided. *St. Martin-in-the-Fields, Trafalgar Sq. Rubbing fee from 50p according to size of brass selected. Open Mon.–Sat. 10–6, Sun. 12–6, closed Good Fri.*

Time Out   **Field's Restaurant,** also in St. Martin's crypt, serves a good range of salads, sandwiches, and pastries throughout the day, hot dishes at lunchtime, and a reasonably priced set dinner in the evening.

Where the southern end of Trafalgar Square slopes toward Whitehall sits a bronze equestrian statue of Charles I, cast in 1633, on a sadly eroded stone base. Before it could be installed, the unhappy Charles was forced from his throne by Oliver Cromwell and his Parliamentarians, and the statue was sold to a scrap dealer. During the puritanical Cromwell's short-lived Commonwealth, this dealer made a small fortune selling mugs and other mementos to clandestine royalist sympathizers made, or so he claimed, from the melted down statue. After Cromwell's little-lamented death in 1658 and the restoration of the monarchy two years later, this same dealer miraculously produced the statue intact and undamaged, and resold it to the authorities. Charles II then had it set up on its present site, the very spot where a number of those responsible for Charles I's execution in 1649—the regicides—had themselves been executed.

St. James's Park and the Mall

❺   The southwest corner of Trafalgar Square leads to, and is dominated by, **Admiralty Arch,** so called because of its proximity to the Admiralty, headquarters of the Royal Navy. The massive gray-black arch, with its three great openings, was built in 1910 to provide a fitting climax to the Mall, the great ceremonial way that leads to Buckingham Palace. The central arch is opened only on ceremonial occasions.

The Mall itself, probably the most splendid and stately avenue in London, is similarly Edwardian, having been laid out in 1904 to provide a grand approach to Buckingham Palace, itself refaced at about the same time. It replaced a more modest street dating from 1660. From the Restoration to the end of the 18th century, the Mall remained by far the most fashionable spot for London's *beau monde* to stroll, to see, and to be seen. Today's street lies a little to the south of the original Mall, which has been preserved as a wide gravel path.

St. James's Park is one of London's smallest parks, but probably the prettiest. It covers 93 acres and was developed at different times by a series of monarchs, having originally been the heart of the royal backyard when Britain's kings and queens lived in the sprawling complex of buildings that was Whitehall Palace. Henry VIII was the first king to develop it, draining the marshes that had made it a handy hunting preserve. Charles I took his last walk across St. James's Park en route to his execution, and it was his son, Charles II, who began to convert it to its present shape. He employed Le Nôtre, a famous French landscape gardener who had worked for Louis XVI, and charged him with remodeling the park. In 1829, John Nash relandscaped the park for George IV, generally giving it the look it has today.

Although St. James's Park is a lovely place in which to wander during the day, with its beautifully maintained flower beds and exotic birds, it is at its best after dark, especially in summer, when the illuminated fountains play and Westminster Abbey and the Houses of Parliament, beyond the trees, are floodlit.

As you walk down the Mall from Trafalgar Square, you will see that much of the right (north) side is occupied by the handsome Regency facade of **Carlton House Terrace,** built by John Nash, an inspired architect and town planner, in 1827–32. Its gleaming white stucco facades and massive Corinthian columns make Carlton House Terrace probably the most imposing and magisterial of all of Nash's many works in London. It stands on the site of Carlton House, built for the Prince Regent shortly before the present buildings went up. Horace Walpole called Carlton House "the most perfect palace in Europe." In fact even the recklessly spendthrift Prince Regent admitted that the cost of the building had been "enormous." Yet no sooner was Carlton House completed than George III, the prince's father, died, and the prince himself came to the throne. He decided that splendid though it was, Carlton House was insufficiently magnificent for the King of England, and instructed Nash to rebuild it. Today, Carlton House Terrace is home to a number of institutions and government offices, among them the Royal Society, the Turf Club, and, at the level of the Mall, the

6 **Institute of Contemporary Arts** (ICA). The ICA offers a varied program of temporary exhibitions, films, and lectures. To attend, you have to be a member, but a one-day membership fee is available. *The Mall, tel. 01/930–3647. Day membership 75p adults, children under 14 free. An additional charge is made for entry to specific events. Open daily 12–11.*

Time Out The **ICA Café** serves delicious lunchtime salads and quiches, and a good selection of desserts.

Dividing Carlton House Terrace in two are the magnificent
7 **Duke of York Steps,** named after the statue of the duke, standing atop a 124-foot column that towers above the steps. The memorial was put up in honor of George III's second son who was commander-in-chief of the British Army at the time of the French Revolution. Although an excellent administrator and soldier, the duke was less successful in managing his private affairs. His debts were so vast at his death that the wits of his time suggested that he was placed on so high a column in order to get him out of the reach of his creditors.

Continuing down the Mall toward Buckingham Palace, you
8 pass **St. James's Palace** on the right (*see* St. James's and
9 Mayfair) and, beyond it, **Clarence House,** home of the

⓾ Queen Mother, and **Lancaster House,** a handsome early 19th-century mansion used for government receptions and conferences.

Buckingham Palace to Parliament Square

Buckingham Palace faces the west end of the Mall and St. James's Park. Planted in the middle of the great traffic circle in
⓫ front of the palace is the **Queen Victoria Memorial,** a huge monument to the Victorian ideals of motherhood, truth, justice, peace, and progress. It was put up in 1911 as part of the remodeling of the Mall. Perhaps one of the best things that can be said for this mammoth celebration of everything but virginity and the right to vote is that it makes a wonderful grandstand from which to view processions and the ceremony of Changing the Guard. The Guard at Buckingham Palace is changed daily April through July and on alternate days during the rest of the year. At 11 AM the Guard marches from Wellington Barracks *(see below)* to Buckingham Palace: The ceremony itself starts at 11:30; arrive early if you want a good view.

⓬ **Buckingham Palace,** backed by some 40 acres of private garden, is the London residence of the Queen. When she is here (usually on weekdays except in January, some of June, all of August, and September, and when she is away on State visits), the Royal Standard flies over the east front. The palace was originally Buckingham House, built in the early 18th century for the duke of Buckingham. In 1762 it was sold to George III. Then, in 1824, Nash was commissioned to remodel the house for George IV, and its name was changed to Buckingham Palace. It was then that it became the permanent London base for the court.

Buckingham Palace is so fixed a symbol of the crown and of London that few pause to think how architecturally dull it is, or at least how dull is the heavy east front added by Sir Aston Webb in 1913. Initially, the building stood on three sides of a courtyard, the east end of which was open to St. James's Park. After Nash remodeled the rear of the building, which the public never sees, a new east end was added in 1847, and in turn reworked by Webb just before World War I. The magnificent interior is completely closed to the public, a great pity, as there are dozens of splendid state rooms inside, including the State Ballroom and, of course, the Throne Room. The royal apartments are in the north wing.

What was formerly the chapel—bombed during World War II
⓭ and rebuilt in 1961—is now the **Queen's Gallery,** adjoining the south side of the palace. This is one of the best small galleries in Europe, with regular exhibitions drawn from the vast and spectacular royal collections. *Buckingham Palace Rd., tel. 01/ 930–4832. Admission £1.20 adults, 60p children and senior citizens. Open Tues.–Sat. 10:30–5, Sun 2–5; closed temporarily between exhibitions.*

About 200 yards from the Queen's Gallery is the **Royal Mews** where the state coaches are on view, including the sumptuous State Coach, an immensely elaborate gilded affair, built in 1761. This is the carriage used for coronations. The Royal Mews are still used for their original purpose as stables, thus you should also be able to see some of the horses that draw the coaches in ceremonial processions. *Buckingham Palace Rd.,* *tel. 01/930–4832. Admission 60p adults, 30p children. Open Wed. and Thurs. 2–4; occasionally closed shortly before state occasions.*

On the right of the palace as you face it is a wide avenue where the tourist buses park. This is **Constitution Hill,** leading alongside Green Park to Hyde Park Corner. Its name came about when Charles II used to take his daily walk—his constitutional —here. Three attempts on the life of Queen Victoria were made on this road.

In the opposite direction, and from the other side of the Victoria Memorial, **Birdcage Walk** leads along the south side of St. James's Park toward Westminster. The first buildings you pass on the right are the **Wellington Barracks,** the Regimental Headquarters of the Guards Division. These are the elite troops traditionally responsible for protecting the sovereign, and which, among many other duties, mount the Guard at Buckingham Palace. **The Guards Chapel** at the far end of the barracks was destroyed by a flying bomb during a service on June 18, 1944, and 121 people were killed. When the dust and rubble settled, it was found that the candles on the altar were still burning. The chapel was rebuilt in the early 1960s, incorporating what was left of the old building. The public is welcome to attend Sunday services, which are held at 11 and 6; the chapel is generally open during the day from about 10 to 3.

The **Guards Museum** occupies an underground set of rooms in the Wellington Barracks. (The entrance to the museum is at the further end of the barracks from Buckingham Palace, next to the Guard's Chapel.) The museum vividly portrays the story of the five regiments of Foot Guards (Grenadier, Coldstream, Scots, Irish, and Welsh), taking the story from the 1660s right up to the present day. There are uniforms, paintings of battle scenes, and all kinds of fascinating memorabilia, including a cat o' nine tails used to punish guardsmen, and a surgeon's kit from the Crimean War. World Wars I and II and the colonial conflicts in Aden, and, most recently, in the Falkland Islands, are all represented. The Royal Case contains the tunic formerly worn by the Queen for the Trooping the Colour *(see below). Wellington Barracks, Birdcage Walk, tel. 01/930–4466, ext. 3271 or 3253. Admission £2 adults, £1 children under 16 and senior citizens. Open 10–4; closed Fri.*

Off Birdcage Walk, to the right, is a little entry that leads into **Queen Anne's Gate,** lined with 18th-century houses. Tucked away here is a somewhat stiff and formal statue of Queen Anne herself.

Birdcage Walk runs into Parliament Square, site of Westminster Abbey and the Houses of Parliament. Before reaching it, however, there's an interesting detour to the left off Birdcage Walk. This takes you along **Horse Guards Road,** which runs between Birdcage Walk and the Mall, with St. James's Park on one side and the Foreign Office and Horse Guards Parade on the other.

The magnificently ornate Italianate edifice that is the **Foreign Office** is the most dominant building here. It was built in the 1860s by Gilbert Scott, an architect much better known for his fantastical Gothic Revival buildings.

Just beyond the Foreign Office, at the end of King Charles Street, is the entrance to the **Cabinet War Rooms,** a fascinating

labyrinth of wartime offices set deep underground to protect
them from German bombing. They have been ingeniously restored and provide a fascinating glimpse into the working of
Britain's wartime High Command. Among the underground
maze of rooms are the Cabinet Room, where many of the most
important wartime decisions were made, the Prime Minister's
Room, where Churchill made many of his celebrated wartime
broadcasts, and the Transatlantic Telephone Room, from
which Churchill spoke directly to President Roosevelt in the
White House. *Clive Steps, King Charles St., tel. 01/930–6961
or 01/735–8922. Admission £2.50 adults, £1.25 children under
16 and senior citizens. Open daily 10–5:50; closed Good Fri.,
May Day.*

⑱ Past the Cabinet War Rooms is **Horse Guards Parade,** a substantial square, open toward St. James's Park, with the elegant
facade of William Kent's mid-18th-century Horse Guards building forming the bulk of the opposite side. Horse Guards Parade
was originally the tilt yard (a place for jousting contests) of
Whitehall Palace, with a small guardhouse standing on the site
of Horse Guards. But the square is most famous as the site of
the Trooping the Colour every June, the great military parade
that marks the Queen's official birthday (her real birthday is in
April, but the monarch traditionally has a second, "official"
birthday). This is one of the most spectacular events of the London year, full of pomp and circumstance. The "Colour" (or flag)
that is on display belongs to whichever battalion is selected to
provide the monarch's escort that year. Until 1986 the Queen
took the salute on horseback, but nowadays, flanked by members of her family, she takes the salute standing. It is a
magnificent occasion, monarchical Britain at its best. Bands
play, soldiers march up and down, and, along the Mall and
Horse Guards Parade, the standards of the member countries
of the Commonwealth flutter in the breeze. You can watch the
parade up and down the Mall if you get there very early, but it's
extremely hard to find a spot from which to view the Trooping
itself, and many prefer to stay home and see it on TV.

Turning back, you soon come to the entrance of **Downing Street,**
a pleasant row of 18th-century houses where Boswell lodged
⑲ when he made his first visit to London. **Number 10 Downing
Street** is the official residence of the Prime Minister, as it has
been since it was presented to Sir Robert Walpole in 1732.
Eleven Downing Street, the adjoining house, is the official residence of the Chancellor of the Exchequer (the U.K. equivalent
of the Secretary of the Treasury). Both buildings were considerably extended in the early '60s, though the facades were
untouched. The center of the complex—the hub of the British
system of government—is the Cabinet Room on the ground
floor of number 10. Unfortunately, Downing Street is currently
railed off, with police in high profile. But you can catch a
glimpse of both houses from Horse Guards Road, or, if you walk
round to Whitehall, from the other end of Downing Street.

On Whitehall sits the other facade of Horse Guards, where the
Queen's Life Guard—cavalry soldiers in magnificent uniforms
—stand duty. The Queen's Life Guard changes here at 11 AM
from Monday to Saturday, and at 10 AM on Sunday.

Until the end of the 17th century, the entire area between
Whitehall and the Thames, from Parliament Square to Trafalgar Square, was one vast palace. Called Whitehall Palace, it

was the principal London residence of the monarch from the reign of Henry VIII to 1698, when virtually the entire complex was accidentally burned down in a fire started by a Dutch washerwoman who knocked over a candle. With its courts, lawns, walks, and buildings that had grown randomly, Whitehall Palace must have been an impressive sight. A contemporary recorded that it was "a glorious city of rose-tinted Tudor brick, green lawns, and shining marble statues." (There is a model reconstruction of what the palace must have looked like in its heyday that you can see in the Museum of London.)

⓴ All that remains of Whitehall Palace today is Inigo Jones's **Banqueting House,** halfway down Whitehall on the east side, opposite Horse Guards. The Banqueting House was built in 1625, and it was in front of this building that Charles I was beheaded in 1649. But to today's visitor it's mainly of interest for the magnificent ceiling frescoes in the main hall on the second floor. These were painted by Rubens for Charles I in about 1630; as a reward Rubens received a knighthood and the princely sum of £3,000. The subject is the glorification of the House of Stuart, with James I—the father of Charles I—and Charles himself taking center stage in god-like splendor; exactly the attitude that Cromwell and the Parliamentarians hated and that led to the downfall and execution of Charles. *Whitehall, tel. 01/ 930–4179. Admission 70p adults, 35p children under 15 and senior citizens. Open Tues.–Sat. 10–5, Sun. 2–5; closed bank holidays.*

㉑ Walking toward Parliament Square, you'll come to the **Cenotaph,** a simple white memorial to the dead of both World Wars. It sits in the center of the street, and on Remembrance Day in November the sovereign lays the first tribute of symbolic Flanders' poppies, followed by other members of the Royal Family, and the country's political leaders.

The Houses of Parliament

For the final few yards before it enters Parliament Square, Whitehall changes its name to Parliament Street. Entering Parliament Square you are faced with one of the most dramatic **㉒** views in London. You have passed, on your right, the **Home Office**—built by Gilbert Scott at the same time as the Foreign Office. On the far side of the square is Westminster Abbey, with the little church of St. Margaret's in front of it. The most magnificent sight of all is in front of you to the left: the towers, spires, and crenellations of Big Ben, Westminster Hall, and the Houses of Parliament.

Parliament Square itself was laid out by Charles Barry, architect of the Houses of Parliament, in the middle of the 19th century. The square is populated with statues, mainly of prime ministers from the 19th century—Palmerston, Disraeli, and Robert Peel—and Winston Churchill from our own day. Opposite these statesmen, outside Westminster Hall itself, are statues of Richard Coeur de Lion and Oliver Cromwell, while on the far side of the square stands Abraham Lincoln.

㉓ The story of the **Houses of Parliament** is intimately bound up with that of Britain's monarchs, as its official name—the **Palace of Westminster**—suggests. In fact, until Henry VIII moved the court to Whitehall Palace in 1512, the Palace of Westminster was the main residence of the monarch. The first palace was built by Edward the Confessor in the 11th century when he moved his court here from the City. This was taken over and expanded by William the Conqueror, Norman conqueror of Britain in 1066, and his son, William Rufus, who built Westminster Hall at the end of the century. **Westminster Hall,** a massively sturdy hall 240 feet long, is the only part of the original building to have survived, though it has been substantially altered over the centuries, not least by Richard II, who added the fine hammer-beam roof in 1397. Thereafter, the Palace of Westminster was successively rebuilt and expanded through the years, becoming, in the process, the meeting place of the Lords and the Commons, the two Houses of Parliament. Originally, Westminster Hall was used as the meeting place for Parliament, but following the Reformation in the 16th century, the deconsecrated St. Stephen's Chapel became the home of the Commons, while the Lords used the White Chamber. This makeshift arrangement continued until 1834, when a great fire swept through the palace, reducing it overnight to a smoking ruin. Apart from Westminster Hall, all that survived was the crypt of St. Stephen's Chapel, since reconsecrated, and the medieval Jewel Tower.

The rebuilding was one of the great triumphs of early Victorian architecture. The project—which offered the opportunity to rebuild the Houses of Parliament in a manner befitting their status and to provide better facilities in place of the ramshackle and inconvenient maze of rooms, corridors, and buildings with which the Commons and Lords had had to contend—roused enormous public interest. It was specified that the new building be ". . . in the Gothic or Elizabethan style," chiefly to ensure that it harmonized with neighboring Westminster Abbey and that it reflected the historic roots of Parliament.

Charles Barry was selected as architect, though he was known only as the designer of classical buildings. He had the good sense, or fortune, to ally himself with Augustus Pugin, the volatile young champion of the Gothic Revival. While Barry was responsible for the overall plans of the building, Pugin was given charge of its detailing and decoration. Barry himself was later to claim that the Houses of Parliament were really no more than a classical building in Gothic disguise. "All Greek, sir!" he was heard to exclaim. "Gothic details on a classic body!" Be that as it may, the building has about it that timeless, seemingly inevitable air of having always been there.

The interior is every bit as lavish and splendid as the exterior, though unfortunately not easy for the public to see. Visitors are admitted to the Public Gallery of each House, but usually only after waiting in line for several hours (the line for the Lords is generally much shorter than that for the Commons), or if they have managed to secure tickets through their embassy. But the effort is well worth making for anyone with an eye for history and a taste for mid-Victorian art. The most sumptuously decorated part of the building is the **House of Lords.** This upper chamber is the loose equivalent of the U.S. Senate, though its members are either appointed or take their seats through birth and enjoy considerably less power than American senators. Deep, rich paneling, gorgeous carving and gilding, and rich crimson leather benches set the tone. The **House of Commons,** on the other hand, where the elected members of Parliament meet, is a plainer affair, with much less in the way of decoration, and simple green benches for the members. Restoration following extensive wartime bombing did away with some of the more striking bits of decoration. Some of the most interesting parts of the interior are the public areas, which you will walk through on your way to the Public Galleries, especially those decorated with enormous frescoes, commissioned by Prince Albert, depicting stirring scenes from British history. There are delightful touches throughout, many of them inspired by Pugin, whose thoroughness even extended to designing special Gothic inkwells and umbrella stands, but for security reasons, public tours of the Palace of Westminster are no longer available.

The most famous features of the Houses of Parliament are the towers at each end of the vast complex. At the southern end is the 336-foot high **Victoria Tower,** reputedly the largest square tower in the world. Whenever Parliament is in session a Union Jack flies from its summit during the day. The tower at the other end is **Big Ben,** or, more properly, St. Stephen's Tower: Big Ben is actually the nickname of the tower's 13-ton bell on which the hours are struck. It was named for Sir Benjamin Hall, Commissioner of Works when the bell was installed. A light shines from the topmost point of the tower during night sessions of Parliament.

Westminster Abbey

Directly across from the Houses of Parliament is the unmistakable shape of **Westminster Abbey.** The abbey is both the most ancient of London's great churches and the most important. It is here that Britain's kings and queens are crowned, a tradition that dates back to the coronation of William the Conqueror on Christmas Day, 1066. It is here also that many of these same kings and queens are buried.

The first authenticated church on this site was a Benedictine abbey, founded in 970 and dedicated to St. Peter (the official title of the abbey is still the Collegiate Church of St. Peter). But recent historical research indicates that there may have been an earlier church here, built by the 6th-century Saxon king, Sebert. Some experts contend that this site was "holy" long before Sebert's time, even long before Christianity itself came to Britain; they believe it may have been a place of worship to pagan gods long since forgotten.

What *is* certain is that when Edward the Confessor moved his court to Westminster in 1040, he rebuilt the Benedictine abbey, and it was in this new church that William the Conqueror was crowned. Edward's abbey stood for 200 years more until, in 1245, Henry III began the slow process of rebuilding it, determined to make it the largest and most magnificent church in the kingdom. Much of the east end of Henry's building was complete at his death in 1272, but then work came to a halt for another century. In 1376, Abbot Littlington raised enough money to continue the project, and by about 1420, the abbey was largely complete.

There were two later major additions. The first was the construction of the chapel to the Virgin Mary (at the rear of the building) by Henry VII from 1503 to 1519 and generally known simply as the Henry VII chapel. This exquisite late-Gothic chapel is probably the finest example of its type in Britain. The

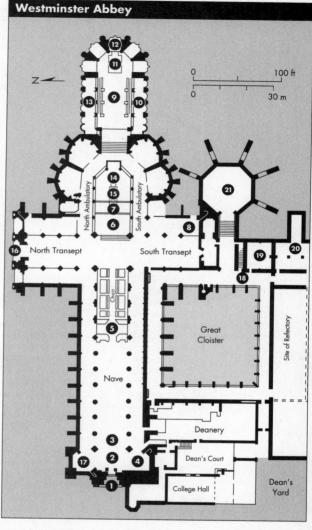

Westminster Abbey

second addition came in the mid-18th century when Nicholas Hawksmoor built the twin towers over the west entrance, the main entrance to the abbey. Though a classical architect, Hawksmoor didn't have much difficulty adapting himself to the task in hand and his towers blend happily with the dark and somber medieval building behind.

Westminster Abbey is a place for serious wandering, but, like all great London buildings, the abbey is also very popular, filled from dawn to dusk with visitors from all over the world, the latest count being three million in a year! To many the abbey is no more than just another sight to be seen. That it is a holy place and a place of worship seems of little importance to the hordes of tourists who charge in and out as though it were a department store. To experience the abbey fully, attend a service here, and try to ignore the distractions.

The first thing that strikes you as you enter the abbey is the proliferation of monuments, tombs, statues, and tablets. At various points the building takes on the aspect of a stonemason's yard. Many of these relics make it difficult to appreciate the splendor of the interior, and are of little interest to anyone but an ardent genealogist. To add insult to artistic injury, many of the memorials are not even marking real graves. H.L. Mencken was annoyed to realize that "when you examine it, you find that two-thirds of the graves haven't even got a dead man in them."

Just inside the great west door is a **memorial to Winston Churchill.** (His burial site is at Bladon in Oxfordshire, just outside Blenheim, where he was born.) Straight ahead, in the center of the nave, is the **Tomb of the Unknown Warrior,** a nameless World War I soldier buried in earth brought with his corpse from France. It is one of the very few floor-level tombs in the abbey over which the countless visitors do not walk. By the tomb hangs a **U.S. Congressional Medal,** a counterpart to the Victoria Cross awarded by Britain to the Unknown Soldier in Washington.

As you wander up the right aisle, you will see memorials to such diverse figures as Baden-Powell, creator of the Boy Scouts; the Wesleys, founders of Methodism; William Congreve, the 18th-century playwright; and Major John André, honored by the British, though a traitor to Americans. Farther on, in the south transept, you come to **Poet's Corner,** filled with memorials to many of Britain's finest writers and composers. Not many of them are actually buried here. The first poet to be honored was Geoffrey Chaucer in 1400. The 16th-century playwright Ben Jonson actually lived in the residential part of the Abbey precincts, and naturally wished to be buried here. However, being a modest man, he declared "Six feet long by two feet wide is too much for me; two feet by two feet will do for all I want." So the Dean obligingly buried him standing upright, giving him the delightful double entendre epitaph "O rare Ben Jonson," *orare* also being the Latin for "pray for." Shakespeare, Dryden, Samuel Johnson, Sheridan, Browning, and Tennyson are also remembered here. Because of the disreputable lives that poets sometimes lead, a few of Britain's finest poets have not been considered suitable for commemorating in a church by the Dean, so they have had to wait until a Dean of more lenient views was in charge. The plaque to Dylan Thomas arrived in Poet's Corner only at the prompting of an American president, Jimmy Carter, who visited the Abbey and expressed surprise that his favorite poet had no memorial. There are also two American-born writers commemorated here— Henry James and T.S. Eliot—both of whom became British citizens. One oddity in Poet's Corner is the memorial to "Spot" Ward, whose only claim to fame was that he cured George II of a sore thumb.

Behind the high altar lie two of the most interesting areas of the abbey: the Chapel of Edward the Confessor and Henry VII's Chapel. This is the area of the royal tombs. Here you'll find a roll call of the royally romantic past, with many of the striking effigies bringing the dead to life: Edward the Confessor himself, lying in his own church in the spot to which he was transferred in 1268; Queen Elizabeth I and her sister "Bloody" Mary; Mary, Queen of Scots, magnificently entombed by her son James I; Henry V, his effigy missing the solid silver head that was stolen at the time of the Reformation (it was replaced by a fiberglass copy in 1971); Queen Anne, who had to wear layers of leather petticoats at her coronation here to keep out the abbey's bitter damp; Richard II, one of the very first carved portraits of an Englishman extant, lying beside his wife, Anne of Bohemia; Edward III, his life of conquest and tumult a contrast to this figure of patriarchal peace. The recent cleaning and repainting of most of the abbey's memorials gives us a wonderful idea of their original splendor.

The focal feature of the **Chapel of Edward the Confessor**, apart from his own massive tomb, is the **Coronation Chair**. This extremely uncomfortable seat was hastily made in about the year 1300 by order of Edward I. The chair encloses the **Stone of Scone** (pronounced "Skoon"), or Stone of Destiny, which has long been a source of friction between England and Scotland. The kings of Scotland were crowned on it and it was used for the coronation of Macbeth's stepson at Scone in 1057. It was carried away from Scotland by Edward I in 1296 but has, over the centuries, become a symbol of Scottish independence. It has been removed from the abbey only three times: once to Westminster Hall for the installation of Oliver Cromwell as Lord Protector, once for safety from German bombers in 1940, and finally by Scottish Nationalists, who stole it one night in 1950 and smuggled it north of the border. (It was discovered and returned six months later.)

Henry VII's Chapel is one of the miracles of Western architecture, and should be savored. It represents the last riot of medieval design in England, and is very un-English in its exuberant richness. A pair of binoculars will help you appreciate the small saints and other delightful details too high up to be seen from ground level. The tomb of Henry VII and his wife, Elizabeth of York, is a masterpiece of the Renaissance by Torrigiano (1472–1528), an Italian artist who is otherwise famous for having broken Michelangelo's nose in a brawl and was banished from Florence because of it. *Broad Sanctuary, tel. 01/222 –5752. Admission into nave free, to Poet's Corner and Royal Chapels £1.80 adults, 40p children (Royal Chapels free Wed. 6–8 PM). Open Mon.–Fri. 9–4, Sat. 9–2, 3:45–5; Sun. all day for services only; closed weekdays to visitors during services.*

Outside the west front of the abbey is an archway leading to **Dean's Yard,** a quiet green courtyard, once part of larger gardens. An entry through the buildings that border the yard leads into Little Dean's Yard (private). The area on this side of the abbey was formerly the living quarters for the monks, and now makes up the quarters of **Westminster School,** one of England's prestigious Public Schools. (In England a Public School is an intensely *private* school.) The original school was founded in medieval times to train the abbey clerks. It was first mentioned in 1339, and received a new charter from Queen Elizabeth in 1560. Through the centuries its most famous schoolboys have included Ben Jonson, Judge Jeffreys, who gained a terrible reputation for conducting the Bloody Assizes after a rebellion in 1685, and more recently the actor Peter Ustinov.

On the south side of Dean's Yard is **Church House,** which dates from 1940. Inside is the Hoare Memorial Hall, where both Houses of Parliament met during World War II after the Palace of Westminster was bombed.

In the northeast corner of Dean's Yard, immediately to your left as you come in, is the entrance to the **Cloisters.** After the time you have spent absorbing impressions in the abbey itself, a quiet session in the Cloisters is refreshing before emerging into the bustle of London. Here, in medieval times, the monks walked and discussed affairs of state and of their souls. It is here, perhaps, more than anywhere else in Westminster, that you just might recapture a sense of the past. There are many nooks and crannies and lovely views to find.

The Cloisters also contain a good **brass-rubbing center** where you can take impressions from facsimiles of several fine old tombs, an ideal memento of your visit to the Abbey. *Tel. 01/ 222-2085. No admission charge; fee charged for each brass rubbed, approx. £2.50–£6.50. Open late Mar.–late Oct. Mon.– Sat. 9–5; late Oct.–late Mar. Mon.–Sat. 10–4:30; closed Good Fri.*

In the Norman **Undercroft,** off the Cloisters, there is an excellent small museum, reopened in 1987 after extensive renovation. Among its treasures are some royal effigies, dressed in their robes, that used to be carried in funeral processions. Since the faces were taken from death masks, they give an impressive idea of how these monarchs actually looked, among them Charles II. Next door is the **Pyx Chamber,** now restored to its ancient function as the Abbey's treasury. Some fine examples of silver and silvergilt vessels, mainly 16th- and 17th-century pieces, are on display.

Off the Great Cloister is the **Chapter House,** an octagonal structure that was once the center of the abbey's religious life. But it has also been called "the cradle of all free Parliaments," because the King's Council, and later Parliament, met here from 1257 until the reign of Henry VIII. It is one of the great interiors in Europe, not only for its feeling of space, but also for the daring design that was employed, with a single column, like a frozen fountain, sustaining the roof. *Undercroft, Pyx Chamber and Treasury, tel. 01/222-5152. Joint admission £1.20 adults, 60p children under 16 and senior citizens. Open daily 10:30–4; closed Good Fri.*

Just north of Westminster Abbey, on the edge of Parliament Square, is the ancient church of **St. Margaret's,** where Sir Walter Raleigh lies buried. When he was beheaded in nearby Old Palace Yard, he remarked, as he saw the blade above him, "This is a sharp medicine, but it is a physician for all diseases." His wife then kept his head in a velvet bag to show to visitors with the macabre words, "Have you met Sir Walter?" William Caxton, the father of English printing, who had two presses nearby, is also buried here. The east window of the church, made in Flanders in 1509, was a gift from Ferdinand and Isabella of Spain. The church is traditionally popular for weddings; Pepys, Milton, and Sir Winston Churchill were all married here. In a niche on the facade of the church is a lead bust of Charles I, looking across the square with a reflective air at the statue of Cromwell, the man who had the monarch executed.

The large domed building across the road from the west front of Westminster Abbey is **Central Hall,** headquarters of the Methodist Church in Britain. The building, now used mostly for concerts and meetings, was the site of the first General Assembly of the United Nations in 1948. The modern building next to it is the **Queen Elizabeth Conference Centre,** opened in 1986. The largest of its seven conference rooms can accommodate 1,100 delegates. The government-owned building is used for both official and commercial functions, including fashion shows, product launches, and exhibitions.

Westminster Cathedral and the Tate Gallery

There are two detours that can be made from Parliament Square. The first is to Westminster Cathedral and, a little further afield, the second is to the Tate Gallery.

For Westminster Cathedral, head south down Victoria Street from the west front of Westminster Abbey. **Victoria Street** was driven through an area of dreadful slums in about 1862, connecting Westminster with Victoria Station at its southern end. Today, very little remains of the fine Victorian and Edwardian buildings that gave it so much character. They have mostly been replaced by dreary steel and glass. On the right as you walk toward Victoria is **New Scotland Yard,** a far cry from the rather romantic late-Victorian building on the Thames that Sherlock Holmes knew as Scotland Yard.

27 **Westminster Cathedral** is on the left of Victoria Street, set back about 100 yards from the road. The area in front of the recently cleaned cathedral has been paved and turned into a pleasing piazza.

Westminster Cathedral is the main Roman Catholic cathedral in London, seat of the Cardinal of Westminster, head of the Roman Catholic Church in Britain. The major part of the building dates from between 1895 and 1903, though it is still partly unfinished inside. It was designed in a richly Byzantine idiom, as foreign a style as can be imagined in the heart of London. A choral service, especially on a great religious occasion, with the choir singing from its place behind the main altar, provides a memorable experience.

Unfinished as it is, the interior is a slightly mysterious and shadowy amalgam of brick, marble, and mosaic. The marbles come from all over the world—Greece, Italy, Ireland, even Norway. The nave of the cathedral, the widest in the country, is topped by three shallow domes of blackened brick. It is unlikely that the building will ever be finished. The tower **campanile,** on the north side of the church, can also be visited; an elevator will take you up to the top. *Ashley Pl., tel. 01/834–7452. Admission to tower 70p adults, 40p children and senior citizens. Cathedral open daily, tower open Apr. through Sept.*

The Tate Gallery is a more substantial undertaking. London's most important gallery of modern art calls for a lengthy visit, or a series of visits, so we don't recommend trying to squeeze it into an otherwise busy day. From the House of Parliament or Westminster Abbey there are two approaches to the Tate. One 15–20 minute walk takes you due south from the Houses of Parliament down Abingdon Street, with the Victoria Tower Gardens on your left, past Lambeth Bridge and on to the Tate. Except for the walk along the gardens, it is a pretty dull trip, with a series of increasingly unattractive modern buildings lining the route and only the view over the Thames providing much variety.

The second route is more complicated. Head down Abingdon Street past the front of the Victoria Tower and take the first right down Great College Street. Here, take the first left, down Barton Street. Between Barton Street and Smith Square, the principal destination of this mini-walk, are a series of delightful little early 18th-century town houses, the sort of houses that Dr. Johnson would have known. Today, many of them have been bought by M.P.s and others with business at Westminster. From Barton Street continue down to the end of the road—about 50 yards or so—turn left and then right and head straight down Lord North Street. Ahead of you is Smith

(28) Square and the Baroque **church of St. John**, or at least what used to be a church. Today, it has been deconsecrated and is used for concerts, and a more delightful concert hall would be hard to find. The church was originally built around 1710. From Smith Square head left up Dean Stanley Street. This brings you out to Millbank, and back to the main route to the Tate Gallery.

(29) The **Tate Gallery** was opened in 1897, and has been extended four times as its holdings have grown. The paintings divide into two main groups, the British collection, an unrivaled series of British paintings from Elizabethan times to the present, and the modern collection, a comprehensive assemblage of modern European and American works. There are also regular special exhibitions devoted to an individual painter or theme. Don't miss the Turner collection, housed in the new **Clore Gallery** opened in 1987. J.M.W. Turner (1775–1851) bequeathed the works that remained in his studio at his death to the nation with the stipulation that they should be displayed in one place. The bequest consisted of 100 finished oil paintings, 200 unfinished ones, and 19,000 drawings, watercolors, and sketches. The new gallery, whose design caused a lot of controversy, shows these works in rotation.

Other highlights among the British collections include works by Hogarth, Reynolds, Gainsborough, Zoffany, Lawrence, Constable, Blake, and the pre-Raphaelites. The modern collections are the equal of any in the world, with every major 20th-century artist represented. This is an essential stopover for anyone with an interest in modern art. The Tate has been busy carving a reputation for itself as a fearless champion of modern artists, and a number of debatable exhibits here have attracted letters of outrage to the press. *Millbank, tel. 01/821–1313 or 01/821–7128 (recorded information). Admission free; admission charged for special exhibitions. Open Mon.–Sat. 10–5:50, Sun. 2–5:50; Clore Gallery, Tues.–Sat. 12–5; closed Good Fri., May Day.*

Time Out The cafeteria in the Tate Gallery basement is a pleasant place to relax after the exertions of picture-gazing; it has a good selection of cakes, sandwiches, and light lunches. The attractive restaurant, decorated with murals, is another question. It's fairly pricey, must be booked in advance, and is not handy for an ad hoc meal. However, the menu has some interesting old English recipes, and the wine list is mouth-wateringly long.

St. James's and Mayfair

The areas covered in this section make up the very heart of London's West End, where the capital's classiest hotels, choicest restaurants, most glamorous shops, and plushest offices jostle for space along the crowded streets—a natural habitat for those with a taste for sophisticated urban living.

As with so much of the center of London, there's no single obvious route into or around any of the sections covered here. Look at any map and you'll quickly see what a random pattern these streets make. The easiest approach is the serendipitous one—follow your instincts and see where they take you.

St. James's

Of the areas covered in this chapter, St. James's is the most historic, with a street plan that has barely changed since it was laid out in the late 17th century. Bounded by Green Park to the west, Haymarket to the east, Piccadilly to the north, and the Mall to the south, St. James's is the ultimate enclave of the gentleman's London. This is where you will find the capital's most celebrated and distinguished men's clubs and shirt, shoe, and hat shops (though not tailors, they're just a step north in Mayfair's Savile Row). Likewise, the area is liberally sprinkled with discreet art galleries. *(See* The London Art Scene in Portraits of London.) St. James's, in short, exudes an air of dusty elegance and old-fashioned charm.

1 Begin your tour of St. James's from **Trafalgar Square,** though you could just as easily begin from Piccadilly or the Mall. From Trafalgar Square, take Cockspur Street or Pall Mall East, on either side of Canada House, to the foot of **Haymarket,** so named because of the horse fodder sold here until 1830. This is a wide and busy thoroughfare, sloping up to Piccadilly Circus at its northern end. It boasts two theaters—Her Majesty's and **2** the elegant 1820 **Theatre Royal**—plus the Design Centre (which shows examples of the best of modern British design), a clutch of movie theaters, the American Express offices, and New Zealand House, a highrise at the end of the street. Behind **3** this last building is Nash's **Royal Opera Arcade,** home of some very English little shops selling fishing tackle, old prints, cashmere, and books.

Heading east along Pall Mall for 100 yards or so, past the stately cream facade of the Institute of Directors on your left, you come to the elongated square that is **Waterloo Place.** The column to your left is the **Duke of York memorial** at the head of the **4** **Duke of York Steps** *(see* Westminster and Royal London), and around it, a cluster of statues. There's Florence Nightingale, the Lady with the Lamp and nurse-heroine of the Crimea; the two luckless explorers Sir John Franklin, who led an expedition to find the Northwest Passage in 1845 that ended with the death of every man under his command, and Captain Scott, who presided over another British polar fiasco, this time in the Antarctic in 1911–12; three monarchs: Edward VII, Victoria, and George VI; Sir John Burgoyne, son of the General Burgoyne who surrendered at Saratoga; Sir Colin Campbell, who led the relief of Lucknow during the Indian Mutiny; and Lord Curzon, the "most superior person," who lived around the corner at 1 Carlton House Terrace.

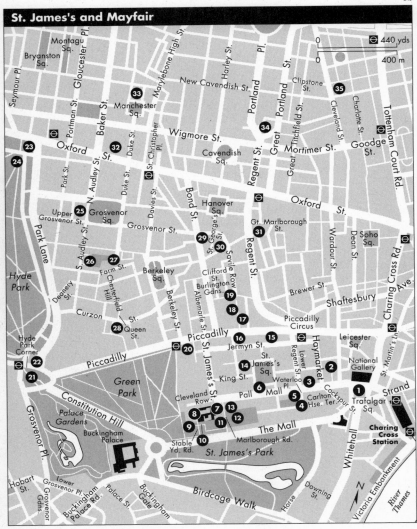

St. James's and Mayfair

⑤ Diagonally opposite this collection of frozen worthies is the glistening facade of the **Atheneum,** with a colored copy of the Parthenon frieze running around its upper stories. The Atheneum signals the start of an exploration of London clubland. None of these exclusive haunts is open to the general public, and membership is not easy to come by. But almost all of the clubs are housed in handsome, sturdy buildings, and you can sometimes peek through the open windows. Around the corner from the Atheneum is the **Travellers' Club** and, next door, the

⑥ **Reform Club,** perhaps the most famous of all and certainly the most attractive, housed in a sooty and stately Italianate building designed by Charles Barry, architect of the Houses of Parliament.

From the Atheneum, **Pall Mall,** a dignified, elegant road, runs west to St. James's Palace. The name Pall Mall, like that of the parallel Mall, comes from the early form of croquet—*pail mail* or *pell mell*—that was played here from the beginning of the 17th century to the Restoration. Heading down Pall Mall, you pass, on your left, the **RAC Club,** another of the great St. James's clubs, and, a little beyond it, a series of handsome 17th-century facades. Thomas Gainsborough, the 18th-century painter, lived at #80–82.

⑦ Pall Mall ends at **St. James's Palace.** For a century or more this lovely brick palace has taken a back seat in the affairs of the nation: Its only remaining claims to fame are that a number of royal functionaries have offices here, and various court functions are held in the State Rooms. However, all foreign ambassadors to Britain are still officially accredited to the "Court of St. James's"—though the court exists in name only. The palace originally took its name from the leper hospital that stood here in the 11th century. In the 1530s, Henry VIII knocked it down and began work on the present building. Although it remained a royal residence, it was overshadowed by the sprawling mass of nearby Whitehall Palace. St. James's partly regained royal favor when Whitehall burned down in 1698, despite the preference of the reigning monarchs—William and Mary—for Kensington Palace and Hampton Court. But Queen Victoria finally downgraded St. James's when she came to the throne in 1837 and moved into Buckingham Palace. If St. James's Palace no longer has a prominent role to play, it nonetheless remains the most romantic of London's palaces, especially the facade fronting Pall Mall, made all the more picturesque by the guardsmen standing sentinel outside.

Inside the palace is the **Chapel Royal,** said to have been designed for Henry VIII by Holbein, though heavily redecorated in the mid-19th century. The ceiling still has the initials H and A, intertwined, standing for Henry VIII and his second wife, Anne Boleyn, the mother of Elizabeth I and the first of Henry's wives to lose her head. *It is possible to attend the Sun. morning services here at 8:30 and 11:15 between the first week of Oct. and Good Fri.*

⑧ If you continue along Cleveland Row (the extension of Pall Mall), **York House**—the home of the duke and duchess of Kent— is on the left. A left turn into Stable Yard Road will bring you to

⑨ **Lancaster House.** This was originally built for the duke of York in the 1820s and was then enlarged in 1833–41. Today it is used by the government for official receptions and conferences. It has been open to the public in the past, but for the moment it remains closed.

⑩ On the other side of Stable Yard is **Clarence House,** so called because it was designed by Nash and built in 1825 for the future king, William IV, then the duke of Clarence. It was restored in 1949, and is now the home of the Queen Mother.

Walk back along the Mall toward Admiralty Arch past the south side of St. James's Palace. This Mall frontage was designed by Wren in the 17th century and contrasts well with the Tudor frontage on Pall Mall. To continue your exploration of this little enclave of royal houses, turn back up Marlborough Road, toward Pall Mall again. On the left is the open-sided **Fri-**
⑪
⑫ **ary Court** of St. James's Palace, opposite **Marlborough House,** the latter built by Wren for the duke of Marlborough in 1709 and now the Commonwealth Conference Centre; the building will be closed for essential repairs until about 1990.

⑬ Just in front of Marlborough House is the **Queen's Chapel,** built for Henrietta Maria, the Roman Catholic wife of Charles I. The chapel is one of London's forgotten glories—small but exquisite. It was built by Inigo Jones between 1623 and 1627, among the first purely classical buildings in the country. *You can attend Sun. services here between Easter and the end of July; Holy Communion is celebrated at 8:30 and either Sung Eucharist or Morning Prayer at 11:15.*

St. James's continues north from here, up the hill to Piccadilly, by way of **St. James's Street,** which features several more exclusive clubs, including White's at #37–38, the oldest London club (founded in 1736); Boodle's, #28; Brooks on the corner of Park Place; and the Carlton, #69. Lobb's, at #9, is a world-famous bespoke shoemaker *(custom shoemaker)*, and James Lock, at #6, has been making hats for more than 200 years. The window of this classic shop is always a slightly dusty delight. In contrast to these old-fashioned glories is a startlingly modern, copper-colored building halfway up St. James's Street on the left, looking like a group of organ pipes posing as space rockets.

There are two good ways into the heart of St. James's from here: one down King Street, the other down Jermyn Street. Both run right (eastward) off St. James's Street. **King Street** will take you past the solemn 18th-century facade of Christie's, the fine art auctioneers. The building is open to anyone who cares to step inside and wander around the sale rooms. There's nearly always something of interest about to come under the hammer, including, from time to time, works that will fetch millions. Past Christie's, you come to Duke Street on your left, home to a series of exclusive little galleries; further on lies **St. James's Square,** one of the oldest and most pleasing of London's elegant leafy squares. When first laid out in about 1670, it was probably the most fashionable address in the whole of London, and by 1720 no less than seven dukes and seven earls had houses here. Bomb damage in World War II flattened a number of the original 18th-century buildings, but enough remain to give a strong sense of this locale's plush past. The cramped building in
⑭ its northwest corner is the **London Library,** the most exclusive and probably the best private lending library in London, with about a million volumes lining its creaking shelves.

Take the center exit on the north side of St. James's Square up to **Jermyn Street** and you'll find yourself surrounded by London's best tie- and shirtmakers, as well as stores selling traditional ivory-backed hairbrushes, silk robes, cashmere sweaters, beautiful handmade shoes, and a host of other essential gentlemen's accessories. From Jermyn Street it is no more than a couple of minutes' walk up to Piccadilly, the next stop on our tour.

Piccadilly

Piccadilly Circus, once the hub of the West End and a symbol of London worldwide, makes a convenient starting point for the walk down Piccadilly itself or for a foray northwest into the center of elegant Mayfair. For our purposes, we treat Piccadilly as separate from Mayfair, but, walking its length, you can head north into Mayfair at any point up any one of the dozen or so streets off Piccadilly.

For all its international fame, Piccadilly Circus is not a place to linger—it exudes an air of Times Square grime and squalor. But the famous statue of Eros is worth a look. It has been repaired, cleaned, and, as part of a long-delayed traffic improvement plan, has been moved to a new site slightly south of where it originally stood. The statue is not actually of Eros at all, but is rather an allegory of Christian Charity, a reference to the original building of Piccadilly Circus and Shaftesbury Avenue in the last century under the patronage of Lord Shaftesbury, a notable philanthropist, who swept away some of the capital's worst slums. The name Piccadilly is said by some (although there are several theories) to be derived from the tailor's shop that stood there in the 17th century, and which sold lace collars or "piccadells."

Piccadilly Circus lies at the junction of four major roads: Piccadilly, Regent Street, Shaftesbury Avenue, and Lower Regent Street. Of these, **Piccadilly** is the largest and most prominent. From the Circus it runs due west down to Hyde Park Corner forming the final stretch of the principal route into London from the West Country. Care is needed when crossing it as buses go westward against the eastward flow of the rest of the traffic. It is lined by a mixture of stores, airline offices, learned societies, and large hotels—including one of London's most famous, the Ritz.

⑮ Walking from Piccadilly Circus, the first building to notice, on the left, is **St. James's Church,** one of Wren's churches, revealing his hand in every elegant line. It was built between 1676 and 1684, but was damaged during the Blitz and since restored. The spire was not replaced until 1968 and, believe it or not, is made of fiberglass. There is a wealth of beautiful craftsmanship inside, including a limewood reredos (an ornamental screen behind the altar) by Grinling Gibbons, who also carved the organ case and font. The church is surrounded by a paved garden where you can rest in the middle of a busy day. A crafts market is held here on weekends. The church also offers a lively program of talks, discussions, and recitals, held both on weekdays and weekends.

Time Out **The Wren at St James's** is a pleasant little café attached to St. James's Church. Sandwiches and pastries are always on sale, and at lunch you can buy salads, soup, and a hot dish.

⑯ Continuing along Piccadilly, you'll pass some famous shops, including **Hatchard's,** one of the best bookshops in London, and **Fortnum and Mason,** the Queen's grocer. Fortnum's has three tea shops of varying degrees of elegance (and price) for mid-sightseeing snacks. Here, too, is the **Piccadilly Arcade,** with tall, glass-fronted shops. It's not as famous as its big brother across the road—the **Burlington Arcade**—but it's worth investigating all the same.

On the north side of Piccadilly is the Italianate bulk of **Burlington House,** home of the **Royal Academy of Arts.** The Academy (otherwise known as the RA) mounts prestigious loan exhibitions, as well as the famous—or infamous, depending on your artistic point of view—Summer Exhibition of mixed amateur and professional works, a highlight of the London social season. There are also some fine works in the permanent collection, but the prize is a bas-relief sculpted disk, or tondo, by Michelangelo: the *Madonna Taddei.* Around the courtyard of Burlington House are several other societies: the Geological Society, the Chemistry Society, the Linnean Society, the Society of Antiquaries, and the Royal Astronomical Society. In short, Burlington House represents nothing less than a little corner of 18th-century inquiry and investigation in the middle of London. *Burlington House, Piccadilly, tel. 01/734–9052. Admission price varies according to exhibition. Open daily 10–6; closed Good Fri.*

Time Out The Royal Academy's restaurant is a pleasant place to have mid-morning coffee, afternoon tea, or a light lunch snack. You can use it without having to buy an entrance ticket to the current exhibition.

Running up beside Burlington House is **Burlington Arcade,** a long, covered walkway of delightful little shops. This is the place to wander on a wet day, or to search for the slightly extravagant present to take home. Most of the shops stock traditional British-crafted goods with an emphasis on woolens, linen, glass, and china. It was the first shopping precinct of its kind in the country, and was built for Lord Cavendish in 1819. The Regency atmosphere has been retained right down to the uniformed watchmen (beadles).

If you turn right at the top of the Burlington Arcade, you will find the **Museum of Mankind,** the British Museum's Department of Ethnography, housed at the back of Burlington House. It contains a large part of the British Museum's collection of Aztec, Mayan, African, and other ethnic artifacts, all imaginatively displayed. The museum deserves to be better known, and is often pleasantly uncrowded, in contrast with many of London's other major collections. *6 Burlington Gardens, tel. 01/437–2224. Open Mon.–Sat. 10–6, Sun. 2:30–6; closed Good Fri.*

At 21 Albermarle Street, two blocks past the Arcade, off Piccadilly, is **Faraday's Laboratory and Museum,** dedicated to the work of the great scientist, Michael Faraday, with a unique collection of original apparatus. *21 Albermarle St., tel. 01/409–2992. Admission adults 40p, children 20p. Open Tues. and Thurs. 1–4.*

Along Piccadilly there are more shops and airline offices, including that of Aeroflot with a cooly conceived modern equestrian statue by Elizabeth Frink outside, for the next few blocks until **The Ritz** hotel looms on the left.

Here, on the south side of Piccadilly, is the northern edge of **Green Park,** a 53-acre expanse of grass and trees that was added to the Royal Parks by Charles II, replacing St. James's

Park as the fashionable airing spot of London. On weekends its railings facing Piccadilly are festooned with art and artifacts of all kinds, lending a little color (but not a lot of class) to an otherwise staid stretch.

At the western end of Piccadilly you come to **Hyde Park Corner,** a perpetual maelstrom of traffic at the junction of several major roads. The center of this traffic whirl, however, is an island of surprising tranquility. There's a few fine statues here, but the center piece is the **Wellington Arch,** a triumphal arch that was originally intended as a sort of monumental back gate to Buckingham Palace. It used to have a large statue of Wellington on the top—perhaps to pair with Nelson on his column in Trafalgar Square. However, this was replaced in 1912 by the present *Peace in Her Chariot,* a suitably heroic group. (By the way, London's smallest police station is located in the arch.) In order to cross the roadways here, you'll have to use the network of pedestrian underpasses.

On the north side of Hyde Park Corner, just by the park itself, is **Apsley House,** now the **Wellington Museum.** It was built in the 1770s by Robert Adam, though refaced and extended in the 1820s, by which point it had passed into the hands of the duke who kept it as his London house until his death in 1852. In 1847 it was acquired by the nation, when it became the Wellington Museum. The interior is much as it was in the Iron Duke's day, full of heavy and ornate pieces, some perhaps more impressive than beautiful, though there's also a fine equestrian portrait of Wellington by Goya, painted during the Peninsula Campaign. *149 Piccadilly, tel. 01/499–5676. Admission £2 adults, £1 children under 16 and senior citizens. Open Tues.–Sun. 11–5; closed bank holidays.*

Mayfair

Mayfair represents all that is gracious in London living, with an unmistakable air of wealthy leisure, even on the busiest days. Like neighboring (but low-life) Soho, it is one of the few areas of London whose borders are quite distinct. And, again like Soho, it is laid out on the next best thing to a grid pattern London can offer. This makes it easy to find your way around, but where you actually start an exploration of the area is up to you. Mayfair is bound by Piccadilly on the south, Park Lane on the west, Oxford Street on the north, and Regent Street on the east. From all these main roads many streets lead into Mayfair, all equally useful in taking you into this desirable heart of moneyed London.

For simplicity's sake, begin your exploration of Mayfair at Hyde Park Corner. Head north from here up Park Lane, the western border of Mayfair. **Park Lane,** with its expansive views over Hyde Park, was one of the most distinguished Mayfair addresses. But its town houses have mostly been demolished, replaced by a looming series of hotels and office blocks. Yet two groups of the original early 19th-century houses remain overlooking the park, all with delightful bow fronts and wrought iron balconies.

Continue up Park Lane to **Marble Arch** at the meeting point of Oxford Street and Bayswater Road, another traffic whirlpool. The arch was brought here from Buckingham Palace in 1851, and was sited near the place where the public gallows known as

Tyburn Tree once stood. To the west of Marble Arch, at the
(24) northeastern corner of Hyde Park, is **Speakers' Corner,** a large
open space where anyone with the compulsion to air his or her
views in public can do so on Sunday afternoons. As the preserve
of every kind of eccentric, this is one of the best free shows in
London. From Marble Arch you can either head down Oxford
Street (*see below*) or, to penetrate the heart of Mayfair, back-
track four blocks down the east side of Park Lane to Upper
Brook Street. This will bring you to **Grosvenor Square** and the
(25) **U.S. Embassy.** This large, graceful square was laid out in 1725–
31, and has at its center a statue of Franklin D. Roosevelt,
erected in 1948. The British public had a soft spot for Roosevelt, which they demonstrated by the speedy way they raised
money for the statue. The embassy takes up the whole of one
side of the square. When the building first went up in the late
'50s there were many wry comments about the huge gold eagle
poised over the center of the facade, as if waiting to pounce on
the London pigeons. John Adams, first American ambassador
to Britain and second President of the United States, lived at
the corner of Brook and Duke streets.

From Grosvenor Square walk down South Audley Street. Just
(26) over Mount Street is the charming little **Grosvenor Chapel,**
built in 1730 and used by American forces in World War II. To
the left of the church is an entrance to **St. George's Gardens,** a
peaceful spot with a fountain in the middle. If you cross the gar-
(27) dens to Farm Street you will find the Jesuit **Church of the Im-
maculate Conception,** built in the mid-19th century and noted
today for its fine music. Chesterfield Hill and then Queen
Street will take you down to **Curzon Street,** which crosses Mayfair from west to east. This street retains some old houses amid
the modern office blocks. On its south side is an area of consid-
(28) erable charm—**Shepherd Market,** a network of narrow streets
with attractive houses and shops. You won't find any sheep
there nowadays, though something of a village atmosphere remains, but there are a couple of rousing pubs, and the vestiges
of Shepherd Market's red light days.

Time Out **L'Artiste Musclé** (1 Shepherd Market) is a popular wine bar/
restaurant with above average French meals.

At the end of Curzon Street, Fitzmaurice Place curves into
Berkeley Square (pronounced "Barkly"). It was once one of London's most distinguished residential squares, and former inhabitants include the prime minister Robert Walpole (1676–
1745) and Clive of India (1725–74). It remains one of the capital's most prestigious addresses, though these days savvy
realtors and other money-spinning organizations make this historic square their home.

The heart of modern Mayfair is **Bond Street** (from Berkeley
Square, walk along Bruton Street). It is divided into Old and
New Bond Street. (Old Bond Street was laid out some 20 years
before New Bond Street, in 1690 to be exact.) The older street
hasn't lost its air of slight superiority, and today it is the home
of many of London's most luxurious shops. Internationally
known names like Asprey's and Cartier's are here, as well as
some of the top art dealers, and the great auction house of
(29) **Sotheby's.** This is a shopping street par excellence.

Near the top of Bond Street, Brook Street leads east to **Hanover Square.** Turn south down St. George's Street, and you'll
(30) pass the lovely church of **St. George's,** still a top choice for socie-

ty weddings. Further down, Clifford Street will take you through to **Savile Row,** renowned for fashionable tailoring since the mid-19th century—though proposed property taxes threaten to force the tailors out into suburbia.

Regent and Oxford Streets

The eastern border of Mayfair is **Regent Street,** originally laid out around 1825 as the central section of the triumphal way through London intended to connect Carlton House Terrace with Regent's Park. Like the park, Regent Street is named after the Prince Regent, later George IV, a man of considerable taste (witness the Royal Pavilion in Brighton) but little staying power. The original grandiose plan was never more than half realized, and then only at vast expense and amid bitter public criticism. Very little of the original street survives today; most of the elegant houses were swept away at the beginning of the century and replaced by anonymous and dreary blocks. Regent Street is the location of those airline offices not located on Piccadilly, and some good shops of which the best is **Liberty,** a store filled with rich silks and high fashion. The Regent Street frontage is surmounted by impressive carvings and a 115-foot frieze celebrating trade with exotic places. Around the corner in Great Marlborough Street, the mock Tudor facade masks a rich interior, partly built from the carved timbers of old fighting ships.

At its northern end, Regent Street meets Oxford Street at **Oxford Circus,** one of the major traffic junctions in the West End, despite its relatively small scale. **Oxford Street** itself extends west from Oxford Circus to Marble Arch and east to Tottenham Court Road. For most of its length it is closed to all traffic other than buses and taxis, though this does not affect the enormous crowds of people that throng up and down it. Whatever the season, Oxford Street will be packed solid with shoppers. It claims to be the capital's premier shopping street, but, despite the presence of some good department stores, the majority of the shops here are unmemorable and offer cheap fashions at high prices. Some of the best shopping areas here are Wigmore Street and St. Christopher's Place to the north, and Mayfair to the south. Three stores (*see* Shopping) worth fighting the crowds for are **Selfridges,** founded by an American businessman; two branches of that English institution **Marks and Spencer;** and **John Lewis.** To avoid the worst of the crowds, try to do your browsing first thing in the morning.

There are two interesting detours to be made north from Oxford Street. The first is to the **Wallace Collection,** one of the most delightful and unexpected art galleries in London. To reach it, head north from Oxford Street up Duke Street, beside Selfridges, into Manchester Square, a typical mid-18th-century London square, with a garden in the center and fine townhouses all around. On the northern side is the handsome Hertford House, home of the Wallace Collection. The house itself, built toward the end of the 18th century but extensively renovated in the middle of the 19th, was the London home of the marquesses of Hertford, the second, third, and fourth of whom were astute and successful art collectors, the fourth marquess especially. From the end of the 18th century to 1870, these energetic aristocrats assembled one of the finest private collections in the country, though much of it was housed in their

Paris home until about 1870. Then the entire collection was transferred to London and to Hertford House, where it has remained ever since. In 1900, the collection passed to the nation.

Because it was first and foremost a private house, the Wallace Collection has none of that intimidating formality that so many grand picture galleries possess. Not unlike the Frick Collection in New York, the works here blend happily with their sumptuous surroundings, making the entire place a pleasure to walk around, quite irrespective of the paintings themselves. Nonetheless, it is these that constitute the principal attraction, and a pretty astonishing one at that. At the heart of the collection are the 18th-century French works—all snapped up at bargain prices by the second marquess during the French Revolution. Boucher, Watteau, Fragonard, and Chardin are all well represented, forming a collection of greater value than its counterpart in the National Gallery. But there are also a number of very fine Rubens and Rembrandts, Frans Hals' *Laughing Cavalier*, an exquisite Poussin, some stirring Van Dycks, an extensive series of Canalettos, and a whole host of lesser Dutch works from the 17th and 18th centuries. There are also various rooms of fine porcelain and china, arms and armor, and magnificent furniture. As if this were not enough, The collection is almost always uncrowded. *Hertford House, Manchester Sq., tel. 01/935–0687. Admission free. Open Mon.–Sat. 10–5, Sun. 2–5; closed Good Fri., May Day.*

The other side trip from Oxford Street is up Regent Street north of Oxford Circus to **Portland Place,** of interest to any student of architecture. Heading up Regent Street you see the distinctive circular portico and spire of **All Souls, Langham Place** about 400 yards in front of you. Like Regent Street, this too was built as part of the aborted triumphal way to Regent's Park. Unable to secure all the land in a direct line between Oxford Circus and the entrance to the park, the architect, John Nash, was forced to bend his route left and then quickly right around the spot where his church now stands. In order to lessen the effect of this unfortunate kink, Nash designed the church with its circular portico to carry the eye around the corner, while its spire was intended to act as a natural focal point looking north up Regent Street.

Directly to one side of the church is **Broadcasting House,** headquarters of the BBC, the British Broadcasting Corporation. Here, Regent Street becomes Portland Place, one of London's most elegant thoroughfares. It was designed by the brothers Adam in the 1780s, and, when built, was London's widest street. Many of its houses are today in varying states of disrepair, while some have been replaced by slab-like prewar blocks.

Time Out The George (55 Great Portland St.), just round the corner from the BBC, is a pub serving steak pie, omelets, chicken, and scampi among other tempting lunch dishes; arrive early to avoid the crowds.

Clipstone Street (which runs off Great Portland Street) will provide you with a startling view of a modern building of a very different sort—the Post Office Tower, now officially the **British Telecom Tower.** A pencil-thin glass tube built in 1965 and some 620 feet high, it is London's principal telecommunications center. It can be seen from all over London, peeping out from behind even the tallest buildings. However, the best complete

top-to-bottom view is along Clipstone Street. The viewing platform at the top was closed to the public some years ago after a
bomb incident.

The northern end of Portland Place gives way to Nash's beautiful Park Crescent, the Marylebone Road, and Regent's Park
(*see* Regent's Park and Hampstead).

Knightsbridge and Kensington

This route takes the London explorer through two fashionable
quarters: Knightsbridge and Kensington. High society, with
its snazzy shops and eating-places, is the keynote, although
there are also some historic sites to explore. This is an ideal
route for a sunny spring or fall day, when London is at its best.

Knightsbridge

Take the Underground to Knightsbridge station and come out
the Sloane Street exit. Don't let the chaotic traffic send you
back below! One way leads south down Sloane Street to Sloane
Square and Chelsea, with the Cadogan Hotel half-way down—
where Oscar Wilde foolishly allowed himself to be arrested.
Another way, **Knightsbridge,** leads along the south side of
Hyde Park and the high rise that is the Hyde Park Barracks.
You might look up and see horses on what appears to be a balcony, for this is the headquarters of the Household Cavalry—
perhaps the most glamorous regiment in the British Army,
whose gorgeous plumed helmets, sparkling breastplates, and
proud, high-stepping horses are always so striking a feature of
London's royal occasions. The soldiers regularly exercise their
horses in the park, usually first thing in the morning. If you can
time your walk to reach the barracks at 10:28 on a weekday
morning (9:28 on Sundays—precision is a virtue of military
time-keeping), you should be able to see mounted guards leaving the barracks on their ride to Horse Guards Parade, where
the guard is changed at 11 AM (10 on Sundays—*see* Westminster and Royal London).

But it is the third branch off the traffic swirl—on the left as you
leave the station—that is the route we describe. **Brompton Road**
runs down to Harrods and then on to the great museum complex of South Kensington. This is an area of ritzy shops, with
❶ **Harrods** leading the bunch. Most visitors will buy something
here, however small, just to get one of the famous green-and-
gold bags. One of the main points of interest is the ground-floor
Food Hall, with its fine tiled ceiling and decorative array of edi-
bles. But, as a modern luxury store, Harrods doesn't really
compare with some of the best in the States. It is also desperately crowded, especially at sale time.

Time Out   **Le Metro** (28 Basil St.), close to Harrods, is a comfortable wine
bar where a croissant-and-coffee (or hot chocolate) breakfast is
served until 11, followed by lunch, at which you can take your
choice from salads and pâtés or heartier cooked dishes.

There are a few other highlights along Brompton Road, especially Beauchamp (pronounced "Beecham") Place, with dress
and shoe boutiques for the well-lined purse, and a generous
sprinkling of restaurants and wine bars. Walton Street, run-

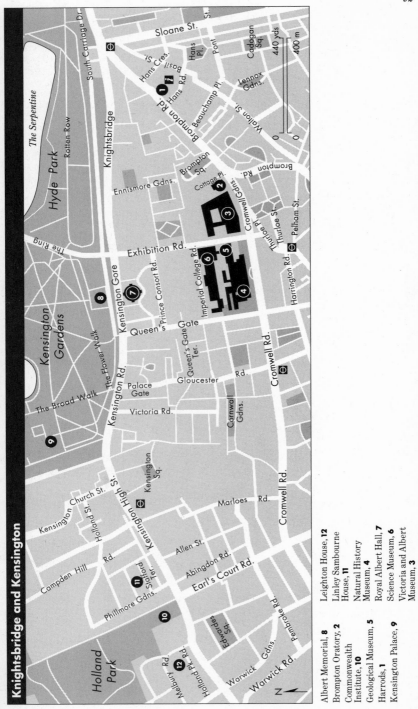

Knightsbridge and Kensington

The Serpentine

Hyde Park

Rotten Row

South Carriage Dr.

Sloane St.

Hans Cres.

Basil St.

Hans Pl.

1 **i**

Brompton Rd.

Beauchamp Pl.

Pont

Walton St.

Lennox Gdns.

Cadogan Sq.

Knightsbridge

Brompton Sq.

Brompton Rd.

Ennismore Gdns.

Cottage Pl.

2

Cromwell Gdns.

Thurloe St.

Pelham St.

The Ring

Exhibition Rd.

3

Cromwell Pl.

Harrington Rd.

Kensington Gardens

Kensington Gore

8

Prince Consort Rd.

7

Imperial College Rd.

6

5

4

The Flower Walk

Queen's Gate

Queen's Gate Ter.

The Broad Walk

Kensington Rd.

Palace Gate

Gloucester   Rd.

Cornwall Gdns.

9

Victoria Rd.

Cromwell Rd.

Kensington Church St.

Holland St.

Kensington High St.

Stafford Ter.

Kensington Sq.

Marloes Rd.

Cromwell Rd.

Campden Hill   Rd.

Allen St.

Abingdon Rd.

Earl's Court Rd.

Holland Park

11

Phillimore Gdns.

10

Edwardes Sq.

Warwick Gdns.

Melbury Rd.

12

Holland Pk. Rd.

Pembroke Rd.

Warwick Rd.

N

0 ———— 440 yds
0 ———— 400 m

Albert Memorial, **8**
Brompton Oratory, **2**
Commonwealth Institute, **10**
Geological Museum, **5**
Harrods, **1**
Kensington Palace, **9**

Leighton House, **12**
Linley Sambourne House, **11**
Natural History Museum, **4**
Royal Albert Hall, **7**
Science Museum, **6**
Victoria and Albert Museum, **3**

ning off Beauchamp Place, is also a happy hunting ground for the discriminating shopper.

② Further along Brompton Road, on the right, is the **Brompton Oratory,** a very Italianate Roman Catholic church both inside and out, though lacking the sparkle and glamor of its southern counterparts. It was built in that late-Victorian period (1876–84) when English Roman Catholics, who had suffered eclipse and worse for centuries, were emerging into the light of tolerance. The gentle statue outside is of Cardinal Newman (1801–90), the standard-bearer of the vast upsurge in Roman Catholic activity in the mid-19th century.

③ The next building is the **Victoria and Albert Museum,** cliff-like and surmounted by cupolas, structured like a cross between a crown and a wedding cake. This is the heart of the South Kensington Museum Complex. It would seem strange that there can be two museums such as the British Museum and the V&A (as it's always called) in the same city, but they really do serve two different purposes. In some realms they overlap a little, as with drawings and watercolors, but the main function of the V&A is to act as a "Museum of Ornamental Art," with the object of "the application of fine art to objects of utility and the improvement of public taste in design." It is essentially a teaching museum, heavily committed to design from every age and country. As such it has an unrivaled collection in many spheres, and one can spend hours wandering through its endless rooms, surrounded on all sides by artistic treasures from France, Italy, the East and, of course, Britain itself. Have an idea of what you want to see and arm yourself with a free plan when you go in or you could quickly lose yourself in the endless maze.

The collection is so vast, and so rich, that it is difficult to pick out the most exciting elements. The paintings of Constable rank very high on any list; so do the jewel rooms, especially the massive Baroque jewels; the delicate miniatures, with some of the loveliest painted in Elizabeth I's reign; the medieval church art, with its elaborate workmanship and occasional glimpses into a world haunted by the fear of death and damnation; a profusion of Renaissance art, especially a series of magnificent Raphael cartoons; costumes from many periods, excellently exhibited in the Costume Hall; musical instruments bewildering in their complexity and craftsmanship, and frequently played in fascinating recitals; Chinese, Islamic, and Indian art; Japanese art in a new gallery; the huge collection of sculpture reproductions . . . the list is endless. But the V&A is far from stuffy, as the Henry Cole Wing with its photographic exhibitions clearly demonstrates. It is, in fact, a very progressive place, and an ideal museum in which to wander and ponder. *Cromwell Rd., tel. 01/938–8500 or 01/938–8441 (recorded information). For admission a donation is requested but is not required. Open Mon.–Sat. 10–5:50, Sun. 2:30–5:50; closed Good Fri., May Day.*

Time Out The attractively decorated museum cafeteria is a pleasant—some would say essential—place for refreshment after time spent absorbing the wonders of the museum. You can buy anything from a pastry or sandwich to a full meal.

Next to the V&A come the three museums devoted to science—the Natural History Museum, the Geological Museum, and the Science Museum. The most spectacular, from the outside at **④** any rate, is the **Natural History Museum,** a marvelous late-

Victorian building by Alfred Waterhouse with ultra-modern additions. Note the little animals carved into the cathedral-like entrance. The collections are excellent and very instructive for kids, with dioramas and a massive, full-size model of a blue whale. *Cromwell Rd., tel. 01/589–6323 or 01/725–7866 (recorded information). Admission £2 adults, £1 children under 15 and senior citizens. Open Mon.–Sat. 10–6., Sun. 2–6; closed Good Fri., May Day.*

5 The **Geological Museum** is strictly the domain of the enthusiast. The main themes are the earth's history and the general principles of geological science. There is also a large collection of gemstones. *Exhibition Rd., tel. 01/938–8765. Admission £1 adults, 50p children under 15 and senior citizens. Open Mon.–Sat. 10–6, Sun. 1–6; closed Good Fri., May Day.*

6 The **Science Museum** has consistently proved itself highly popular, with working models, changing exhibitions, and a popular policy of providing both instruction and fun for kids with a "hands on" exhibit area. An enormous range of topics is covered, from locomotives and computers to space technology and the history of medicine. *Exhibition Rd., tel. 01/589–3456; 01/938–8123 and 01/930–8111 (recorded information). Admission free. Open Mon.–Sat. 10–6, Sun. 2:30–6; closed Good Fri., May Day.*

Time Out **Daquise** (20 Thurloe St.), at the southern end of Exhibition Road (near South Kensington tube station), is a colorful Polish restaurant, serving morning coffee, tea, and pastries as well as traditional East European dishes at lunch and dinner. It's long been a haunt of the Polish community in the United Kingdom.

Exhibition Road, the wide thoroughfare that runs up north beside the V&A, will take you through the heart of this cultural complex—and that's exactly what it is and was planned to be by the serious Victorians, taking their cue from the pedagogical Prince Albert—on to Kensington Gardens. On the right side of Exhibition Road is the large Mormon Chapel with a thin spike covered in gold leaf. On the left is the Imperial College of Science, now part of London University. At the center of the college campus is the **Queen's Tower,** all that remains of the Imperial Institute, which was demolished in the early 1960s after the Imperial Institute became the Commonwealth Institute (*see* Kensington section below), and moved to Holland Park. There is an uninterrupted view of London from the upper gallery, and displays relate the history of the tower; the belfry contains a peal of 10 bells. *Imperial College, Exhibition Rd., tel. 01/589–5111. Admission 60p. Tower open daily July–Sept. 10–5:30.*

Prince Consort Road runs left off Exhibition Road. Above it **7** stands the massive bulk of the **Royal Albert Hall,** named for Victoria's consort and nowadays scene of the summer series of Promenade Concerts (known as the Proms) that have been running for nine healthy decades. These concerts, now sponsored by the BBC, form one of the most comprehensive festivals of music in the world. They last for eight weeks with a concert every day. The huge amphitheater, resplendent in wine-red and gold, is a truly Victorian temple to art and science. If you are not able to get to a concert, it is still worth wandering round the **8** outside and across the road to look at the **Albert Memorial** and to walk into Kensington Gardens (*see below*). Beside the statue of Albert at the back of the hall—there are statues of Albert everywhere—is the restored **Royal College of Organists** (1875) and the modern **Royal College of Art** where there are sometimes exhibitions worth seeing.

Kensington

Even in these democratic days, you occasionally hear someone say that the *only* area where one could *possibly* live in London is "north of the river and south of the park." The park is Hyde Park; the area, the Royal Borough of Kensington (amalgamated with Chelsea). Though the district is now a very mixed bag, this still sums up the basic tone: It is a grand residential area. Many of the more stately houses have been divided into apartments, but the feeling of stuccoed wealth, the pillared porches, and the tree-filled squares remain.

King William III, who suffered from asthma, found the Thames mists that frequently veiled Whitehall very trying. So in 1689 he bought Nottingham House, as it was then called, sited in the rural village of Kensington, where he was able to breathe more easily. Renamed Kensington Palace, and enlarged from time to time, it still acts as the spiritual heart of the neighborhood.

With the arrival of royalty the village "flourished almost beyond belief," according to a chronicler writing in 1705. Court functionaries hurried to follow the royal example, and **Kensington Square** (just behind the House of Frazer department store) was built to accommodate them. In the reign of Queen Anne (1702–14), the demand for lodging became so pressing that at one time an ambassador, a bishop, and a physician occupied apartments in the same house in the square.

⊙ **Kensington Palace** was greatly extended and improved by both the monarchs who subsequently lived here, the Hanoverians George I and George II. (The latter had the misfortune to die here while sitting on the lavatory, though the public announcement had it that he was on the throne at the time.) On and off for more than a century, leading architects were employed in remodeling the palace, and their work is to be seen in those state apartments that are open to the public. It was here, too, that the young Princess Victoria was called from her bed on the night of June 20, 1837, by the Archbishop of Canterbury and the Lord Chamberlain, to be told of the death of her uncle, William IV, and her accession to the throne. Today the palace is the London home of the Prince and Princess of Wales, and of Princess Margaret.

Some rooms in the **state apartments** are furnished as they were in the 1830s when the young Victoria lived out her restricted childhood with her dominating mother and governess. Visitors can also see the **Court Dress Collection,** which consists of "Ladies' and Gentlemen's Court Dress and Uniforms from 1750 to the 1950s" displayed in period settings. Both court dress and court behavior were governed by strict rules, and the exhibition opens this curious world of rigid etiquette to the public. *Kensington Gdns. tel. 01/937–9561. Admission £2.60 adults, £1.30 children under 16, £1.70 senior citizens. Open Mon.–Sat. 9–5, Sun. 1–5; closed Good Fri.*

Immediately behind the palace runs **Kensington Palace Gardens** (called Palace Green at the south end), a wide and leafy avenue of large houses set in their own grounds and mostly the work of the leading architects of the 1850s and '60s. Thackeray, the novelist—author of *Vanity Fair*—died at #2, in a house he had designed for himself. It is now the Israeli Embassy. This is one of the few private roads in London, with a uniformed guard at either end, and its secluded nature makes it ideal for those foreign countries who have a need for extra security—Israel, Romania, Czechoslovakia, and the Soviet Union among them.

Just past the towering, modern Royal Garden Hotel is **Kensington Church Street,** which runs up to the right, with St. Mary Abbots Church on the corner. It looks genuinely medieval, but was built on the site of a much earlier church in the 1870s by Gilbert Scott, who also designed the Albert Memorial. This is rich territory for the antiques enthusiast. All the way up this winding road are shops specializing in everything from Japanese armor to Victorian commemorative china. Tucked away behind the church is Kensington Church Walk (go down Holland Street, take the second street on the left), which is a microcosm of the area, containing tiny shops full of dolls and prints, pottery, and pictures. Holland Street itself is attractive, with an excellent pub and a tiny little flowered cul-de-sac almost opposite. A little further on is the modern and massive brick bulk of the municipal offices. .

| Time Out | **Andronica's Coffee Shop** (35 Kensington High St.) makes a pleasant refuge from the crowds of shoppers; breakfasts, pastries, and cream teas are the specialties. |

If you turn back down to Kensington High Street, now a busy and flourishing, if slightly tacky, shopping area, and follow it westward, you will come eventually to the **Commonwealth Institute.** You'll recognize it by the huge, tent-like copper roof, standing back from the street in its own spacious grounds. Although the Commonwealth plays a much less important role in British affairs nowadays (just as British influence on other Commonwealth members has diminished), this institute is very much alive, with excellent, attractively displayed exhibits from the member countries, and frequent concerts and film shows. *230 Kensington High St., tel. 01/603-4535. Admission free. Open Mon.–Sat. 10–5:30, Sun. 2–5; closed Good Fri.*

Behind the institute lies **Holland Park,** the grounds of Holland House. The building was mostly destroyed by incendiary bombs during World War II, but the grounds have been preserved, with their peacocks and ducks, rabbits and chickens all running wild. Some of the best flower beds in London are here, too, with a fine display of roses in June and July. The house was first built in Tudor times, and was the lively center for artists and wits during the residence of the third Baron Holland between 1773 and 1840. The brilliant circle was largely attracted there by his wife, a dynamic hostess though an impossible woman. There is a fetching restaurant in what is left of Holland House called **The Belvedere.** It's an attractive place for alfresco dining. (*See* Dining.)

On the eastern side of Commonwealth Institute is the **Linley Sambourne House,** a little masterpiece of Victoriana. Managed by the Victorian Society, this fascinating survival was sold intact to the City of London by the countess of Rosse, mother of Lord Snowdon and the granddaughter of Mr. Sambourne, who built and furnished the place in the 1870s. For over 30 years, Linley Sambourne was the main political cartoonist for the satirical magazine *Punch*. For anyone interested in the Victorian era a visit here is a must. *18 Stafford Terr., tel. 01/994–1019. Admission £1.50. Open Mar.–Oct., Wed. 10–4, Sun. 2–5.*

A little farther along High Street, on the other side, is **Edwardes Square**. It was developed in about 1802—in perfect taste, though entirely English in atmosphere and architecture—by a Frenchman named Changier. The story goes that Changier was really one of Napoleon's agents and that he built the square to house the imperial civil servants once England had been successfully invaded!

Time Out   A very pretty pub on the corner of Edwardes Square, the **Scarsdale Arms** is an ideal spot for a summer drink.

A little way past Commonwealth Institute, on the same side of High Street, is a turning called Melbury Road that leads to **Holland Park Road**. Here, at #12, on the right-hand side, lived Lord Leighton, the Victorian painter par excellence. You can still recapture some of the exotic richness of the artistic life of the last half of the 19th century in the interior decorations of ⓬ **Leighton House,** especially in the Arab Hall, lavishly lined with Persian tiles and pierced woodwork. The rest of the house was somewhat neglected, but, thanks to the generosity of John Paul Getty III, it is being refurbished. This small neighborhood was one of the principal artistic colonies of Victorian London. If you are interested in domestic architecture of a century back, wander through the surrounding streets. You will find a lot to enjoy. *12 Holland Park Rd., tel. 01/602–3316. Admission free. Open Mon.–Sat. 11–5 (Mon.–Fri. 11–6 during exhibitions); closed bank holidays.*

Hyde Park and Kensington Gardens

The Royal Parks are among London's unique features: Great swathes of green in the middle of the city, where it really is possible to escape from the noise and urgency of the metropolis. The description "royal" is somewhat paradoxical, for today these are the most democratic of places, where Londoners of every class and background come to relax. Yet the parks owe their very survival to monarchical origins. Having first been established as places where royalty hunted, walked, or rode, they acquired a privileged status and remained immune from the greedy clutches of property developers during London's many phases of expansion.

This section describes a walk through the two largest Royal Parks in central London (Richmond Park, on the capital's western edge, is larger; *see* The Thames Upstream).

Hyde Park and Kensington Gardens are technically separate, but on the ground it is impossible to know when one stops and the other begins. For St James's Park and Green Park see the section on Westminster and Royal London, and St. James's and Mayfair. For Regent's Park to the north, see the section Regent's Park and Hampstead.

Hyde Park covers 361 acres, stretching from the Bayswater Road in the north to Knightsbridge in the south, and bounded by Park Lane in the east. To the west lies Kensington Gardens, another 273 acres, once the private grounds of Kensington Palace, but now the continuation of Hyde Park; together the two areas form the largest open space in central London. Both parks have fine trees—though they were badly damaged and many destroyed in the terrible storm of October 1987—plus some attractive areas of flower beds, seasonally replanted, and a surprisingly large variety of birds.

Though there are gates all around the park, most of them splendidly decorative, the main entrance to Hyde Park is **Decimus Burton's Gateway** at the southern end of Park Lane, just by **Apsley House** (*see* St. James's and Mayfair). To the left, as you enter, is **Rotten Row,** a long avenue that runs along the bottom of the park. It's a sandy track with paths on each side that used to be a popular strolling place, especially on Sundays after church. Today it is used almost exclusively for riding—the odd name is an English corruption of *route du roi,* for this was the route taken by the king's carriage when going from Whitehall to Kensington Palace.

Henry VIII was the first monarch to use the area as a royal hunting ground, and deer roamed the park until the middle of the last century. Charles I transformed it from a hunting ground into a place where fashionable society could see and be seen; a circular drive was laid out for carriages to parade around. Later the park became a locality for duels. In 1851 the first Great International Exhibition was held here in the magnificent surroundings of the specially constructed Crystal Palace (much to the horror of *The Times* which forecast that Hyde Park would become "a bivouac of all vagabonds. Kensington and Belgravia would be uninhabitable and the [social] season would be ruined").

Heading into the center of the park from Apsley House, you will come across the statue of **Achilles,** standing 20-feet high. This was yet another tribute to Wellington, paid for by subscriptions from the admiring women of Britain. The assembled ladies must have had a shock when this colossal nude, cast from the metal of guns captured during some of the duke's famous victories, was finally unveiled in 1822.

Farther along is the start of a long, man-made, crescent-shaped lake called the **Serpentine** in Hyde Park and **Long Water** in Kensington Gardens. The poet Shelley's first wife, Harriet Westbrook, drowned herself here in 1816 when she was pregnant.

Strolling along the edge of the Serpentine is one of the most enjoyable rural pleasures that London has to offer. At any season of the year the lake has its own atmosphere: In summer it's almost a seaside scene, the grass strewn with deck chairs and the water busy with boats; in winter it takes on an air of gentle melancholy, the trees sketching bare traceries against the gray sky, the water visited by swooping gulls.

Past the swimming area you will arrive at the **bridge** that carries the main road across the park. This is an elegant structure, built in 1826, which looks like a stage set come to life among the trees, especially at night. From here you get a good view of Westminster's skyline to the southeast.

Once across the bridge you are in **Kensington Gardens.** These began as the private grounds of Kensington Palace, and were landscaped by Queen Caroline, wife of George II, who created

Hyde Park and Kensington Gardens

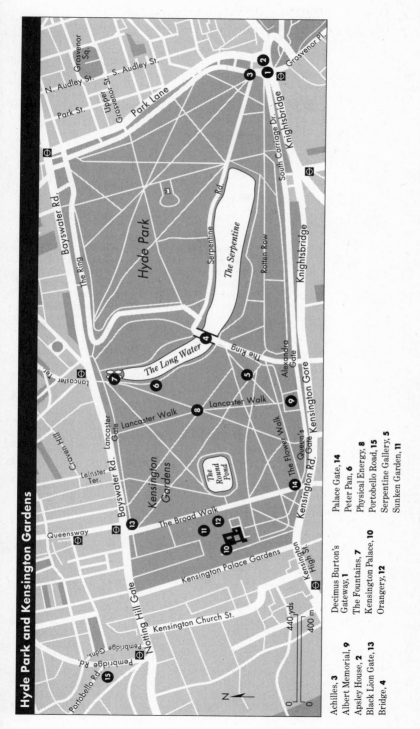

Achilles, **3**
Albert Memorial, **9**
Apsley House, **2**
Black Lion Gate, **13**
Bridge, **4**

Decimus Burton's
Gateway, **1**
The Fountains, **7**
Kensington Palace, **10**
Orangery, **12**

Palace Gate, **14**
Peter Pan, **6**
Physical Energy, **8**
Portobello Road, **15**
Serpentine Gallery, **5**
Sunken Garden, **11**

most of their present features. Just south of the bridge is the
⑤ **Serpentine Gallery,** an art gallery that houses regular exhibitions, usually of interesting modern works. *Kensington Gdns., tel. 01/402–6075 or 01/723–9072 (recorded information). Open in summer daily 10–6, winter 10–4.*

Time Out   **The Dell** restaurant at the eastern end of the Serpentine has a self-service counter with hot dishes and salads on the menu, but the location is the best thing about the place.

If you walk northward along the western (left) bank of the
⑥ Long Water, you will pass the statue of **Peter Pan,** who was supposed to live on an island in the Serpentine. His creator, J.M. Barrie, had a house just north of the park, at 100 Bayswater Road. At the end of the lake you will reach a paved Italianate
⑦ garden called **The Fountains.**

The southwesterly walkway from here will take you past an obelisk memorial to the explorer J.H. Speke, who discovered the source of the Nile. **Lancaster Walk** to the south from here will lead you to a huge bronze equestrian sculpture by G.F. Watts
⑧ ⑨ called **Physical Energy,** and then on to the **Albert Memorial,** at the southern extremity of the gardens. This monument—the physical expression of Queen Victoria's obsessive reverence for her dead husband's memory—was for many years considered the ugliest landmark in the country. Tastes change, however, and many have developed a quiet affection for this "memorial of our Blameless Prince." So here Albert sits, 14-feet high, under his ornate canopy, holding a catalogue of the Great International Exhibition, which had been his brainchild. The base is decorated with 169 life-size figures of poets, composers, architects, and sculptors drawn from all ages and lands. The four corners have marble groups symbolizing Agriculture, Manufacturing, Commerce, and Engineering, while at the outer corners of the steps are four more groups representing Europe, Africa, Asia, and America. You may have trouble seeing the details of the memorial, though, as it is badly eroded by air pollution, and often surrounded by scaffolding or hoardings, while experts decide how to preserve it.

From just above the memorial, **Flower Walk** angles westward. The long flower beds bloom for most of the year, with the displays being regularly changed. At the end of the Flower Walk
⑩ the **Broad Walk** bisects the gardens, and beyond it stands **Kensington Palace** (*see* Knightsbridge and Kensington).

⑪ Northeast of the palace is a **Sunken Garden,** dating from 1909
⑫ and surrounded by lime trees, and an **Orangery,** which was built two centuries earlier. On the other side of the Broad Walk from the palace is the **Round Pond,** a favorite spot for ducks, pigeons, and model yachtsmen. The Broad Walk leads north to
⑬ the Bayswater Road through the **Black Lion Gate,** while to the
⑭ south it leads to Kensington Road via the **Palace Gate.**

Black Lion Gate is only a few minutes' walk away from **Notting Hill,** a lively residential quarter with some interesting book-
⑮ shops and antiques shops. Just behind the main road lies **Portobello Road,** where the Saturday market is a magnet for every antiques- and bargain-hunter in London. It's essential to arrive early for the best choice—but at even the busiest times the hunt will be fun, and you might be able to uncover some good buys. The regular antiques dealers along Portobello Road and in the neighboring streets are open normally on weekdays (*see* Shopping).

Time Out Two pâtisseries near the north side of Kensington Gardens are the **Pâtisserie Française, Maison Pechon** (127 Queensway) and, slightly more expensive, **Maison Bouquillon** (41 Moscow Rd). Hot chocolate, strong coffee, and fresh-baked croissants and pastries are specialties of both establishments.

Belgravia and Chelsea

To the southwest of Hyde Park Corner is the aristocratic area of Belgravia. The streets and squares here were laid out in the mid-1800s by Thomas Cubitt, one of England's greatest entrepreneurs, a builder who had as much effect on the appearance of London as Wren and Nash did. If you start at **Hyde Park Corner** tube and take the exit past the shuttered building that was once St. George's Hospital and is waiting to be reborn as a hotel, you will be poised to plunge into Belgravia. Turn right down Grosvenor Crescent and you soon find yourself in Belgrave Square, ringed by imposing mansions that were once the houses of lords and dukes, and are now mostly embassies and discreet offices.

Diagonally across the square, Belgrave Place will lead through to **Eaton Square,** the aptly-chosen locale for the TV series, *Upstairs, Downstairs.* It is no accident that this whole neighborhood of wealth and splendor is grouped around the back of Buckingham Palace. It's worth taking a gentle stroll around the streets leading off Eaton Square north and south; they are full of wine bars, interesting little shops, and fascinating lanes called mews, where the rich once kept their horses and carriages, and where a former stable can now change hands at over half a million pounds. Eaton Square also heralds the start of a long route running westward. Here it is residential, but very soon, after Sloane Square, it becomes the shopping extravaganza of King's Road.

Chelsea

Sloane Square marks the beginning of Chelsea, where many of Britain's most famous artists and writers lived. It was once a seedy but cosmopolitan region of London. It is now a much sought-after residential section, with even very small terrace houses commanding high prices. In one corner of the square, by the tube station, stands the **Royal Court Theatre,** distinguished during the last three decades or so for its commitment to modern drama; it was here that *Look Back in Anger* was first staged in 1956. The works of many of Britain's most interesting new playwrights are still premiered here. On the other side of the square is **Peter Jones,** a major department store that sells everything from fabrics to furniture polish.

From here, the **King's Road** runs west, packed with boutiques, bistros, and antique shops. It is best seen on Saturdays when the sidewalks are crowded with pink- and green-haired punks rubbing shoulders with Gucci-clad yuppies. It has long lost top billing as the trendiest shopping thoroughfare, but it retains an attractively zany atmosphere.

Time Out Part of the fun of a stroll down King's Road is discovering a lively spot for a snack or a light lunch. Here are three suggestions out of a large number of possibilities. **Chelsea Kitchen** (98 King's

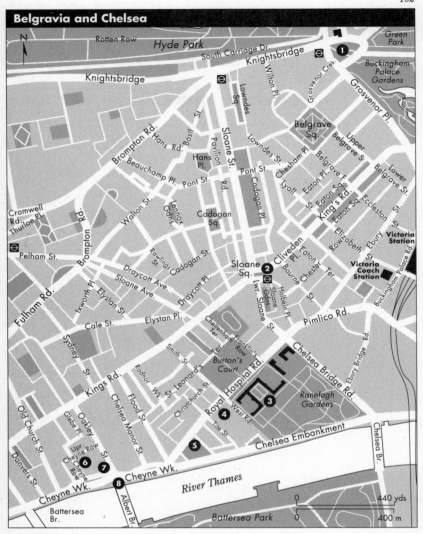

Belgravia and Chelsea

Albert Bridge, **8**
Carlyle House, **6**
Physic Garden, **5**
Hyde Park Corner, **1**
More's Statue, **7**

National Army
Museum, **4**
Royal Court Theatre, **2**
Royal Hospital
Chelsea, **3**

Rd.) specializes in inexpensive and nourishing basic food. **Henry J. Bean's** (195 King's Rd.) is a good-quality, fast-food place (the burgers, deep-fried potato skins, and chili are especially recommended), while **La Bersagliera** (372 King's Rd.) is a busy Italian café whose homemade pasta regularly sells out.

A left turn off the King's Road down Cheltenham Terrace and Franklin's Row will lead you to a quite different, and calmer, world. Here you will find the Chelsea Barracks, the Royal Hospital, and the National Army Museum.

❸ The **Royal Hospital Chelsea,** rather like the Royal Naval Hospital at Greenwich, is only a "hospital" in the ancient meaning of the word—a hospice. It was founded in the late 17th century as a home for old and disabled soldiers, and was modeled on the Hôtel des Invalides in Paris. Its oldest inhabitant today served with the British Army well before World War I, and altogether there are now 405 pensioners, wearing their traditional uniform with its black three-cornered hat and red jacket usually weighed down with medals. The Royal Hospital was built by Sir Christopher Wren between 1682 and 1691, and had the seal of approval of Charles II; there is some evidence to support the legend that the king was influenced to build the hospital by his mistress Nell Gwynn. The fine **statue of the Merry Monarch** by Grinling Gibbons is on the grounds. The statue is decked with oak leaves on May 19 each year, Oak Apple Day, in commemoration of the time when Charles hid in an oak tree to escape the troops of Oliver Cromwell.

The hospital, its old pink bricks mellowing in the sun, is a peaceful place, and you can understand why it is that old soldiers never die but only fade away; it would be a fine spot to fade in. The building itself is worth visiting, and the manicured grounds are ideal for a quiet stroll. In May each year, the Chelsea Flower Show is held here; vast tents are erected, and thousands of plants brought in. Garden-lovers (whose numbers rival those of dog lovers in Britain) troop to the show to see the latest developments in gardening and to carry away samples and ideas. *Royal Hospital Rd., tel. 01/730–0161. Admission free. Open Mon.–Sat. 10–12 and 2–4, Sun. 2–4 only Apr. through Sept.; closed bank holidays.*

❹ The **National Army Museum** is just past the hospital, on Royal Hospital Road. This museum celebrates the exploits and achievements of the British Army from 1485 to 1982, the year of the Falklands conflict. It is an excellently conceived display, and for anyone who finds the changes in the art of warfare over the centuries interesting, it will prove a rich mine. Separate rooms are devoted to weapons, uniforms, and military art. The sad thing about it is that the outside of the building is monumentally ugly, and, since it stands in close proximity to the work of one of the world's greatest architects, uncharitable thoughts about the modern army's taste are unavoidable. *Royal Hospital Rd., tel. 01/730–0717. Open Mon.–Sat. 10–5:30, Sun. 2–5:30; closed Good Fri., May Day.*

Two blocks past the museum, on the corner of Chelsea Embankment and Royal Hospital Road, is a botanical garden, started by the Society of Apothecaries in 1673 to provide "physic" in the healthy air. A statue of Sir Hans Sloane (1660–1753), an eminent doctor who provided the land, stands in the **❺** middle. The **Physic Garden** (entrance on Swan Walk) is a fascinating place to stroll and relax, and proves a source of inspiration to enthusiastic gardeners. Sadly the hurricane that raged through southern England in October 1987 left the garden badly damaged. *Royal Hospital Rd., tel. 01/352–5646. Admission £1.50 adults, £1 children. Open approximately mid-Apr.–mid-Oct., Sun. and Wed. 2–5; daily 12–5 during the Chelsea Flower Show in the third week of May.*

One of the most intriguing parts of Chelsea, especially for the visitor who is attracted to houses with histories, is the riverside walk from here to past Battersea Bridge. This parade of houses overlooking the river is **Cheyne Walk** and has been the haunt of poets, painters, writers, and composers for several centuries. Here you will see many of the round blue ceramic plaques put up on the facades of buildings all over London to commemorate famous residents. Starting at #4 with the novelist George Eliot (1819–80), you continue with the artist and poet Dante Gabriel Rossetti (1828–82), who lived at #16 for 20 years and kept a small zoo in the garden; Captain Scott (1868–1912), doomed explorer of the Antarctic, lived at #56 Oakley Street, just around the corner. Thomas Carlyle (1795–1881), the Victorian historian and pundit, lived in Cheyne Row at #24, which is open to the public. The American writer Henry James (1843–1916), a passionate anglophile, died in Carlyle Mansions

6 in World War I. *Carlyle House, 24 Cheyne Row, tel. 01/352–7087. Admission £1.60 adults, 80p children under 17. Open Apr.–Oct., Wed.–Sun. 11–5; closed Mon. and Tues. (but open bank holiday Mon.), Good Fri.*

Suddenly you'll come face to face with one of the area's most famous inhabitants, Sir Thomas More (1473–1535), the Man for

7 All Seasons. **More's statue,** looking out across the river, is modern, set up in 1969, but it has a strongly Tudor look to it— square, gilded, and hierarchic, portraying More the saint, rather than More the richly humorous, warm human being. The statue stands outside **All Saints' Church,** which was badly damaged in the Blitz (1940) and then rebuilt, and which contains many interesting memorials that survived nearly untouched. More and his family lived in **Crosby Hall,** which was moved from its original site in Bishopsgate and re-erected on the Chelsea Embankment in 1910 on the land that used to be More's orchard. His first wife is buried in All Saints', part of which he designed.

8 The **Albert Bridge,** an 1873 suspension bridge, is especially attractive when lit up at night. You could cross it for a quiet walk in **Battersea Park,** which stretches on the opposite bank.

Cheyne Walk continues westward. It was along here that the artists J.M.W. Turner (1775–1851) and the American James McNeill Whistler (1834–1903) lived (#118 and #96 respectively). The misty light on the river formed the subject of many of Whistler's best paintings. Turner, who lived here under the name of Booth, was also captivated by the quality of the light, and painted views of the former Battersea Bridge, which lay outside his windows. The present bridge was built in 1890 and keeps watch over a stretch of the river made interesting by the many houseboats that are moored here.

Soho and Covent Garden

By turns seedy, stylish, and salacious, Soho, like its much grander neighbor Mayfair on the other side of Regent Street, has the unusual distinction of being one of the very few areas of London whose borders are quite clear. It also has the distinction of being laid out on the nearest thing to a grid plan that London has to offer, which makes this, the most concentrated and international district of London's West End, a pretty easy place to get around.

Soho's unusual name is believed to derive from the days when this was hunting land attached to the nearby Palace of Westminster, "So-Ho!" being a common hunting cry of the time. By the late 17th century, as London grew more rapidly, the open fields of Soho quickly became urbanized, a process boosted by the influx of immigrants from the Continent and a great flood of refugees made homeless by the Great Fire of London in 1666.

The trades practiced by these early residents are still remembered in many street names here: Glasshouse Street marked the site of a large bottling factory, while there were several breweries conveniently located in nearby Brewer Street. Like the similarly tawdry areas around the Moulin Rouge in Paris, Soho also had its *moulin*, or windmill, in Great Windmill Street, just off Shaftesbury Avenue. In the days of the 16th and early 17th centuries, Leicester Square was the local public green, used by the locals to hang their washing out to dry.

Soho has always had a substantial immigrant population. The first foreigners to settle here were Greeks escaping from the Turkish oppression of the Ottoman Empire, and the French Huguenots (Protestants) fleeing Catholic oppression in their homeland. Later waves of French came after the revolutionary upheavals at the end of the 18th century and the Paris Commune of 1870. In fact, one of Soho's most celebrated restaurants, Wheelers in Old Compton Street, was started by one of Napoleon's chefs. Many famous refugees and temporary visitors to London have lived in this area—Karl Marx, Wagner, and Haydn.

Today, the predominant foreign influences are Italian and Chinese. The Italian influence is apparent almost everywhere in Soho, but the Chinese community is gathered in only one corner, around Gerrard Street, to the south of Shaftesbury Avenue. Here, a cluster of Chinese restaurants and supermarkets, Chinese-style phone boxes, a pagoda, and other street decorations combine to create London's mini version of Chinatown.

Soho owes its slightly exotic air to the cosmopolitan nature of the people it has welcomed within its borders, an air that makes it subtly, but distinctly, different from the rest of staid, insular London. In addition to the film, record, and advertising companies, restaurateurs, and other high profile folk who have made this their natural territory, it should be no surprise that Soho has also long had a reputation as London's premier red-light district. This was never a situation that local residents have been happy about, and recent clean-up campaigns have greatly improved matters, though some strip clubs, a few soft-porn movie houses, and several fairly discreet sex shops remain. For Londoners at least, Soho without sex is as difficult to imagine as the city without rain.

Soho and Covent Garden

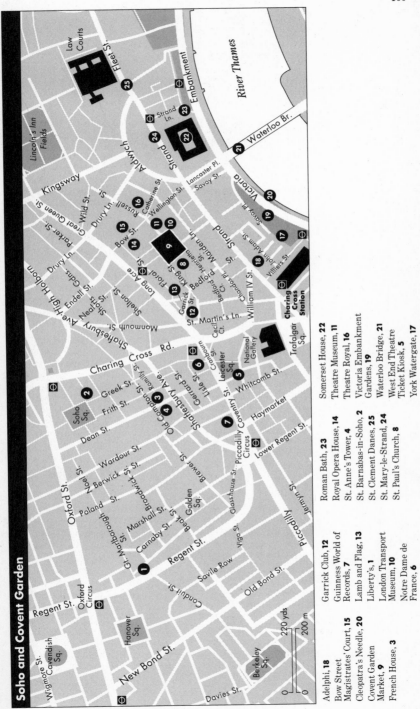

Adelphi, **18**
Bow Street
Magistrates' Court, **15**
Cleopatra's Needle, **20**
Covent Garden
Market, **9**
French House, **3**

Garrick Club, **12**
Guinness World of
Records, **7**
Lamb and Flag, **13**
Liberty's, **1**
London Transport
Museum, **10**
Notre Dame de
France, **6**

Roman Bath, **23**
Royal Opera House, **14**
St. Anne's Tower, **4**
St. Barnabas-in-Soho, **2**
St. Clement Danes, **25**
St. Mary-le-Strand, **24**
St. Paul's Church, **8**

Somerset House, **22**
Theatre Museum, **11**
Theatre Royal, **16**
Victoria Embankment
Gardens, **19**
Waterloo Bridge, **21**
West End Theatre
Ticket Kiosk, **5**
York Watergate, **17**

Soho

You can choose practically any point from which to launch an expedition into Soho; it's not a large area and all the most interesting points are easily reached. Given that there's no ideal point from which to start—and because you've got to start somewhere—our description of Soho begins at **Oxford Circus,** which, if nothing else, is very easy to find.

❶ Head south down Regent Street a couple of hundred yards from Oxford Circus and make a left into Great Marlborough Street. This leads you past the black-and-white facade of **Liberty's** department store *(see* Shopping) to the north end of **Carnaby Street.** Carnaby Street's dizzy heyday as a fashion and pop music mecca back in the Swinging Sixties evaporated almost entirely without trace many years ago, leaving today's pedestrian-only street a poor imitation of its former self. Worth investigating, however, is the small network of lanes off to the left, where there are several interesting little craft shops, among them the **Craftsmen Potters Association's store** on parallel Marshall Street, where there are some fine examples of craftsmanship on display *(see* Shopping).

The Romantic poet and painter William Blake was born at #74 Broadwick Street in 1758. This street leads to Berwick (pronounced "Berik") Street, scene of a thriving daily market. Pick your way past the crowded stalls, trying not to slip on the squashed cabbage leaves, to reach Old Compton Street. This is one of Soho's major thoroughfares—the other is Wardour Street—famed in about equal measure for its cafés, restaurants, and sex shops.

Attractions lie to both the north and the south. To the north, up Frith Street, is the prettiest and probably the most interesting square in the area, **Soho Square.** It was laid out in about 1680 and became fashionable in the 18th century; only two of the original buildings are left. The garden in the middle is distinguished for the tiny cottage that seems to come straight from Disney's *Snow White*—it's actually a toolshed that was put up in the last century. At the corner of Soho Square and Greek
❷ Street is **St. Barnabas-in-Soho,** a charitable institution whose fine 18th-century house is open to the public. The plasterwork, staircases, and fireplaces are well worth a look. *1 Greek St., tel. 01/437-1894. Open Wed. 2:30-4, Thurs. 11-12:30.*

❸ To the south of Old Compton Street, on Dean Street, is another famous Soho landmark, the **French House.** This pub is run with impeccable panache by one of Soho's most celebrated characters, the redoubtable Gaston. It's nearly always packed with various Bohemian types, but it's worth fighting your way to the bar for a glass of pastis or a *vin ordinaire.* During World War II, the pub was a London rendezvous of de Gaulle's Free French Forces. The walls are hung with signed photographs of French boxers and cycle racers.

❹ Directly opposite the pub is the **tower of St. Anne's church,** all that remains of this once famous church, probably designed by Wren. The building was hit by German bombs in 1940, leaving only the tower standing. The garden on the other side of the tower at Wardour Street, originally the graveyard, adds a welcome touch of green, as well as a place to sit for a while.

Dean Street runs south into Shaftesbury Avenue, which effectively divides the main body of Soho from the Chinese area based around Gerrard Street. Shaftesbury Avenue is the heart of London's theaterland *(see* London's Theater's in Portraits of London).

Time Out   The area just above Shaftesbury Avenue is a good place for tea shops or *pâtisseries*, since they are mostly of French origin. Two worth sampling are **Maison Bertaux** (28 Greek St.) and, just around the corner, **Pâtisserie Valerie** (44 Old Compton St.). Prices aren't low, but the cakes are delicious (some of the stickiest and creamiest in London!) and the cafés are a good place to watch the world go by.

South of Shaftesbury Avenue and Gerrard Street is **Leicester Square** (pronounced "Lester"). It's among the oldest and most famous of London's squares, having been laid out originally as early as 1630. By the 19th century it had gained a reputation as a place of slightly disreputable theaters, restaurants, and dance halls. It still performs its traditional role as an entertainment center, though now its theaters have become cinemas and its dance halls discos. Despite its faint hint of Times Square, and its generally characterless buildings, it remains a reasonably likable place, not least for the still handsome garden in its center. There's a statue of William Shakespeare in the center, with the bard looking rather out-of-sorts; busts of the artists Hogarth and Reynolds; and a small, lively statue of Charlie Chaplin. On the west side of the square is the **Society of West End Theatres' ticket kiosk,** where you can buy half-price tickets for many London theaters on the day of the performance. Leicester Place, on the northeast corner of Leicester Square, contains the French church of **Notre Dame de France.** One of the side chapels is decorated with a mural by the great French artist and poet Jean Cocteau.

Also off the northwest corner is the **Trocadero Centre**—an entertainment complex with shops and no less than three separate exhibitions, all specially designed to provide family entertainment. **Guinness World of Records** is a three-dimensional recreation of the odd and amazing facts and figures, records and achievements, catalogued in the world-famous *Guinness Book of World Records.* The **London Experience** uses state-of-the-art electronic media to recreate in sound and vision the story of London since the foundation of the city, while **Light Fantastic** claims to be the world's largest permanent exhibition of holography. There are over 100 exhibits demonstrating illusions created by pure technology, including plasma spheres—a form of sculpture in light that is meant to be touched—and a laser light show. *Guinness World of Records, Trocadero, tel. 01/439-7331. Admission £3.50 adults, £2 children under 16, £2.50 senior citizens. Open daily 10–10. The London Experience, Trocadero, tel. 01/439-4938. Admission £2.50 adults, £2.00 children under 16 and senior citizens. Shows daily 10:20–10:20; late night show June–Sept. at 11. Light Fantastic, Trocadero, tel. 01/734-4516. Admission £2.50 adults, £1.75 children and senior citizens. Open daily 10–10.*

Just beyond the Trocadero is Piccadilly Circus *(see* St. James's and Mayfair).

Cranbourn Street, at the northeast corner of Leicester Square, will lead you to Charing Cross Road, the eastern border of Soho and, like Shaftesbury Avenue, laid out in the 19th century. Heading left (north) up Charing Cross Road you pass a series of new and secondhand bookstores. Just above busy Cambridge Circus is #84, which gave the title to Helen Hanff's memorable book (subsequently a movie), sadly now a record store.

Finally, though not strictly speaking in Soho, you might like to explore the little courts and alleyways running off the Charing Cross Road, among them **Cecil Court** and **Bedford Court.** They are lined with print shops, secondhand bookstores, and some record stores. This is the place to find old theatrical posters, programs, and books on every subject under the sun. It is also an excellent area for pubs. Try the **Salisbury,** the **Black Horse,** or the wonderfully named **Green Man and French Horn** on St. Martin's Lane, just across from the end of Cecil Court.

Covent Garden

St. Martin's Lane makes a convenient point from which to head into Covent Garden. Or, if you plan to explore Covent Garden without having first been to Soho, just take the tube to Covent Garden station. In any event, you should begin your exploration of this ever more characterful chunk of central London at the born-again old **Covent Garden Market.**

Originally, the "Convent Garden" belonged to the 13th-century Abbey of St. Peter at Westminster, for which it produced fruit and vegetables. Following the dissolution of the monasteries in the mid-16th century, the Crown took possession of the lands and awarded them in 1552 to John Russell, first earl of Bedford. In 1630 the fourth earl (later the duke of Bedford—dukes outrank earls) commissioned Inigo Jones, the leading architect of the day, who was also responsible for the Banqueting House on Whitehall, to lay out a square on the site. **St. Paul's Church** was at one end, with tall, elegantly colonnaded houses on the north and east sides, and the plain rear wall of Bedford House (the earl's London residence) filling in the south side. This was the first of London's great squares, and it influenced the design and construction of many subsequent London squares. Sadly, of the buildings, only the church remains today.

With the opening of Westminster Bridge in the mid-18th century, Covent Garden became well established and grew to be one of the world's foremost fruit, vegetable, and flower markets. However, after World War II, as the market expanded, it became clear that the surrounding narrow streets and buildings were acting as a straitjacket to development and creating the most appalling traffic jams. And so, in 1974, market operations were moved to a new site at Nine Elms, south of the Thames, leaving the deserted Covent Garden ripe for redevelopment. The area was very nearly turned into yet another jungle of glass-and-concrete high-rise office blocks, but after a prolonged protest campaign, a plan of small-scale development was adopted, which has generally been very successful.

At the heart of Covent Garden is the market building itself, overlooked by the back of St. Paul's, whose main entrance is on Bedford Street. St. Paul's is a rather stark church, inside and out, but worth visiting for the memorials to famous theater folk that line the walls. It is popularly known as "the actors' church." The portico facing the market building provides an excellent stage for open-air entertainment—jazz musicians, jugglers, fire- eaters, and mime troupes.

9 The **market building** is the centerpiece of the whole area, and was built for the duke of Bedford in 1840. Following the move of the vegetable and fruit markets to Nine Elms, it was carefully restored and reopened in 1980, having been converted into an unusual shopping center, with boutiques and craft shops, health-food bars, and gift shops galore. On its south side is the lively and much less formal Jubilee open-air market, catering to artists and craftsmen and selling food, records, toys, and a multitude of flea-market goods. The best time to visit it for crafts is on the weekend. There are plenty of restaurants and cafés nearby, or, if you just need to rest your legs, you can sit on the steps and watch the people go by.

10 On the southeastern corner of the square stands the old Flower Market, now the **London Transport Museum.** It contains an extensive collection of vehicles, including an original omnibus, trains (including a steam locomotive used on the Underground as long ago as 1866), trams, and buses. This is a real "hands-on" museum, and you are encouraged to try out many of the exhibits, which makes it a popular place with children. *39 Wellington St., tel. 01/379–6344. Admission £2.40 adults, £1.10 children under 16 and senior citizens. Open daily 10–6.*

11 The long-awaited **Theatre Museum** opened next door on Shakespeare's birthday, April 23, 1987. It is devoted to the British theater from Shakespeare to the present day in all its many facets—not merely straight drama, but also musical comedy, opera, rock and pop, circus, pantomime, and music hall (vaudeville). The main exhibition contains theatrical memorabilia of every kind, including prints and paintings of the earliest London theaters, early play scripts, costumes, and props. One interesting feature is the re-creation of a dressing room, stuffed full of memorabilia such as tap shoes and a traveling makeup case, all belonging to former stars. The Paintings Gallery, designed in the style of an ornate theater foyer, contains a collection of paintings of performers in character. There is a well-stocked bookshop, a box office that sells seats for all the main London theaters, and an attractive café. *Russell St., tel. 01/831–1227. Admission £2.25 adults, £1.25 children under 16 and senior citizens. Open Tues.–Sun. 11–7; closed Good Fri.*

Time Out Besides selling salads, pastries, muffins, and open sandwiches, the café on the entrance floor of the Theatre Museum is an excellent spot to recuperate from visiting the museum or shopping in the market; the café is open to all, so you don't have to buy a ticket for the museum. There are lots of cafés and restaurants in and around the market, and part of the fun is to wander around and discover one that you like the look of. A few worth trying are **Crank's** (11 Covent Garden Market), part of the whole-food chain; **Boswell's Coffee House** (8 Russell St.); and **Tutton's** (11–12 Russell St.), where you can eat outside during the summer (prices in the downstairs restaurant are more expensive).

The streets leading away from the market building, into and around the rest of Covent Garden, are equally intriguing. To the north—walk up James Street past the back of the Royal Opera House—is **Long Acre,** running east/west. A way down to

your left is **Dillons Arts Bookshop,** a good bet for books, posters, and postcards; and, nearly next door, **Stanfords** has
the best collection of travel books, guidebooks, and maps in
town.

⓬ Turn left again at the end of Long Acre into Garrick Street. On
the right is the grave facade of the **Garrick Club,** one of the
city's best-known gentlemen's clubs. It's famous today as an actors' club (Laurence Olivier is one of the longest-serving
members), though Dickens, Thackeray, and Trollope all belonged to it in their day. Continue down Garrick Street to Rose
⓭ Street, a tiny alley on the left, at the end of which is the **Lamb
and Flag,** one of London's few remaining authentic Dickensian
pubs.

Time Out **The Calabash** (38 King St., which leads off Garrick St.) serves
authentic African dishes at reasonable prices. It's in the basement of the Africa Centre, a cultural center where all kinds of
talks, lectures, and performances are given; there's also a shop
that stocks reasonably priced African arts and crafts.

To get back to the heart of Covent Garden from Garrick Street,
walk down the narrow passage by the side of the Lamb
and Flag pub and turn right along Floral Street, which will
bring you back to James Street. From here, continue north
across Long Acre, into Neal Street, or turn right onto Long
Acre.

Neal Street is full of little shops, restaurants, and craft galleries. The **Contemporary Applied Arts building,** a block up on the
left on the corner of Earlham Street, has regular exhibits of
pottery, jewelry, and textiles. Some items are for sale, though
they can be expensive.

Time Out **Neal's Yard,** off Short's Gardens, the third turning on the left
off Neal Street, is a small yard full of enticing little shops. At
the **Bakery and Tea Room** you can buy fresh scones and cakes,
either to eat on the premises or to take out. Across the yard a
small café sells hot lunch dishes and baked potatoes with delicious fillings. It's fun to perch on the seats in the yard while you
eat—but beware the greedy pigeons.

If instead of taking Neal Street you turn right down Long Acre,
you will come to the **Glasshouse** where all day long you can
watch glassblowers practicing their craft and purchase any
piece that catches your eye. **Bow Street** will then be on the
right. It is known for two things: the Royal Opera House and,
practically opposite it, the Magistrates' Court.

⓮ The present theater, today the **Royal Opera House,** opened in
1858. There had been two previous theaters here since the 18th
century. One, built in 1732, burned down in 1808, a common
theatrical event in the days before electricity. Its replacement
suffered the same fate in 1856. The existing theater then became England's principal opera house, and adopted its present
name of the Royal Opera House in 1936. In 1956 its two resident
companies, the Sadler's Wells Ballet and the Covent Garden
Opera Company, became the Royal Ballet and the Royal Opera
Company, respectively. The rear of the building was extended
in 1981—at a huge cost—providing much needed rehearsal
space and dressing rooms. This finally put to an end the all-too-
frequent sight of internationally known singers and dancers

changing (on occasion even rehearsing) in the corridors. The theater's atmosphere and acoustics are superb, with the rich Victorian gilt decorations and plush seats setting off performances to their best advantage. *(See* Arts and Nightlife.)

⑮ Bow Street Magistrates' Court was established in 1749 by Henry Fielding (1707–54), a noted magistrate, but also a journalist and prolific novelist who wrote *Tom Jones*. Fielding employed a band of private detectives, the "Bow Street Runners," and paid them out of the fines that were imposed in the court. In 1829, the Home Secretary, Sir Robert Peel, formed the first regular police force; it was based at #4 Whitehall, backing onto a courtyard known as Scotland Yard. It was not until 1879 that a police station was established next to the Magistrates' Court in Bow Street.

⑯ Head down Bow Street and turn left into Russell Street. Straight ahead you'll see the **Theatre Royal,** the largest theater in London, and probably the most famous. It's the fourth theater built on this site, the original dating from 1660. It was granted a Royal Patent by Charles II in 1663 but burned down the following year and was rebuilt by Sir Christopher Wren. His theater survived until 1776 before it, too, burned down. The third theater was built for the playwright Sheridan. When *it* burned down in 1809, the playwright was seen sitting in the window of a nearby tavern watching the flames. His explanation for this display of sangfroid was simply, "Where else should a man drink but by his own fireside!"

The Strand and Embankment

To the south of Covent Garden is **The Strand,** one of London's most historic streets, though today little more than a broad thoroughfare lined with office blocks and shops. Its historic significance lies in the vital role it used to play as the main route between the City to the northeast and Westminster. Its name comes simply from the fact that originally it was a "strand," or beach, along the banks of the Thames. Since the building of the parallel Victoria Embankment along the north bank of the Thames in the 1870s, the Strand lost its links with London's great river, and its historic role disappeared with the arrival of alternate routes to the City. From the 15th to the 17th century this stretch of riverbank was the site of some of London's most aristocratic houses, though the only reminder now of those
⑰ palmy days is the **York Watergate** at the western end of the Victoria Embankment Gardens. Built in about 1625, it was the river entrance to the duke of Buckingham's mansion, York House. In those days, before the Victoria Embankment was built, the Watergate was actually on the Thames.

Down at the south end of the Strand is **Charing Cross Station,** one of London's main train stations. A 19th-century copy of an elaborate medieval memorial-cum-cross stands outside it. The original was put up by the 13th-century king Edward I to mark the resting place of the coffin of his wife, Eleanor, on its way to her funeral at Westminster Abbey.

⑱ Between the Strand and the river, just beyond Charing Cross Station, is the area called the **Adelphi,** built in the late 18th century by the Scottish architect brothers, John and Robert Adam. Though most of their elegant brick town houses have since been knocked down, enough remain to give a taste of the days when the "People of Quality" flocked to live here (look especially at those on Adam Street).

(19) Behind the Adelphi is the York Watergate in the **Victoria Embankment Gardens,** a quiet haven where many office workers spend their lunch hour in the summer. The flower beds are beautifully kept, while the shrubs and trees filter the noise of the Embankment traffic. The gardens are interesting also for the statues they contain, further proof of the Victorians' obsession with preserving the memories of the great and the good. There are several interesting statues, including one to Robbie Burns, who sits on a tree stump being inspired by his muse.

Fronting the gardens is the **Victoria Embankment,** one of the most durable and characteristic of all the improvements made to London by the Victorians. It was laid out between 1868 and 1874 by the indefatigable Sir Joseph Bazalgette, otherwise best remembered as the man who built London's sewers (almost all of them still functioning, though beginning to show signs of wear). Running from Westminster to the City, its bold engineering and ornate cast-iron street lamps became the talk of London. The Victorians (always conscious of the need for symmetry) constructed the contemporary and parallel Albert Embankment on the opposite bank of the Thames, a little upstream.

(20) The principal point of interest now on the Victoria Embankment is **Cleopatra's Needle,** a weathered pink granite obelisk that has no connection whatsoever with Cleopatra. It is the oldest out-of-doors object of any kind in London by a clear 1,000 years or more. Standing 68 feet high and tipping the scales at 180 tons, it was carved in about 1450 BC at Heliopolis in Egypt for Thothmose III. In 1819 the obelisk was presented to Britain by Mohammed Ali, the Viceroy of Egypt. Only in 1878 did it finally arrive in England, though not without many alarms en route. Being so heavy, the Needle could not be carried on board ship. Instead, a torpedo-like casing was built to carry it, which was towed behind a tug. A storm blew up during the journey, the tow-line parted, and the Needle was reluctantly abandoned. To everyone's surprise, it was rescued a few days later, and the journey safely completed.

Conscious of its great antiquity and eager that their own civilization should prove as durable, the Victorians buried a number of contemporary articles and mementos under the Needle before it was put up, among them a railway guide and photographs of the 12 most beautiful women of the time. Some of the seats along this stretch of the Embankment carry on the Egyptian theme, with camels as supports.

(21) Continuing eastward, **Waterloo Bridge** provides one of the best river viewpoints in London—around the bend of the Thames in both directions to the City and to Westminster. And from here also you get the best view of the spectacular 18th-century **(22)** facade of **Somerset House,** on the Strand east of Waterloo Bridge. Begun by Sir William Chambers in 1780, it stands on the site of a massive Tudor palace built in 1550 for Lord Protector Somerset, who ruled England while Edward VI, the son of Henry VIII, was a child. Until the Victoria Embankment was built in the last century, the Thames at high tide lapped at the foot of the building, adding greatly to its charm, as contemporary pictures make clear. Until 1973, Somerset House was headquarters of the Registrar General of Births, Deaths, and Marriages, and also contained a number of other government offices. Today, plans to transfer the magnificent art collections of the Courtauld Institute of Art to the stately public rooms of Somerset House are in the final stages, though no definite date has been set.

㉓ Next door to Somerset House, in Strand Lane, is the so-called **"Roman Bath."** It probably dates from the 17th century, rather than from Roman times. Nonetheless, it is thought that the Romans knew and used the spring that feeds the bath. It is owned by the National Trust today, and can be viewed from a pathway.

Opposite Somerset House lies the **Aldwych,** a substantial crescent containing three theaters and the massive **Bush House,** the home of the BBC World Service. The eastern end of the island formed by the Aldwych and the Strand is occupied by **Australia House,** the London headquarters of the Commonwealth of Australia.

This end of the Strand is graced by two of London's prettiest churches, both forming unusual little islands in the middle of the road. The most westerly, almost opposite Somerset House, **㉔** is **St. Mary-le-Strand,** an attractive early 18th-century church. **㉕** The other, more easterly, church is **St. Clement Danes,** designed by Wren, with a tower added later by James Gibbs, who designed St. Mary-le-Strand, and containing the tuneful bells that provided the inspiration for the nursery rhyme "Oranges and lemons, say the bells of St. Clement's." Inside there's a statue of Dr. Johnson, once a regular worshipper here. Today St. Clement's is the principal church of the RAF, the Royal Air Force, and guards a book containing the names of 1,900 American airmen killed during World War II.

Time Out **The India Club** (143 Strand) is not a club at all but an unassuming little canteen-type restaurant serving excellent, cheap Indian dishes; it's very popular with students. The entrance is difficult to spot, and the dining room itself is halfway up a rickety staircase.

Just beyond the Strand are the imposing Gothic towers and turrets of the Law Courts *(see* Bloomsbury and Legal London) and the Temple Bar, gateway to Fleet Street and the City *(see* The City).

Bloomsbury and Legal London

Bloomsbury is a pleasant, partly residential district tucked between the bustle of the West End and the City. It is most notable today as the site of two of the great educational institutions of London, the British Museum and the University of London. The area is perhaps also equally famous as the former haunt of the celebrated Bloomsbury Group, a self-centered cultural clique that thrived here in the early decades of the century and included such figures as Virginia Woolf, Lytton Strachey, E.M. Forster, Bertrand Russell, Maynard Keynes, and Rupert Brooke.

Architecturally, the elegant and spacious 17th- and 18th-century squares of Bloomsbury, some of the finest in London, are the area's most distinctive features. The earliest, **Blooms-bury Square,** was laid out in 1660. Lined with huge trees, the square now hides a vast underground parking lot. The other leafy squares of Bloomsbury—Russell, Bedford, and Woburn, all named after associations with their original aristocratic landlords—have had almost equally distinguished pasts.

Bloomsbury

The heart of Bloomsbury and of learned London is located just a little to the east of Tottenham Court Road, a substantial and busy thoroughfare that forms the western border of Blooms-bury. Beginning from the Tottenham Court Road tube station, the first turning off to the right up Tottenham Court Road is Great Russell Street. Walk along it and turn left into **Bedford Square,** laid out by Robert Adam in the late 18th century, and currently the home of several major publishers. If you continue along Great Russell Street, you will reach the sooty expanse of
❶ the **British Museum,** the only major London museum housed in a building worthy of its magnificent collections.

Founded in 1753, the museum was originally based in Monta-gue House, on the same site as today's museum. But by 1820 its collections had expanded to the point where a larger building had to be constructed. Finished in 1847, the monumental and severely Greek design alone is almost worth the journey to London. The building is enhanced enormously by the absence of new development in the area, allowing its massive and state-ly presence to dominate the surrounding buildings as it did when originally designed.

The collections here are so varied and so vast that there's not much point in trying to do more than sample just a few—at least on a first visit. Savor what you can, and hope to return at some future date. Arm yourself with a free floor plan if you hope to navigate around its maze-like interior with any suc-cess.

The British Museum is not only one of the world's great muse-ums, it also houses one of the great libraries, and on both scores has been enriched by the natural acquisitiveness of the British over two centuries. The library—**The British Library** as it is now officially called—was split off from the museum in 1973 to become a separately managed organization. Like the museum, however, its incomparable riches are greatly enhanced by its setting, especially that of the main Reading Room, beneath whose huge copper dome some of the greatest scholars and thinkers in the world have worked. While the average visi-tor won't be able to see the Reading Room itself, the display of manuscripts, bindings, and rare illuminated and printed books in the King's Library in the museum itself is always fascinat-ing. The library started in 1757 with the gift of the then Royal Library by George II to the fledgling museum. Along with the priceless volumes went the right to have a copy of every book published in Britain. The Reference Division alone has around 10,000,000 volumes, and still they flood in.

Among the most precious treasures in the museum are the **Elgin Marbles.** They are an unrivaled collection of ancient Greek sculptures, housed in a specially built gallery donated by the art dealer Lord Duveen. The sculptures date from about 450 BC, the Golden Age of Athens, and were the work of Phidi-as, greatest of all Greek sculptors. These magnificent carvings originally decorated the Parthenon in Athens, from where they

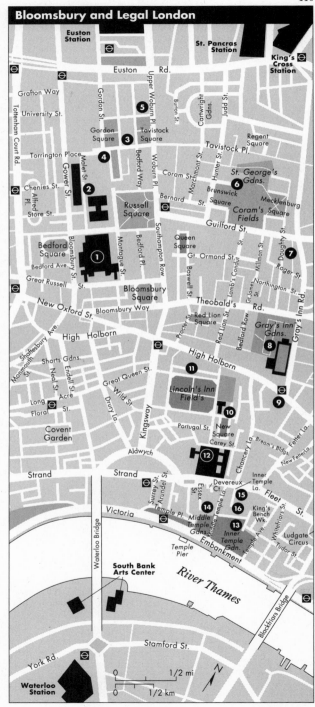

British Museum, **1**
Courtauld Institute
Galleries, **4**
Dicken's House, **7**
Foundling Hospital, **6**
Gray's Inn, **8**
Inner Temple, **13**
Jewish Museum, **5**
Law Courts (Royal
Courts of Justice), **12**
Lincoln's Inn, **10**
Middle Temple, **14**
Percival David
Foundation of Chinese
Art, **3**
Prince Henry's
Room, **15**
Soane Museum, **11**
Staple Inn, **9**
Temple Church, **16**
University of London, **2**

Bloomsbury and Legal London

were removed in 1811 by Lord Elgin, British Ambassador to Greece. He had found them lying neglected around the building, ignored by Greek and occupying Turk alike. Today, they are the subject of a dispute between Britain and Greece, the latter's government lobbying fiercely for their return. However, it is unlikely that they will ever leave London.

Apart from these magnificent sculptures, the museum counts among its prized possessions a superb collection of Egyptian relics. The **Rosetta Stone,** with its parallel inscriptions in three languages, which helped archaeologists to interpret Egyptian hieroglyphics, stands in pride of place at the beginning of the exhibition.

Upstairs, one of the most instructive displays is that of Roman Britain, including the **Mildenhall Treasure,** a cache of Roman silver found in a Suffolk field in 1842. On this floor, too, are rooms full of Greek and Roman art; some grisly remains of ancient Egyptians; and antiquities found on the site of Ur of the Chaldees—the home town of Abraham—by Sir Charles Leonard Woolley in the 1920s.

In 1985, seven new basement galleries were opened, displaying sculpture which had been in storage since 1939 when it was put away to protect it from World War II bombing. The mostly Greek and Roman riches in this collection are worth a visit on their own.

The museum's other treasures include one of the original copies of the **Magna Carta,** a collection of drawings from virtually every European school since the 15th century, and Renaissance displays of metalwork, jewelry, coins, pottery, and glass.

Just inside the Great Russell Street entrance to the museum is a shop selling books, catalogues, postcards, posters, slides, and small reproduction pieces. *Great Russell St., tel. 01/636–1555; 01/580–1788 (recorded information). Admission free. Open Mon.–Sat. 10–5, Sun. 2:30–6; closed Good Fri., May Day.*

Time Out In mid-1988 the museum opened a new self-service restaurant and café that serves attractively presented food prepared with fresh ingredients. The restaurant is decorated by a plaster cast of a part of the Parthenon frieze that Lord Elgin didn't remove. (Open 12:15–4:15, hot lunches available until 2:30. The average cost of a lunch is £4 per head.) There is also a coffee shop that is open from 10–4.

Around the University of London

The rear exit from the British Museum leads on to Montague Place. If you walk north up Malet Street, you will pass the main
② entrance of the **University of London.** It was founded by royal charter in 1836 as simply an examining body, but came to incorporate a number of schools and colleges. This was the first university in the country to admit women on the same footing as men (in 1878). The university includes several fine art col-
③ lections which are open to the public. The **Percival David Foundation of Chinese Art** is at 53 Gordon Square, and the
④ **Courtauld Institute Galleries** is in Woburn Square (both to the north of the university complex). The Courtauld exhibits Impressionist paintings, sculpture, furniture, tapestries, and carpets, and is one of the most peaceful galleries in London. It's easily appreciated on one visit, it's rarely crowded, and there are plenty of comfortable sofas to sit on while enjoying the pictures. *Percival David Foundation of Chinese Art, 53 Gordon*

*Sq., tel. 01/387–3909. Admission free. Open Mon.–Fri. 10: 30–
5 (sometimes closed 1–2 for lunch); closed weekends and bank
holidays. Courtauld Institute Art Galleries, Woburn Sq., tel.
01/580–1015. Admission free. Open Mon.–Sat. 10–5, Sun. 2–5;
closed bank holidays.*

At the top of Malet Street is **University College,** founded in 1826
by advocates of religious tolerance, and the first college in England to admit Jews and Roman Catholics. University College
was incorporated into the University of London in 1907. The
main courtyard and portico are in Gower Street opposite University College Hospital, a fine red-brick Victorian building.
Behind University College (reached from Gower Street via
Torrington Place) is **Gordon Square,** which, together with the
adjoining Tavistock Square, was home to many members of the
Bloomsbury Group. In Upper Woburn Place you will find the
⑤ Jewish Museum, founded over 50 years ago, and illustrating the
long history of Jewry in Britain (dating back to the 13th century). The collection consists mainly of objects connected with
the celebration of Jewish ritual, many of them precious antiques, survivals of the terrible times through which Jews have
passed over the centuries. There are manuscripts, embroidery,
and silver, many of the items of great intrinsic worth, and all of
them of interest. *Woburn House, Tavistock Sq., tel. 01/
388–4525. Admission free. Open late Oct.–late Mar., Tues.–
Thurs. 10–4, Fri. 10–12:45, late Mar.–late Oct. Tues.–Fri.
10–4; Sun. 10–12:45; closed Sat., Mon., and bank holidays.*

At the bottom of Woburn Place is **Russell Square,** Bloomsbury's
largest square. Bedford Place connects back with Bloomsbury
Square, where you began.

Time Out | **Pizzeria Amalfi** (107 Southampton Row) is a cheerful Italian
restaurant offering reasonably priced pasta dishes.

Leading out of the east side of Russell Square, Guildford Street
takes you to **Coram's Fields,** seven acres of open space, including a huge sports field, mostly used for children's soccer.
Coram's Fields were opened in 1936 by the Queen Mother—
then the duchess of York—and are on the site of the former
⑥ Foundling Hospital, founded in 1742 by Captain Thomas Coram. Captain Coram was a friend of the composer George
Frederick Handel, who donated proceeds from his early performances of *Messiah* to help support the work of the
orphanage. Another early supporter of the hospital was the
artist William Hogarth, who gave paintings to the hospital and
persuaded a number of his friends to do the same. When the old
building was pulled down, the unique collection was transferred to the present one, including a staircase and the interior
of the Court Room, with its paintings by Hogarth, Gainsborough, and Reynolds. Handel's original keyboard is on display,
as well as a special *Messiah* score Handel prepared for the hospital children to perform. Although the orphanage was closed
in 1956, the foundation continues to act as an adoption and fostering agency. *40 Brunswick Sq., tel. 01/278–2424. Admission
50p adults, 25p children and senior citizens. Open Mon.–Fri.
10–4 unless being used for meetings or functions; check in advance. Closed bank holidays.*

Halfway along Guilford Street is **Lamb's Conduit Street,**
which has a pleasant old pub, the Lamb, usually very crowded
in the summer. To the right off Lamb's Conduit Street is Great
Ormond Street and the famous **Hospital for Sick Children,** to
which Sir James Barrie made a gift of the copyright of his *Peter*

Pan in 1929. East of, and parallel to, Lamb's Conduit Street, Great James Street has some fine examples of domestic Georgian architecture of the 1720s; many of the original glazing bars and fanlights remain. Other streets in the neighborhood, such as Northington Street and John Street, have more of the same. The latter leads into **Doughty Street** where you will find the house that Charles Dickens lived in (#48) from 1837 to 1839. He finished writing *Pickwick Papers*, and wrote the whole of *Oliver Twist* and *Nicholas Nickleby* here. The house contains a good library and a museum. *48 Doughty St., tel. 01/405–2127. Admission £1.50 adults, 50p children under 16. Open Mon.–Sat. 10–5; closed bank holidays.*

Legal London—The Inns of Court

Continuing down Doughty Street, which changes its name to John Street about half way along, you reach Theobald's Road and the start of one of the most delightful and surprising walks London offers, along the interlinking chain of leafy gardens, quiet courts and alleyways, magnificent halls and townhouses that make up the heartland of England's legal profession. Known collectively as the Inns of Court, the area consists of four separate "Inns." From north to south they are **Gray's Inn, Lincoln's Inn,** the **Middle Temple,** and the **Inner Temple** (mysteriously, there's no Outer Temple). In all, they represent the finest grouping of almost unspoiled historic buildings in London. They might not be able to boast any undisputed architectural masterpieces, but the cumulative effect of these dignified, time-honored buildings standing in their peaceful gardens is unequaled anywhere else in London.

Their curious names are quite easily explained. Just as medieval tradesmen naturally gathered together, partly for protection, partly to make it easier for potential customers to find them—a kind of primitive Yellow Pages—so London's medieval lawyers banded together in the area still occupied by the Inns of Court. The term "inn" is self-explanatory; these early lawyers needed food and lodging, which they found in commercial inns. Eventually the inns were taken over by the lawyers, and became more or less permanent residence and office space combined. The two "Temples"—the Inner and the Middle—derive their names from the fact that the land where they now stand, slightly south of the other two inns, was owned by the Knights Templar, a chivalric order founded at the time of the First Crusade in the 11th century. Here, in the 12th century, they built the Temple Church, modeled on the Church of the Holy Sepulcher in Jerusalem. In time, the Knights were disbanded, but the lawyers remained.

The atmosphere of the Inns of Court is as close to an Oxford or Cambridge college as anywhere outside those two ancient universities. This is hardly surprising given that not only are the Inns of Court much the same age as Oxford and Cambridge, but that originally, at least, they fulfilled a similar function. Today, the Inns of Court still retain an important educational role. Those hoping to become a barristers (to be called to the Bar) must pass a series of examinations here. More obscurely, they must also eat a certain number of dinners in the Hall of the Inn to which they are attached, in order to fulfill the attendance requirements. Today, no more than a tiny number of barristers actually live in the Inns of Court, but practically every practicing barrister has "chambers"—his or her offices—here.

8 Entering **Gray's Inn** by the north gate from Theobald's Road, you are faced by the long Georgian bulk of Raymond Buildings. It is entirely typical of the office buildings of the Inns of Court, down to the signboards on every doorway—or staircases as they are confusingly called—with the name of each resident painted on them. Architecturally, Gray's Inn is generally felt to be the least distinguished of the Inns of Court. Its great glory is its garden—quiet, calm, and spacious. The Hall of Gray's Inn, badly bombed in World War II but successfully restored, does boast a fine carved oak screen from the reign of Elizabeth I that survived the war unscathed. The hall was the scene of the first performance of Shakespeare's *Comedy of Errors* in 1596. *Holborn, tel. 01/405-8164. Visits to the hall and library only by advance written application to the librarian. Chapel open Mon.–Fri. 10–4; closed bank holidays.*

Leaving Gray's Inn, you emerge into the noise and bustle of High Holborn which, with the Strand, is one of the two main roads into the City from Westminster and the West End. To **9** your left is **Staple Inn,** no longer one of the Inns of Court, but, with its black-and-white half timbering and overhanging gables, one of the finest Elizabethan buildings in London. It was seriously damaged by bombs in 1944, but was excellently restored. One of its two inner courts was occupied for a time by Dr. Johnson.

10 The next of the Inns of Court, **Lincoln's Inn,** lies three blocks west along High Holborn. Turn to the left down Great Turnstile Row. Lincoln's Inn is probably the most beautiful of the inns. Fortunately, it was also lucky enough to escape almost unharmed from the bombs of World War II. It is one of the oldest inns, known to have been associated with the law as far back as 1292; written records go back to 1424. The buildings date from a variety of periods, the oldest, **Old Hall** and **Old Buildings,** dating from the end of the 15th century, and the newest, the neo-Tudor **New Hall and Library,** from the mid-19th century. But there's also a fine 18th-century court, **Stone Buildings,** and a 15th-century chapel, which Inigo Jones remodeled in 1620. Completing the architectural delights is **New Square,** the only complete 17th-century square in London. *Chancery La., tel. 01/405-1393. Permission must be obtained in advance to visit the halls and library. Gardens and chapel open Mon.–Fri. 12:30–2:30; the public may also attend Sunday service (at 11:30) in the chapel during legal terms; closed bank holidays.*

A detour here, through the western gate of Lincoln's Inn, leads to the adjoining **Lincoln's Inn Fields,** London's largest and oldest surviving square, surrounded by some handsome buildings. On the south side is a magnificent 1806 portico. On the west side, 56–60 make up Lindsay House, believed to have been built by Inigo Jones. But the great attraction in Lincoln's Inn **11** Fields is to be found on the north side of the square. This is **Sir John Soane's Museum,** one of the most idiosyncratic and fascinating museums in London. It was formed by Sir John Soane, whose house this was from 1790 until his death in 1831. Soane was an immensely learned and gifted architect and, as a collector, a magpie of genius. His portrait hangs in the dining room of the house. The exhibits include a superb series of Hogarth paintings; *The Rake's Progress,* displayed on ingenious hinged screens; and the sarcophagus of Seti I, which Soane bought for £2,000 after the British Museum had foolishly refused it. Almost as interesting is the house itself, much of it remodeled by Soane. The terms of the bequest which led to the creation of the museum stipulated that the building be left exactly as it was on

Soane's death, allowing a rare glimpse of the life and surroundings of a learned and inquiring Englishman. *13 Lincoln's Inn
Fields, tel. 01/405-2107. Admission free. Open Tues.-Sat.
10-5; closed bank holidays.*

Just to the southwest of Lincoln's Inn Fields in Portsmouth
Street is another oddity, the 16th-century antiques shop that
Dickens reputedly used as the model for his *Old Curiosity
Shop.*

Back on the major route, leave Lincoln's Inn by its southern
gate and walk into Carey Street. Here you are confronted by
the immense brick back of the **Royal Courts of Justice,** or **Law
Courts** as they are more commonly called. The Law Courts are
to civil law what the Old Bailey in the City is to criminal law.
The sensational murder trials are heard over at the Old Bailey,
but it is here that fraud trials and other financial cases are decided, less gripping perhaps but even more lucrative to the
lawyers who dispute them. The building looks as though it
could have been built in the Middle Ages, but it is in fact Victorian, the masterpiece of George Edmund Street, whose death
from a stroke in 1881 is said to have been hastened by the frus-
trations and delays that surrounded its construction (1871-82).
The main hall—238 feet long and 80 feet high—is magnificently opulent, dwarfing the bewigged and gowned figures that
scurry through it. There is a small exhibition of judges' robes
on view. *Strand, tel. 01/936-6000. Admission free. Building
open Mon.-Fri. 9-4:30; closed bank holidays.*

The main facade of the Law Courts fronts onto Strand at the
Temple Bar, the principal entrance to the City. Opposite, and
actually in the City, are the **Inner** and **Middle Temples.** There
are four entrances to the Temple from the Strand and Fleet
Street (the Strand becomes Fleet Street once it enters the
City). The first, opposite the Law Courts, leads to **Devereux
Court,** and from there to the 17th-century **New Court** and then
on to **Fountain Court,** which takes its name from the fountain in
its center. From here the great lawns of the Middle Temple
Gardens slope majestically down to the Victoria Embankment
and the Thames, bordered on the east by the **Middle Temple
Hall.** This superb Elizabethan hall has a wonderful hammer-
beam roof and carved screen; unfortunately the hall is not open
to the public, although you may be able to gain admittance
through a member of the Middle Temple. The second gateway
is more imposing, but leads to a less interesting area—**Middle
Temple Lane,** the approximate border of the Middle and Inner
Temples, going all the way to the Thames. The third entrance
to the Temple—the **Inner Temple Gateway** located on Fleet
Street—is the most rewarding. At its entrance is a fine early
Jacobean half-timbered building, containing, in **Prince Henry's
Room,** an elaborate and very rare plaster ceiling from the same
period. *17 Fleet St., tel. 01/353-7232. Admission 10p. Open
Mon.-Fri. 1:45-5, Sat. 1:45-4; closed all bank holidays.*

From the Inner Temple Gateway, head down Inner Temple
Lane to the **Temple Church,** the original church built here by
the Knights Templar in the 12th century. It is one of only three
round churches in Britain, as splendidly atmospheric as it is
precious. The choir was extended in about 1250, in the Early
English style, a particularly pure form of Gothic, and this is
probably the country's finest example. *The Temple, tel. 01/
353-8462. Open daily 10-4; closed bank holidays.*

Inner Temple Lane leads on to Church Court, site of one of the
very few modern buildings in the Inns of Court, the **Inner Tem-**

ple Hall (1955), not open to the public. Unfortunately, the same goes for the magnificent gardens of the Inner and Middle Temples, but they make a striking background to the buildings.

Regent's Park and Hampstead

Regent's Park and Hampstead in north London contain some of the prettiest and most rural parts of the city, as well as fine architecture and some important historical sights. For the sheer pleasure of idle exploring they are hard to beat.

To get you going in the right direction, we begin in the less-than-lovely surroundings of **Marylebone Road** (pronounced "Mar– le–bun"). A wide, nondescript, and noisy thoroughfare laid out in the last century to link Paddington to the west with Islington to the east, it is of interest only as the home of the London Planetarium and Madame Tussaud's, London's world-famous wax museum. **Madame Tussaud's** has long maintained its reputation as one of the most popular attractions in London, as the lines of tour buses outside make very clear. If an ever-changing parade of famous figures from the past and present is your cup of tea, this is the place for you. Madame Tussaud herself originally made her reputation at the court of Louis XVI in France. Swept up by the tumult of the French Revolution, she continued her art by making casts of guillotined heads. She arrived in London in 1802, and a number of her original wax heads are still on view here. *Marylebone Rd., tel. 01/935–6861. Admission £4.20 adults, £2.80 children under 16, £3.15 senior citizens. Joint ticket with planetarium (see below) £5.60 adults, £3.40 children, £4.20 senior citizens. Open Easter–end Sept. daily 9:30–5:30, Oct.–Easter daily 10–5:30.*

The **London Planetarium,** adjoining the wax museum, is in some ways more interesting. The night sky of both hemispheres is vividly brought to life, taking you on a journey through time and space. In addition, there are excellent lectures and displays of holography. In the evening the planetarium becomes a "Laserium" with laser light shows. *Marylebone Rd., tel. 01/486–1121. Admission £2.20 adults, £1.40 children under 16, £1.70 senior citizens. Joint ticket with Madame Tussaud's £5.60 adults, £3.40 children under 16, £4.20 senior citizens.*

Devotees of Sherlock Holmes might like to continue west from Madame Tussaud's about 200 yards to **Baker Street,** which runs at right angles to Marylebone Road. Head left down Baker Street to the Abbey National Building Society, located at what would, if it existed, be 221b Baker Street, home of the celebrated Victorian sleuth. The Abbey National still receives hundreds of letters every year addressed to the detective and asking for help.

From Madame Tussaud's and the London Planetarium, walk east along Marylebone Road for about a quarter of a mile. On your right is **Park Crescent,** two magnificent neo-Classical terraces that swing north from Portland Place toward Regent's Park. They were planned by John Nash as the final flourish of that architect's great triumphal way through London from Carlton House Terrace to Regent's Park. Though badly bombed in the war, they have since been excellently restored and comprise perhaps the best example of that prolific architect's more restrained work. From Park Crescent, the entrance to the park is just a step away over the Marylebone Road.

Camden Lock, **8**
Church Walk, **10**
Freud Museum, **9**
Highgate Cemetery, **14**
Keat's House, **11**
Kenwood House, **13**
London Planetarium, **2**
London Zoo, **7**
Madame Tussaud's, **1**
Open-Air Theatre, **6**
Park Crescent, **3**
Queen Mary's Gardens, **5**
Royal College of Physicians, **4**
Spaniard's Inn, **12**

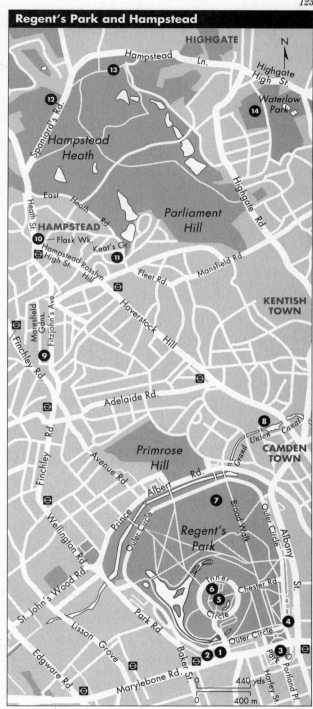

Regent's Park and Hampstead

Regent's Park and the Zoo

Regent's Park is the youngest of London's great parks, named in honor of the Prince Regent. It was laid out in 1812 by Nash. His plans were both innovative and ambitious, calling for a series of magnificent terraced houses overlooking the park as though they were country houses overlooking their landscaped grounds. The country-loving English gentry, for whom these stately buildings were intended, would thus have London homes that resembled their homes in the country. The park is still fringed with serried ranks of Nash's lovely stucco marvels, grandiose and verging on the florid at times, but typical of the quite unique designs that flowed from Nash's busy drafting pen.

Enter the park by the gate, centrally placed between Park Square East and Park Square West. Just across the road is the **4** **Royal College of Physicians,** a strange structure designed by Denys Lasdun—who was also responsible for the National Theatre on the South Bank—which could easily be taken for a temple of some dark cult.

Once you are into the park, London drops away like a discarded life; peace reigns, and you can stroll among the flowers to your heart's content. The flower displays between the gate and Chester Road, which crosses the park, are all formal ones. Like those in other London parks, they are regularly replanted as the seasons pass, and you will be able to see stunning displays of fuchsias, for example, if you are there at the right time of year (June through September). The park also contains a semipermanent display of large pieces of sculpture by British artists. The main avenue, called the **Broad Walk,** is geographically a long, leafy continuation of Portland Place.

When you reach Chester Road, turn left and walk toward the **Inner Circle.** This road is lined with cherry trees, which are magnificent for a few weeks in spring. When you reach the Inner Circle you will be opposite the wrought-iron gates to **Queen** **5** **Mary's Gardens.** If you have time to visit only one London park, this should be the one. The gardens are not extensive, but within their spherical boundary they are very richly planted. Their chief glory comes in May, June, and July when the endless beds of roses are at their peak. The scent and the shadings of color are enough to send the most casual visitor into a Persian dream. Evergreens, heathers, and azaleas make a visit worthwhile the year round.

6 Hidden behind a high hedge is the **Open-Air Theatre,** where Shakespeare is performed in mid-summer. It is a magical location for the plays, especially *A Midsummer Night's Dream*, with its open-air setting. As the sun sinks behind the trees and the stage lights take over, the sense of being in an enchanted place is very strong. Substantial refreshments are available before and after the performance, as well as during intermissions. The evenings can be chilly, so go prepared, or rent a blanket once you're there.

The easiest way to reach the Zoo is to return to Chester Road and turn left onto Broad Walk. It is quite a way up to the Zoo—there are, after all, 472 acres in the park.

7 The **Gardens of the Zoological Society of London,** known simply as the Zoo, were started over 150 years ago absorbing, en route, other collections, such as that of the royal menagerie, which used to be housed in the Tower of London. The Zoo itself is one of the busiest mazes in the world, and you can wander around for hours. Major attractions are: (1) the Mappin Terraces, which were built some 70 years ago as a natural habitat for animals such as goats, pigs, and bears; (2) the Children's Zoo, where children can play with the smaller animals; (3) the Snowdon Aviary, designed by Lord Snowdon in 1965 when he was married to Princess Margaret; (4) the Lion Terraces; (5) the Elephant and Rhino Pavilion, an oddly delicate name for such a massive, castle-like structure; (6) the Small Bird House; and (7) the Tropical House, with its darting hummingbirds. One fascinating and unique exhibit is the Moonlight World, on the lower floor of the Charles Clore Pavilion. Here nighttime conditions are simulated so that visitors can watch nocturnal animals during the day. The process is reversed at night, when the cages are lit, and the animals take up their daytime activities. A visit to the Zoo could last hours and, for an interested child, even a whole day. Although it is one of London's major tourist attractions, the Zoo is actually the private gardens of the Royal Zoological Society, and the society has increasing difficulty in finding the necessary funds—a fact reflected in the high cost of admission. *Regent's Park, tel. 01/722333. Admission £3.90 adults, £2 children under 16 and senior citizens. Open Apr.–Sept. daily 9–6 (bank holidays 9–7), Oct.–Mar. 10 –dusk.*

If you walked to the Zoo, it may be fun to take a waterbus to Little Venice, near Warwick Crescent. The **Regent's Park Canal** (properly called the Grand Union Canal) borders the whole northern side of the park, adding to the countryside feel. (For more on Canal Trips *see* Guided Tours in Essential Information.)

From the north of the Zoo, cross Prince Albert Road, to **Primrose Hill.** Though compact by comparison with the other Royal Parks, the park rises to a height of 206 feet. On November 5th each year, the hill comes to life as the setting of a massive Guy Fawkes Night fireworks display, complete with a huge bonfire. The festivities are countrywide, and celebrate the failure of the Gunpowder Plot, an attempt to blow up the king and parliament in 1605.

The **Camden Town** district of London, lying close by Primrose Hill, was one of the first areas in London to be gentrified in the 1960s. Today, it is still a colorful and lively place for an afternoon's stroll. Most of the action centers around **Camden Lock,** just to the north of Camden Town station. This is a busy area during the week, with its crafts shops and small restaurants, but the area really comes alive on weekends, with an antiques market alongside the Lock itself. (From here you can take a barge up the Regent's Canal, via the Zoo, as far as Little Venice.) Aside from the market, there are craft stalls, boutiques, cafés, art galleries, and secondhand clothes shops.

Time Out Part of the fun at Camden Lock is choosing an attractive restaurant or café: There are plenty here, and they're all full of atmosphere. Popular spots include **Pasta Underground** (214 Camden High St.), where healthy portions of pasta plus other Italian dishes are served, and **Marine Ices** (8 Haverstock Hill), home of the best Italian ice cream in town.

Hampstead

Before visiting Hampstead proper, there is one place of interest to see. At the foot of Fitzjohn's Avenue, which runs up to Hampstead from Swiss Cottage tube, is the **Freud Museum,** in a side turning, Maresfield Gardens. Here the great Austrian master spent the last year of his life, having fled Vienna in 1938 to escape Nazi persecution. He lived here in the company of his daughter, Anna, until he died, just a few months later in 1939. Anna Freud remained until her own death in 1982. In the short time that he occupied the house, Freud managed to decorate it and install his eclectic collection of statues, his library, and, of course, his celebrated couch—and here they all are still, lovingly preserved exactly as they were when he died. The place does have a somewhat sanctified and mummified air, but the owners ensure that lectures, study groups, and special exhibits are held, to make the museum more than just a relic of the past. *20 Maresfield Gdns., Hampstead, tel. 01/435-2002. Admission £2 adults, £1 children 12-16 and senior citizens. Open Wed.-Sun. 12-5; closed bank holidays.*

The "village" of Hampstead rises to the north of Camden Town and Kentish Town. (Hampstead is no longer a village, of course, nor are the other two towns. They are just names for sections of London's northward sprawl.) The fastest way to get there is by tube to Hampstead station, which has the distinction of being the deepest Underground stop in London with an elevator shaft that goes down 181 feet.

Hampstead, about four miles from the city center, has always had the reputation of being a place apart from the rest of the capital. The sense of separateness is more than the result of geographical distance; the place has long had a refreshingly different, almost countrified atmosphere. Over the years it has exerted a special attraction for writers and musicians and for those wishing to enjoy both the excitement of London and the peace of a more rural setting. Hampstead's rural atmosphere owes a lot to the Heath—800 acres of extensive grass and forested areas, twisting walks, and lakes, complete with the stately home of Kenwood.

In the Middle Ages, Londoners flocked to Hampstead from London to avoid the plague, seeking its cleaner, fresher air. By 1700 Hampstead spring water was being sold in London in the way that Perrier is sold now. In 1736 thousands of Londoners plodded up the hill to Hampstead to get a grandstand view of the widely forecast "end of the world," heading home again that evening more disappointed than relieved. By the mid-18th century, Hampstead had become established as a fashionable place to live, particularly among writers. This 18th-century atmosphere is still strong today.

Of special interest is **Church Walk,** just off High Street, possibly the finest (and certainly the prettiest) row of 18th-century houses in London. And there are many more delights: atmospheric little alleyways, hilly streets, quiet courtyards, and shaded gardens. **Flask Walk** and **Keats Grove**—the latter where the poet lived—are just two such treasures. *Keats House, Wentworth Pl., Keats Grove, tel. 01/435-2062. Admission free. Open Mon.-Fri. 2-6, Sat. 10-5, Sun. 2-5; closed Good Fri., Easter Sat., open other bank holidays 2-5.*

Time Out   Hampstead is another part of London packed with eating places of all kinds and prices. For light meals, morning coffee, and teatime snacks, try **Hampstead Patisserie & Tea Rooms** (9 South End Rd.) at the southern edge of the Heath near Keats House; **The Coffee Cup** (74 Hampstead High St.) and a pleasant, if somewhat disorganized, café in the basement of **Burgh House,** a handsome 18th-century house in New End Square that is now a community arts center.

12   Off the northwest edge of the Heath itself, on Hampstead Lane, is the **Spaniard's Inn,** an ancient pub little changed (save for the addition of a substantial parking lot) since the days when the notorious highwayman, Dick Turpin, was reputed to eat and drink here.

13   The principal sight on **Hampstead Heath** is **Kenwood House,** a fine country house standing in landscaped grounds which were united with the Heath in 1924 when the house was opened to the public. The original 17th-century building was substantially remodeled by Robert Adam, a greatly talented exponent of classical decoration, at the end of the 18th century. He refaced much of the exterior and added the handsome library, a gorgeously colored and gilded room with unusual curved ends. The chief treasures at Kenwood, however, are the pictures, which once belonged to the Earl of Iveagh, who gave them to the nation in 1927. Like the Wallace Collection just off Oxford Street, this magnificent collection gains by being displayed in the kind of grand, country-house atmosphere for which many of the paintings were originally intended. This is certainly true of the superb portraits by Reynolds, Lawrence, Van Dyck, and Gainsborough, though there are also marvelous works by Rembrandt, Vermeer, Guardi, and Turner here, too. Upstairs is a small collection of jewelry and accessories such as antique shoe clips and buckles.

The lawns in front of the house run down to a small lake crossed by a charming bridge, just the sort of stage scenery that delighted the 18th-century upper class. The lake itself is the setting for some of London's celebrated open-air summer orchestral concerts, many including a spectacular fireworks finale. *Hampstead La., tel. 01/348–1286. Admission free. Open Apr.–Sept. daily 10–6; Oct. daily 10–5; Nov.–Jan. daily 10–4; Feb. and Mar. daily 10–5. Closed Good Fri.*

Time Out   The café in the former stables at Kenwood serves a selection of sandwiches, salads, light lunches, and pastries. The chocolate cake, served with a dollop of whipped cream, is delicious.

14   To the east of Hampstead, and also topping a hill, is the former village of **Highgate,** which has some fine houses, and retains a period atmosphere, too. What Highgate is particularly known for is its **cemetery,** the chief attraction being Karl Marx's grave, a ponderous modern tomb, topped by an oversized bust of the German philosopher. Parties of Russian and Chinese visitors are fond of posing for photographs in front of the tomb to show comrades back home that they have made the pilgrimage to this hallowed ground. In the older, overgrown, western part, enormous ornate Victorian tombs and memorials are inscribed with heart-rending messages of farewell. In addition to many ordinary Londoners, the cemetery contains the graves of the poet Christina Rossetti; Carl Rosa, founder of the opera company that bore his name; the scientist Michael Faraday; and Tom Sayers, the last of the barefist boxers, whose grave carries the effigy of his huge dog. Fifteen years ago the cemetery was forgotten by all but vandals and the occasional film company in search of a ghoulish setting for a horror film. Since then, local volunteers have restored the grounds without spoiling the unique atmosphere of the cemetery. It's well worth following one of their tours. *Swains La., Highgate, tel. 01/340–1834. Admission free, but voluntary contribution requested. Tours of the western side summer daily 10–4, winter daily 10–3. Tours of the eastern side summer daily 10–5, winter daily 10–4.*

Time Out   The restaurant in **Lauderdale House** in nearby Waterlow Park serves cheap lunches and a good variety of snacks. The house, now a community and arts center, was originally built in the 16th century by a master of the Royal Mint.

The City

The City of London is nothing if not confusingly named. Mention it to most Britons and they'll assume you're talking about the great financial institutions based here, always collectively referred to as "the City," the British version of Wall Street. Mention it to most visitors and the odds are they'll just think you mean London as a whole. In fact, the City (note the capital letter) is a distinct and precise area of London. Much more than just another district, it is an administrative and legal entity in itself, in many important respects quite separate from the rest of London.

Such status suggests a special history. And indeed the City is the most ancient part of London, site of the original Celtic settlement that the Romans built up into their great commercial and cultural center of Londinium. Emerging from the chaos of the Dark Ages (the Anglo Saxons are known to have feared the haunted, derelict Roman buildings that remained, calling them the "work of giants"), the City remained first and foremost a commercial center, a role emphasized when, in the 11th century, King Edward the Confessor moved his palace a couple of miles upstream to Westminster. This effectively fixed the City's role as a commercial center, as distinct from the administrative and legal center that Westminster became. William the Conqueror further underlined these different roles after his conquest of Britain in 1066, when he followed Edward's example and made Westminster his residence. Separated from the seat of royal power, the City was free to concentrate its energies on trade.

Commerce has always been the lifeblood of the City. The Romans built their settlement here principally for military reasons—the Thames was relatively narrow, shallow, and easy to cross here, and there were two easily defended strong points. But the Romans were not slow in appreciating the natural advantages for trade the site possessed: A great river far enough from the sea to be secure from raiders, but still near enough to make commerce easy. From the Norman Conquest (1066) onward, trade continued to dominate the life of the City, becoming increasingly international as the centuries passed.

Today, the Lord Mayor and the Corporation of London hold much more than merely ceremonial positions. They watch over a community that is one of the leading financial centers of the world, rivaled only by New York, Tokyo, and Zurich.

City Background

Often called the Square Mile (though it is neither square nor a mile in area), the City lies to the east of central London, stretching from the Temple Bar at its western border to the Tower of London in the east, and from Smithfield in the north to the Thames in the south. Its 677 acres are jammed with a multitude of buildings both ancient and modern. Yet, though it is crowded by day, at night an almost ghostly emptiness pervades its ancient streets. Its permanent population numbers less than 8,000.

A combination of age—at least 2,000 years—and continuous habitation have inevitably meant that a great many of its older buildings and districts have been rebuilt or destroyed over the years as it constantly renewed itself. Natural disasters and wars have played their part in reshaping the character of the City. The most famous, or infamous, moment of destruction occurred in September 1666 when for four days the Great Fire raged, destroying almost every structure in the area. Among the buildings lost was the great Gothic cathedral of St. Paul's. But in destroying the medieval city, the fire also made possible a dynamic new wave of building, much of it the work of Sir Christopher Wren. *(See* Wren and the Great Fire of London in Portraits of London.) The City was rebuilt largely following the original medieval street plans, and Wren did more than anyone to transform its appearance, building 51 new churches, among them his masterpiece, St. Paul's.

The City was again devastated nearly 300 years later by German bombing in World War II. Fifty-seven days and nights of near continuous bombing during the Blitz wiped out large areas, though miraculously St. Paul's and the Tower of London escaped the worst of the damage. The opportunity for intelligent rebuilding was largely squandered, as the featureless, ugly buildings that have appeared since clearly show. Nonetheless, enough of the essential character of the City has survived to give the visitor a vivid sense of the colorful and often turbulent history of this most historic part of London.

Temple Bar to Ludgate Hill

❶ The main gateway to the City is **Temple Bar** in Fleet Street. Its significance stems from the fact that it was this western approach that was the most direct route for travel to and from Westminster and the City. But its curious name is misleading. First, there's no temple here. The term refers to the nearby Temple area *(see* Bloomsbury and Legal London). Second, there is no bar, and there hasn't been since 1870, when the handsome Baroque gateway built by Wren in 1670 was dismantled as an obstruction to traffic. Even this wasn't really a bar, but a ceremonial entryway. Today, a bronze griffin, emblem of the City, marks the site where Wren's gateway stood (similar griffins mark all the traditional entries to the City). It is here

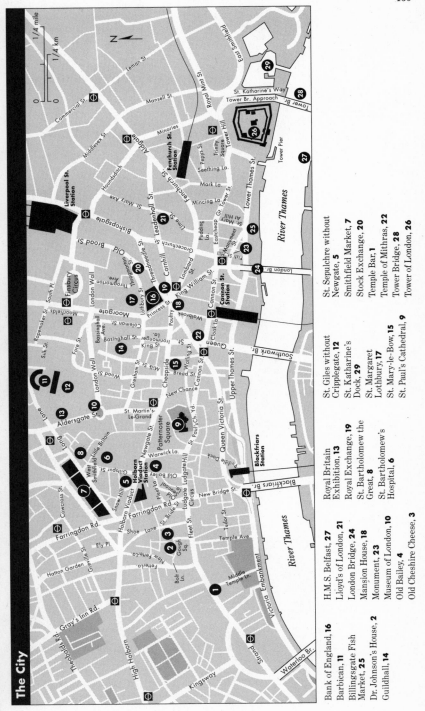

The City

Bank of England, **16**
Barbican, **11**
Billingsgate Fish Market, **25**
Dr. Johnson's House, **2**
Guildhall, **14**

H.M.S. Belfast, **27**
Lloyd's of London, **21**
London Bridge, **24**
Mansion House, **18**
Monument, **23**
Museum of London, **10**
Old Bailey, **4**
Old Cheshire Cheese, **3**

Royal Britain Exhibition, **13**
Royal Exchange, **19**
St. Bartholomew the Great, **8**
St. Bartholomew's Hospital, **6**

St. Giles without Cripplegate, **12**
St. Katharine's Dock, **29**
St. Margaret Lothbury, **17**
St. Mary-le-Bow, **15**
St. Paul's Cathedral, **9**

St. Sepulchre without Newgate, **5**
Smithfield Market, **7**
Stock Exchange, **20**
Temple Bar, **1**
Temple of Mithras, **22**
Tower Bridge, **28**
Tower of London, **26**

that by ancient custom the monarch must ask permission of the Lord Mayor of London to enter the City.

Fleet Street itself follows the course of the little river Fleet, which ran from Hampstead, up in the north of London, to the Thames. There's no trace of it today, and hasn't been since 1765 when it was boarded over. The fame of Fleet Street derives from its traditional role as the center of Britain's newspaper business. Today, spiraling rents and labor costs have forced virtually all the newspapers away from Fleet Street, most of them having relocated to the massive redevelopment areas around London's docklands.

❷ Halfway along Fleet Street, on its north side, turn down narrow Bolt Lane and follow the winding alley to **Dr. Johnson's House** in Gough Square. Here, in a 17th-century house, the writer lived in the 1750s while he was compiling his great dictionary. *17 Gough Sq., tel. 01/353–3745. Admission £1.30 adults, 80p children under 16 and senior citizens. Open May–Sept., Mon.–Sat. 11–5:30; Apr.–Oct., Mon.–Sat. 11–5; closed bank holidays.*

❸ Around the corner from Gough Square, in Wine Office Court, is the **Old Cheshire Cheese** pub, with its historic beams and ancient fireplaces. This also dates from the 17th century, and was a favorite watering hole of Dr. Johnson and Boswell, his biographer and companion. Try a pint of their real ale—and a slice of cheese, of course.

Time Out **El Vino's** wine bar (47 Fleet St.) was the traditional haunt of Fleet Street journalists, and, even though most newspaper offices have moved, some newspapermen still return to this favorite bar, although you're more likely to see City business types here. At lunch you can eat in the small restaurant or get sandwiches from the bar. The management has had to abandon its decades-long resistance to serving women at the bar but still applies a dress code: jacket, collar, and tie for men; skirts for women.

At the foot of Fleet Street is **Ludgate Circus,** a drab traffic circle, which gets its name from the Lud Gate, believed to have been built by King Lud in 66 BC, who is today also commemorated by the **Old King Lud** pub on the corner. Ahead of you now is Ludgate Hill and St. Paul's.

❹ Fleet Street runs into **Old Bailey,** at the northern end of which stood one of London's grisly prisons, Newgate Prison. The building was demolished in 1902 to make way for the **Central Criminal Court,** or the Old Bailey as it is commonly called. The imposing Edwardian building, extended in the 1970s, is famous mainly for the gilt statue of Justice on the dome: the blindfolded figure impassively holding the scales and sword of justice in her hands. To watch a trial, head for courts 1–3, the old courts, where the juiciest trials usually take place. Courts 4–19 are modern, with restricted view from all but the front seats. *Public Gallery open 10–1, 2–4; stand on line at the Newgate St. entrance. Check the day's hearings on the sign outside.*

❺ Continuing north from Old Bailey, cross Newgate Street and head up Giltspur Street. Immediately on the left here is the church of **St. Sepulchre without Newgate.** It is the resting place of Captain John Smith, "sometime Governor of Virginia and Admiral of New England," whose life was saved by Pocahontas, the 17th-century Native American who married an Englishman.

A little farther up Giltspur Street, to the right, is **St.**
⑥ Bartholomew's Hospital, one of the oldest charitable foundations in London and today a leading teaching hospital. It dates back to 1123. Though originally a religious foundation, it was spared by Henry VIII in the 16th century when he so rigorously suppressed the country's other religious foundations. Appropriately, there is a statue of him in the niche above the main gateway.

Just to the northwest of St. Bart's, as the hospital is called, is
⑦ Smithfield, London's main meat market. The area has been a market of sorts since the 12th century when this grassy spot (or "Smoothfield") just outside the then City walls was used as a horse market. In the mid-1800s the area was notorious for its stench and filth and for the drunkenness of the traders. The Victorians put a stop to all that when they built a new market in 1868, and banned the sale and slaughter of live animals. Following a fire after World War II, the market was again rebuilt, reopening in 1963.

Time Out **Rudland and Stubbs** (35–37 Greenhill Rents) is a friendly fish restaurant in the heart of the meat market; you can lunch at the bar on fishy snacks or eat in style in the restaurant. The **Hand and Shears** (1 Middle St.) offers traditional pub food to City workers; watch for the lurid pub sign.

⑧ Just to the east of Smithfield is the church of **St. Bartholomew the Great,** the second oldest church in London. It was founded, like its namesake the hospital, in 1123 by the Normans. The church is approached through an attractive gateway with an Elizabethan timbered facade. For many years this was covered by plaster, coming to light unexpectedly in 1915 when a bomb from a German zeppelin blew the plaster off. The interior of the church has undergone considerable rebuilding and restoration over the years, notably in the 16th and 19th centuries, leaving the choir as the only remaining section of the original Norman building. It possesses a monumental charm, not unlike the Chapel of St. John in the White Tower in the Tower of London. The church is often used for concerts, and to hear Bach or Handel performed in such surroundings can be a memorable experience.

St. Paul's Cathedral

⑨ Backtracking to Ludgate Hill, turn and walk up toward **St. Paul's.** Built by Sir Christopher Wren between 1675 and 1710, Wren's building replaced the earlier Gothic cathedral that had stood here since the Middle Ages before its destruction in the Great Fire of 1666. The building is Wren's greatest work, and its instantly recognizable dome has been the greatest landmark on the London skyline for nearly 300 years. Fittingly, the architect himself is buried in the crypt, under the simple epitaph composed by his son: *Lector, si monumentum requiris, circumspice*—Reader, if you seek his monument, look around you.

Despite its vast size—520 feet long and 365 feet from the crown of the lantern on the dome to the ground—the church was built in the relatively short time of 35 years, which accounts for its

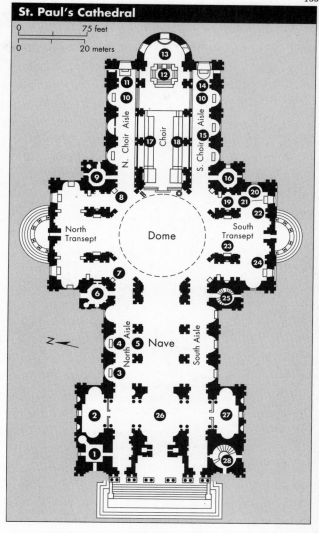

St. Paul's Cathedral

unusually unified quality. Wren himself, well aware of the parsimony of his paymasters, can claim much of the credit for this. He insisted that all the foundations be laid from the start, thus ensuring that the dimensions of the building could not subsequently be altered. Equally striking is the consistently high level of craftsmanship, both inside and out. For the interior, Wren was very lucky to have the services of the great Dutch wood carver, Grinling Gibbons. His exquisitely carved choir stalls are particularly fine, as are the black and gold wrought-iron screens by the French master, Jean Tijou.

Wren's designs for the building went through three distinct stages. His original plan was rejected, but the second, later called the Great Model, reached the stage of having a massive and beautifully detailed wooden model made of it, which is now on display in the crypt. The third design, or the Warrant Design as it came to be known, was the one finally chosen. But Wren made significant alterations to it during its construction, notably the substitution of a dome for the giant steeple he had originally designed. The construction of the dome itself was a difficult technical undertaking, with an elaborate brick cone built between the inner and outer skins to strengthen and support both. The interior of the dome presents another curiosity. Words whispered from one side of the aptly named **Whispering Gallery** can be clearly heard on the other side, 112 feet away. It's worth climbing the spiral steps to the Whispering Gallery, not only for the chance to test the remarkable acoustics, but also for the view down to the chancel and the nave. More steps climb up from the Whispering Gallery to the exterior **Stone Gallery**, some 70 feet above the Whispering Gallery, and then higher still to the **Golden Gallery** just below the lantern, ball, and cross. This last series of steps is very steep and, though quite safe, should not be attempted by the faint-hearted. From bottom to top you will have climbed 627 steps! There are good views from both the Stone and Golden Galleries across the City and beyond. Try to pick out the distinctive steeples of Wren's many other City churches, and imagine the view in his time, centuries before the development of high rises, when St. Paul's dominated the City skyline. These galleries are also a good spot from which to study more closely the details of Wren's unusual and imaginative design; there are close views to be had of the flying buttresses and western towers, and you can see the brick cone that divides the inner and outer dome while you are on the steps leading up to the Golden Gallery.

The interior of the church is crowded with memorials, some indifferent, some good, almost all of them large and elaborate. Dr. Johnson; John Donne, the poet and dean of St. Paul's, whose effigy, wrapped in its shroud, is the only one to have survived the destruction of the Gothic cathedral; the artists Reynolds and Turner (in Painters' Corner); the duke of Wellington; Nelson; even George Washington—all are commemorated. One of the most impressive memorials is the American Memorial Chapel in the area behind the high altar (there's an admission charge). This chapel was dedicated in 1958 to the 28,000 Americans stationed in Britain who lost their lives on active service. The Roll of Honor was presented to St. Paul's by General Eisenhower in 1951. The walls are decorated with carvings of plants and birds indigenous to the United States. Henry Moore's sculpture *Mother and Child*, given to St. Paul's by Moore in 1984, stands near the entrance to the ambulatory.

Many of the most interesting tombs, including Wren's, are in the crypt. The most splendid is probably that of the duke of Wellington, the Iron Duke, victor of the Battle of Waterloo in 1815. As contemporary accounts relate, his funeral here in 1852 was among the most magnificently staged events in the building's long history, rivaled for pomp and ceremony only by Winston Churchill's funeral in 1965. Also buried in the crypt are two other celebrated British military leaders: Nelson, who was killed at the battle of Trafalgar in 1805, and Lord Kitchener, World War I military supremo, who died when the cruiser he was traveling in was struck by a mine off the Orkneys in 1916. The crypt also contains an exhibition of gold and silver plate, and ecclesiastical robes. *Tel. 01/248-2705. Admission to* *ambulatory (American Chapel) 60p adults, children free; to crypt and treasury 80p adults, 40p children; to galleries £1 adults, 50p children; **Super Tours** runs tours of the cathedral weekdays at 11, 11:30, 2, and 2:30, £3.50 adults, £2.50 children. Cathedral open Mon.–Sat. 7:30–6, Sun. 8–6; the ambulatory, crypt, and galleries Mon.–Fri. 10–4:15, Sat. 11–4:15.*

The areas immediately around St. Paul's, many of which were flattened during World War II, present a depressing contrast to the cathedral itself, despite—or perhaps because of—the earnest attempts of architects and planners after the war to make them a fitting showcase for modern British architecture. There are plans to redevelop the worst offender, Paternoster Square, but these probably won't take effect for some years.

The Museum of London and the Barbican

Heading north from St. Paul's up St. Martin's-le-Grand, you come to **London Wall,** a street so named because it follows the line of the old Roman wall, though only a few remains are still visible. (Proof of the durability of the Romans' construction methods is amply provided by the fact that large portions of their original city walls survived until well into the 18th century. Archaeological preservation was not high on the list of priorities then, so a lot of what remained was pulled down to make way for new buildings.) Ironically, despite its proximity to some of the most venerable and ancient remains of London, London Wall itself ranks high among the ugliest postwar redevelopments in the City. A row of gaunt and poorly designed high rises stretches the length of the street, discouraging all but the most determined visitors to search for the Roman remains.

⑩ But one modern building is worth seeking out here: the **Museum of London.** It traces the history of London, especially its social history, from the city's earliest days. Not to be missed among its imaginative displays are the statues from the Roman Temple of Mithras, the Lord Mayor's Ceremonial Coach, the diorama of the Great Fire of London, and the Cheapside Hoard of Jacobean jewelry, which was very likely buried for safekeeping during an outbreak of plague. The museum tells the whole of London's history, from earliest times to the present day, in chronological order. The sections on the history of the capital in the present century include a Woolworth's counter and elevators from Selfridges; both stores were founded by Americans and had quite an impact on the day-to-day life of Londoners. *London Wall, tel. 01/600–3699. Admission free. Open Tues.–Sat. 10–6, Sun. 2–6; closed bank holidays.*

Time Out   **Millburn's,** the museum's restaurant, entered down stairs from the forecourt, provides acceptable light refreshments in an area of the City that doesn't offer much in the way of family eating places.

⑪ Just to the north of the Museum of London is another of the City's rebuilt regions, the **Barbican,** a vast residential and arts complex that is best known today as the London home of the Royal Shakespeare Company and the London Symphony Orchestra. It takes its name from the watchtower that stood here in the Middle Ages, just outside the city walls. Architecturally, about all that can be said for the Barbican is that the arts center has the largest flat roof in Europe. The residential sectors tend to be empty and dispiriting. Many residents use their apartment here as a London pied-à-terre, escaping to their country homes on weekends and holidays; those who live here year-round often comment on the lack of any sense of community. Furthermore, the area's gloomy concrete walkways and empty echoing plazas are no place to linger at night.

There is more life in the Barbican Arts Center, even if it does have the feel of an air terminal run by well-heeled conservative troglodytes. Only three of the eight levels are actually below ground, but as there are very few windows the whole place has a subterranean atmosphere to it. The interlocking stairs and terraces seem to lead even deeper into the bowels of the earth. The combination of hammered concrete walls, soft carpets, and massive girders (used decoratively as well as structurally) combine with strangely low ceilings to give one the feeling of being in an underground city. The only airy space in the whole building is the huge conservatory on the roof, open to the public only on weekends and bank holidays. Guided tours of the center take place regularly, and are a good way of seeing something of life behind the scenes.

If you can adjust to this curious atmosphere, the facilities here are unrivaled. The performances in the Royal Shakespeare Company's two auditoriums are usually well worth a visit; the main house stages a wide variety of productions in one of the most imaginatively designed auditoriums in the world. The little Pit, buried in the bowels of the building, is a small theater-in-the-round, for experimental work.

Concerts take place in the Barbican Hall every evening. Symphony concerts predominate, but the programs range over a very wide spectrum. Less conventional music can be heard in the regular program of intriguing and lively "foyer events," which has something for almost every taste. In a single week you might hear jazz, African music, the songs of Shakespeare's time, and a saxophone quartet playing classical pieces. The Barbican Cinema shows a mixture of quality new-release films and revivals, and the Art Gallery stages large-scale temporary exhibitions on a variety of themes. Small artwork exhibitions, often displaying the creations of just a couple of artists or craftspeople are mounted in the Sculpture Court and in small exhibition spaces dotted around the building. *Silk St., tel. 01/ 638–4141. Admission free. Open Mon.–Sat. 9–11, Sun. and bank holidays 12–11. For theater, concert, and cinema bookings, tel. 01/638–8891 or 01/628–8795. Box office open daily 10–8. Prices vary. Barbican Gallery, tel. 01/638–4141, ext. 306 or 346. Prices vary according to exhibition. Open Mon.–Sat. 10–6:45, Sun. and bank holidays 12–5:45. For advance booking for tours of the center, tel. 01/638–4141 ext. 218. Price £2. Mon.–Sat. 11–7, Sun. 12–7.*

Time Out   Each of the three restaurants in the Barbican caters to different tastes, and to different purses as well. **The Cut Above** serves full-scale meals; **Wine on Six** is the center's informal wine bar, while the **Waterside Café**, pleasantly situated next to the terrace and pool, is the place to go for a light meal, afternoon tea, or morning coffee. There are also a number of bars and coffee bars in the center.

⓬ About the only building in this part of London that survived the Blitz, and then only partially, is the evocatively-named **St. Giles without Cripplegate,** St. Giles being the patron saint of cripples. Today it is the parish church of the Barbican, and stands just to the south of the main complex, looking somewhat forlorn among the surrounding concrete and brick. Only the church tower and walls are original, the remainder having been destroyed by German bombs and rebuilt in the 1950s.

⓭ **Royal Britain** is a newly opened permanent exhibition on the edge of the Barbican Centre, opposite Barbican Underground station in Aldersgate Street. To reach it from the Barbican Centre, take the road tunnel (Beech Street) and turn right onto Aldersgate Street. It attempts to bring to life more than a thousand years of royal history, from semi-mythical figures such as Queen Boudicca and Prince Arthur to the Royal Family of today: "The Family Firm," as Prince Philip has called it. The exhibition uses the latest techniques to provide a "unique and evocative audio-visual experience." For instance, the visitor is taken back to 1587 to experience the last moments on earth of Mary Queen of Scots, as she walks down the paneled corridors of Fotheringay Castle to confront her executioner. *The Barbican, tel. 01/588–0588. Admission £5 adults, £3 children and senior citizens. Open daily 9–5:30.*

The Guildhall and the Financial Center

⓮ Return to London Wall and head south down Coleman Street to Basinghall Avenue. Here, turn right, continue to Bassinghall Street, and you come to the **Guildhall.** This is the home of the Corporation of London, the City's governing body, presided over by the Lord Mayor of London. The building itself originally dates from about 1410, but in the course of a long and eventful life has probably sustained more damage and destruction and undergone more restoration, renovation, and outright rebuilding than any other historic building in London. It was severely damaged in the Great Fire of 1666, only the exterior stone walls surviving intact. Having been rebuilt after the fire, it underwent numerous alterations throughout the 18th and 19th centuries. Then, in 1940, it was again nearly destroyed when German bombs blew the roof off. Lavish restoration in the '50s and later again in the '70s produced the building you see today. It is the scene of the election of the Lord Mayor every year and of other City officers, and is where the City stages banquets in honor of visiting heads of state and various other bigwigs, with carriages, liveried flunkies, gold plate, and a lot of pomp and circumstance.

Visitors can see the 152-foot-long hall with its magnificent stone-arched roof. The roof itself was constructed in the 1950s, but sits upon walls dating from the Middle Ages; steel trusses hidden within the stone arches carry the weight of the roof. High up in the west gallery, well placed to observe all the ceremony below, stand Gog and Magog, 9-foot wooden giants. The present statues replaced two from the early 1700s that were destroyed in World War II. Gog and Magog have presided over the Guildhall since the early 1400s; Gog represents an inhabitant of ancient Britain, while Magog is a Trojan invader. *Gresham St., tel. 01/606–3030. Open Mon.–Fri. 9–5; closed bank holidays.*

The new west wing of the Guildhall, built in the 1970s, houses the **Guildhall Library**—full of books and documents relating to the history of the City—and the small **Museum of the Worshipful Company of Clockmakers,** which contains watches and clocks from several centuries. *Tel. 01/606–3030. Admission free. Open Mon.–Fri. 9:30–5; closed bank holidays.*

The Guildhall takes its name from the many City Guilds, or trade associations, later known as Livery Companies (from their ceremonial clothes or livery—not their rich diets) that met from the Middle Ages onward to discuss their business and the affairs of the City. Their prosperity and influence, especially following Henry VIII's dissolution of the religious and monastic bodies based in the City in the 16th century, ensured them a dominant voice in the administration of the City. Remarkably, despite their seeming archaism—their members include the Fan Makers' Company, the Gold and Silver Wyre Drawers' Company, the Scriveners' Company, and the Tallow Chandlers' Company—the City Guilds are still a potent force in the City's life. Though their role is often only ceremonial today, they help support a number of charities and influential City schools. Only members of a guild may elect the Lord Mayor.

From the Guildhall continue south down Milk Street to **Cheapside.** Memories of Saxon times haunt the streets here. The very name Cheapside is of Saxon origin, *ceap* meaning barter. All around Cheapside the street names—Bread Street, Ironmonger Lane, Wood Street—indicate the busy trades that flourished here from the 11th century onward. Here you will also find the church of **St. Mary-le-Bow.** There's been a church on this site since at least 1091 (contemporary records relate that its roof blew away in a gale that year), but the present building is the work of Wren. Like so many of the City's churches, it was badly damaged in the war. Tradition has it that to be a true Cockney, or native of London, you must be born within the sound of Bow bells. With such a tiny permanent population in the City now, the numbers of bona-fide Cockneys have certainly been reduced.

Continue east down Cheapside and you come to the seven-way intersection that marks the center of the City. Here, the large almost windowless classical building on your left is the **Bank of England,** "the old lady of Threadneedle Street," as it has been popularly known for well over a century. The present building, which incorporates a very few parts of the original 18th-century bank, was completed just before World War II. The bank plays a leading role in Britain's economic fortunes, as well as monitoring and, when necessary, directing the multifarious goings-on of the City. It was a privately-owned operation until 1946, when it was nationalized.

For a long time, it has been almost impossible to visit the small, semi-private museum run by the bank; bookings have been taken literally years ahead. A new museum and exhibition center has been promised for the fall of 1988. Full details were not available at press time. *Tel. 01/601–4878 or 01/601–3695 for further information.*

Just behind the bank in the narrow street called Lothbury, is the little church of **St. Margaret Lothbury.** The church was rebuilt by Wren after the Great Fire but is interesting mainly for the collection of decorative woodwork—rood screens, pews, a reredos—from a number of other Wren churches since demolished. Much of the finest work is by Grinling Gibbons.

18 Facing the bank, and occupying the southern flank of the intersection, is the **Mansion House,** built in the early 18th century. This is the official residence of the Lord Mayor of London. His term of office lasts just one year, and it's said that the lavish entertainments he is expected to provide are so costly that few could afford to hold the office longer. The building is not open to the public.

19 At the northern end of the intersection, standing at right angles to the Bank of England, is the handsome classical facade of the **Royal Exchange.** Like so much else, the first exchange was destroyed in the Great Fire of 1666. The replacement, designed along similar lines and completed in 1669 (and one of the first City buildings to be re-erected), was itself burnt down in 1838. Queen Victoria opened the present exchange in 1844, when it acquired its royal title; once again, the pattern of a central courtyard, now roofed over, was retained. After Lloyd's (*see below*), which had occupied space in the exchange since the 1770s, moved out to its own headquarters in 1927, the exchange experienced several decades of neglect, and was used for everything from an exhibition space for paintings by City workers to offices for an insurance company.

In 1981, the exchange reverted to something very close to its original role, becoming the home of the **London International Financial Futures Exchange.** LIFFE, as it is popularly known, enables businesses to hedge their risk in the currently volatile European market; the older Financial Futures Exchange in Chicago covers the North American market. Even if you don't understand the arcane complications of financial dealing, a trip to the Visitors' Gallery is worthwhile. Watching the trading on the floor below is like attending a performance by a combined modern dance troupe and a roaring baseball crowd. *Royal Exchange, tel. 01/623–0444. Admission free. Visitors' Gallery open Mon.–Fri. 11:30–1:45; closed bank holidays.*

Time Out If you want to mingle with the sharp young lads from the exchange floor while they take a break from all that frantic buying and selling, join them for champagne at the **Greenhouse Steak Bar** (expensive snacks are also served) at the back of the Royal Exchange. Or go to Finch Lane for a couple of pints at the **Woolpack,** a basic, smoky pub, with not much more food than a cheese or ham roll, but plenty of opportunity for eavesdropping.

20 The raison d'être of the City has always been to trade and to make money, and LIFFE is but one of the latest and most successful manifestations of that purpose. If you head down Threadneedle Street between the Bank of England and the Royal Exchange, you will reach a much more venerable trading institution, the **London Stock Exchange.** There has been a stock exchange in London since at least the beginning of the 18th century. It moved from one location to another as it grew, settling here in 1801. The present building, opened in 1972, is the third on this site. Trading in stocks and shares used to take place on the trading floor, which often became hectic and confused. Following the so-called "Big Bang" in the fall of 1986, when a number of reforms of stock exchange trading practices were implemented, trading has moved off the floor. Business is now done almost exclusively over the telephone; the offices of all the stock exchange member companies are linked by a sophisticated electronic network that gives up-to-the-minute information on the share prices of some 7,000 companies all over the world. As a result, a visit to the Viewing Gallery is likely to be disappointing, as only one corner of the trading floor is now regularly used; this is for the Traded Options Market. Short talks are given on the workings of the stock exchange (now the largest exchange in the world, executing, on average, 30,000 orders each working day), and there are regular films, but modern technology has left the gallery behind, and it doesn't have much atmosphere. *Old Broad St., tel. 01/588-2355. Admission free. Open Mon.-Fri. 9:45-3:15; closed bank holidays.*

Another of London's great financial institutions, **Lloyd's,** has its headquarters here in Leadenhall Street. To reach it from the stock exchange, turn right into Gracechurch Street and then take the first left into Leadenhall Street. This route takes you near **Leadenhall Market,** where there has been a market since the 14th century. The present building, all glass and brightly painted cast iron, dates from 1881.

㉑ **Lloyd's of London** has been in the insurance business since the end of the 17th century. But as if to belie its long and distinguished history, the firm's new headquarters are anything but traditional. Finished in 1986, they are the work of the modernist architect Richard Rogers, whose other well-known buildings include the Pompidou Center in Paris and the headquarters of the Hong Kong and Shanghai Bank in Hong Kong.

Even though the building has been the target of considerable criticism, apparently a large majority of the 4,000 to 6,000 people who work here have said that they're happy with it—as well they might considering the £163 million it cost! The building is the most lively and imaginative of all the new blocks in the City, with far more visual interest than, say, the monolithic **National Westminster Bank Tower** a short distance to the north. The main feature of Lloyd's is a 200-foot-high barrel vault made of sparkling glass specially treated to make it appear "alive" from wherever you see it, inside or out, and in all weather. The barrel vault houses a central atrium, or court, around which are wrapped 12 tiers of galleries stretching toward the sky. From inside, you feel as if you're in a majestic medieval cathedral, with light streaming in through the great glass window. Almost as striking are the six satellite towers, all metal and exposed pipes, which accommodate the building's services.

The public visit to Lloyd's starts with a ride in one of the many external glass-sided observation elevators, another novel (for London) feature of the building. Then you can visit an exhibition that tells the history of Lloyd's from its origins at the end of the 17th century in Edward Lloyd's coffee house on nearby Tower Street, where insurance was arranged for trading ships and their cargoes. Lloyd's is not a conventional insurance company but a society of underwriters (more than 30,000) that provides not only marine insurance but covers every risk imaginable: fleets of aircraft, factories, oil rigs, and all kinds of "oddballs," such as a wine-taster's palate; Marilyn Monroe even insured her legs at Lloyd's. The underwriters, who are personally liable for the risks they insure, do not deal with the public directly; they work only with accredited Lloyd's brokers who obtain business from all over the world. (Lloyd's receives £20 million in premiums every working day, about 75% of which originates outside the United Kingdom) The culmination of the visit is the view from one of the galleries down into the great atrium and lower galleries.

There is an exhibition with memorabilia such as the Nelson Collection, which includes silver plate presented by the company to the great sea captain following his victory at the battle of the Nile in 1798. The Lutine Bell, traditionally rung to announce the loss at sea of a vessel insured with Lloyd's, now stands in the center of the atrium and is only rung occasionally —two strokes for good news, one for bad. *1 Lime St., tel. 01/623 –7100, ext. 6210 or 5786. Open Mon.–Fri. 10–2:30; closed bank holidays.*

Time Out **Lloyd's Coffee House,** at the foot of the new office building, serves virtually anything throughout the day: breakfast, a full lunch, afternoon tea, or just coffee and pastries. Despite its name, there's no connection, even in terms of decor, with the 17th-century coffee house where Lloyd's originated.

Mithras, the Monument, and London Bridge

Most of our route so far has been over the area once occupied by the Roman settlement. During the last 40 years or so, archaeologists have been able to piece together a fairly comprehensive picture of the Roman city; one of the last pieces was fitted into the jigsaw early in 1988 when the remains of an amphitheater were discovered on a construction site in front of the Guildhall. It is hoped that these newly discovered remains, part of one of the most important buildings of Roman Londinium, will eventually be incorporated into some form of permanent exhibition. Naturally enough, there is scarcely any visible evidence of the period of Roman occupation on the present-day streets; some of the archaeological finds are on display in the Museum of London, from which you can also view a section of the Roman city walls. However, if you retrace your steps to the Bank of England and then head southwest down Queen Victoria Street for **22** a couple of hundred yards, you'll reach the **Temple of Mithras,** unearthed during construction work in 1954. Further Roman remains are on show in **Cannon Street,** just around the corner. Here is the **London Stone** set, oddly enough, into the wall of the Bank of China. Though its origins are unknown, it is believed that this is the ancient Roman milestone from which all distances throughout the province of Britannia were measured.

Continue down Cannon Street and into Eastcheap. From here **23** turn right into Fish Street Hill. Before you is the **Monument,** a massive Doric column of white stone put up in 1667—and designed, naturally enough, by Wren—to commemorate the Great Fire of London, ". . . the better to preserve the memory of this dreadful Visitation," as the Act of Parliament that allowed for its construction put it. The Monument stands 202 feet high, with its base exactly 202 feet from the small bakery shop in Pudding Lane where the fire started. At the summit is a gilt urn with flames leaping from it. You can climb up to the top (311 steps) and admire the fine view. St. Paul's still dominates the skyline, though now it has to compete with modern tower blocks. *Monument St., tel. 01/626–2717. Admission 50 p adults, 25p children. Open Apr.–Sept., Mon.–Fri. 9–5:40, Sat. and Sun. 2–5:40; Oct.–Mar., Mon.–Sat. 9–3:40; closed Good Fri., May Day.*

24 A little to the south of the Monument is **London Bridge.** A bridge has been at or near the site of the present London Bridge since Roman times, although the exact location of the earliest bridge is unknown. Recent research suggests that it was probably a little downstream from today's bridge. A second wooden bridge certainly existed in Saxon times, and this is the one that seems to have given rise to the nursery rhyme *London Bridge is Falling Down*, which it really did in 1014. The first stone bridge was constructed in 1176. It rapidly sprouted houses along both sides of its narrow width and stood until 1831, when it was finally pulled down to make way for an elegant, classical structure. The opening ceremony took the form of a banquet on the bridge itself, to which 15,000 people were invited. This bridge was in turn replaced in 1967 when it could no longer cope with the volume of traffic, and was sold to the McCulloch Oil Corporation of California who reconstructed it at Lake Havasu City, in a corner of America's Arizona desert; rumor has it the company mistakenly thought that they were buying the infinitely more spectacular Tower Bridge. The present London Bridge is more than 100 feet wide and divides the Port of London, downstream, from King's Reach, upstream.

25 From London Bridge head down Lower Thames Street to what was, until 1982, **Billingsgate Fish Market.** Beside the old market building, now hardly recognizable as it is undergoing a thorough reconstruction, is the Custom House, built early in the last century. Just to the east of here, back in Lower Thames Street, substantial remains of a wooden Roman jetty were unearthed a few years ago. The bulk of the finds are now in the Museum of London.

The Tower of London

26 From Lower Thames Street it's an easy five minute walk to the most famous of the City's sights, the **Tower of London.** Of all the historic monuments and buildings of London, the Tower of London (or simply the Tower, as it is generally known) is perhaps the most impressive and rewarding to visit—a dramatic and beautiful series of buildings intimately bound to the story of London.

The Tower began life as a fortress and palace, and it remains one of the Royal Palaces (in which capacity it still guards the Crown Jewels). The Queen does not live here, of course, though every British monarch from William the Conqueror in the 11th century to Henry VIII in the 16th did. At other times the Tower has been the site of the Royal Mint, home to the Public Records, the Royal Menagerie, the Royal Observatory, and most famously a prison and scene of countless executions. Those who were incarcerated here included Anne Boleyn; Queen Elizabeth I, before she came to the throne; Sir Walter Raleigh, who spent 13 years here; and Robert Devereux, earl of Essex and long-time favorite of Elizabeth I. The little Princes in the Tower may also have also met their fates here.

Its splendor and the richly historic associations that invest it, make the Tower a hugely popular tourist attraction. It gets *very* crowded, especially in the summer. So be prepared for long lines, and allow at least three hours for a visit. A good time to arrive is early in the morning, when the Tower opens; if you head straight for the Crown Jewels, you should have some time to see them in relative peace before the crowds build up. Remember that the Jewel House is normally closed throughout February.

The best and most interesting way to see the buildings, at any rate on a first visit, is to tag along on one of the many free tours given by the "Beefeaters," the popular name for the Yeoman Warders of the Tower. They wear a distinctive and picturesque Tudor-style uniform of dark blue and red and, on special occasions, an even more magnificent one of scarlet and gold. Tours start from the Middle Tower about every 30 minutes; they last approximately one hour, and, as the Warders' commentary is full of factual detail, are not always suitable for small children.

The Tower straddles almost exactly the line of the old Roman city walls of London, fragments of which can be seen at the little **Wardrobe Tower** at the southeast corner of the White Tower and alongside the **History Gallery;** this is a walk-through display of Tower history situated south of the White Tower.

The **White Tower** is the heart of the entire complex, and in some ways the most impressive, certainly the most conspicuous, building here. It is also the oldest, begun in 1078 by William the Conqueror, the first Norman king of England. When completed in about 1097, it dominated the surrounding buildings of London, underlining only too clearly the military might of the victorious Normans. Its brooding presence was not softened by the later enlargement of the windows and the addition of elegant cupolas on the four corner towers. The interior has been greatly altered—except for the **Chapel of St. John,** which is the original Norman chapel, as beautiful as it is rare. It is a structure of great simplicity, almost entirely lacking in ornamentation, built in characteristically heavy Norman style. It is one of the great treasures of London and should not be missed.

The rest of the White Tower is occupied by the **Royal Armouries,** Britain's national museum of arms and armor. One of the original functions of the Tower was to serve as a great arsenal, which in the Middle Ages supplied armor and weapons to the kings of England and their armies. The collection was started under Henry VIII, who restocked the arsenal and also established a workshop at Greenwich, a few miles down the Thames, to make fine armor for himself and his court. The collection was opened to the public during the reign of Charles II in the second half of the 17th century, which makes the Tower Armouries Britain's oldest public museum. The armor and weapons on display come from both Britain and the rest of Europe, and date from Saxon and Viking times up to the present day. Among the highlights are the earliest known English cannon, made in about 1450; Henry VIII's armor made for him at Greenwich in 1540, with decorations designed by the court painter Hans Holbein; and armor belonging to Robert Dudley, earl of Leicester, and to Charles I. Armor from Asia and the Islamic World is on show in the **Oriental Armoury** in the **Waterloo Barracks.** Gruesome and realistically displayed instruments of torture and punishment can be seen in the **Bowyer Tower,** while in the **New Armouries** there are examples of almost every weapon made in the Tower for British forces between the 17th and 19th centuries.

Surrounding the White Tower are other fortifications and buildings, dating from the 11th to the 19th centuries. Starting

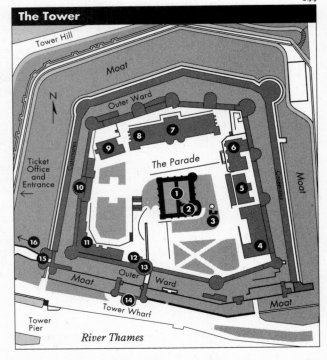

from the main entrance (by the shop), the first and most obvious feature is the **moat.** Until it was drained under the direction of the duke of Wellington in 1843, the moat was foully polluted, obstinately resisting all attempts to flush it with water from the Thames.

Across the moat a series of gateways—the **Middle Tower** and the **Byward Tower**—form the principal entrance on this, the landward approach. A little further on the right you will reach **Traitors' Gate,** which used to be the main river entrance. Its name comes from the time when it was the main entrance to the Tower, for the Thames acted as London's chief thoroughfare, and condemned prisoners, or those under suspicion, were delivered by water to their grim fate.

Immediately opposite Traitors' Gate is the misleadingly named **Bloody Tower.** Begun in about 1280, it was originally known as the Garden Tower, and its present name can be traced back only as far as 1571. Its most famous inmates were the little Princes in the Tower, monstrously murdered on the orders of their uncle, Richard III—or so the story goes. Nobody really knows who was responsible for their deaths, but there is little reason to doubt that they did die either here or somewhere else in the Tower. Sir Walter Raleigh was also a prisoner here between 1603 and 1616, and spent his time writing a *History of the World*. His imprisonment was not quite the gruesome ordeal you might imagine: His wife and two sons sometimes lived with him, the younger boy was actually christened in the Tower chapel of St. Peter, and Raleigh was permitted to keep two servants. The spacious rooms where he lived are today much as they were during his prison term. Sir Walter was released from the Tower in 1616 to lead an expedition to seek for El Dorado. The failure of his mission led to his return to the Tower two years later and his execution at Westminster.

Next to the Bloody Tower is the **Wakefield Tower,** a ponderous circular structure built in the 13th century. Originally it contained the king's private apartments. Henry VI was allegedly murdered here in 1471, another of the many victims of the Wars of the Roses, England's bloody medieval civil war.

Once inside the inner wall, or ward, you are faced by the great bulk of the **White Tower.** The first things you might notice are the somewhat sinister-looking ravens, long a feature of the Tower. Legend has it that the disappearance of the ravens will signal the disintegration of the kingdom. Though picturesque, the birds are not exactly friendly; they have been known to attack visitors, so be on your guard.

Running the length of the inner ward on the east side is a series of buildings dating from the 17th, 18th, and 19th centuries. These are the **New Armouries,** the **Old Hospital,** and the **Museum of the Royal Fusiliers.** The north side is occupied by the gloomy 19th-century bulk of the **Waterloo Barracks.** These house the **Oriental Gallery** (mentioned above) and the **Heralds Museum,** the latter open only between April and September.

By far the most famous exhibit here—for many people the principal attraction in the whole Tower—is the Crown Jewels, a priceless and breathtakingly beautiful collection of regalia, precious stones, gold, and silver, all housed in the high-security buildings known as the **Jewel House.** Perhaps the most startling exhibits are the Royal Scepter, containing the largest cut diamond in the world, weighing in at no less than 530 carats, and the Imperial State Crown, made for the coronation of Queen Victoria in 1838 and containing some 3,000 precious stones, mainly diamonds and pearls, including the second-largest cut diamond in the world. Like that in the Royal Scepter, it was cut from the Cullinan diamond—the Star of Africa. Almost as extraordinary is the immense Koh-i-noor diamond, set in the crown made for the coronation of Queen Elizabeth (now the Queen Mother) in 1937.

Stories of attempts to steal the Crown Jewels abound. The bulk of them are 19th-century fictions, but one at least is true, though considerable mystery surrounds it. In 1671 Colonel Thomas Blood managed to get as far as the wharf with the jewels before he was apprehended. His punishment was remarkably mild, taking the form of a Royal Pension. This led to speculation that King Charles II, short of ready cash as usual, was behind the plot.

To the west of the Waterloo Barracks is the little chapel of **St. Peter ad Vincula,** which can be visited only as part of a Yeoman Warder tour. This is the third church on the site, and, though it dates from the 16th century, it has been extensively altered. St. Peter ad Vincula is the resting place of the many people who were executed at the Tower. A plaque on the rear wall details many of the more celebrated. Being "traitors," however, they were not accorded normal burial, and their corpses were simply dumped under the flagstones. In all, some 2,000 bodies are thought to have been buried here.

Directly outside the chapel is **Tower Green,** used both as an overflow burial ground when it eventually became impossible to accommodate more corpses in the chapel, and as the site of the very small number of private executions that were carried out at the Tower. A small bronze tablet marks the spot where the block is believed to have been positioned. It was a rare honor to be granted the privilege of a private execution on Tower Green. Most people were unceremoniously executed outside the Tower on nearby Tower Hill: Apart from anything else, it afforded a much better view for the thousands who regularly flocked to the executions.

To the west of Tower Green is the **Beauchamp Tower,** built by Edward I (reigned 1272–1307). Constructed essentially as just another defensive tower, it quickly came to house prisoners of importance, and here as much as anywhere in the Tower the sense of the centuries unfolding is most vivid. The walls are liberally strewn with graffiti and inscriptions carved by prisoners. Many are in Latin, but there are also names—including one that has traditionally been assumed to refer to Lady Jane Grey, England's "nine-day Queen," executed in the Tower in 1554.

Immediately to the south of the Beauchamp Tower is an L-shaped row of black-and-white Tudor houses. The center one is known as the **Queen's House,** and was built in 1530 for the governor of the Tower. By tradition, Anne Boleyn was imprisoned here before her execution, and it was here that the conspirators of the 1605 Gunpowder Plot to blow up Parliament were interrogated.

An excellent overview of the Tower can now be had from the battlements. A walk along the walls of the inner ward, beginning at the **Wakefield Tower** and taking in many of the defensive towers, provides a fitting climax to a visit to the Tower of London. *H.M. Tower of London, tel. 01/709–0765. Admission £4.50 adults, £2 children under 16, £3 senior citizens; reduced admission charges apply during Feb. when the Jewel House is closed. Small additional admission charge to the Fusiliers Museum only. Open Mar.–Oct., Mon.–Sat. 9:30–5:45, Sun. 2–5:45; Nov.–Feb., Mon.–Sat. 9:30–4:30. Closed Good Fri.*

Yeoman Warder guides daily from Middle Tower, no charge, but a tip is always appreciated. Subject to weather and availability of guides, about every 30 minutes until 3:30 in summer, 2:30 in winter.

㉗ From riverside walk in front of the Tower; there is a good view across to *H.M.S. Belfast* and the new building developments along the south bank of the Thames (*see* The South Bank).

Tower Bridge and St. Katharine's Dock

㉘ **Tower Bridge,** just to the east of the Tower of London, is relatively young, having been begun in 1885 and opened with due pomp and ceremony nine years later by the then Prince of Wales, the late Edward VII. It's unusual among London's bridges in that it is the only bridge that can be raised to allow ships to pass. Today, of course, with the virtual extinction of trade and ship movements on the Thames in London, the complex lifting mechanism is rarely used, and then generally only on ceremonial occasions (the visit of a warship or the tall sailing ships, for example). The bridge is also one of only a handful

over the Thames built in the Gothic style. This was done principally to ensure that it harmonized with the nearby Tower of
London, but it is also the major reason why so many people have
inadvertently assumed that the bridge actually dates from the
Middle Ages, and mistake it for London Bridge.

The upper sections of the bridge are now open to the public.
The tour starts in the North Tower, where an elevator takes
you most of the way to the top. There are exhibitions on the history and engineering design of the bridge, and on the development of London's docklands. Then comes a dramatic trek along
the high-level walkways connecting each side of the bridge,
with superb views up and down the river and across the City.
There are more exhibitions in the South Tower, including a display of photographs taken during the construction of the
bridge. Another elevator ride takes you back to ground level
and the last stage of the visit. This is to the machine room,
where the original machinery—boilers, steam and hydraulic
engines, pumps and accumulators—are all beautifully preserved in full working order; a video explains the operation of
the bridge. *Tower Bridge, tel. 01/403–5386 or 01/403–3761. Admission £2 adults, £1 children under 16 and senior citizens.
Open Apr.–Oct., daily 10–6:30; Nov.–Mar., daily 10–4:45.
Closed Good Fri.*

㉙ To the east of the Tower is **St. Katharine's Dock.** The best route
from the Tower is along the wharf, underneath Tower Bridge
and then along the path in front of the Tower Hotel. The Dock
was opened in 1828, but was never very successful, partly because, as you can still see today, the entrance from the river
was too small to accommodate large ships. The Dock closed in
1968, and after a lot of controversy the site was redeveloped;
sadly most of the handsome warehouses that once lined the
dockside were demolished and replaced with a combination of
modern shops, offices, flats, and a large hotel; the docks themselves are used as a marina. Compared with the new developments currently springing up along each bank of the Thames
on the sites of former docks further east, St. Katharine's seems
ragged around the edges these days.

The South Bank

Southwark, which lies on the south bank of the Thames immediately opposite the Tower of London and St. Paul's Cathedral,
is London's oldest suburb. It is almost as old as London itself,
for a settlement grew up here as soon as the Romans built the
first London Bridge. Being outside the City proper and not
subject to its regulations, the area acquired a name for easy living. In the Middle Ages, Londoners used to come across the
river to enjoy a night in one of the many inns—Southwark was
famous for its good, strong beer—or to sample the pleasures of
the Southwark "stews" (not casseroles, but brothels!). Bear-
baiting and the theater were other forms of entertainment
available on the south bank. The Globe, where Shakespeare
was both actor and shareholder, and where many of his plays
were staged, was one of several playhouses that flourished here
in the first half of the 17th century.

Despite its lively history, the South Bank, with the exception
of the arts complex upstream (west), has until recently hardly

been worth recommending to visitors. Southwark suffered heavy bombing in World War II, and then experienced a general economic decline as port activity moved downstream away from the center of London. For 30 years or more, nobody did anything to improve the area, and its 19th-century warehouses, narrow streets, and alleyways, with their commanding views across the Thames, became increasingly run down and neglected.

All this has altered dramatically since 1983, once both the local authorities and the real estate developers belatedly realized the value of this tract of near-derelict waterfront. Now several mammoth new developments are already complete, others are under construction, and yet more are in the design stages.

Butler's Wharf to Old St. Thomas's

❶ The route starts at the south end of **Tower Bridge,** just a few minutes' walk from the Tower of London and at the exact end of the tour around Tower Bridge. If you are walking across the bridge, take the steps that descend to the riverside as soon as the bridge reaches the south bank of the river and walk downstream, or east, away from the Tower. (It's at this point that we should apologize for any possible imprecision in the description of this route; given the rate at which new buildings and roads are being created in this part of London, it's impossible to be absolutely up to date.) The development ahead of you is
❷ known as **Butler's Wharf.** When completed, it will contain attractive speciality shops, restaurants, and bars, as well as the Design Museum, riverside apartments, a university hall of residence, and substantial office space. Butler's Wharf was formerly a large warehouse, and until 1982 there was also a brewery here; the brewery tower has been incorporated into the new development.

The displays at the **Design Museum,** due to open in mid-1989 and claiming to be the first of its kind in the world, will focus on the history and current evolution of mass-produced goods and services: everything from furniture to cars, perfume to packaging, clothing to electrical equipment. Films, sound recordings, posters, and other advertising material will be used to put the exhibits in their contemporary social and cultural context. As well as the main museum, the **Boilerhouse** will show temporary thematic exhibitions; a third exhibition space, known as the **Design Review,** will stage quickly-changing "shop window" displays of the latest design ideas. There will also be regular lectures and films and a riverside café with panoramic views. *Butler's Wharf, London, tel: 01/403–6933. Probable admission £1.80 £1.80 adults, £1.20 children and senior citizens. Probable opening times Tues.–Sun. 11–6:30 (later on some nights). Telephone for up-to-date information.*

Now retrace your steps to Tower Bridge and then continue up-
❸ stream to *H.M.S. Belfast,* either along the river or inland along **Tooley Street** and then right along Morgans Lane. The *Belfast,* which can also be reached by a ferryboat service from the Tower of London, was the largest and among the most powerful cruisers ever built for the British Royal Navy. She was present off Normandy on D-Day, when Allied troops launched the long-awaited second front against the Germans, and after the war she served in the Far East. When her active career ended in

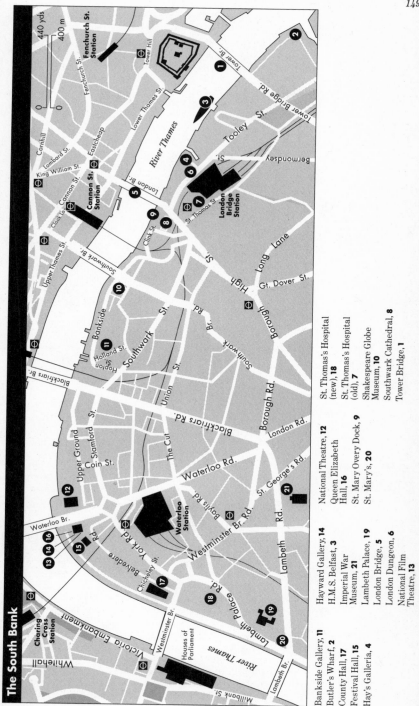

The South Bank

440 yds

400 m

Bankside Gallery, **11**
Butler's Wharf, **2**
County Hall, **17**
Festival Hall, **15**
Hay's Galleria, **4**

Hayward Gallery, **14**
H.M.S. Belfast, **3**
Imperial War
Museum, **21**
Lambeth Palace, **19**
London Bridge, **5**
London Dungeon, **6**
National Film
Theatre, **13**

National Theatre, **12**
Queen Elizabeth
Hall, **16**
St. Mary Overy Dock, **9**
St. Mary's, **20**

St. Thomas's Hospital
(new), **18**
St. Thomas's Hospital
(old), **7**
Shakespeare Globe
Museum, **10**
Southwark Cathedral, **8**
Tower Bridge, **1**

1963 she was destined for the scrapyard but was saved through the efforts of the Imperial War Museum.

Visiting the *Belfast* can take up to two hours. As well as the mess decks, punishment cells, and operations room, the tour includes the engine room with its massive, gleaming boilers and the armaments. *Symon's Wharf, Vine La., Tooley St., tel. 01/407–6434. Admission £3 adults, £1.50 children under 16 and senior citizens. Open mid-Mar.–mid–Oct. daily 11–5:30; mid-Oct.–mid–Mar. daily 11–4:30; closed Good Fri.*

④ From the *Belfast*, it is a short walk along the river to **Hay's Galleria.** The galleria, which opened in the late summer of 1987, is the public face, as it were, of a massive new office development known as **London Bridge City,** which runs from here to London Bridge. Beneath a spectacular 100-foot-high, 300-foot-long glass barrel-vault roof are grouped specialty shops and a few restaurants and pubs. The developers are obviously hoping to create a second Covent Garden by the Thames, with snack-food stalls and street entertainment. It's a little too soon to comment on how well the galleria works—it hasn't yet had time to evolve its own particular atmosphere and so far the shops aren't as wide-ranging as those in Covent Garden—but there is no denying the drama of the building. In the center is a massive kinetic sculpture, *Navigators*, created by David Kemp, embodying a telescope and quadrant, paddlewheel flanges, and a massive bronze fish-head. These objects recall the three centuries of history of Hay's Wharf, the oldest wharf in the port of London, dating back to 1651.

Time Out Reasonably priced lunch spots are disappointingly thin in the galleria. The best bet is **The Horniman at Hay's,** which serves reasonable pub food. Alternatively, you can eat a take-away snack on one of the benches overlooking the river and enjoy the view across to the Custom House.

Walking westward from the galleria, follow the riverside path that runs in front of the Cottons building—the offices are wrapped around a 100-foot-high atrium, decked out with a lush water garden. Next comes the London Bridge Hospital, and then No. 1 London Bridge, with its twin towers clad in polished **⑤** granite. Steps take you up onto **London Bridge** itself—take care, this must be one of the windiest spots in London.

The far, or land, side of Hay's Galleria could hardly be a greater contrast to all this high-tech, high-cost architecture. **Tooley Street** is a busy, battered highway that looks as if it has been untended for decades. It is, however, home to two unusual attractions, both calculated to appeal to children. **Space Adventure** was due to open in mid-1988, shortly after this book went to press; it promised a "multi-sensory electronic extravaganza," allowing "the traveler to experience all the thrills of countdown and launch, G-forces, interplanetary travel, re-entry, and landing." *64–66 Tooley St., tel. 01/403–7417. Admission £3.50 adults, £2 children under 15 and senior citizens. Open daily 10–6; winter closing time will probably be earlier.*

⑥ A few doors along is the **London Dungeon,** which is devoted to recreating, as vividly and as scarifyingly as possible, scenes of medieval torture and execution, disease and persecution; there is also a realistic recreation of the Great Fire of London of 1666. The dungeon is one of London's most popular tourist spots—

there are usually long lines to get in. It's not somewhere to go if you are squeamish, or sensitive to cruelty and horror. Teenagers love it! *28–34 Tooley St., tel. 01/403–0606. Admission £3.50 adults, £2 children under 14 and senior citizens. Open Apr.–Sept. daily 10–5:30, Oct.–Mar. daily 10–4:30.*

If you make your way from the dungeon along Joiner Street, under the railway viaduct (the line, incidentally, was London's first railway, constructed in 1836) and then turn right in **St. Thomas Street,** you will reach, on your right, a short row of elegant houses. This is all that remains of the old **St. Thomas's Hospital,** which occupied this site from the early 13th until the mid-19th centuries. St. Thomas's moved to its present site upstream in Lambeth (*see below*) when its site was needed to extend the railway. Virtually all the hospital buildings were demolished—except for a single operating theater for female patients, opened in 1821. Being in a loft, it was simply blocked off and then forgotten for more than a century. It has now been restored to its original state—and what a state that was! The surgeon worked in an apron stained with blood, washing facilities scarcely existed, and operations were watched by medical students who crowded onto benches around the operating table. Most gruesome of all is the sawdust box underneath the table, which caught blood as it flowed from the patient; when it was full, the surgeon called for "more sawdust." Next door the herb garret, where medicinal herbs were dried and stored, has also been restored. This is one of London's less well-known museums, but it throws more light on what life was *really* like than only more popular attractions. *St. Thomas St., tel. 01/739–2372. Admission £1 adults, 50p children and senior citizens. Open Mon.–Sat. 10–6, Sun. 2–6.*

Southwark Cathedral to Coin Street

On the far side of London Bridge stands **Southwark Cathedral,** the largest Gothic church in London after Westminster Abbey; it is also the earliest, as building began in 1220. This is the fourth church on this site; all its predecessors were destroyed by fire. The first dated from as early as the 7th century. The chief feature of interest for American visitors is the Harvard Chapel, which commemorates John Harvard, founder of Harvard University, who was baptized here in 1608. Shakespeare's younger brother Edmund is buried here, as are the Elizabethan dramatists John Fletcher and Philip Massinger. Look for the funny faces carved on the bosses, which were removed from the roof of the nave and are on display.

The churchyard is a pleasant place to eat a lunchtime sandwich on a sunny day, as many local office-workers do. You'll also catch the smells from **Borough Market,** a small early morning wholesale fruit and vegetable market held underneath the railway viaduct.

Around the corner is another massive new office development, **St. Mary Overy Dock.** There has always been a wharf here, and the maritime connection is maintained by the *Kathleen & May,* the last surviving wooden three-masted topsail schooner, permanently moored in an enclosed dock here. Hundreds of ships like the *Kathleen & May* plied the coasts of Britain in the early part of this century, carrying coal, cement, pit-props, even gunpowder, from port to port. On board, there is an exhibition on the history of Britain's coasting trade under sail and, particularly interesting, a rare film of the *Kathleen & May* herself. *St. Mary Overy Dock, tel. 01/403–3965. Admission £1 adults, 50p children under 14 and senior citizens. Open Mon.–Fri. 10–5, Sat. and Sun. 11–4.*

Alongside the innkeepers, prisoners, and ladies of easy virtue, bishops also lived in medieval Southwark. A number of provincial bishops built grand London palaces along the riverbank. The massive west wall of the great hall of the Palace of the Bishops of Winchester has been incorporated into the new development; you can see the outline of a once-lovely rose window.

Time Out **The Old Thameside Inn,** just by the *Kathleen & May,* serves morning coffee and pastries, lunches, and old-fashioned high tea. Around the corner in Cathedral Street, an unremarkable entrance, distinguished only by a small sign saying **Dining Room,** leads down to a pleasant basement vegetarian restaurant, open Tuesday–Friday.

Now walk west along **Clink Street,** where one of Southwark's several prisons stood, past the Bankside Pub and under Cannon Street Railway Bridge and Southwark Bridge. There are good views across to the north bank and St. Paul's Cathedral. On the left, a narrow street called Bear Gardens leads to the ⑩ **Shakespeare Globe Museum,** the advance guard of a massive project that the American actor and film director Sam Wanamaker has been nursing for more than two decades. His aim—and it is now at long last being realized—is to rebuild Shakespeare's Globe Playhouse to its original open-roof design of 1599, using, as far as possible, authentic Elizabethan materials and craft techniques. A second, entirely new theater will also be built. Called the Inigo Jones Theatre, this is a small indoor theater designed by the 17th-century architect for masques and other courtly entertainments but never built at that time. The new theaters are scheduled to open in the early 1990s, so for the moment there is little to see. However, the museum fills in the background—if in a rather academic way—to what 300 years ago was a lively and exuberant center of theatrical activity. *Bear Gdns., tel. 01/602–0202 or 01/925–6342. Admission £1 adults, 50p children and senior citizens. Open Apr.–Sept. Mon.–Fri. 10–5, Sat. 10–5:30, Sun. 2–6. Telephone in advance to check winter opening times.*

Continue to follow the river upstream, past **Cardinal's Wharf,** where Christopher Wren lived while St. Paul's Cathedral was being built, and along **Bankside,** past Bankside Power Station, ⑪ now no longer in use. The **Bankside Gallery** is the headquarters of two celebrated artistic societies, the Royal Society of Painter-Etchers and Engravers, and the Royal Society of Painters in Water-Colour. There is a small regular exhibition, and changing displays of members' work. *48 Hopton St., tel. 01/928 –7521. Admission varies according to exhibition. Open Tues.–Sat. 10–5, Sun. 2–6; closed bank holidays.*

Descend the steps on the far side of **Blackfriars Bridge** and follow the path along the front of the Sea Containers building and past the **Oxo Tower,** another London landmark whose future is in doubt at the time of writing. The pub on the bridge, **Doggetts,** is named after Doggetts Coat and Badge Race, an annual rowing contest over four-and-a-half miles along the

Thames that is said to be the oldest annual event in British sport; it was founded by Thomas Doggett, a comic actor who left money for the prizes on his death in 1721. Beyond the Oxo Tower is yet another building development. But this one is a surprise, for here are several rows of tiny family houses with little gardens, and a small park: the absolute antithesis of the usual high-tech, yuppy-oriented, high-price developments elsewhere in London. **Coin Street,** as this small area is called, is the happy result of a long, local campaign to prevent the site from falling into the hands of commercial developers who would, inevitably, have put up a mixture of offices and high-cost dwellings.

The South Bank Arts Complex

A short walk along the recently opened, wide embankment promenade, past the modern headquarters of Thames Television and the IBM building, brings you to the **National Theatre,** the first of the many concrete bunker-style buildings that make up the South Bank Arts Complex. Although the first proposals were made in 1907 and a foundation stone was laid in 1951, the National Theatre Company was not formed until 1962 and only moved to its present purpose-built home in 1976. The building is open all day and evening, six days a week, to everyone, not just to playgoers. The foyers are intricately varied, full of character (though their very intricacy can be confusing to the first-time visitor), and *very* busy, with several bars and snack counters, a bookshop, and exhibitions. There are three auditoriums —the **Olivier,** a cavernous open stage, partly in the round; the **Lyttleton,** with a traditional proscenium arch; and the **Cottesloe,** where studio productions are staged. As plays are performed on a repertory system, there is always a wide choice of productions to see. Try to catch a performance here; some of the nation's best actors work at the National, and, although the company is sometimes uneven, its best work can be electrifying. *South Bank, tel. 01/928–2252 (box office); 01/928–8126 (recorded information); 01/928–033 (administration). 1½-hour tours of the theater, normally five times daily between 10:15 and 6; £2.50 adults, £1.75 children and senior citizens. Open Mon.–Sat. 10 AM–11 PM.*

Time Out The coffee bars, lunch spots, and bars of the National Theatre are ideal places to rest and relax at any time of the day; there's at least one open throughout the day, and you don't have to have tickets for a performance.

Immediately west of the National, directly underneath Waterloo Bridge, is the **National Film Theatre** (N.F.T.) and the new **Museum of the Moving Image** (M.O.M.I.). The N.F.T.'s two auditoriums present a staggering number of films, mainly drawn from its huge archives. If you are interested in the art of the cinema, it is well worth getting a temporary membership. M.O.M.I. is a brand-new museum (due to open in fall 1988, after this guide went to press). It celebrates every aspect of the art and techniques of the moving image, from Chinese shadow plays of 2500 BC to the latest fiber optics and satellite images, but concentrating, of course, on cinema and television. The emphasis is on participation, with visitors taking part in film- and television-making processes in a Moving Image Workshop; costumes, equipment, and other movie artifacts are on display.

South Bank, tel. 01/928–3535. Admission £3.25 adults, £2.50 people under 20 and senior citizens. Open Tues.–Sat. 10–8, Sun. 10–6; last admission 1½ hours before closing time. Closed bank holidays.

Time Out The N.F.T. restaurant and cafeteria is a popular place for lunch or an evening meal—and you don't have to be a member to use it. The salad bar, where you can help yourself to as much as you can cram onto your plate, is especially good value.

⑭ The rest of the arts complex, on the far (west) side of Waterloo Bridge, consists of the **Hayward Gallery,** where temporary large-scale exhibitions of art are staged, and three concert halls. The gallery is surmounted by a tall, skeletal sculpture made of neon tubing. At night hectic colors run up and down this erection, their speed and intensity governed by the velocity of the wind playing through an anemometer at the top. *Belvedere Rd., tel. 01/928–3144 or 01/261–0127 (recorded information). Admission varies according to exhibition. Open Mon.–Wed. 10–8, Thurs.–Sat. 10–6, Sun. 12–6; closed Good Fri., May Day.*

⑮ The largest of the three concert halls is the **Royal Festival Hall,** which is used principally for symphony concerts, ballet performances, and other large scale musical entertainments. It has to be said that neither the auditorium nor the foyers at the Festival Hall are as exciting as those of the National Theatre. Still, there is now a well-stocked bookshop, a disc store, and exhibition space.

Time Out The Royal Festival Hall's eating places include a salt beef bar, a pasta counter, a salad bar, and a coffee shop, as well as a more conventional cafeteria.

⑯ The other two concert halls occupy a separate building, close to the Hayward Gallery. The **Queen Elizabeth Hall** is a medium-size auditorium, generally used for chamber concerts and choral performances, while the program of the small **Purcell Room** consists largely of chamber and solo recitals, experimental works, and lectures.

Westminster Bridge to the Imperial War Museum

The next stretch of the embankment offers highly photogenic views across the river to Big Ben and the Houses of Parliament. Before reaching **Westminster Bridge,** the path runs in front of **⑰ County Hall.** This mammoth building was formerly the seat of the local government of Greater London (the Greater London Council, or G.L.C.), basically the whole of London excluding the City. After considerable controversy, the G.L.C. was abolished in 1986, and the building's future remains undecided, with proposals ranging from making it a hotel to turning it into commercial offices. The chill, classical facade facing the river was built in 1932.

⑱ The river frontage on the far side of Westminster Bridge is occupied by **St. Thomas's Hospital,** which moved here from Southwark in the mid-19th century. St. Thomas's is one of London's several major "teaching hospitals," which means that medical students do their training here. Severe bomb damage in the war left few of the older buildings intact, and much of the hospital today is brand new. At the time of writing, plans were well under way for the creation of a **Florence Nightingale Museum** in the hospital, which is scheduled to open during 1989. The museum will contain displays on Florence Nightingale's life and work. Although she is best known for her work during the Crimean War (1854–56), she spent another 20 years campaigning for better living and health conditions for the army. The museum will also feature the evolution of modern nursing techniques. The centerpiece of the museum will be a reconstruction of the barrack ward in Scutari where wounded soldiers from the Crimean battlefield were nursed. *Lambeth Palace Rd., tel. 01/928–9292, ext. 3124. Telephone for details of opening times and admission charges.*

⑲ Beyond St. Thomas's, for the most part hidden behind high walls, stands **Lambeth Palace,** which for centuries has played an integral, though little-known, part in London's history. The building has been the London residence of the Archbishop of Canterbury, the senior archbishop of the Church of England since the early 13th century, and remains so still. It is rarely open to the public; the fine Tudor gatehouse can be admired, however, from outside. The building has had an eventful history; it was overrun during the 1381 "Peasants' Revolt" against the hated poll tax, three years after John Wycliffe, the reformer and translator of the Bible, was tried for heresy in the chapel; Archbishop Cranmer wrote the English Prayer Book here (1549); and for centuries the building was the scene of power struggles between the secular and religious arms of government.

⑳ Next to the palace is **St. Mary's,** a former church (it was deconsecrated in 1972) with a long history. Captain Bligh of *Bounty* fame lies buried in the churchyard. St. Mary's Church now houses the Tradescant Trust's **Museum of Garden History.** This is another of London's specialist museums, and its enthusiastic supporters have worked hard to build up a unique collection, including a replica of a 17th-century knot garden containing only period plants, especially those grown by the Tradescants. The garden is a hidden haven only a few yards from the everyday bustle and roar of contemporary London life. *St. Mary-at-Lambeth, Lambeth Palace Rd., tel. 01/261–1891. Admission free. Open early Mar.– early Dec. Mon.–Fri. 11–3, Sun. 10:30–5; closed early Dec.–early Mar.*

㉑ This walk along the Thames, London's oldest highway, ends here, at the south side of Lambeth Bridge. There is, however, one additional attraction worth mentioning, though its subject matter may not be to everyone's taste. The **Imperial War Museum** is only a short walk down Lambeth Road. This major museum of warfare concentrates on the two world wars, with equipment, photographs, medals, paintings, and other memorabilia of the British and Commonwealth armed forces. Among the hardware on display are a World War I tank, a Battle of Britain Spitfire, a midget submarine, and a VI Flying Bomb. While many of the displays concentrate on the story of particular campaigns and battles, the social side of war—what life was like for the soldiers and for the families they left at home— is not neglected. The museum also holds a fine collection of often very moving paintings by Britain's official war artists, and countless documents and relics, including the Surrender Document signed by the Argentinians at the conclusion of the Falklands campaign in 1982. A major redevelopment program got under way during 1988 to improve the museum's ramshackle display areas, and work may be continuing during 1989. When complete it will allow more of the museum's collection to be shown in a much more up-to-date manner. *Lambeth Rd., tel. 01/735–8922 or 01/582–2525. Admission charges are being introduced in 1989; rates not available at press time. Open Mon.– Sat. 10–5:50, Sun. 2–5:50.*

Greenwich

Greenwich, some seven or eight miles downstream (that is, east, toward the sea) from central London, provides the perfect day out. The attractions here range from the old Royal Observatory, where Greenwich Mean Time was born, to the magnificence of *Cutty Sark*, proudest of the great clipper ships that plied between the China Seas and Britain. In fact, Greenwich's principal raison d'être is maritime. It is the site of the Royal Naval College—the most splendid complex of Baroque buildings in England—and of the National Maritime Museum. There's also a large, rambling park here, ideal for a summer day's stroll and picnic, and rich in history.

By far the most dramatic approach to Greenwich is by boat from Westminster Pier or Tower Bridge. The river scene as you pass by the former docks, now being rapidly developed with offices and expensive apartment blocks, is fascinating; but most compelling of all is the view as you round a bend in the river and see, spread out in front of you, the imposing vista of the Royal Naval College, with the park behind. The river trip from Westminster Pier takes about 45 minutes; from the Tower of London, about 25 minutes. *Details of times and other information can be obtained from the London Tourist Board's recorded riverboat information service, tel. 01/730–4812.* During 1989, Thames Line, which runs high-speed riverbuses between Chelsea and east of Tower Bridge, will be extending its service to Greenwich. Greenwich is also just 10 minutes from central London by overground Network SouthEast train from Charing Cross. This route is London's oldest railway line— which makes a neat contrast with the newest way of getting to Greenwich, via the Docklands Light Railway, the elevated railway opened in 1987 that runs north of the river through Docklands. The London terminus is at Tower Gateway, close to the Tower of London and just a couple of minutes' walk from Tower Hill Underground station. One branch of the Light Railway terminates at Island Gardens, on the north bank of the Thames immediately opposite Greenwich. In the gardens, a modest domed building conceals the entrance to a pedestrian tunnel under the river, which brings you out close to the *Cutty Sark (see below)* on the Greenwich side. The tunnel itself is only a few hundred yards long, and you can descend and ascend again in a marvelously old-fashioned elevator.

❶ The heart of Greenwich is the buildings of the **Royal Naval College,** started in 1694 as a home, or "hospital," for old sailors and which, in 1873, became the Royal Naval College. They are the work of Wren and his two assistants, Hawksmoor and Vanbrugh, and embody all that is most heroic and dynamic in Baroque architecture. Huge, stately, and splendid, the buildings more than repay close inspection. Be sure to visit the **❷** **Painted Hall,** the College's dining hall, probably the best, and certainly the most complete, illusionistic decorative scheme in

England. It was painted by Sir James Thornhill (1675–1734)
3 between 1707 and 1717. In the opposite block is the **College
Chapel,** whose interior dates from the end of the 18th century
and is correspondingly more restrained, though no less attractive than its noble neighbor. At Christmas 1805, Nelson's body
lay in state here, following the battle of Trafalgar. Occasional
concerts are held in the chapel, which is one of the most splendid places to hear music in London.

At the south end of the Naval College, and framed by Wren's
4 buildings, is the **Queen's House,** diminutive in comparison. It
was built by Inigo Jones from 1616 for Henrietta Maria, wife of
Charles I. Though simple in the extreme—no more really than
an elegant classical rectangle—it is usually cited as the first
genuinely classical building in England; that is, the first building that used the lessons of Italian Renaissance architecture. It
is difficult to overestimate its significance in the history of English architecture. Nowadays the Queen's House forms part of
the National Maritime Museum (*see below*), to which it is linked
by an elegant arcade. Extensive repairs and restoration work
are currently in progress, and the building is unlikely to be reopened to the public before late 1989. *Royal Naval College,
King William Walk, tel. 01/858–2154. Admission free. Open
daily except Thurs. 2:30–4:45.*

5 The **National Maritime Museum** is a must for anyone with salt
in the veins. It's a treasure house of paintings, models, maps,
globes, sextants, uniforms, and relics of old sea dogs, all chart-
ing Britain's illustrious maritime heritage. A good place to
begin a visit might be the **New Neptune Hall,** where the *Reli-
ant,* a paddle tug launched in 1907, has been preserved. Other
highlights of the museum include the ornate royal barges, used
by the Royal Family and senior Admiralty officials to visit the
former Royal Dockyards in the Greenwich area, and a sophisticated slide presentation called *The Way of a Ship,* which
explains just how a sailing vessel works. *Romney Rd., tel. 01/
858–4422. Joint admission with Royal Observatory, £2.20
adults, £1.10 children and senior citizens. Open late Mar.–late
Oct. Mon.–Sat. 10–6, Sun. 2–6; late Oct.–late Mar. Mon.–Sat.
10–5; Sun. 2–5; closed Good Fri., May Day.*

Time Out The **Dolphin Coffee Shop** on the museum grounds is a good
place to recuperate after the rigors of the museum; non-
museum visitors are also welcome.

By the riverbank itself are two real ships, each of considerable
6 historical interest. The ***Cutty Sark,*** sole survivor of the great
fleets of clipper ships that raced to all corners of the globe in the
19th century, was moved to Greenwich in the 1950s and placed
in dry dock here. It's possible to explore almost the entire ship;
visitors can see the holds, where 5,000 bales of wool were
stowed for the trip from Australia to England, and the cramped
quarters of the crew. The officers, by contrast, did rather better, with some quite elegant accommodations, and even a coal
fire. *King William Walk, tel. 01/858–3445. Admission £1.30
adults, 70p children under 16 and senior citizens. Open late
Mar.–late Oct. Mon.–Sat. 10–5:30, Sun. 12–5:30; late Oct.–
late Mar. Mon.–Sat. 10–4:30, Sun. 12–4:30.*

7 Beside the *Cutty Sark* is the very much smaller ***Gipsy Moth IV***
in which Sir Francis Chichester sailed single-handed around

Greenwich

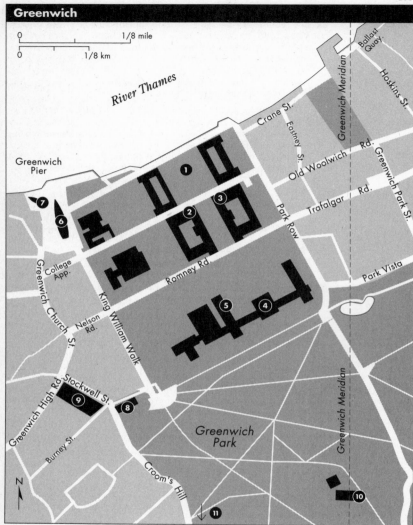

0 — 1/8 mile
0 — 1/8 km

River Thames

Greenwich Pier

Crane St.

Eastney St.

Old Woolwich Rd.

Greenwich Meridian

Hoskins St.

Ballast Quay.

Greenwich Park St.

Park Row

Trafalgar Rd.

Park Vista

Romney Rd.

College App.

Greenwich Church St.

Nelson Rd.

King William Walk

Greenwich High Rd.

Stockwell St.

Burney St.

Croom's Hill

Greenwich Park

Greenwich Meridian

N

College Chapel, **3**
Cutty Sark, **6**
Fan Museum, **9**
Gipsy Moth IV, **7**
Greenwich Theatre, **8**
National Maritime
Museum, **5**

Old Royal
Observatory, **10**
Painted Hall, **2**
Queen's House, **4**
Ranger's House, **11**
Royal Naval College, **1**

the world in 1966. Inside you can admire the ingenious way all the equipment Chichester needed was packed into a tight space, along with some equally needed luxuries. *King William Walk, tel. 01/853-3589. Admission 20p adults, 10p children and senior citizens. Open Apr.-Oct. Mon.-Sat. 10-6, Sun. 12-6; closed Nov.-Mar.*

There are some attractive shops in the center of Greenwich; books and antiques one speciality, crafts another. A craft market is held every Saturday and Sunday from 10 to 5 in the attractive Victorian **covered market,** only a few steps away from *Cutty Sark.* Here you can browse and have the additional pleasure of buying something from its creator. There's also a well-known open-air **antiques and bric-a-brac market** at the corner of Greenwich High Road and Crooms Hill, just beyond St Alfege's Church, on most Saturday and Sunday mornings.

8 The **Greenwich Theatre** at the foot of Crooms Hill is a lively modern theater built on the site of a Victorian music hall. A wide selection of plays are performed, often with notable West End stars, and an evening here is a pleasant way of rounding off a day spent exploring Greenwich. *Tel. 01/858-7755 or 01/858-3800 for reservations.*

Time Out   The **Theatre Restaurant** serves good food, and is specially well known for its salad bar. You can eat here at lunchtime, or before or after a show.

9 Immediately opposite the theater, in two newly restored houses dating from the 1820s, is the **Fan Museum.** This museum, due to open in the late summer of 1989, is the only one in the world devoted solely to fans. The displays, which will draw on a collection of over 2,000 items, will focus on the history and manufacture of fans; a workshop and study center are being established. *10-12 Crooms Hill, tel. 01/305-1441 or 01/858-9540. Telephone for information about opening times and admission.*

10 Now head up the hill in **Greenwich Park** that overlooks the Naval College and the Maritime Museum to the **Old Royal Observatory.** It was founded in 1675, though most of the buildings date from a slightly later period and are the work of the ubiquitous Wren. The functions of the observatory were moved to Sussex after World War II when the smoke-laden atmosphere of London made astronomical observations too difficult. However, many original telescopes and other instruments have been retained and are imaginatively displayed, especially in Wren's elegant Octagon Room. And the prime meridian—the zero longitude—still runs through the courtyard of the observatory; you can stand straddling the line, with one foot in each hemisphere. And if you're here in the middle of the day, remember to check your watch at exactly one o'clock, when the red ball on the observatory roof, known as the Greenwich time ball, drops as a signal to river traffic; when it was erected in 1833, this was the first visual time signal in the world. *Greenwich Park, tel. 01/858-4422. Joint admission with National Maritime Museum, £2.20 adults, £1.10 children and senior citizens. Open Apr.-Oct. Mon.-Sat. 10-6, Sun. 2-6; Nov.-Mar. Mon.-Sat. 10-5, Sun. 2-5; closed Good Fri.*

The **park** itself is one of London's oldest Royal Parks, and had been in existence for well over 200 years before Charles II commissioned the French landscape artist Le Nôtre to redesign it in what was, in the 1660s, the latest French fashion. The Flower Garden, on the southeast side of the park, and the deer enclosure nearby are both attractive. Look also for **Queen Elizabeth's Oak** on the east side, around which Henry VIII and his second queen, Anne Boleyn, Elizabeth's mother, are said to have danced.

Just outside the park boundaries, on the northwest side, stands the **Ranger's House,** a handsome early 18th-century mansion. The house is so called because during the 19th century it was the official residence of the ranger, or keeper, of Greenwich Park. It now houses a collection of Jacobean portraits and another of early musical instruments; concerts are regularly given here. *Chesterfield Walk, Blackheath, tel. 01/853–0035. Open daily 10–5; closed Good Fri.*

The Thames Upstream

The Thames is Britain's longest river, and for much of its extent, as it winds its way through the Cotswolds, past the "dreaming spires" of Oxford, and majestic Windsor Castle, it is an attractive country river rather than a busy urban waterway, suggesting lazy summer days spent messing around in boats. Traveling west, upstream, from central London, you reach a series of attractive little waterside villages, such as Chiswick and Kew. The word "village" may seem anachronistic, particularly in this part of London where your explorations will be to the roar of aircraft descending to land at Heathrow Airport a few miles further west. But until relatively recently, say the beginning of this century, these were independent settlements, surrounded by fields, and they still retain something of this rural atmosphere, especially where parkland runs down to the riverbank. The royal palaces and grand houses that abound in this area were built as country residences, not town houses, in the days when the river was one of the main means of traveling into London.

The places described below would make, at the very least, a good single day's excursion—though there's so much to visit that it would be better to make two or three trips or, if you can spare only a single day, be selective in what you visit; Kew Gardens, for instance, can claim at least half a day of anyone's time. The area is well served by public transport. The District Line of the Underground runs out to Kew and Richmond, while you can get overground Network SouthEast trains from Waterloo Station to those places and also to Twickenham, Brentford, and Hampton Court. Chiswick House can be reached by tube to Turnham Green, then the E3 bus; or by tube to Hammersmith and the #290 bus.

Of course the obvious, and in many ways the most pleasant, way to travel is on the river itself. There are on average seven boats a day from Westminster Pier (just by Big Ben) to Kew, and three to Richmond and Hampton Court. *For more detailed information call the London Tourist Board's riverboat recorded information service at 01/730–4812 or the operators at 01/930–4721.* But a few words of caution: river travel is slow—it takes 1½ hours to reach Kew from central London, 1½ to three hours to travel to Richmond, and anything up to four to get to Hampton Court. With times like these, the trip itself becomes the principal item on the day's program, rather than the places of interest to see when you get off the boat. In addition, even on a summer's day it can be quite chilly on the water; and, although some stretches of the river are interesting to look at, there are others that can be monotonous.

Chiswick and Kew

Chiswick is the nearest of these Thames-side destinations to London, with Kew just a mile or so beyond it. Much of Chiswick today is a nondescript suburban district, developed at the beginning of this century. But, incongruously stranded among the terraced houses, a number of fine 18th-century houses and a charming little village survive. The chief attraction is **Chiswick House,** built in about 1725 by the earl of Burlington, and surrounded by rambling gardens. Here Burlington entertained his smart friends, the writers Pope, Swift, and Gay, and the composer Handel among them.

The significance of Chiswick House in the history of English architecture is considerable. Burlington—after whom the Burlington Arcade on Piccadilly and Burlington House, home of the Royal Academy, are named—was a connoisseur and patron of brilliance, fascinated above all by the architecture and art of the Italian Renaissance and Ancient Rome. Having completed the obligatory Grand Tour of Italy as a young man, he returned to England determined to import to his own country the lessons he had learned there, above all in the realms of architecture. He set about building for himself what was in essence an Italian villa modeled closely on Palladio's famous villas around Venice. He had the help of William Kent (1685–1748), an architect, interior designer, and landscape artist of genius. Despite its small scale—it's a curiously pokey and cold house—Chiswick House sparked off an enormous interest in Britain in what came to be known as Palladian architecture, and is the direct ancestor of many hundreds of English stately homes both small and large. *Burlington La., tel. 01/995–0508. Admission £1 adults, 50p children under 17, 75p senior citizens. Open Apr.– Sept. daily 9:30–6:30; Oct.–Mar. Mon.–Sat. 9:30–4, Sun. 2–4.*

To one side of Chiswick House is **Hogarth's House,** the 18th-century painter's country retreat, a small, charming house with a pretty garden. Probably more than any other historic building in London, Hogarth's House has been overtaken by the march of time. It stands forlorn between the Great West Road—still, as in Hogarth's time, the principal highway from London to the West Country, though what was then little more than a dusty track is now a six-lane highway—and a modern office building. The painter's ghost no doubt contemplates the ravages of progress from the safety of his tomb (located in the graveyard of St. Nicholas's Church, across the highway in Church Street) with the same skeptical but benign eye that Hogarth brought to his satirical paintings and prints. *Great West Rd., tel. 01/994– 6757. Open Apr.–Sept. Mon. and Wed.–Sat. 11–6, Sun. 2–6; Oct.–Mar. Mon. and Wed.–Sat. 11–4, Sun. 2–4; closed Good Fri., first 2 weeks in Sept., and last 3 weeks in Dec.*

Church Street (reached by an underpass) is the nearest thing to a sleepy country village street in all London, despite its proximity to the Great West Road. Follow it down to the Thames at its foot and turn left. This brings you into **Chiswick Mall,** with a series of sturdy 18th-century houses overlooking the river. The walk along here for a half mile or so is one of the capital's greatest pleasures: calm, serene, and elegant.

Time Out There are several riverside pubs along this stretch of the Thames. One of the most attractive is the **Dove,** a mile or so downstream (toward Hammersmith and central London), close to **Kelmscott House,** where the writer, artist, and craftsman William Morris lived from 1877 to 1896.

A mile or so to the west, a similarly attractive walk can be had along **Strand on the Green,** an 18th-century river frontage that leads to Kew Bridge and the Royal Botanic Gardens at Kew. Here a series of small houses look over the narrow towpath and the river, their tidy brick facades covered with wisteria and roses: a positively bucolic scene.

Time Out Two pubs along the riverbank, the **Bull** and the **City Barge,** are ideal for a summertime drink.

Strand on the Green ends at Kew Bridge. Across the river is **Kew Green**—a trim, grassy open space used by local cricketers (Sunday afternoon cricket is an institution here) and surrounded by fine 18th-century houses, with, in its center, a church where the painters Gainsborough and Zoffany (1733–1810) lie buried.

The village atmosphere of Kew is still quite distinct, helping to make this one of the most desirable areas of outer London. But Kew is known chiefly for the **Royal Botanic Gardens** (Kew Gardens), the country's leading botanical institute, and a public garden covering 300 acres and containing more than 60,000 species of plants. There are strong royal associations here. Until 1840, when Kew Gardens was handed to the nation, it had been the grounds of two royal residences: the White House, or Kew House as it was originally known, and Richmond Lodge, or the Dutch House, further to the west. George II and Queen Caroline lived at Richmond Lodge in the 1720s, while their eldest son Frederick, Prince of Wales, and his wife, Princess Augusta, came to the White House during the 1730s. The royal wives were the keen gardeners. Queen Caroline got to work on her grounds, while next door Frederick's pleasure garden was developed as a botanic garden by his widow after his death. She introduced all kinds of "exotics," foreign plants brought back to England by botanists on the exploration expeditions that were then being sent out all over the world. Caroline had the assistance of a skilled head gardener and of the architect Sir William Chambers, who built a series of pretty temples and follies, as well as, in 1761, the **Chinese Pagoda,** a splendidly eccentric work that can be seen for miles around. Under the unofficial directorship of a celebrated botanist, Sir Joseph Banks (1743–1820), Kew developed rapidly as both a beautiful landscaped garden and an important center of study and research.

George III, who had largely been brought up at Kew, united the two neighboring estates. In 1802, he knocked down the White House, intending to rebuild it on a more lavish scale. While the work progressed, he and his queen lived in the nearby Dutch House. But as George grew progressively mad, the new palace was abandoned, then pulled down. The Dutch House, or **Kew Palace** as it subsequently became known, remains quietly domestic, unlike a royal palace. It has been carefully and evocatively restored; one can easily imagine George III, that most domesticated of all English monarchs, at home here, surrounded by his brood of children. The little formal gardens to its rear were redeveloped in 1969 as a 17th-century garden. These, too, are a pleasure to see, with their trim hedges, statuary, and carefully laid-out plants and flowers. *Tel. 01/940–3321. Admission 80p adults, 40p children under 16 and senior citizens. Open Apr.–Sept. daily 11–5:30.*

To some extent, though, the greatest architectural glories of Kew are its two giant 19th-century greenhouses: the **Palm House** and the **Temperate House.** These were both built in the mid-19th century by Decimus Burton (1800–81)—an architect with a talent for utilizing the then modern building materials of iron and glass—to house the many exotic species the gardens were rapidly accumulating. The Palm House is generally the more celebrated of the pair, with its ornate cast iron supports and gently curving roofs, although both stand as potent reminders of the Victorians' daring engineering and taste. Along the front of the Palm House stand a row of massive heraldic animals, replicas of the Queen's Beasts, created to decorate Westminster Abbey for the coronation of the present Queen in 1952. At present the Palm House is closed while it undergoes a massive restoration program: Reopening is scheduled for 1990. While the Palm House is shut, visit instead the Temperate House; you can climb the spiral staircase to the walkway running just underneath the roof and look down on the mass of foliage and fruits below.

The **Princess of Wales Conservatory** is the latest, and the largest, plant house at Kew, opened in 1987 by the Princess herself. Under its bold glass roofs, designed to maximize energy conservation, there are no less than 10 climatic zones, their temperatures all precisely controlled by computer. Within a few minutes you can move from the humid pool and swamp habitats, where the Amazon waterlily flourishes, to the cloud forest zone, which reproduces the conditions found on the upper reaches of tropical mountains, through to the savannah of eastern Africa.

Due to open in the early summer of 1989 is an exhibition area in the **Centre for Economic Botany** in the newly constructed Joseph Banks Building. The majority of the building will be devoted to Kew's research collection on economic botany and to its library, but the public will be able to enjoy exhibitions on the theme of plants in everyday life; the first will be on cellulose, which is used to make such diverse things as wrapping paper and eyeglass lenses. *Kew Gdns. Admission free. Open Mon.–Sat. 9:10–4:30, Sun. 9:30–5:30.*

Apart from the plant houses, the gardens are a splendid spot to wander and relax, and perhaps to enjoy a picnic. (Kew's catering facilities, traditionally poor, are slowly improving.) The spring flowers make a splendid display; a little later in the year the **Rhododendron Dell** and the **Azalea Garden** are the places to make for, while during the summer the roses and waterlilies are magnificent. In the fall, the heather garden, near the pagoda, is attractive, and the colors, including every shade of brown and gold, are unforgettable. It really is the case that there will be something to see at whatever time of year you come. Unfortunately, the terrible storm of October '87 did maximum damage to the ancient and extremely rare trees of Kew; altogether about 1,000 were destroyed or very badly damaged. *Royal Botanic Gdns., tel. 01/940–1171. Admission 50p. Gardens open at 9:30 daily, glasshouses at 10. Closing times as follows: late Mar.–mid Sept. 6:30 PM (Sun. and bank holidays 8 PM); Mar. and mid-Sept.–late Oct. 6 PM; late Oct.–end Jan. 4 PM.*

Osterley Park

There's an interesting visit to be made to **Osterley,** which can be reached by tube on the Piccadilly Line, five stops before Heathrow Airport; there is a 15-minute walk from the station. Osterley Park is in essence a Tudor house encased within an 18th-century shell; the four corner pepper-pot towers still bear a Tudor stamp, while Robert Adam, in 1760, built a magnificent classical portico, a great ceremonial entryway, on the main front. (The original Tudor stable block stands beside the main house and holds a handy cafeteria.) The interior is probably the best and most complete example of Adam's full-blown style. Adam himself described it as being all "delicacy, gaiety, grace, and beauty," with "fanciful figures and winding foliage." And indeed it is a superb creation, especially the characteristic colored stucco work, immensely complex and ornate. But Adam had the unusual opportunity of planning his interiors as complete wholes—not only would he design the principal features of a room, he would design all the furniture, and often the carpets, as well. The work having taken 20 years or so to complete, Osterley also illustrates well the evolution of Adam's style, from relative simplicity to astonishing elaboration. As with Ham House (*see below*), Osterley is today maintained by the Victoria and Albert Museum. *Isleworth, tel. 01/560–3918. Admission £2 adults, £1 children under 16 and senior citizens. Open Tues.–Sun. and bank holiday Mon. 11–5; closed Good Fri.*

Richmond

Richmond has long been a desirable and attractive suburb, with many fine houses and pretty streets. Much of the reason for its charm lies in its proximity to the Thames, and in the sweeping views over the river from **Richmond Hill,** the latter lined with a series of handsome homes and antiques shops (as well as some less lovely apartment blocks). The hill leads up to **Richmond Park,** 2,470 acres of heathland still roamed by herds of deer. The park originally belonged to Richmond Palace, though it was open land until 1637 when Charles I had it enclosed. By the time of George II, however, the public had been granted access to it, and so it remains today, its ancient oaks the last vestiges of the vast medieval forests that once crowded in on London. Three houses remain in the park, all of them originally royal residences. One, **Pembroke Lodge,** is now a restaurant. **White Lodge,** now the Royal Ballet School, was where Edward VIII was born, and was also the home of the present Queen's parents. The third, **Thatched House Lodge,** is still the property of the Crown, and is the home of Princess Alexandria and her husband Angus Ogilvy.

Time Out **The Cricketers** on Richmond Green serves a good pub lunch and provides morning coffee and afternoon tea in a coffee shop called **Stumps.** Two other pleasant places for a snack are the

Café Mozart in Church Court, an Austrian pâtisserie, and **Mrs. Beetons** on Hill Rise, which serves traditional dishes from the best of British cooking.

Ham House and Marble Hill House

To the west of Richmond Park, overlooking the Thames and nearly opposite the oddly named Eel Pie Island, is **Ham House.** It was rebuilt in the late 17th century by the duke and duchess of Lauderdale, who had the unenviable reputation of being the least loved couple in London. Despite their excessively nasty dispositions—a contemporary called the duchess "the coldest friend and the most violent enemy that ever was known"—they created an exquisite late-Jacobean house, whose superb location is matched only by the sumptuousness of its interior. Rich, heavy furnishings, powerfully carved furniture, period portraits, and great swirling stucco work combine to produce an overwhelming sense of opulence and luxury. Both the interior and the gardens are today largely as they were when the duchess died in 1698, and are now expertly managed by the Victoria and Albert Museum. You can reach Ham from Richmond either by road or by a riverbank walk of half an hour or so; this is one of the most pleasant rural walks in the whole of London. *Ham St., Richmond, tel. 01/940–1950. Admission £2 adults, £1 children under 16 and senior citizens. Open Tues.–Sun. and bank holiday Mon. 11–5; closed Good Fri.*

On the northern bank of the Thames, almost opposite Ham House, stands another mansion, this one an almost perfect example of a Palladian villa. **Marble Hill House** was built in the 1720s by Frederick, Prince of Wales, for his mistress, the "exceedingly respectable and respected" Henrietta Howard. Henrietta lived there happily for the rest of her life. After her death in 1767, many years after Frederick, the house had a variety of owners before falling into disrepair in the late 19th century. It was rescued in 1901, and now its furniture and decorations closely resemble the originals. It is a perfect place to visit for all admirers of 18th-century taste and graciousness. A ferry service operates during the summer from Ham House across the river, after which it is a short walk along the river. By road, access is across Richmond Bridge. *Richmond Rd., Twickenham, tel. 01/892–5115. Admission free. Open Mon.–Thur. and Sat. and Sun. 10–5.*

Time Out   The **Ferry Inn** is an intimate riverside pub serving real ale and good food. It's a short walk upstream along the north bank from the ferry over from Ham.

Hampton Court Palace

Some 20 miles or so from central London, on a loop of the Thames upstream from Richmond, lies **Hampton Court,** a mellow red-brick palace, bristling with turrets and twisted chimneys in the very best Tudor tradition. The house was begun in 1514 by Cardinal Wolsey, the ambitious and worldly chancellor of England, who intended it to surpass in size and opulence all other private residences. His master, Henry VIII, however, coveted the great house once it was completed, and made Wolsey an offer he couldn't refuse. The king added a great hall and

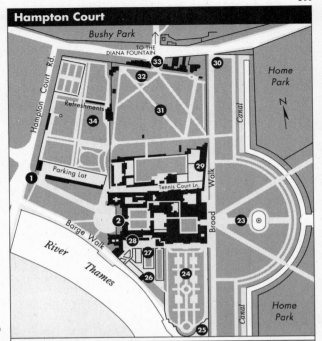

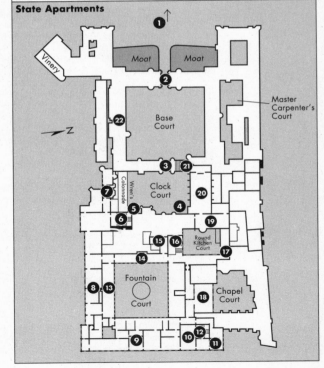

chapel, and lived much of his rumbustious life here. Further improvements were made by James I at the beginning of the 17th century, but by the end of the century the palace was getting rather run-down. Plans were drawn up by William and Mary to demolish the building and replace it with a still larger and more splendid structure in conscious emulation of the great palace of Versailles in France. However, the royal purse was unable to stretch quite that far and it was decided to keep the original buildings but add a new complex adjoining them at the rear. The ever-present and ever-ready Wren was commissioned as architect, and his graceful additions are among the most pleasing of the whole palace. (A serious fire at Easter 1986 badly damaged some of Wren's chambers, which will be closed for several years while restoration is done.) William and Mary—Mary especially—loved Hampton Court and much of their life here is still in evidence, especially the collections of Delftware and other porcelain.

The site beside the slow-moving Thames is perfect. The old palace itself, steeped in history, hung with priceless paintings, full of echoing cobbled courtyards and cavernous Tudor kitchens—not to mention a couple of royal ghosts, the luckless shades of Jane Seymour and Catherine Howard, two of Henry's unfortunate queens—is set in a park alive with dappled deer and tall ancestral trees, with magnificent ornamental gardens, an elegant Orangery, and the celebrated maze.

In a very real way Hampton Court not only enshrines some of the best architecture that England can show, but is also a microcosm of much that was excellent in three centuries of English art and art collecting. To progress from the Tudor part of the palace, with its roundels of Roman emperors, its allegorical tapestries, its ornate woodwork, and tiny, almost claustrophobic chambers, into Wren's gracious state apartments, opening one out of the other like a chain of airy boxes, with spacious views over the gardens and parks, is to walk through a central part of English history. But it must also be said that many of the rooms are rather empty (and some might also say endless), and that a good number of the paintings are hung so high on the walls that it is well nigh impossible to see them, a problem compounded by the inevitable red rope that prevents you from approaching close to them. Nonetheless, some rooms are furnished with many excellent pieces, especially the bedrooms, with their four-poster beds surmounted by plumes and rearing like enormous catafalques.

Royalty ceased to live here with George III. He, poor man, preferred the seclusion of Kew, where he was finally confined during his madness. However, the private apartments that range down one side of the palace are occupied by pensioners of the crown. Known as "grace and favor" apartments, they are among the most attractively placed homes in the country, with a veritable surfeit of peace and history on their doorsteps. *East Molsey, tel. 01/977–8441. Admission £2.80 adults, £1.40 children under 16 and senior citizens; charge includes admission to maze. Open late Mar.–late Oct. daily 9:30–6; late Oct.–late Mar. daily 9:30–4.*

Sightseeing Checklists

Historic Buildings and Sites

Buckingham Palace. *See* Westminster and Royal London.
Clarence House. *See* St. James's and Mayfair.
Downing Street. *See* Westminster and Royal London.
Lambeth Palace. *See* The South Bank.
Lancaster House. *See* St. James's and Mayfair.
Mansion House. *See* The City.
Marlborough House. *See* St. James's and Mayfair.
Palace of Westminster. *See* Westminster and Royal London.
St. James's Palace. *See* St. James's and Mayfair.
Somerset House. *See* Soho and Covent Garden.

Museums and Galleries

Bank of England Museum. *See* The City.
Bankside Gallery. *See* The South Bank.
Banqueting House. *See* Westminster and Royal London.
Barbican Gallery. *See* The City.
Bear Gardens Museum and Arts Centre. *See* The South Bank.
H.M.S. Belfast. *See* The South Bank.
Bomber Command Museum. *See* **Royal Air Force Museum.**
British Museum. *See* Bloomsbury and Legal London.
Cabinet War Rooms. *See* Westminster and Royal London.
Carlyle's House. *See* Belgravia and Chelsea.
Centre for Economic Botany. *See* The Thames Upstream
Chelsea Royal Hostpital. *See* **Royal Hospital and Museum.**
Chiswick House. *See* The Thames Upstream.
Clock Museum. *See* The City.
Commonwealth Institute. *See* Knightsbridge and Kensington.
Court Collection. *See* **Kensington Palace.**
Courtauld Institute Art Galleries. *See* Bloomsbury and Legal London.
Crown Jewels. *See* **Tower of London.**
Cutty Sark. *See* Greenwich.
The Design Museum. *See* The South Bank.
Dickens' House. *See* Bloomsbury and Legal London.
Dulwich College Picture Gallery. *See* Off The Beaten Track.
Fan Museum. *See* Greenwich.
Faraday's Laboratory and Museum. *See* St. James's and Mayfair.
Florence Nightingale Museum. *See* The South Bank.
Foundling Hospital Art Treasures. *See* Bloomsbury and Legal London.
Freud Museum. *See* Regent's Park and Hampstead.
Geffrye Museum of Furniture and Decorative Arts. Sequence of rooms furnished with pieces dating from the 16th century to the 1930s, plus staircases, paneling, and portraits from old London houses; the museum is located in a row of 18th-century almshouses. *Kingsland Rd., E2, tel. 01/739–8368. Open Tues.– Sat., bank holiday Mon. 10–5, Sun. 2–5; closed Good Fri.*
Geological Museum. *See* Knightsbridge and Kensington.
Gipsy Moth IV. *See* Greenwich.
Guards Museum. *See* Westminster and Royal London.
Guildhall. *See* The City.
Ham House. *See* The Thames Upstream.
Hampton Court Palace. *See* The Thames Upstream.

Hayward Gallery. *See* The South Bank.

Heinz Gallery. Gallery of the Royal Institute of British Architects with changing program of architecture-based exhibitions. *21 Portman Sq., tel. 01/580–5533. Open Mon.–Fri. 11–5, Sat. 10–1; closed bank holidays and Aug.*

Hogarth's House. *See* The Thames Upstream.

Horniman Museum and Library. *See* What To See and Do With Children.

House of St. Barnabas-in-Soho. *See* Soho and Covent Garden.

Imperial War Museum. *See* The South Bank.

Institute of Contemporary Arts. *See* Westminster and Royal London.

Iveagh Bequest. *See* Regent's Park and Hampstead.

The Jewish Museum. *See* Bloomsbury and Legal London.

Dr. Johnson's House. *See* The City.

Kathleen & May. *See* The South Bank.

Keats House and Museum. *See* Regent's Park and Hampstead.

Kensington Palace and Court Collection. *See* Knightsbridge and Kensington.

Kenwood House. *See* **Iveagh Bequest.**

Kew Palace. *See* The Thames Upstream.

Leighton House Museum and Art Gallery. *See* Knightsbridge and Kensington.

Linley Sambourne House. *See* Knightsbridge and Kensington.

London Toy and Model Museum. *See* What To See and Do With Children.

London Transport Museum. *See* Soho and Covent Garden.

Marble Hill House. *See* The Thames Upstream.

The Monument. *See* The City.

Museum of Garden History. *See* The South Bank.

Museum of London. *See* The City.

Museum of Mankind. *See* St. James's and Mayfair.

Museum of the Moving Image. *See* The South Bank.

National Army Museum. *See* Belgravia and Chelsea.

National Gallery. *See* Westminster and Royal London.

National Maritime Museum. *See* Greenwich.

National Portrait Gallery. *See* Soho and Covent Garden.

National Postal Museum. Major collection of stamps from all over the world, with emphasis on British and Commonwealth issues; Penny Blacks, etc. *King Edward St., tel. 01/432–3851. Open Mon.–Thur. 9:30–4:30, Fri. 9:30–4; closed bank holidays.*

Natural History Museum. *See* Knightsbridge and Kensington.

North Woolwich Old Station Museum. *See* Off The Beaten Track.

Old Royal Observatory. *See* Greenwich.

Old St. Thomas' Hospital Operating Theatre Museum. *See* The South Bank.

Osterley Park House. *See* The Thames Upstream.

Percival David Foundation of Chinese Art. *See* Bloomsbury and Legal London.

Pollocks Toy Museum. An 18th-century house containing a treasure trove of dolls, dolls' houses, toy theaters, teddy bears, and folk toys. *1 Scala St., tel. 01/636–3452. Admission 60p adults, 30p children under 19. Open Mon.–Sat. 10–5. Check for bank holiday opening.*

Prince Henry's Room. *See* Bloomsbury and Legal London.

Public Records Office Museum. Selected documents, e.g. one copy of the Magna Carta, from Britain's official government records. *Chancery La., tel. 01/876–3444. Open Mon.–Fri. 9:30–4:45; closed bank holidays, first half of Oct.*

Queen's Gallery. *See* Westminster and Royal London.
Queen's Tower. *See* Knightsbridge and Kensington.
Ranger's House. *See* Greenwich.
Royal Academy of Arts. *See* St. James's and Mayfair.
Royal Air Force Museum. *See* Off The Beaten Track.
Royal Hospital and Museum. *See* Belgravia and Chelsea.
Royal London. *See* The City.
Royal Mews. *See* Westminster and Royal London.
Royal Naval College. *See* Greenwich.
St. Bride's Crypt Museum. *See* Bloomsbury and Legal London.
Science Museum. *See* Knightsbridge and Kensington.
Serpentine Gallery. *See* Hyde Park and Kensington Gardens.
Sir John Soane's Museum. *See* Bloomsbury and Legal London.
Tate Gallery. *See* Westminster and Royal London.
Theatre Museum. *See* Soho and Covent Garden.
Tower Bridge. *See* The City.
Tower of London. *See* The City.
Victoria and Albert Museum. *See* Knightsbridge and Kensington.
Wallace Collection. *See* St. James's and Mayfair.
Wellington Museum. *See* St. James's and Mayfair.
Westminster Abbey Undercroft, Pyx Chamber, and Treasury.
See Westminster and Royal London.
Whitechapel Art Gallery. East end gallery staging changing art exhibitions, often of the work of 20th-century artists. *White-chapel High St., tel. 01/377–0107/5015. Admission varies according to exhibition. Open Tues.–Thurs. and Sun. 11–5, Wed. 11–8; closed all bank holidays.*
William Morris Gallery. An 18th-century house in northeast London where the artistic polymath William Morris (craftsman, painter, and writer) lived for eight years. Contains many examples of his work and of his fellows in the Arts and Crafts movement. *Lloyd Park, Forest Rd., tel. 01/527–5544, ext. 4390. Open Tues.–Sat. 10–1, 2–5, first Sun. each month 10–12, 2–5; closed bank holidays.*
Wimbledon Lawn Tennis Museum. Displays on the history and development of the game in a building immediately behind the celebrated Center Court. *Church Rd., tel. 01/946–6131. Admission £1.50 adults, 75p children under 16 and senior citizens. Open Tues.–Sat. 1–5, Sun. 2–5; closed bank holidays and during the Championship fortnight each June.*

Parks and Gardens

London is full of intimate little patches of green; part of the fun of exploring the city is to find such oases, generally only known to natives.

The majority of London's large open spaces are the **Royal Parks,** now administered by a government department but formerly all owned by the royal family and used for hunting and other relaxations. Those in central London are:
Green Park (*see* St. James's and Mayfair)
Hyde Park (*see* Hyde Park and Kensington Gardens)
Kensington Gardens (*see* Hyde Park and Kensington Gardens)
Primrose Hill (*see* Regent's Park and Hampstead)
Regent's Park (*see* Regent's Park and Hampstead)
St. James's Park (*see* Westminster and Royal London)

The Royal Parks in outer London are:
Bushey Park, near Hampton Court
Hampton Court Park (*see* The Thames Upstream)
Richmond Park (*see* The Thames Upstream)
All the above parks are open daily from dawn to dusk.

Also well worth exploring is **Hampstead Heath** on the range of hills overlooking central London to the north (*see* Regent's Park and Hampstead).

Two specialist gardens regularly open to the public are:
Chelsea Physic Garden (*see* Belgravia and Chelsea)
Royal Botanic Gardens (*see* The Thames Upstream)

Churches

The following is no more than a small selection of London's many interesting historic churches. Note that since most small churches are staffed entirely by voluntary helpers, opening times may vary. Visitors are always welcome to attend Sunday services; remember that, in the City especially, weekday services are frequently held as well. Admission to churches is nearly always free, but donations are always welcome; churches receive no state assistance to maintain their buildings and generally have to rely on the money they can raise themselves.

All Saints, Margaret Street. Outstanding example of ornate mid-19th century Gothic Revival style. *Margaret St., tel. 01/636–1788. Open daily 7–7, closed after morning service bank holidays.*

All Souls, Langham Place. *See* St. James's and Mayfair.

Chapel Royal, St. James's Palace. *See* St. James's and Mayfair.

Ely Chapel. *See* St. Etheldreda.

Grosvenor Chapel. *See* St. James's and Mayfair.

Guards Chapel. *See* Westminster and Royal London.

The Oratory. Ornate Baroque late 19th-century Roman Catholic church. *Brompton Rd., tel. 01/589–4811. Open daily 6:30 AM– 8PM, bank holidays 8–1.*

Queen's Chapel. *See* St. James's and Mayfair.

St. Bartholomew the Great. *See* The City.

St. Clement Danes. Church celebrated in the "Oranges and Lemons" nursery rhyme: church of the Royal Air Force, built by Wren in the 17th century, with spire added in the 18th. *Strand, tel. 01/242–8282. Open Mon.–Fri. 8–5, Sat.–Sun. 8–4:30.*

St. Etheldreda (Ely Chapel). A 13th-century chapel restored to Roman Catholicism in the 19th century and renovated in the 1930s. Oldest Roman Catholic place of worship in London. *Ely Pl., tel. 01/405–1061. Open daily 7–7.*

St. George, Hanover Square. *See* St. James's and Mayfair.

St. James's, Piccadilly. *See* St. James's and Mayfair.

St. Margaret's Westminster. *See* Westminster and Royal London.

St. Martin-in-the-Fields. *See* Westminster and Royal London.

St. Mary-le-Bow. *See* The City.

St. Mary-le-Strand. *See* Soho and Covent Garden.

St. Mary Woolnoth. Damaged in the Great Fire, this church was repaired by Wren but rebuilt by Hawksmoor in the 1720s on an Egyptian plan. *Lombard St., tel. 01/626–9701. Open Mon.–Fri. 8–5; closed Sat., Sun., bank holidays.*

St. Paul's Cathedral. *See* The City.

St. Stephen Walbrook. Rebuilt by Wren after the Great Fire, and used by him to experiment with ideas for the dome of St. Paul's. Interior restored in 1987 with new altar—a huge circular block of marble wrought by the sculptor Henry Moore. The Samaritans movement was launched here by the present incumbent, Chad Varah. *Walbrook, tel. 01/283-4444. Open Mon.- Thur. 9-4, Fri. 9-3, and for Sun. services.*

Savoy Chapel. Early 16th-century chapel rebuilt in the mid- 19th century that serves as the private chapel of the Queen in her position as duke of Lancaster; also chapel of the Royal Victorian Order. *Savoy Hill, Strand. Open Tues.-Sat. 11:30- 3:30, Sun. services 11:15.*

Southwark Cathedral. *See* The South Bank.

Temple Church. *See* Bloomsbury and Legal London.

Westminster Abbey. *See* Westminster and Royal London.

Westminster Cathedral. *See* Westminster and Royal London.

Other Places of Interest

Barbican Arts Centre. *See* The City.

Brass Rubbing Centre. *See* Westminster and Royal London.

Chessington World of Adventures. *See* What To Do and See With Children.

Gardens of the Zoological Society of London (the Zoo). *See* Regent's Park and Hampstead.

Guinness World of Records. *See* Soho and Covent Garden.

Highgate Cemetery. *See* Regent's Park and Hampstead.

Light Fantastic. *See* Soho and Covent Garden.

Lloyd's of London. *See* The City.

The London Brass Rubbing Centre. *See* Westminster and Royal London.

London Dungeon. *See* The South Bank.

The London Experience. *See* Soho and Covent Garden.

London International Financial Futures Exchange. *See* The City.

London Planetarium. *See* Regent's Park and Hampstead.

London Stock Exchange. *See* The City.

Madame Tussaud's. *See* Regent's Park and Hampstead.

Space Adventure. *See* The South Bank.

Thames Barrier Visitor Centre. *See* Greenwich.

Wembley Stadium. *See* Off The Beaten Track.

What to See and Do With Children

On London's traditional sightseeing circuit, make for the **Royal Mews** (*see* Westminster and Royal London), where some of the Queen's horses can be seen up close, the **Whispering Gallery** in St Paul's Cathedral (*see* The City), where it is fun to try the echo, and the gruesome instruments of torture on show in the **Bowyer Tower** in the **Tower of London** (*see* The City). Climb the 311 steps to the top of the **Monument** (*see* The City), or take the elevator to the high walkways of **Tower Bridge** (*see* The City). At **Hampton Court** see who can find their way out of the maze first.

Museums of specific interest to children include the **London Transport Museum** in Covent Garden (*see* Soho and Covent Garden); the **Science Museum,** where there are lots of opportunities for hands-on discovery; the **London Toy & Model Muse-**

um north of Kensington Gardens, where there is a train in the garden and a mass of manufactured toys and models on display; the **Bethnal Green Museum of Childhood** in east London, which has traditional toys, dolls, dolls' houses, and puppets; and the **Horniman Museum,** an educational museum in south London with well-displayed ethnographic and natural history collections.

Many other museums, e.g., the Natural History Museum, National Gallery, provide children's quizzes and holiday-time activities.

London Toy & Model Museum, *21–23 Craven Hill, tel. 01/ 262–9450. Admission £2.20 adults, 80p children under 15 and senior citizens. Open Tues.–Sat. 10–5:30, Sun. 11–5:30; closed all Mons. except bank holidays, Good Fri.*
Bethnal Green Museum of Childhood, *Cambridge Heath Rd., tel. 01/980–3204, 01/981–1711, 01/980–4315, 01/980–2415 (recorded information). Open Mon.–Thur. and Sat. 10–6, Sun. 2:30–5.*
Horniman Museum, *100 London Rd., Forest Hill, tel. 01/699– 1872/2339. Open Mon.–Sat. 10:30–6, Sun. 2–6.*

Other attractions of interest include **Guinness World of Records** and **Light Fantastic,** both in the Trocadero Centre at Piccadilly Circus (*see* Soho and Covent Garden); **Space Adventure** and the **London Dungeon,** both in Tooley Street (*see* The South Bank)— the latter is not suitable for young children or for sensitive children of any age; and the London **Zoo** in Regent's Park (*see* Regent's Park and Hampstead).

A novel idea might be to try brass-rubbing, at the **Brass Rubbing Centre** in Westminster Abbey or at the **London Brass Rubbing Centre** at St. Martin-in-the-Fields Church in Trafalgar Square (*see* Westminster and Royal London).

There are two sophisticated theme parks on the very edge of the built-up area of the capital city: **Chessington World of Adventures,** to the south, where there is also a zoo, and **Thorpe Park** toward the west.

Chessington World of Adventures, *Leatherhead Rd., Chessington, Surrey, tel. 03727/27227. Admission £6.25 adults, £5.25 children and senior citizens. Open daily 10–5; from Oct.– Mar. the zoo alone is open.*
Thorpe Park, *Staines Rd., Chertsey, Surrey, tel. 0932/562633. Admission £6.50 adults and older children, £3.50 senior citizens, children less than 3 feet tall free. Open daily late Mar.– mid-April and beginning of June–mid-Sept. 10–6, till 8 PM late July–end Aug.; mid-Apr.–end May and mid-Sept. open Sat. and Sun. only 10–6. Closed Oct.–late Mar.*

Chiselhurst Caves, on the southeastern edge of the city, are the remains of old chalk mines said to date from Roman times; the tours take place by lamplight. *Old Hill, Chiselhurst, tel. 01/ 467–3264. Admission £1.50 adults, 75p children under 16, 75p senior citizens weekdays only. Open Easter–end Sept. daily 11–5; Oct.–Easter Sat. and Sun. only 11–5.*

Hampstead Heath (*see* Regent's Park and Hampstead) is a superb place for a walk. Join the kiteflyers on Parliament Hill Fields on the southern slopes of the heath throughout the year, and if there's snow get your hands on a toboggan—this is one of London's best tobogganing spots.

Another fun outdoor activity is swimming or boating on the **Serpentine,** the lake in **Hyde Park** (*see* Hyde Park).

Places where children might actually enjoy shopping are **Covent Garden** and **Hamley's,** the huge toy shop in Regent's Street. At Christmas, the grotto and visit to Father Christmas in **Selfridges,** on Oxford Street, is generally reckoned to be the best in London; be prepared for lengthy crowds in December—those in the know come in late October or early November.

Off the Beaten Track

Regent's Canal From **Camden Lock,** follow the towpath of the **Regent's Canal** (*see* Regent's Park and Hampstead) east for a fascinating view of London and Londoners at home. The canal runs past the elegant houses of Islington and then through increasingly less prosperous areas, eventually reaching the Thames at Limehouse. There's a great deal of interest for the curious observer —private homes and semi-secret back gardens running down to the water, wide views south to the tower blocks of the City, and old industrial areas. The canal runs alongside Victoria Park in Hackney, one of the capital's first public parks. There are numerous exits from the canal towpath to the surrounding streets.

Docklands London's **Docklands** are the fastest-growing part of the capital. The old docks had lain derelict for several decades after the main port of London had moved downstream to the areas near the mouth of the Thames, and have only been revived since the early 1980s by a combination of government action and commercial development. Now the area is claimed to be Europe's largest building site, where huge high-tech offices and smart apartments and town houses are being built cheek by jowl with the still run-down homes of the area's original inhabitants.

The **Docklands Light Railway** is a new overhead rapid-transit railway running through the whole area. Use it to explore the neighborhood and to enjoy some stunning views as it runs above the old docks, many now turned into marinas and recreational areas. The central London terminus of the railway is at Tower Gateway, a few minutes' walk from the Tower of London and from Tower Hill station on the Underground. Island Gardens station, at the end of one branch, is just opposite Greenwich, to which it is connected by a foot tunnel under the river (*see* Greenwich). The London Dockland Development Corporation (LDDC) runs regular coach tours through Docklands, including the areas to the east that are still awaiting development. *Tours leave Tower Hill Underground on Wed. and Sat. at 10 (length 2¼ hours, cost £8) and on Tues. and Thurs. at 6:30 (length 2½ hours, cost £11). It is essential to confirm details and book places at least 24 hours in advance; tel. 01/515– 3000 or 01/538–0022.*

Dulwich **Dulwich Village** in southeast London has handsome 18th-century houses strung out along its main street; most of the land around here belongs to the Dulwich College Estate—founded in the early 17th century by the actor Edward Alleyn —which keeps strict control of modern development. The village is a pleasant place to wander on a sunny summer day. **Dulwich Park** is a well-kept municipal park with a particularly fine display of rhododendrons in late May. Opposite the park gates is the **Dulwich College Picture Gallery,** a lovely small gallery with works by Rembrandt, Van Dyck, Rubens, Poussin, and Gainsborough among others; the gallery was designed by Sir John Soane (*see* Bloomsbury and Legal London). To get to Dulwich take the Network SouthEast surface train from Victoria to West Dulwich or from London Bridge to North Dulwich. *College Rd., tel. 01/693–5254/5. Admission £1.50 adults. Open Tues.–Sat. 10–1, 2–5, Sun. 2–5; closed all bank holidays.*

If you have enough energy left after exploring Dulwich and the Picture Gallery, walk through the park and then south for about half a mile to another delightful small museum, the **Horniman Museum** (*see* What To Do and See With Children).

The Royal Air Force Museum

The Royal Air Force Museum in north London is a must for flying and military enthusiasts. The story of the R.A.F. is told in great detail, and there are uniforms, guns, and radar equipment on display, as well as detailed sections on World War I and World War II exploits, including the work of the Bomber Command. The **Battle of Britain Museum** in the same complex (no extra charge) explains how the R.A.F. fought off the German threat in 1940. *Grahame Park Way, Hendon, tel. 01/205–2266. Admission £3 adults, £1.50 children under 16 and senior citizens. Open daily 10–6.*

The Thames Barrier

The Thames Barrier is a mammoth piece of civil engineering designed to prevent the Thames from flooding the extensive low-lying parts of central and south London. The barrier, which has a span of 520 meters and contains enough concrete to build about 10 miles of six-lane freeway, is sited a few miles downstream (east) of Greenwich. An exhibition and video display explain why the barrier is necessary and the technology it employs, and visitors can walk along the riverbank close to it, although, unfortunately, the gates and control room are not open. The best view is gained on the short cruise from the visitors' center. An enjoyable way of traveling to the barrier is by boat, either from Greenwich or from Westminster or Tower Piers in central London; the train station is Charlton, reached by Network SouthEast trains from Charing Cross Station. *Unity Way, off Woolwich Rd., tel. 01/854–1373. Admission £1 adults, 50p children under 16 and senior citizens. Open Mon.–Fri. 10:30–5, Sat. and Sun. 10:30–5:30.*

North Woolwich Old Station Museum

After visiting the barrier, make your way east into Woolwich, take the open-deck car ferry across the river, and visit the **North Woolwich Old Station Museum.** This has displays on the history of railways in east London with locomotives, rolling stock and a reconstructed 1910 booking office. Return to central London by overground train from North Woolwich. *Pier Rd., N. Woolwich, tel. 01/474–7244. Admission free. Open Mon.–Sat. 10–5, Sun. 2–5, bank holidays 2–5.*

5 Shopping

Shopping Districts

Chelsea Chelsea means first and foremost the King's Road, less glamorous now than a few years ago, but still a mecca for those in search of up-to-the-minute fashion. Chelsea is also a happy hunting ground for the antiques lover, and the discriminating home furnisher will find some very classy fabrics on offer. A Saturday on the King's Road may well open your eyes to some of the weirder trends among London's youngsters. It's still the haunt of the remnants of the punk generation.

Covent Garden Craft shops and stores selling eccentric designs, plus trendy boutiques have made a natural home for themselves here, especially in and around the elegantly restored 19th-century market. But this is one of those delightful areas where simply strolling around, window-shopping, and people watching are as much fun as the shopping itself.

Kensington Antiques are the real draw here, especially up Kensington Church Street. The serious antiques hunter in search of large items will be spoilt for choice, but there are also many shops with small pieces for sale to delight the gift seeker. Kensington High Street itself, though it may have seen better days, still has a number of good clothes stores.

Knightsbridge This is very much a home away from home for the committed shopper. Heading the list is Harrods, its great gaudy Edwardian bulk dominating Brompton Road. But there are delights all around. Sloane Street—for fashions and fabrics—Beauchamp Place, neighboring Walton Street, and a whole host of greater and lesser streets from Hyde Park corner to South Kensington are all tried and tested, long-term favorites.

Mayfair Mayfair means Bond Street (Old and New), South Molton Street, Savile Row, and the Burlington Arcade in an area lying between Piccadilly and Oxford Street. The emphasis is very much on traditional British goods for men and women, with South Molton Street adding a raffish, modern accent. Prices and quality are tip-top. A shopping area for the hardened case.

Oxford Street Despite its claims to being Britain's premier shopping street, Oxford Street is to be endured rather than enjoyed. Selfridges, Marks and Spencer, and John Lewis are all good department stores here, while little St. Christopher's Place, almost opposite the Bond Street tube, adds a chic touch. But otherwise the crowds, the noise, the traffic, and the unmistakable tattiness of stretches Oxford Street itself, combine to produce a very much less-than-lovely atmosphere.

Piccadilly Though the actual number of shops here is really quite low for a street of its length—after all Green Park takes up almost half of one side—Piccadilly still boasts a number of classy outfits, Simpsons, Hatchards, and Fortnum and Mason chief among them. Also in the Piccadilly area are several very elegant shopping arcades, with the Burlington Arcade leading the pack.

Regent Street China, clothes, fabrics, good department stores, and wide sidewalks have all helped make Regent Street an appealing alternative to neighboring Oxford Street. The crowds are just as thick on the ground, but the presence of perennials such as Liberty's—probably the city's most appealing department store—more than compensate.

Shopping A (Mayfair, Soho, and Covent Garden)

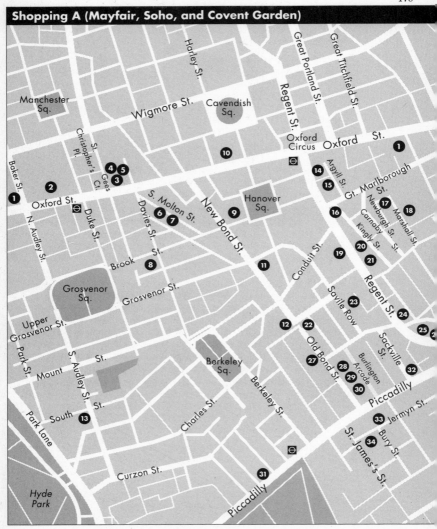

Aquascutum, **25**
The Armoury of St. James's, **33**
Asprey's, **27**
Authentics, **39**
Browns, **6**
Burberrys, **19**
Butler and Wilson, **7**
Cartier, **11**

Coleridge, **31**
The Coppershop, **43**
Craftsmen Potters Shop, **18**
Dorin Frankfurt, **38**
Droopy Browns, **4**
F. Fwd., **17**
Garrard, **24**

Gered, **21**
Gray's Antique Market, **8**
Grosvenor Prints, **45**
Halcyon Days, **9**
Hamleys, **20**
Hat Shop, **3**
Henry Sotheran's, **32**
Herbert Johnson, **22**

Irish Linen Co., **30**
John Lewis, **10**
Kilkenny, **12**
Laura Ashley, **15**
Liberty, **16**
Lord's, **29**
Marks and Spencer, **1**
Maud Frizon, **28**

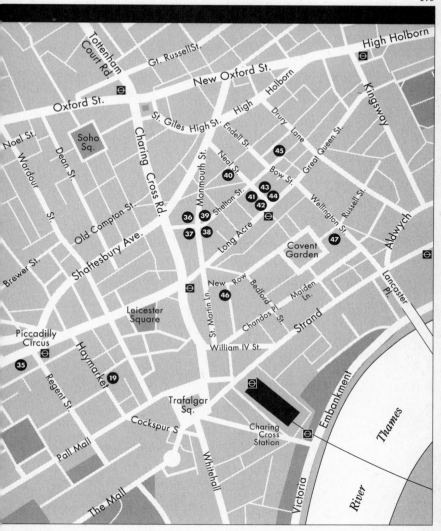

180

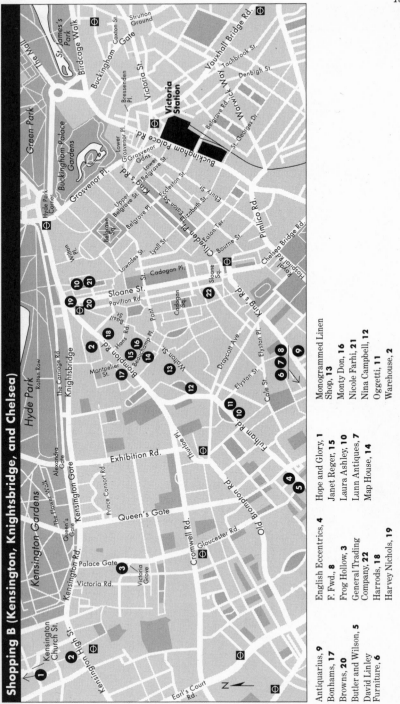

Shopping B (Kensington, Knightsbridge, and Chelsea)

Antiquarius, **9**
Bonhams, **17**
Browns, **20**
Butler and Wilson, **5**
David Linley
Furniture, **6**

English Eccentrics, **4**
F. Fwd., **8**
Frog Hollow, **3**
General Trading
Company, **22**
Harrods, **18**
Harvey Nichols, **19**

Hope and Glory, **1**
Janet Reger, **15**
Laura Ashley, **10**
Lunn Antiques, **7**
Map House, **14**

Monogrammed Linen
Shop, **13**
Monty Don, **16**
Nicole Farhi, **21**
Nina Campbell, **12**
Oggetti, **11**
Warehouse, **2**

St. James's Though his suits may be made in Savile Row, this is where the English gent comes for the rest of his clothes. Superb shoes, classic shirts, silk ties, magnificent hats, and all manner of accessories have kept St. James's a front runner for timeless English clothes. Naturally the prices mirror the quality on offer.

Stores Arranged by Category

Antiques London can provide a fruitful vacation for any antiques buff. Two excellent areas for exploration are the Camden Passage Market (*see* Street Markets in this section), and Kensington Church Street, which is lined with antiques stores of every description and price range. Out of the hundreds of stores available in town we list five to whet your appetite. (*See* Prints.)

Antiquarius (135–141 King's Rd., SW3) at the Sloane Square end of the King's Road, is an indoors antiques market with over 200 stalls that offers a wide variety of collectibles, including metalware, meerschaum pipes, ceramics, Art Nouveau bric-à-brac, period clothing, and lace. (*See* map B.)

A real find for our enthusiast is the **Gallery of Antique Costume and Textiles** (2 Church St., NW8). Here you can forage at leisure amid tapestries, shawls, table linens, and, above all, costumes. Nothing after the 1930s. It lies off our maps, but is easily found, three blocks north of Edgware Road subway station.

Gray's Antique Market (58 Davies St., W1 and around the corner at 1–7 Davies Mews, W1) is a vast gaggle of small boutiques, loaded with curios and collectibles. This is a hunting ground for the keen searcher for treasure trove—but allow yourself plenty of time. (*See* map A.)

For any collector of china and glass who also has a taste for history, **Hope and Glory** (131A Kensington Church St., W8) should figure high on the visiting list. The stock here is of commemorative china and glass from the period 1887–1953. (*See* map B.)

At the Parson's Green end of King's Road, and thus off the edge of our map, lies **Lunn Antiques** (86 New King's Rd., SW6). You will find this a treasure chest of antique linen and lace, drapes, pillowcases, tablecloths, and period clothing making the trek out here worthwhile. Their stock consists of highly attractive items of near-museum quality. (*See* map B.)

China and Glass All London's department stores carry excellent lines of china and glass, mostly of the classic Wedgwood or Minton varieties, or of their less expensive competitors. There are, of course, plenty of stores that sell nothing else, and here are three possibilities.

For superb British glass, with a strong accent on originality, try **Coleridge** (192 Piccadilly, W1), which carries a stock of both practical and display pieces, rather like a small London version of Steuben. (*See* map A.)

Gered (158 Regent St., W1) are the people to go to for that wedding gift. A huge selection of designs to choose from, with a heavy emphasis on Wedgwood, many of whose most popular designs date back to the 18th century. (*See* map A.) There are also branches at 112 Regent St., W1, and 173 Piccadilly, W1.

To find formal china and elegant crystal all in one store, visit **Thomas Goode** (19 S. Audley St., W1). Their very best crystal comes with a hefty price tag, but the range is fairly wide, and shoppers on a tighter budget should find something to please them. (*See* map A.)

Clothing London is one of the top cities for women's fashion. Clothes are on offer here in every price range and every style, and many leading international houses have major branches in the city. Space does not allow us to list more than a few stores that might interest you, though we have selected them to try and cover the picture in outline. Remember that most of the large department stores have fashion clothing floors, especially Harvey Nichols, Harrods, and Selfridges, while John Lewis, Simpsons, and Liberty can all provide more traditional, though still stylish, clothes.

What is true for women's wear goes even more for men's. London is still renowned for its male fashions, especially in the more sober, traditional categories.

General **Aquascutum** (100 Regent St., W1), which is celebrated for its high-style, expensive rainwear, also sells a superb range of clothes for both sexes. An ideal goal for the traditional executive with plenty of moolah. (*See* map A.)

To shop at **Burberrys** (165 Regent St., W1, and 18–22 The Haymarket, SW1) is rather like visiting a comfortably familiar country house, where closets and drawers overspill with classic, quality clothing for men and women. Famous for its tartan trademark and its magnificent raincoats. (*See* map A.)

Herbert Johnson (30 New Bond St., W1) has every kind of hat, especially for that old-fashioned head. Trad "titfers" for men, for huntin', shootin', and fishin'; fancier, more delicate creations for women. Drop by if you intend to go to a formal garden party, or visit Ascot races. The Royal Navy cap worn by Prince Charles for his wedding was from Herbert Johnson. (*See* map A.)

Lord's (66–70 Burlington Arcade, W1). A very good reason for visiting this seductive arcade is Lord's softly irresistible supply of cashmere for men and women—plus shirts, ties, and scarves in abundance. It's amazing how much these small Arcade stores manage to pack in. Their paisley patterned robes would have made Noël Coward's eyes gleam. (*See* map A.)

Marks & Spencer (458 Oxford St., W1 and 173 Oxford St., W1). This major chain of stores is an integral part of the British way of life—sturdy practical clothes, good materials and workmanship, and basic accessories, all at moderate, though not bargain basement, prices. "Marks and Sparks," as they are popularly known, has never been renowned for their high style, though they have recently formed an alliance with Brooks Brothers. There are two major branches on Oxford Street, one recently restyled, #458 near Marble Arch (with a new home-furnishing branch across the road), and the other, #173, just east of Oxford Circus. (*See* map A.)

Simpson (203 Piccadilly, W1) is a quiet, pleasant store, with a thoughtful variety of designer and leisure wear, luggage, and gifts. It is the home of the Daks' brand of classic British design. There's a barbershop, restaurant, and wine bar to add to the store's conveniences. It's just a block west of Piccadilly Circus. (*See* map A.)

Women's Wear **Browns** (23–37 South Molton St., W1) is the firm that put the South Molton Street pedestrian mall on the map, and is a very good bet for the trendy shopper on the lookout for the latest designer clothes. Here you'll find styles by Azzedine Alaïa, Sonia Rykiel, Romeo Gigli, and all the latest from France, Italy, Germany, the United States and, of course, Britain. Also at 6C Sloane St., SW1. (*See* both maps.)

Dorin Frankfurt (46 Monmouth St., WC2) has affordable designs in one-size ladies' wear—simple lines, individual style, and soft fabric to suit all ages. The store's weird in the extreme, but the fashions by Ron Arad might very well be just what you are looking for. (*See* map A.)

Droopy Browns (St. Christopher's Pl., W1). Ladies fashions for all ages with more than a touch of theatricality. Sumptuous colors and fabrics, striking styles, and dresses for most occasions —weddings, balls, cocktails, or just everyday wear. Also at 99 St. Martin's La., WC2. (*See* map A.)

English Eccentrics (155 Fulham Rd., SW3) is an intriguing store, with a very keen eye to unusually designed prints and odd historical patterns. Specializes in sweaters, clean-cut jersey separates, and highly covetable scarves, mainly for women, but with increasing attention being paid to the male market. (*See* map B.)

The Hat Shop (9 Gees Court, W1). A store with rows of cubbyholes brimming with ladies' hats for every occasion, from feasts to funerals. Friendly assistants to help you with that difficult choice. Also at 58 Neal St., WC2. (*See* map A.)

Janet Reger (2 Beauchamp Pl., SW3). It was Janet Reger who pioneered the surge of luxurious lingerie that now froths out from every store. This is the one, though, to visit for the real thing. (*See* map B.)

Laura Ashley (256–258 Regent St., W1, also at 183 Sloane St., SW1, and other branches). Design from the firm founded by the late high priestess of English traditional. Country dresses, blouses, and skirts, plus wallpapers and fabrics in dateless patterns that rely heavily on flowers, fruit, leaves, or just plain stripes, that have captured the nostalgic imagination of the world. (*See* both maps.)

Maud Frizon (31 Old Bond St., W1). Our choice for ladies' shoes. Fashionable, dainty footwear radiates on circular display tables here, in tantalizing colors and materials. (*See* map A.)

Nicole Farhi (193 Sloane St., SW1). A store specially recommended for the career woman of taste; Nicole Farhi stocks a desirable range of practical clothes, some prices on the high side, but with some affordable wear as well. Also available are children's clothes in the French Connection range. Also at 25–26 St. Christopher's Pl., W1. (*See* both maps.)

Rebecca (66 Neal St., WC2). The ladies' version of Sam Walker's (*see* Menswear). A rather pricey way of buying secondhand clothes, but they have been selected with care, and are in tip-top condition. The styles go back to the '30s, and, though you aren't likely to find a bargain on the racks, if you are into nostalgia, this is your place. Beautiful lingerie and cashmere, with most of the period attire coming in unusual shades. (*See* map A.)

Warehouse (19 Argyll St., W1). Warehouse stocks practical, stylish, reasonably priced separates, in easy fabrics and basic colors. But if that sounds dreary, don't be fooled. This place is a working girl's heaven. The stock changes very quickly, so it always presents a new face to the world. Also at 76 Brompton Rd., SW3, and Barker's Arcade, 63–67 Kensington High St., W8. (*See* both maps.)

Menswear All the stores we list above under General Clothing stock excellent menswear. Try Aquascutum, Burberrys, and Simpson. All the large department stores, too, carry a wide range of men's clothing, Selfridges and Harrods especially.

Moss Bros. (21–26 Bedford St., WC2). "Moss Bros," as you will always hear this store called, made their name renting out tuxedos, complete morning suits for fancy weddings, and all kinds of formal wear for the busy man—and woman—on the move. They will save you having to pack your tux just in case of that formal date. The store also stocks an excellent range of menswear for sale, both formal and leisure, mostly in a middle range of prices. (*See* map A.)

Sam Walker (41 Neal St., WC2) provides a refined way to buy secondhand clothes. He specializes in men's vintage clothing at prices that *almost* reflect their near-museum quality. Naturally, most of the stock is well pre-World War II, and carries period nostalgia in every fold. (*See* map A.)

Tommy Nutter (18 Savile Row, W1). One of London's contemporary tailoring legends. Ideal for the modern, well-dressed yuppie. (*See* map A.)

Crafts In the wake of the current interest in the alternate way of living, health foods, and preserving the environment, has come an enormous increase in public awareness of the value of traditional crafts. London now boasts many stores devoted to selling the best craftwork available. Here are six specializing in different fields.

The Coppershop (48 Neal St., WC2) is a small place, which gleams from floor to ceiling with burnished copper, every kind of cooking pot, and a fair selection of ornamental items, too. Enthusiastic service and advice on copper care from the owner. (*See* map A.)

Some of the best British potters joined to found the **Craftsmen Potters Shop** (7 Marshall St., W1) as a cooperative venture to market their wares. The result is a store that carries a wide spectrum of the potters art, from thoroughly practical jugs, plates, and bowls, to ceramic sculptures. Prices range from the reasonable to way up. (*See* map A.)

Princess Margaret's son, David Linley, and his partner Matthew Rice, run **David Linley Furniture** (1 New King's Rd., SW6) a workshop/store that specializes in handcrafted items of furniture, mainly on commission. Their major pieces range from £500 to several thousand pounds, but a range of desktop accessories, with a Venetian design, has been very popular, carrying price tags of much more affordable £10 and up. (*See* map B.)

The delightful best of Irish design and workmanship—Waterford glass, designer clothes, chunky woolens, home accessories —are all brought together in a typically friendly atmosphere at **Kilkenny** (150 New Bond St. W1. *See* map A.)

True to its name, **Naturally British** (13 New Row, WC2) is a good spot to find British crafts at their best. From small, low-priced pottery or wood items to larger pieces such as gloriously carved rocking horses with a high price tag on their aristocratic manes. (*See* map A.)

Anyone with an eye for the decorative attractions of Italian marbled paper will find **Nina Campbell** (9 Walton St., SW3) a must. Address books, all kinds of desk equipment and stationery, plus Edwardian-inspired lamps and fluffy cushions make very tempting gifts. Naturally, the cushions aren't made of paper! (*See* map B.)

Gifts   Gifts are what you make them, and London will come up with everything from plastic salt and pepper shakers shaped like Big Ben to a £3,000 antique print of St. Paul's. Here are some stores where you may be able to find an unusual gift to take home with you. Keep an eye, too, on the larger department stores as you shop around, they can always surprise you with items that you might not have thought to look for. You should also investigate the possibilities of the shops attached to the major museums, most of which have a wide variety of books, posters, postcards, and reproductions of items in their collections.

The Armoury of St. James's (17 Piccadilly Arcade, SW1). The Armoury is a fascinating wee store bursting with impeccably painted toy soldiers, old medals, and military prints. A must for the nostalgic enthusiast. (*See* map A.)
Frog Hollow (15 Victoria Grove, W8). Here's the place to buy superbly made cuddly toys for the small members of the family (Princess Diana does, so the report goes). The accent is on frogs of every description, but there are many other unusual, charming animals here as well (*See* map B.)
General Trading Co. (144 Sloane St., SW1). With a dozen departments to explore, even the most finicky shopper will find something to delight or amuse in this Aladdin's cave. Rumor has it that the Prince and Princess of Wales had their wedding gift list here. General Trading Company buyers range the world—especially the Far East—to discover new suppliers, and their merchandise includes French glass, Indian crafts, Italian lighting fixtures, Chinese toys, and English bone china. This is one of those delightfully absorbing shops where you can spend as little as £5, or as much as your credit card will stretch to, and you will always feel you are walking away with something special. (*See* map B.)
Halcyon Days (14 Brook St., W1) is a charming shop, devoted entirely to small decorative boxes from music to snuffboxes, made of enamel, china, or precious metals. Halcyon Days promises that their boxes of today will be the antiques of tomorrow. They have a very decorative line in commemorative items, which make ideal mementos. (*See* map A.)
Hamleys (188–196 Regent St., W1). Six floors of toys and

games for both children and adults. The huge stock ranges from traditional teddy bears to computer games and all the latest technological gimmickry. (*See* map A.)

Mysteries (11 Monmouth St., WC2) is the spot to find a comprehensive selection of books and paraphernalia for those with a leaning toward the occult—rock crystal balls, oils, incense, and psychic readings, books, tapes, and tarot cards. Just the place to find that gift for your friend on the West Coast. (*See* map A.)

Neal Street East (5 Neal St., WC2). The "East" in the name refers to the Orient—for this rabbit-warren of a store, full of bright and inspiring oriental goods, has a strong Chinese slant. If this kind of design attracts you, then be sure to drop in as you tour the Covent Garden area and explore several floors of soft slippers, embroidery, art materials, toys, books, and pottery. (*See* map A.)

Penhaligon (41 Wellington St., WC2) is a block south of the Royal Opera House in Covent Garden. William Penhaligon—court barber at the end of Queen Victoria's lengthy reign—blended perfumes and toilet waters in the back of his shop, using essential oils and natural, indeed often exotic, ingredients. Today Penhaligon's still makes its traditional preparations—including soaps, talc, and bath oils—following William Penhaligon's original notes, while the elegantly packaged products and equally sumptuous shops both retain a look of high Victoriana. Also at 55 Burlington Arcade, W1, and 20A Brook St., W1. (*See* map A.)

The Tea House (15A Neal St., WC2). Any shop that's devoted to the British national drink has to be worth a visit, and this one certainly is. There's tea of all kinds on sale, but the most striking feature here is the variety of teapots available—classic ones, copies of 17th-century ones, even a pot that caricatures Mrs. Thatcher. It's a great place to find a really unusual gift. (*See* map A.)

Gizmos **Authentics** (42 Shelton St., WC2) is an ultramodern store, all black and steel, which offers high-tech gizmos—lighters, watches, pens, all kinds of potential gifts designed in slick style. (*See* map A.)

F.Fwd. (14A Newburgh St., W1). You got it—Fast Forward! Definitely a store for the gimmick maven, it sells ingeniously designed gifts, mostly pocket sized and medium priced. Very high tech. Also at 261 King's Rd., SW3. (*See* both maps.)

If you're looking for that gift, gadget, or gizmo that stands out in a crowd, then try **Oggetti** (133 Fulham Rd., SW3). Design with that striking indefinably Italian flair abounds, but some of the prices are audacious, too. Also at 100 Jermyn St., SW1. (*See* both maps.)

Jewelry Jewelry—precious, semi-precious, and totally fake—can be had by just rubbing an Aladdin's lamp in London's West End. Here are a few suggestions for baubles, bangles, and beads, only one of which—Sheer Decadence—is truly outrageous.

Asprey's (165–169 New Bond St., W1) has been described as the "classiest and most luxurious shop in the world." It offers a range of exquisite jewelry and gifts, both antique and modern. If you're in the market for a six-branched Georgian candelabrum or a six-carat emerald and diamond brooch, you won't be disappointed. (*See* map A.)

All that glitters at **Butler and Wilson** (20 S. Molton St., W1) isn't gold. This store is cleverly designed to set off its irresistible costume jewelry to the very best advantage—against a dramatic black background. It has some of the best displays in town, and keeps very busy marketing silver, diamonté, and pearls by the truckload. Also at 189 Fulham Rd., SW3. (*See* both maps.)

Cartier (175 New Bond St., W1). The very essence of Bond Street is captured in this exclusive jewelers, which also sells glassware, leather goods, and stationery. It combines royal connections—Cartier's was granted its first royal warrant in 1902—with the last word in luxurious good taste. Many of the duchess of Windsor's trinkets first saw the light of day here. (*See* map A.)

Garrard (112 Regent St., W1). Garrard's connections with the royal family go back to 1722, and they are still responsible for keeping the Crown Jewels in glittering condition. But they are also family jewelers, and offer an enormous range of items in jewelry or silver, from antique to modern. Charles bought Diana her engagement ring here. (*See* map A.)

For very desirable costume jewelry, visit **Monty Don** (58 Beauchamp Pl., SW3) located in a busy, chic shopping street near Harrods. Monty Don's sells animal and insect brooches in rhinestone and huge crystal drop earrings. (*See* map B.)

At **Sheer Decadence** (44 Monmouth St., WC2) you can decorate yourself with a sensational look at a reasonable price. It's a store full of mad, baroque jewelry and accessories—strange materials worked inventively into striking one-of-a-kind pieces. (*See* map A.)

Linen Among the traditional crafts that can still be bought in London, finely wrought linen ranks high. Again, many of the department stores, Liberty and Harrods among them, carry a fair range of linen goods, but here are two specialty stores that you might want to try for a more personal service.

The Irish Linen Co. (35–36 Burlington Arcade, W1) is a tiny store bursting with crisp, embroidered linen for the table, the bed, and the nose. Exquisite handkerchiefs cost from $4.95 to $45. (*See* map A.)

For a wide range of fine Italian bed linen with matching towels, bathrobes, and nightshirts, as well as tablecloths, mats, and napkins—all of which you can have monogrammed—try **The Monogrammed Linen Shop** (168 Walton St., SW3). Proud grandparents may want to buy a superbly embroidered christening gown here. (*See* map B.)

Prints For a gift to take home, a memento of London, or just the delight of owning a beautiful, old object, prints are tough to beat. We list here three out of the many print shops in central London. If you want to find some more, all close together, visit Cecil Court.

Grosvenor Prints (28–32 Shelton St., WC2). Shelton Street lies in the tangle of streets northwest of Covent Garden, where many attractive stores have established themselves. Grosvenor Prints sells antiquarian prints, but with an emphasis on views and architecture of London—and dogs! It's an eccentric collection, and the prices range widely, but the stock is so odd that you are bound to find something interesting and unusual to meet both your budget and your taste. (*See* map A.)

Henry Sotheran's (2–5 Sackville St., W1), just off Piccadilly, is a great place to visit for a pictorial gift. There is a wide selection of antique botanical and ornithological prints in the Princes Arcade Store, 2–4 Princes' Arcade, W1, just off Piccadilly, opposite the Royal Academy. More prints, plus old books of adventure and travel on Sackville Street. (*See* map A.)

The Map House (54 Beauchamp Pl., SW3) is an old established store, and is one of the best places in London to root out a special old map or print. Antique maps can run from a few pounds to several thousand, but the Map House also has excellent reproductions of maps and prints, especially of botanical subjects and cityscapes. (*See* map B.)

Department Stores

London's department stores range from Harrods—which tries to be Bloomingdale's clone—through many serviceable middle-range stores, devoted to the middle-of-the-road tastes of the middle class, to a few cheapjack ones that sell merchandise you would find at a better rate back home. Most of the best and biggest department stores are grouped in the West End, around Regent's Street and Oxford Street, with two notable exceptions out in Knightsbridge.

We begin with our favorite, **Liberty** (200 Regent St., W1), easily the most splendid store on Regent Street, and one of London's most attractive. Liberty is a labyrinthine building, full of nooks and crannies, all stuffed with goodies like a dream of an eastern bazaar realized as a western store. Famous principally for its fabrics, it also has an Oriental department, rich with color; menswear that tends to the traditional; and women's wear that stresses the chic and recherché. It is a store hard to resist, where you may well find an original gift—especially one made from those classic Liberty prints. (*See* map A.)

A short distance from Liberty, on Oxford Street and two blocks west, is **John Lewis** (278 Oxford St., W1), a store whose motto is "We are never knowingly undersold," and for sensible goods at sensible prices they take a lot of beating. For the visitor to London who's handy with the needle, John Lewis has a wonderful selection of yard goods. Many's the American home with John Lewis drapes. (*See* map A.)

Ten blocks west on Oxford Street—10 crowded blocks in the middle of the day or at sale time—lies **Selfridges** (400 Oxford St., W1). This giant, bustling store is London's upmarket version of Macy's. It has virtually everything you could want for the home and the family. There's a food hall catering to every taste, and a frenetic cosmetic department that seems to perfume the air the whole length of Oxford Street. In recent years, Selfridges has made a specialty of high-profile popular designer fashion. Even more important for the visitor to town, there's a branch of the London Tourist Board on the premises, a theater ticket counter, and a branch of Thomas Cook, the travel agent, in the basement. (*See* map A.)

Our last two selected department stores are southwest of Oxford Street, in fashionable Knightsbridge. **Harrods** (87 Brompton Rd., SW1) is one of the world's most famous department stores, and is currently owned by an Egyptian family. Harrods lives up to its motto, *Omnia Omnibus Ubique*—everything, for everyone, everywhere. Though Harrods may not be so unabashedly sumptuous as in times past (nor so peaceful!), it still reigns supreme among British stores. Visit especially the astounding food halls to see the extensive selections, the elaborate displays—the seafood arrangements, in particular, are stunning—and the lovely floor, wall, and ceiling tiles. Harrods is popular with members of the Royal Family, but don't be misled into thinking that you might rub shoulders with the Queen. When she visits the 15-acre store, it opens an hour early, just for her. (*See* map B.)

Harvey Nichols (109 Knightsbridge, SW1). Harvey Nichols is renowned for its range of household furnishings, stationery, and jewelry, but most of all for its fashions. It has a pleasantly glitzy atmosphere for browsing, with a fun young "Zone" in the basement. The Princess of Wales has often been seen shopping here, and it is a very acceptable alternative to Harrods, if you can't take crowds. (*See* map B.)

Street Markets

The street markets of London are not only great places for bargains—or at least you can kid yourself that they are!—but are full of genuine bedouin Londoners, from the Cockney stall holders selling vegetables or antiques, their Jaguars parked in a nearby street, to the locals out buying their Sunday dinners. The markets are also a rich source of free entertainment, tasty snacks, and insights into the way London works. Naturally, there is a lot of rubbish on view, imported plastic from Hong Kong or cheesecloth shirts from Bombay, but there is also a seemingly endless supply of attractive plates and grubby—but delicately cut—glass, small Victorian jewel boxes, and brass candlesticks. The stalls that line the bustling streets never seem to be empty, and the language of the hucksters is even more colorful than their wares, with the captivating line of badinage and friendly banter that they have.

Street markets are mainly a weekend pastime, and, as many of them are open on Sunday morning, they provide something to do on a day that can be extremely dull and dreary in London. A wander through one of the markets, followed by a good Sunday lunch, then an afternoon in a park or by the river, makes a classic London way of cheering up the sabbath.

Bermondsey (Tower Bridge Rd., SE1). Also known as the New Caledonian Market, this is one of London's largest market sites. There are hundreds of stalls selling a wealth of junk and treasures from Britain's attics. Note that this market is held on Friday only starting at the unearthly hour of 4 AM, and it's then that the really great buys will be snapped up. You should still be able to find a bargain or two if you turn up a bit later. *To get there, take the #15 or #25 bus to Aldgate, then a #42 over Tower Bridge to Bermondsey Sq., or take the tube to London Bridge and walk. Open Fri. 4:30 AM–noon.*

Camden Lock (Dingwalls) Market (NW1). This is just the place to pick up an unusual and inexpensive gift, besides being a picturesque and pleasant area to wander around, with its cobbled courtyards and the attractive lock nearby. There's an open-air antiques market here on Saturday and Sunday, though the individual craft shops are open during the week as well. It does get horribly crowded on weekends. *You'll need to take the tube or #24 or #29 bus to Camden Town. Shops open Tues.–Sun. 9:30–5:30.*

Camden Passage (Islington, N1). The endless rows of little antiques shops here are the places to head for, particularly if you're interested in silverware and jewelry, though the market is by no means confined to these alone. Saturday is the big day for stalls; during the rest of the week only the shops are open. *A #19 or #38 bus or tube to The Angel will get you there. Open Wed.–Sat. 8:30–3.*

Greenwich Antiques Market (Greenwich High Rd., SE10). If you're planning to visit Greenwich, then combine your trip with a wander around this open-air market near St. Alfege Church. You'll find one of the best selections of secondhand and antique clothes in London—good quality tweeds and overcoats can be had at amazing value. But, as in any self-respecting London market, you'll also find a wide range of other items, ranging from the worthless to the wonderful. The market for antiques is open on Saturday and Sunday only. *Take a British Rail train to New Gate Cross and then a #117 bus, or a bus direct to Greenwich. Antiques, crafts, and clothes Sat. and Sun. 9–5; fruit and vegetables Mon.–Fri. 9–5.*

Leadenhall Market (EC3). The draw here is not so much what you can buy—plants and food mainly—as the building itself. It's a handsome late-Victorian structure, ornate and elaborate, with lashings of atmosphere. *To get there take the tube to Bank or Monument. Open Mon.–Fri. 7 AM–3 PM.*

Petticoat Lane (Middlesex St., E1). Petticoat Lane doesn't actually appear on the map, but it's the commonly used name of this famous market on Middlesex Street. On Sunday it becomes Petticoat Lane, where you can pick up all sorts of bargains. Look for good quality, budget-priced leather goods, dazzling knitwear, and cut-price fashions. There are also luxury goods such as cameras, videos, and stereos at exceptional prices. *Liverpool St., Aldgate, or Aldgate East tubes are the closest. Open Sun. 9–2.*

Portobello Market (Portobello Rd., W11). This is no longer the place it once was for bargains, but Saturday is the best day to search the stalls for a not-quite-bargain-priced treasure in the way of silverware, curios, porcelain, and jewelry. Some of the clothes stalls are excellent value, selling well-known labels at knock-down prices. It's always crowded, there are street entertainers, and authentic hustle-and-bustle atmosphere, and, since it is firmly on the tourist route, you'll hear as much German or Texan as you will Cockney. The market is open all week except Thursday afternoon. *You'll need to take a #52 bus or the tube to Ladbroke Grove or Notting Hill Gate. Fruit & vegetables Mon.–Wed. and Fri., 8–5, Thurs. 8–1; antiques Fri. 5–3; both on Sat. 8–5.*

VAT Refunds

To the eternal fury of Britain's shopkeepers, who struggle under cataracts of paperwork, Britain is afflicted with a 15% Value Added Tax. Foreign visitors, however, need not pay VAT if they take advantage of the Personal Export Scheme. Of the various ways to get a VAT refund, the most common are **Over the Counter** and **Direct Export**. Note that though practically all larger stores operate these schemes, information about them is not always readily forthcoming, so it is important to ask. Once you have gotten onto the right track, you'll find that almost all of the larger stores have export departments that will be able to give you all the help you need.

The easiest and most usual way of getting your refund is the **Over the Counter** method. There is normally a minimum value for goods you purchase of £75, below which VAT cannot be refunded. You must also be able to supply proof of your identity—your passport is best. The sales clerk will then fill out the necessary paperwork, Form 407 VAT. Keep the form and give it to Customs when you leave the country. Lines at major airports are usually long, so leave plenty of time. The form will then be returned to the store and the refund forwarded to you, minus a small service charge, usually around $3. You can specify how you want the refund. Generally, the easiest way is to have it credited to your charge card. Alternatively, you can have it in the form of a sterling check, but your bank will charge a fee to convert it. Note also that it can take up to eight weeks to receive the refund.

The **Direct Export** method—whereby you have the store send the goods to your home—is more cumbersome. You must have the VAT Form 407 certified by Customs, police, or a notary public when you get home and then send it back to the store. They, in turn, will refund your money.

If you are traveling to any other EEC country from Britain, the same rules apply, except in France, where you can claim your refund as you leave the country.

Clothing Sizes

Men Suit, shirt, and shoe sizes in the United Kingdom are the same as U.S. sizes.

Women
Dresses and Coats

U.S.	4	6	8	10	12	14	16
U.K.	6	8	10	12	14	16	18

Blouses and
Sweaters

U.S.	30	32	34	36	38	40	42
U.K.	32	34	36	38	40	42	44

Shoes

U.S.	4	5	6	7	8	9	10
U.K.	2	3	4	5	6	7	8

6 Dining

Introduction

Our Dining advisor, Mark Lewes, is a longtime Fodor contributor, who has been eating his way around the world for 40 years—writing gourmet articles en route.

Once upon a time, eating in London was an experience to be endured rather than enjoyed. Things are very different now. There are restaurants offering cuisine from all over the world —and even, be it said in reverent tones, from Britain itself. There have always been Italian and French restaurants, some dating back three-quarters of a century, solid reliable places, with solid reliable menus. But now there are literally hundreds of possibilities offering exciting, adventurous cooking.

It is difficult to say what brought about this complete *volte face*. One of the more obvious reasons is the great influx into Britain in the last decade of new citizens who have brought their own cooking with them. That might explain the opening of what seems like endless Tandoori restaurants, but in no way deals with the fact that Britons are becoming more conscious of what they eat. There one would have to look to a worldwide change in attitudes to food. In Britain, as in so many countries, not least the United States, the adage "you live to eat, not eat to live" is now a passionately held credo.

Whatever your personal version of this creed, it is likely to find satisfaction in London. It cannot necessarily be said that your purse will be as happy as your stomach. Rents and local taxes being what they are, restaurants find that they have to charge more and more just to make ends meet. The result has inevitably been that fewer Londoners are able to eat out, unless they are on expense accounts or celebrating. It has also meant that restaurants which have reasonable prices and still give value-for-money and courteous service are treasured. It is much more difficult to find a reasonably priced, friendly little restaurant in London than it is in New York.

Many London restaurants have set lunch menus that are half the price of their normal ones. This makes dining in some of the very fanciest eating places within the budget of almost any visitor. The one thing to be sure of is that you don't hike up the cost with the bar check.

A serious problem to dining in London is that it is difficult to do so on Sundays or late at night. You should always check if a restaurant is open on Sunday; it could save you a wasted journey.

A law obliges all U.K. restaurants to display their prices, including VAT, outside their establishments. Most do now, and if you are on a very tight budget, it's wise to read them carefully. Look for the hidden extras such as service, cover, and minimum charge that are usually at the bottom of the menu in small type.

The most highly recommended restaurants are indicated by a star ★.

Category	Cost*
Very Expensive	£35 and up (way up!)
Expensive	£25–£35
Moderate	£10–£25
Inexpensive	under £10

per person without VAT, service, or drinks

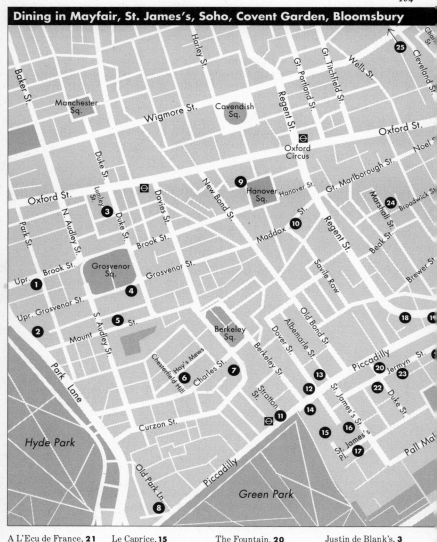

Dining in Mayfair, St. James's, Soho, Covent Garden, Bloomsbury

A L'Ecu de France, **21**
The Agra, **26**
Alastair Little, **32**
Auntie's, **25**
Bertorelli's, **46**
Le Boulestin, **48**
Café des Amis
du Vin, **45**
Café Pacifico, **41**

Le Caprice, **15**
Champagne
Exchange, **7**
Chez Gerard, **27**
Chiang Mai, **33**
Chicago Pizza Pie
Factory, **9**
Connaught Hotel Grill
Room, **4**
Crank's, **24**
Dukes, **17**
Food for Thought, **43**

The Fountain, **20**
Frith's, **31**
Le Gavroche, **1**
Gay Hussar, **30**
Green's, **22**
The Greenhouse, **6**
Hard Rock Café, **8**
Inigo Jones, **42**
Jam's, **13**
Joe Allen's, **51**

Justin de Blank's, **3**
Langan's Brasserie, **11**
Ley-Ons, **34**
Lindsay House, **35**
L.S. Grunt's, **49**
Mandeer, **29**
Manzi's, **39**
Meridien Oak Room, **19**
Mon Plaisir, **40**
My Old Dutch, **54**
Neal Street
Restaurant, **44**

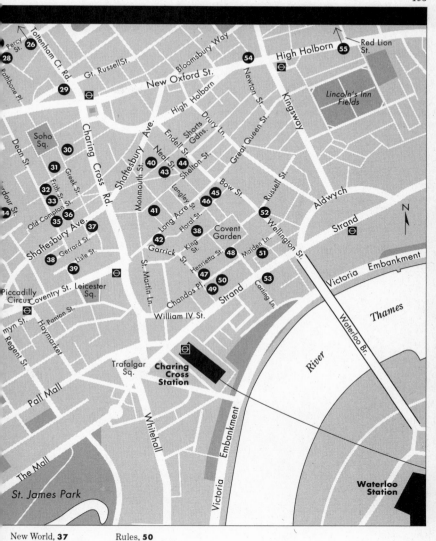

New World, **37**

90 Park Lane, **2**

North Sea Fish
Restaurant, **55**

Orso, **52**

Pizzeria Condotti, **10**

Poon's, **38**

Porter's, **47**

The Ritz, **14**

Rules, **50**

Savoy Grill, **53**

Scott's, **5**

Smollensky's
Balloon, **12**

Soho Brasserie, **36**

Suntory, **16**

Veeraswamy, **18**

White Tower, **28**

Wilton's, **23**

Dining in South Kensington, Knightsbridge, and Chelsea

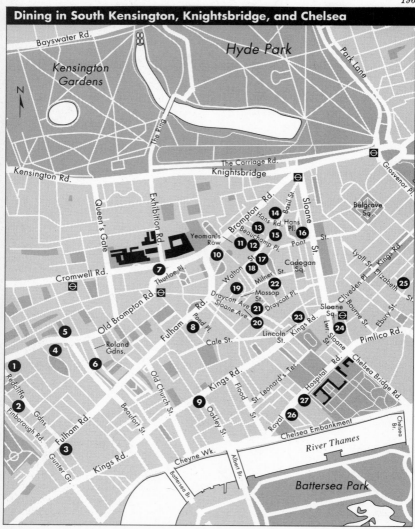

Blake's, **6**

The Capital, **14**

Drake's, **8**

Drones, **16**

English Garden, **23**

English House, **22**

Foxtrot Oscar, **27**

Gavvers, **24**

Henry J. Bean's, **9**

Hilaire, **5**

Lou Pescadou, **1**

Luba's Bistro, **11**

Ma Cuisine, **17**

Ménage à Trois, **13**

Mijanou, **25**

19, **19**

O Fado, **12**

L'Olivier, **2**

Parson's, **3**

Reads, **4**

St. Quentin, **10**

Stockpot, **15**

Le Suquet, **21**

La Tante Claire, **26**

Tui, **7**

Waltons, **18**

Zen, **20**

Bill Bentley's, **11**
Bubb's, **2**
Coates' Café, **7**
Corney and Barrow, **9**
Gallipoli, **10**
Ginnan, **4**
Oscar's Brasserie, **3**
Le Poulbot, **5**
Rouxl Britannia, **8**
Rudland & Stubbs, **1**
Sweetings, **6**

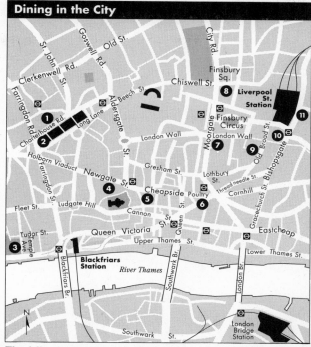

Dining in the City

Credit Cards The following credit card abbreviations are used: AE, American Express; DC, Diners Club; MC, MasterCard; V, Visa.

St. James's

Very Expensive
French

A L'Ecu de France. This is one of the citadels of traditional French fare in London. The decor, with its paneling and rich upholstery, will take you back to 1910. The service, expert but friendly, and the perfectly prepared classic cuisine come with a high price tag on them. You may also need a bank loan to enjoy the wine list, but the set menus can often soften the blow. The simplest dishes are often the best—tournedos Rossini or filet de boeuf en croûte. There are five elegant private rooms available for special occassions. *111 Jermyn St., SW1, tel. 01/930–2837. Jacket and tie required. Reservations needed. AE, DC, MC, V. Closed for lunch Sat. and Sun.*

French/
Traditional English

The Ritz. The Ritz has the most magnificent dining room in London—marble-and-gold Louis XVI—and you look out onto Green Park as you eat. In the evening there's a live cabaret. Chef Keith Stanley produces amazing concoctions—tips of fresh asparagus and smoked salmon glazed with a pink peppercorn and pink champagne sauce is one of the simplest! The wine list is offputtingly pricey. *Piccadilly, W1, tel. 01/493–8181. Jacket and tie. Reservations essential. AE, DC, MC, V.*

Japanese

Suntory. A large and stylishly decorated Japanese restaurant where the waitresses wear kimonos. You can either dine formally in the upper rooms, or watch the chefs at work in the

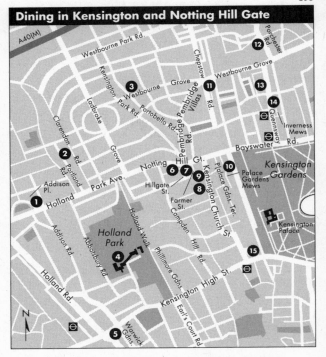

Dining in Kensington and Notting Hill Gate

teppan yaki room, Japanese food fahs will go into raptures over
the sukiyaki (fresh seafood and meat with rice and soy sauce,
cooked in front of you). *72–73 St. James's St., SW1, tel. 01/409–
0201. Dress: casual smart. Reservations advised. AE, DC,
MC, V. Closed Sun., Christmas, New Year, Easter, public holidays.*

Traditional English   **Dukes Restaurant.** The small dining room is decorated with antiques inside the quiet, charming Edwardian Dukes Hotel. It
concentrates mainly on traditional English food such as feuillete of salmon in a mild Stilton sauce, or bread-and-butter pudding. *35 St. James's Pl., SW1, tel. 01/491–4840. Dress: casual
smart. Reservations advised. AE, DC, MC, V.*

Expensive   **Le Caprice.** Just behind the Ritz, LeCaprice is furnished in so-
French   phisticated black-and-white Art Deco, and your fellow diners
could be equally stylish. The menu accommodates itself to all
tastes, whether you're into crudités, or hamburgers, or main
courses with elaborate sauces (salmon fishcakes with sorrel
sauce). Finish up with a mousse of dark and white chocolate.
And it's also a great place for brunch. *Arlington House, Arlington St., SW1, tel. 01/629–2239. Dress: casual smart.
Reservations essential. AE, DC, MC, V. Closed public holidays for lunch.*

Traditional English   **Green's.** The emphasis is on seafood, but Green's also offers
grills and steaks in the evening. It's a restaurant with the air of
a gentleman's club, and the food is very much in keeping: oysters, crab, pigeon pie, and filling desserts such as sticky toffee
pudding. *36 Duke St., St. James's, SW1, tel. 01/930–4566.*

Dress: formal. Reservations necessary at least 2 days in advance. AE, DC, MC, V. Closed Sun. dinner, public holidays.
Wilton's. The most traditional of traditional British fare (turtle soup, sausages and mashed potatoes, partridge, Stilton) is served in Edwardian surroundings. The oysters are the best you'll find anywhere in London—all the seafood arrives fresh up to four times a day. *55 Jermyn St., SW1, tel. 01/629–9955. Jacket and tie required. Reservations advised 2 days in advance. AE, DC, MC, V. Closed Sat. lunch, Sun., last week in July and first 2 weeks in Aug., 10 days at Christmas.*

Inexpensive
Traditional English

The Fountain. At the back of Fortnum & Mason's famous foodstore is this elegant restaurant decorated in pastel shades and serving delicious light meals, toasted snacks, sandwiches, and ice-cream sodas. During the day, go for a Welsh rarebit or cold game pie; in the evening you can get a fillet steak. Just the place for pre-theater meals. (Full meals are also available in the St. James Room restaurant in the store.) *181 Piccadilly, W1, tel. 01/734–4938. Dress: informal. Reservations accepted for dinner only. AE, DC, MC, V. Closed Sun., public holidays.*

Mayfair

Very Expensive
California Nouvelle

Jam's. A stylish, split-level dining room, serving "colorful, fresh food with a sense of humor" (its parent restaurant is in New York). Try the deep-fried Missouri-style squid with chili mayonnaise, the red pepper pancakes with crême fraiche and red salmon caviar, or the rack of lamb on Chinese leaves with butter sauce and roasted pinenuts. *42 Albemarle St., W1, tel. 01/493–3600. Dress: casual smart. Reservations essential for lunch, advised for dinner. AE, MC, V. Closed Sat. lunch, Sun., public holidays.*

French
★

Le Gavroche. Near the U.S. Embassy, and generally felt to be London's finest restaurant. The excellent service and the discreetly sumptuous decor complement the positively Lucullan haute cuisine—duck with foie gras, lobster and champagne mousse. The dining room is comfortable, hung with oil paintings, and decorated in a restful dark green. *43 Upper Brook St., W1, tel. 01/408–0881. Jacket and tie. Reservations at least 1 week in advance. AE, DC, MC, V. Closed Sat., Sun., 10 days at Christmas, public holidays.*

★

90 Park Lane. Nestled inside the Grosvenor House hotel, the flagship of the Trusthouse Forte chain, is this stylish restaurant with a superb wine list and an interesting menu. Specialties include langoustine ravioli in a saffron and batter sauce, venison with roasted chestnuts, and fillet of lamb with crushed coffee beans. *Park La., W1, tel. 01/499–6363. Jacket and tie. Reservations 2 days in advance. AE, DC, MC, V. Closed Sat. lunch, Sun.*

French/
Traditional English

The Connaught Hotel Grill Room. A charming, mahogany-paneled, velvet-upholstered, and crystal-chandeliered dining room with waiters in tailcoats. Fine English fare (duck pâté, roast beef, salmon stuffed with mushrooms and wild rice) is cooked by a top French chef. *Carlos Pl., W1, tel. 01/499–7070. Jacket and tie. Reservations advised 1 week in advance. MC. Closed Sat., Sun., and public holidays.*

International

Scott's. The specialty here is fish—oysters, ragoût de poisson, poached fillet of sole in white wine sauce with truffles, prawns,

and asparagus. The quality of the food and the impeccably unobtrusive service make it the favorite haunt of diplomats from
the numerous embassies in the area. *20 Mount St., W1, tel. 01/
629–5248. Jacket and tie. Reservations advised. AE, DC, MC,
V. Closed Sun. lunch.*

Expensive
French
★

The Meridien Oak Room. Grand Venetian chandeliers and stylish bleached oak paneling set the tone in Le Meridien Piccadilly
hotel's dining room. The food is top quality haute cuisine: the
langoustine gazpacho and the fig tart are especially good. *Le
Meridien, Piccadilly, W1, tel. 01/734–8000. Jacket and tie.
Reservations advised. AE, DC, MC, V. Closed Sat. lunch,
Sun.*

*French/
Traditional English*
★

The Greenhouse. Located on the first floor of an apartment
block, the Greenhouse is approached along a canopied path,
country-house style. It's ultra-popular and has a clubby feel to
it. The menu, which changes every two months, carries a variety of the traditional (calves' liver with bacon and onions, jam
roly-poly with clotted cream) and more modern (deep-fried
mushrooms with avocado and garlic sauce). *27a Hays Mews,
W1, tel. 01/499–3331. Jacket and tie. Reservations several days
in advance. AE, DC, MC, V. Closed Sat. lunch, Sun., one week
at Christmas.*

Langan's Brasserie. Langan's is usually packed with celebrities
and is as exclusive as it is possible to get. If you manage to get
in, you'll be impressed by the faces at other tables, the range of
original modern art on the walls, and the incredibly vast menu.
Service is usually frank (you may find the waiters putting you
off certain dishes) and the food generous and top quality. Highly recommended are the spinach soufflé with anchovy sauce,
and the stuffed artichokes with hollandaise sauce. *Stratton St.,
W1, tel. 01/491–8822. Dress: casual smart. Reservations necessary up to 6 weeks in advance. AE, DC, MC, V. Closed Sat.
lunch, Sun., Christmas, public holidays.*

Indian

The Veeraswamy. This is London's oldest Indian restaurant,
founded in 1927. Needless to say, the whole place, as well as the
menu, has been de-colonialized and refurbished since then—
you can even get a cocktail before your meal. Give the king
prawn masala (medium hot prawn curry) or a lamb kadai
ghosht (curried lamb with capsicums) a try. *99 Regent St., W1,
tel. 01/734–1401. Dress: casual smart. Reservations advised.
AE, DC, MC, V. Closed Christmas, Dec. 26.*

International

The Champagne Exchange. As its name implies, this restaurant
provides more of an excuse to overdose on champagne than a
regular restaurant does. Soak your Dom Perignon up with
smoked salmon and scrambled egg, or steak-and-kidney pie.
The premises are cool designer-gray with piped jazz, spot-
lights, and lacquered chairs, *17c Curzon St., W1, tel. 01/493–
4490. Dress: casual smart. Reservations advised. AE, DC,
MC, V. Closed Sat. and Sun., Christmas, Easter, public holidays.*

Moderate
French/American

Smollensky's Balloon. This American-style bar restaurant offers fine food and good service, and—a real rarity for London—
air-conditioning. The menu changes weekly, but standards are
the five different types of steak, and a vegetarian selection.
Recommended are the calves' liver with couscous and the
chewy nutcake. Sunday lunch is "A Family Affair"—bring the
kids along and be entertained by a clown, a magician, video car-

toons, and a Punch-and-Judy show. *1 Dover St., W1, tel. 01/ 491–1199. Dress: casual. Reservations advised Fri. through Sun. AE, DC, MC, V.*

Italian **Pizzeria Condotti.** This pizzeria, run by cartoonist Enzo Apicella, is lined with original modern paintings and, of course, cartoons. The figure-conscious can choose salads, such as the insalata Condotti—mixed salad with mozzarella and avocado—rather than the hypercalorific, but first-class, pizzas. *4 Mill St., W1, tel. 01/499–1308. Dress: casual smart. Reservations not accepted. Closed Sun., Christmas, Dec. 26.*

Inexpensive **The Chicago Pizza Pie Factory.** A bright basement spot serving
American huge pizzas with salad and garlic bread at good prices, though the choice of fillings may be a bit limited. Worth trying are the American sausage-and-mushroom pizzas. There's a cocktail bar, rock music, and videos. *17 Hanover Sq., W1, tel. 01/629–2669. Dress: casual. Reservations advised for lunch. No credit cards. Closed Christmas, Dec. 26.*

The Hard Rock Café. A phenomenon, not just a hamburger joint. People (especially tourists) stand on line for hours to get into this huge, split-level room with ceiling fans, pool lamps, long tables, and ear-splitting rock music. Favorites include BLT sandwiches, sodas, and calorific desserts. The hamburgers and steaks are top quality. *150 Old Park La., W1, tel. 01/629 –0382. Dress: informal. No reservations. No credit cards. Closed Dec. 24–26.*

International **Justin de Blank's.** An attractive, upmarket, self-service spot, ideally placed for Oxford Street shopping. The food is all homemade. The crab and cucumber mousse is a favorite in summer; the fruit brulé is delicious, and the chocolate roulade sinful. *54 Duke St., W1, tel. 01/629–3174. Dress: informal. No reservations. MC, V. Closed 9 PM, Sat. dinner, Sun., Christmas, public holidays.*

Knightsbridge

Very Expensive **The Capital.** The elegant, club-like dining room has chandeliers
French and trompe l'oeil floral urns. The menu and the service are
★ staid, in keeping with the ambience, but you'll enjoy the classic French dishes such as lamb aux herbes de Provence, or the red mullet on a bed of tomatoes with basil butter. *22–24 Basil St., SW3, tel. 01/589–5171. Jacket and tie. Reservations advised. AE, DC, MC, V.*

★ **Ma Cuisine.** The dining room is uncomfortably small and narrow, but thanks to the talent of chef Guy Mouilleron, you're in for a culinary treat. Irresistible are the cannelloni with salmon and vegetables or (for the adventurous) chicken breast with pigs' trotters and mustard sauce. *113 Walton St., SW3, tel. 01/ 584–7585. Dress: formal. Reservations at least 1 week in advance for dinner. AE, DC. Closed Sat., Sun., Christmas, public holidays, 4 weeks in July–Aug.*

Traditional English/ **Waltons.** This formal, sumptuous restaurant has miles of mir-
French rors and suave lighting. The seafood sausage and/or the roast
★ duck are a must. *121 Walton St., SW3, tel. 01/584–0204. Jacket and tie. Reservations advised. AE, DC, MC, V. Closed Christmas, Dec. 26, Easter.*

Expensive **Drones.** The clientele here is young; the food imaginative—try
French the fillet steak cooked in Madeira sauce or the Polish fillet of

veal with breast of chicken braised in lime juice with white wine and mushrooms. The cool decor is accented by stained glass windows, white walls, and abundant plants. *1 Pont St., SW1, tel. 01/235-9638. Dress: informal. Reservations advised. AE, DC, MC, V. Closed one week at Christmas, public holidays.*

International **Ménage à Trois.** Starters and desserts only are on the menu at this stylish pink-and-gray restaurant. Recommended is the terrine of leeks, and duck confit served with grilled foie gras. Chocolate addicts won't be able to resist the "chocaholics anonymous"—*six* chocolate puddings on one plate. *15 Beauchamp Pl., SW3, tel. 01/589-4252. Dress: casual smart. Reservations essential for dinner. AE, DC, MC, V. Closed Sat. and Sun. lunches, Christmas, Dec. 26, Fri. before Easter.*

Moderate **St. Quentin.** A highly popular corner of Paris in Knightsbridge, *French* the St. Quentin is frequented by locals and French ex-pats ★ alike. The cuisine is traditional but reliable. Try the feuillete d'escargot with foie gras, the veal kidney with mustard sauce, or the fillet of brill in wine sauce. *243 Brompton Rd., SW3, tel. 01/589-8005. Dress: casual smart to formal. Reservations advised. AE, DC, MC, V.*

Portuguese **O Fado.** This is one of London's few Portuguese locales, in a basement, with live music. Seafood is the specialty—pork with clams makes an unusual variation on a theme. *50 Beauchamp Pl., SW3, tel. 01/589-3002. Dress: informal. Reservations essential for dinner Fri. and Sat. AE, MC, V. Closed 1 week at Christmas.*

Inexpensive **Stockpot.** You'll find speedy service in a large, jolly restaurant, *International* often packed to the brim with young people. The food is filling and wholesome: try a Lancashire hot pot, for example, or an apple crumble. *6 Basil St., SW3, tel. 01/589-8627. Dress: casual. Reservations not required. No credit cards. Closed Christmas, public holidays.*

Russian **Luba's Bistro.** Luba's has been popular for decades with its long wooden tables, basic decor, and authentic Russian cooking —chicken kiev, beef stroganoff, etc. Bring your own wine. *6 Yeoman's Row, SW3, tel. 01/589-2950. Dress: informal. Reservations advised. MC, V. Closed Sun., Christmas, public holidays.*

South Kensington

Very Expensive **Blake's Hotel Restaurant.** This has to be one of London's most *International* glamorous, luxurious dining rooms. Black lacquer, masses of ★ flowers, and subtly lit Thai tribal costumes in display cabinets, give it a romantic, oriental air. Though the wine list is breathtakingly expensive, the cuisine is good and extraordinarily varied. You could start with a langoustine, rucola, and bacon salad, go on to a *gyuniku teriyaki* (marinated beef with wild rice and wasabi sauce), and finish with an iced chocolate-and-almond pudding. *33 Roland Gdns., SW7, tel. 01/370-6701. Dress: casual smart to formal. Reservations advised. AE, DC, MC, V. Closed Christmas, Dec. 26.*

Traditional English **Drake's.** The two-level basement restaurant is bare-bricked, with a glass partition through which you can watch the chefs at work. The food is traditional English—spit roast boar with mustard sauce, beef Wellington, or roast duck on a bed of mushrooms with calvados sauce. *2a Pond Pl., SW3, tel. 01/584-4555.*

Dress: casual smart to formal. Reservations advised. AE, DC, MC, V. Dinner only (except Sun.). Closed Christmas.

Expensive   **L'Olivier.** A light and airy basement restaurant decorated in
French   pale blue with flower paintings and rustic pottery. You ring the
bell to get in. Roast meat and bouillabaisse are the specialties
of the house. *116 Finborough Rd., SW10, tel. 01/370–4183.
Dress: informal. Reservations essential on weekends. AE,
DC, MC, V. Dinner only. Closed Sun.*

Traditional English   **Hilaire.** Here's a foodie's paradise, tastefully decorated in olive
green, with watercolor landscapes of Burma. Chef Bryan Webb
has a winning way with the fresh foie gras and haricots verts,
asparagus, and artichokes. Unlikely though the combination
may seem, there's also a Thai flavor to the menu; try the
steamed salmon with Thai ginger and wild mushroom sauce. *68
Old Brompton Rd., SW7, tel. 01/584–8993. Jacket and tie. Reservations required. AE, DC, MC, V. Closed Sat. lunch, Sun.,
public holidays.*

Moderate   **Lou Pescadou.** Boats are the theme in this Provencal-style res-
French   taurant: boats as lamps, pictures of boats on the walls, and so
★   on. Not surprisingly, fish is the specialty—petite bouillabaisse
(fish soup), or a red mullet poached in tarragon sauce. *241
Old Brompton Rd., SW5, tel. 01/370–1057. Dress: informal.
Reservations not accepted. AE, DC, MC, V. Closed Aug.,
Christmas.*

French/   **Reads.** A husband–wife team runs this small, pretty restau-
Traditional English   rant with a country-house feel (lots of plants and wickerwork).
The roast beef is succulent; the excellent cheeseboard features
English cheeses. *152 Old Brompton Rd., SW5, tel. 01/373–
2445. Dress: informal. Reservations advised. AE, DC, MC, V.
Closed Sun. for dinner, public holidays.*

Thai   **Tui.** Stylish and modern, and just around the corner from the
Victoria & Albert Museum. Wake your taste buds up with a
crab claw and prawn hot pot, or a green beef curry. *19 Exhibition Rd., SW7, tel. 01/584–8359. Dress: informal. Reservations advised. Closed public holidays.*

Kensington and Notting Hill

Very Expensive   **Belvedere.** This stunning, spacious country-house-style restau-
French   rant in Holland Park is particularly appealing in summer, when
the gardens are in bloom. The cuisine is "French creative": you
might begin with a salmon parfait with dill and watercress
sauce, and go on to a fillet of veal with tarragon and gravy.
Look out at the floodlit park by night. *Holland House, Holland
Park, W8, tel. 01/602–1238. Jacket and tie. Reservations essential. AE, DC, MC, V. Closed Sat. lunch, Sun., Christmas,
public holidays.*

Expensive   **Boyd's Glass Restaurant.** Named because it's situated under a
French   conservatory dome, this stylish, summery, modern restaurant
serves delicious classic French cuisine—foie gras salad, beef
with truffle sauce. The menu changes monthly. *135 Kensington
Church St., W8, tel. 01/727–5452. Dress: formal. Reservations
advised. MC, V. Closed Sat., Sun., 10 days over Christmas,
Easter.*

Chez Moi. Sophisticated French food is served in a warm
salmon-pink dining room that makes the ideal location for romantic meals. The tables are discreetly far apart and the
lighting is low and flattering. Try a mouth-watering rack of

lamb stuffed with garlic and mint, or boned quails baked in a pastry case with a white port sauce. *1 Addison Ave., W11, tel. 01/603–8267. Dress: informal. Reservations essential for dinner. AE, DC, MC, V. Closed Sat. lunch, Sun., 2 weeks over Christmas, 2 weeks in Aug., public holidays.*

Michel's Bistro. A hot favorite with the local French population. The dining room's long and whitewashed, and Edit Piaf agonizes in the background. It's good value, especially the set lunch. Recommended are the poached salmon with beurre blanc and the beef entrecote in a Roquefort sauce. *343 Kensington High St., W8, tel. 01/603–3613. Dress: anything goes. Reservations essential for dinner. AE, DC, MC, V. Closed public holidays.*

International   **Clarke's.** Can't make up your mind when faced with a lengthy menu? Then this is the ideal place for you—there's no choice at all! Chef Sally Clarke will have planned the meal according to what was available in the market that day, using the freshest of herbs and the best olive oils. *124 Kensington Church St., W8, tel. 01/221–9225. Dress: casual smart. Reservations advised. MC, V. Closed Sat., Sun., 1 week at Christmas, Easter, 2 weeks in Aug.*

Traditional English   **Julie's.** This restaurant has two parts; an upstairs champagne bar and a basement restaurant, both decorated with Victorian ecclesiastical furniture. The cooking is sound Anglo-French (salmon and halibut terrine, roast pheasant with chestnut stuffing and wild rowan jelly). The traditional Sunday lunches are very popular, and in summer there's a garden for outside eating. *135 Portland Rd., W11, tel. 01/229–8331. Jacket and tie. Reservations advised for dinner, essential on weekends. AE, DC, MC, V. Closed Christmas, Dec. 31, Easter.*

Moderate **L'Artiste Assoiffé.** Stanley and Sally the parrots will abuse you
French   in the bar of this eccentric Victorian house before you proceed to the Cancan room or the Carousel room to eat. The music is usually operatic. Pop stars, actors, and royals come here for the food (fillet of steak, caramelized, with dijon mustard; spinach pancakes with nuts and cheese) as well as for the unique atmosphere. *122 Kensington Park Rd., W11, tel. 01/727–4714. Dress: casual smart. Reservations essential. AE, DC, MC, V. Closed Sun., public holidays.*

French/ **Ark.** Established in the 1960s, the Ark remains popular with
Traditional English the locals. The atmosphere is cordial and the menu reliable: the
★   smoked chicken pancakes and French onion soup are always in demand. It's a wooden shed with wooden tables, and a jumble of photos decorate every available surface. *122 Palace Gardens Terr., W8, tel. 01/229–4024. Dress: informal. Reservations essential. MC, V. Closed Sun. lunch, Christmas, Easter.*

Greek **Kalamaras.** There are two small, friendly, authentic Greek restaurants, one "micro" and one "mega," next door to each other. Micro is unlicensed and cheaper but more cramped than mega. Try a plate of *mezze* for starters, and go on to, say, kebabs and salads. *76–78 Inverness Mews, W2, tel. 01/727–9122. Dress: informal. Reservations advised. AE, DC, MC, V. Closed Sun., public holidays.*

Traditional English **Maggie Jones.** An attractive, country-cottage-style restaurant with scrubbed floorboards and pine tables, Maggie Jones' serves good, fresh, wholesome fare such as steak and kidney pie or baked mackerel in gooseberries, to the sound of English 1930s popular songs. *Old Court Pl., Kensington Church St.,*

W8, tel. 01/937–6462. Dress: informal. Reservations essential for dinner and Sun. lunch. AE, DC, MC, V. Closed Christmas, Dec. 26, Jan. 1, public holidays.

Inexpensive **Hung Toa.** This extremely popular Cantonese restaurant offers
Chinese specialties of roast duck, barbecued pork, and fried oysters. The most popular dishes are so much in demand that you should phone ahead to reserve your dish. *54 Queensway, W2, tel. 01/ 727–6017. Dress: informal. Reservations advised. No credit cards. Closed Christmas, Dec. 26.*

Greek **Costa's Grill.** Come for good value, down-to-earth Greek food
★ such as grilled fish, *kleftiko* (roast lamb on the bone). The atmosphere is lively and great fun. *14 Hillgate St., W8, tel. 01/229 –3794. Dress: informal. Reservations advised for groups of over 4. No credit cards. Closed Sun., public holidays.*

Indian vegetarian **Baba Bhel Poori House.** Go for the set thali meal—a trayful of different vegetables with a dessert—or the *dosai* (spicy pancakes). This is a popular, youthful, friendly place and excellent value. *29–31 Porchester Rd., W2, tel. 01/221–7502. Dress: informal. Reservations not necessary. MC, V. Closed Mon., Christmas.*

International **Wine Gallery.** If you want to see the pictures in this art gallery, you have to eat and drink here, too. The food is a lot more interesting than in the average wine bar (pastry parcels with duck, shallots, and garlic; or blinis with sour cream, smoked salmon, and caviar) and the wine is reliable—the owner's a wine merchant. *294 Westbourne Grove, W11, tel. 01/229–1877. Dress: casual. Reservations not necessary. MC, V. Closed public holidays.*

Seafood **Geales.** This is a cut above your typical fish-and-chips joint.
★ The decor is bare-minimum but the fish were swimming in the sea just a few hours beforehand, even the ones from the West Indies (fried swordfish is a specialty). It's popular with the rich and famous, not just loyal locals. *2 Farmer St., W8, tel. 01/727–7969. Dress: informal. No reservations. MC. Closed Sun., Mon., 2 weeks at Christmas, 3 weeks in Aug., public holidays.*

Chelsea

Very Expensive **La Tante Claire.** Justly famous, but cripplingly expensive. The
French food is superb haute cuisine—hot foie gras on shredded pota-
★ toes with a sweet wine and shallot sauce, or pig's trotter stuffed with mousse of white meat with sweetbreads and wild mushrooms—in attractive, light surroundings. Walk your meal off afterwards along the nearby Thames embankment. *68 Royal Hospital Rd., SW3, tel. 01/352–6045. Jacket and tie. Reservations 3–4 weeks in advance for dinner, 2–3 days for lunch. AE, DC, MC, V. Closed Sat., Sun., Christmas, New Year, 10 days at Easter, 3 weeks in Aug.–Sept.*

Expensive **Zen.** No funny lanterns or gilt dragons here—the glitz is much
Chinese more ambitious: mirrors, pillars, red tablecloths and ceiling, even a tiny waterfall near the entrance. The fresh lobster with ginger and spring onions is irresistible; vegetarians should order the "monk's vegetarian" dish. *Chelsea Cloisters, Sloane Ave., SW3, tel. 01/589–1781. Dress: informal. Reservations advised for dinner. AE, DC, MC, V. Closed Christmas.*

French **Gavvers.** This is one of the successful Roux brothers' restaurants, and a lot less pricey than its older sister, Le Gavroche.

The cuisine is classical (blanquette de poisson, foie gras salad) and the service French. *61–63 Lower Sloane St., SW1, tel. 01/ 730–5938. Dress: informal. Reservations advised. AE, DC, MC, V. Closed for Sat. lunch, Sun., public holidays.*

Mijanou. The haunt of politicians and Whitehall civil servants. Chef Sonia Blech prepares top-quality, elaborate food (quails stuffed with wild rice and pecan nuts, lobster terrine with a mild saffron sauce) behind the scenes. There's a dining room for non-smokers. *143 Ebury St., SW1, tel. 01/730–4099. Dress: casual smart to formal. Reservations advised. AE, DC, MC. Closed Sat. and Sun.*

Le Suquet. A tiny, noisy fish restaurant, with a French seaport atmosphere. Oysters are always good here, or you could try the grilled sea bass. *104 Draycott Ave., SW3, tel. 01/ 581–1785. Dress: informal. Reservations 2 days in advance. AE, DC, MC, V.*

Traditional English **English Garden.** This summery restaurant, just off the King's ★ Road, serves traditional English food to businessmen at lunch and to locals (and tourists) in the evenings. Its specialties are fresh salmon fish cakes with watercress mayonnaise, and saddle of hare with juniper berries. Sister restaurants are the English House (*see below*) and Lindsay House (*see* Soho and Covent Garden). *10 Lincoln St., SW3, tel. 01/584–7272. Dress: casual smart. Reservations essential. AE, DC, MC, V. Closed public holidays.*

★ **English House.** The setting here is charming; a private house decorated in chintz, with antiques and cream linen tablecloths. Authentic recipes include Holm Oak smoked pigeon breast with rhubarb and ginger preserve, and hot toffee and apple tart. *3 Milner St., SW3, tel. 01/584–3002. Dress: formal. Reservations essential for dinner. AE, DC, MC, V. Closed Christmas, Good Fri.*

Moderate **Foxtrot Oscar.** A welcome lunch-oasis when you've been "do-*International* ing" the King's Road. Trendies enjoy the cocktails, the hip atmosphere, the clam fries, the eggs Benedict, hamburgers, and huge salads. Stick to the ground floor dining room—the basement's pretty gloomy. *79 Royal Hospital Rd., SW3, tel. 01/352 –7179. Dress: informal. Reservations advised. MC, V. Closed Christmas, Dec. 26.*

Traditional English/ **19.** This popular, informal bistro serves consistently high-*French* standard, mega-portions of food (fresh salmon and halibut terrine, venison casserole) in attractive English country-cottage surroundings. *19 Mossop St., SW3, tel. 01/589–4971. Dress: informal. Reservations not required. MC, V. Closed Sat. lunch, Christmas, Easter.*

Inexpensive **Henry J. Bean's.** Homesick Americans flock here as if by in-*American* stinct. The food is Tex Mex (*muchos nachos*—ground beef with sour cream, spicy sauce, melted cheese and tortilla chips), hamburgers, etc.; the musak American oldies; the decor typical American-bar—walls covered with newspapers and other ephemera. *195–197 King's Rd., SW3, tel. 01/352–9255. Dress: informal. Reservations not accepted. No credit cards. Closed Christmas, Dec. 26, Dec. 31.*

Parson's. The decor is Edwardian colonial interior—swan-neck lamps, cream walls, plants, fans, antique tables and chairs, big windows. You can eat and drink almost anything here from avocadoburgers to spinach/sweet corn enchiladas; from Australian wine to Japanese beer. The music—classical, folk, African—is equally ecletic. *311 Fulham Rd., SW10, tel. 01/352–0651. Dress: informal. Reservations not accepted. AE, DC, MC, V. Closed Christmas, Dec. 26.*

Soho

Expensive
International

Alastair Little. This is a favorite among Soho media people who feel at home with Nouvelle British designer food, such as venison terrine with onion marmalade, and mascarpone tart with figs. Drawbacks are the paper napkins, the functional-futuristic decor, and the tables packed rather close together in the tiny dining room. *49 Frith St., W1, tel. 01/734–5183. Dress: informal. Reservations advised. No credit cards. Closed Sat. and Sun., Christmas, Easter, 3 weeks in Aug.*

New British

Frith's. Unpretentious and very popular Frith's features imaginative English cooking (roast loin of veal with red onions and pinenuts; scallops and squid with tomatoes, ginger, and Chinese garlic flowers), in pleasant surroundings with linen tablecloths and lots of greenery. *14 Frith St., W1, tel. 01/439–3370. Dress: informal. Reservations essential. AE, DC, MC, V. Closed Sat. lunch, Sun., 10 days at Christmas.*

Traditional English
★

Lindsay House. At this restored 16th-century town house they serve mouth-watering food prepared to traditional English recipes of the 17th century, such as "Brye favors"—brie in pastry with fresh tomato sauce, and salmis of pheasant in a rich vegetable and red wine sauce. Decor is in opulent shades of red and green, with hunting scenes and oil portraits on the walls; decor in the ladies' washroom is like none you'll have ever seen. *21 Romilly St., W1, tel. 01/439–0450. Dress: casual smart. Reservations advised, especially for lunch and after-theater. AE, DC, MC, V. Closed Christmas day.*

Moderate
Hungarian

The Gay Hussar. Supposedly the best Hungarian restaurant outside Budapest. Frequented by politicians and journalists, the small interior is somberly, but solidly, furnished in mock Tudor paneling with plush banquette seats. Helpings are Magyar-sized; try the cold cherry soup, the goulash, or the "heroic minced goose." *2 Greek St., W1, tel. 01/437–0973. Dress: informal. Reservations essential. No credit cards. Closed Sun., public holidays.*

International

The Soho Brasserie. This brasserie is decorated in Art Deco blue-and-cream and divided into two. There's a bar at the front —ideal to meet friends for a coffee or a snack, and open throughout the day—and the restaurant at the back, which serves a mean grilled salmon (with beurre blanc, julienne, and mangetout) and a wicked Bavarian cream with candied ginger. The salads are also recommended. *23 Old Compton St., W1, tel. 01/439–9301. Dress: informal. Reservations advised. AE, DC, MC, V. Closed Sun., Christmas, Easter.*

Seafood

Manzi's. London's oldest and most traditional restaurant has dining rooms on two floors. Downstairs is the more lively and atmospheric. The speed and dexterity with which the waiters weave their way between the tables carrying trays of Dover sole or alligator in butter sauce is truly remarkable. The decor features kitsch Moulin Rouge murals and monstrous plastic lobsters. *1–2 Leicester St., WC2, tel. 01/734–0224. Dress: casual smart. Reservations advised. AE, DC, MC, V. Closed Christmas, Dec. 26.*

Thai **Chiang Mai.** The interior is modeled on a traditional Thai stilt
★ house. The food is delicious and spicy, all freshly cooked and
easy to order from an English menu and excellent value. Risk a
Tom Yum (hot and sour soup) or a Tad Tra Prou (beef/pork/
chicken with fresh Thai basil and chili). *48 Frith St., W1, tel.
01/437-7444. Dress: informal. Reservations advised for dinner. AE, MC, V. Closed Sun., public holidays.*

Inexpensive **Ley-Ons.** Ley-Ons was the first Soho restaurant to serve dim
Chinese sum. Anytime up to 5 PM you can sample over 20 varieties. In
the evening, go for lobster with ginger (though this is a pricey
item) or the Cantonese-style fillet steak. *56 Wardour St., W1,
tel. 01/437-6465. Dress: informal. Reservations advised for
Fri. and Sat. dinner. AE, DC, MC, V. Closed Christmas, Dec.
26.*

New World. A large and cheerfully decorated Cantonese restaurant. They also do Pekinese and Szechuan dishes. New
World serves dim sum on trolleys at lunchtime and tasty specialties such as prawns with a hot curry sauce. *1 Gerrard Pl.,
W1, tel. 01/734-0677. Dress: informal. Reservations not necessary (700 seats). AE, DC, MC, V. Closed Christmas.*

★ **Poon's.** There's a sister restaurant in Covent Garden, but this
one is less expensive and more authentic, and so popular that
you'll always find a long line in the evenings. Wind-dried meats
are the specialty of the house. *4 Leicester St., WC2, tel. 01/
437-1528. Dress: informal. Reservations essential. No credit
cards. Closed Sun., Christmas, Dec. 26.*

Vegetarian **Crank's.** This is a popular vegetarian chain (other branches at
Covent Garden, Great Newport Street, Adelaide Street, Tot-
tenham Street, and Barrett Street), always crowded, with an
extremely nutritious, tasty menu. Lunch is self-service; dinner
is candle-lit waiter service. The Marshall Street branch is open
until 11 PM, but the other branches seem to work on the premise
that vegetarians go to bed earlier than carnivores, and close at
8. *8 Marshall St., W1, tel. 01/437-9431. Dress: informal. Reservations advised for dinner. AE, DC, MC, V. Closed Sun.,
Christmas.*

Covent Garden

Very Expensive **Le Boulestin.** The hautest of French classical haute cuisine is
French served in this grand basement restaurant. Specialties include
roast guinea-fowl with shallots, and fillet of smoked pork,
though the menu changes regularly. The cheese selection and
wine cellar are both magnificent. *La Henrietta St., WC2, tel.
01/836-7061. Jacket and tie. Reservations at least one week in
advance for dinner. AE, DC, MC, V. Closed Sat. lunch, Sun.,
3 weeks in Aug., 10 days at Christmas.*

★ **Inigo Jones.** *The* place for original, beautifully presented
French nouvelle cuisine. You'll be paying dearly for your supreme
of duck with black olive and mushroom puree and lavender
honey sauce, but then again, it's a gourmet's paradise. The
bare brick and glass, and comfortable seating are conducive to
a long, relaxed meal. *14 Garrick St., WC2, tel. 01/836-6456.
Dress: formal. Reservations advised. AE, DC, MC, V. Closed
Sat. lunch, Sun., Christmas through New Year, public holidays.*

French/ **Savoy Grill.** The grill continues to attract more than its fair
Traditional English share of literary and artistic names, as well as the occasional

tycoon. The cooking remains top-notch—order an omelette Arnold Bennett (seafood being the added ingredient) or a fillet of pork with fresh cranberries. The decor is discreet and tasteful; low lighting and yew-paneling. *Strand, WC2, tel. 01/836–4343. Jacket and tie. Reservations advised for lunch, and for Thurs. –Sat. dinner. AE, DC, MC, V. Closed Sat. lunch, Sun.*

Expensive
French **Mon Plaisir.** Gallic enough to serve snails and frogs' legs, but the nervous of palate will want to plump for the coq au vin (chicken in wine sauce) or the *carbonade de boeuf* (stewed beef with cider). There's a magnificent cheese board. *21 Monmouth St., WC2, tel. 01/836–7243. Dress: casual. Reservations advised. AE, MC, V. Closed Sat. lunch, Sun., Christmas, Easter.*

International **Neal Street Restaurant.** This place has been frequented by the chic and fashionable from the contemporary arts/design scene for years. It was an early part of the Conran empire. The food is mostly modern Italian and French; specialties include giant prawns with chili and garlic, and pasta spirals with broccoli sauce, but the restaurant's hallmark is its wild mushrooms that flavor many dishes. *26 Neal St., WC2, tel. 01/836–8368. Dress: casual smart. Reservations essential for lunch. AE, DC, MC, V. Closed Sat. and Sun., Christmas through New Year, public holidays.*

Italian **Orso.** An Italian version of Joe Allen's (*see below*)—a basement restaurant with the same snappy staff and a glitzy showbiz clientele. The menu changes seasonally, but at press time the specialties were a warm scallop and asparagus salad starter, and a grilled fillet of lamb with artichokes and balsamic ginger main dish. *27 Wellington St., WC2, tel. 01/240–5269. Dress: casual smart. Reservations essential. No credit cards. Closed Christmas, Dec. 26.*

Traditional English **Rules.** A London institution—an Edwardian restaurant that was a great favorite of Lily Langtry's, among others. Recently the standard of the cooking here has been mixed, but the restaurant remains unchallenged for its splendid period atmosphere. For a main dish, stick with the roast beef, lamb, or Dover sole; for a dessert you can't do better than a homemade whiskey-and-ginger ice cream. *35 Maiden La., WC2, tel. 01/836–5314. Dress: casual smart. Reservations at least one day in advance. AE, DC, MC, V. Closed Sun., Christmas.*

Moderate
American
★ **Joe Allen's.** This well-known basement café located behind the Strand Palace Hotel, is a great place to spot stage and screen personalities. The Caesar salad and the barbecued ribs are a real treat, and if you eat late (after 9 PM) you'll be entertained by a pianist—if you can hear through the surrounding decibels. *13 Exeter St., WC2, tel. 01/836–0651. Dress: casual. Reservations essential. No credit cards. Closed Christmas, Dec. 26.*

L.S. Grunt's. Chicago deep-dish pizzas are the specialty here. Hungry, homesick tourists should go for a Great Grunter (spiced sausage pizza) or a Memories are Made of This (mushroom pizza). It's a noisy, jokey, popular haunt, and best late at night. *12 Maiden La., WC2, tel. 01/379–7722. Dress: casual. No reservations. MC, V. Closed Christmas, Dec. 26, Jan. 1.*

French **Café des Amis du Vin.** In a lane beside the Royal Opera House, this place is split into three: a wine bar in the basement, the Café on the ground floor, and the Salon restaurant on the first floor. Seating in the Café is rather cramped, but the genuine

French atmosphere and food compensate. The menu offers an interesting choice of regional dishes, salads, and wines; experiment with the calves' liver in onion sauce or the roast guinea-fowl with wild mushroom sauce. The Salon restaurant upstairs is considerably more expensive. There are a few tables outside for summer eating. *11–14 Hanover Pl., WC2, tel. 01/379–3444. Dress: informal. Reservations advised. AE, DC, MC, V. Closed Sun., Christmas.*

Italian   **Bertorelli's.** Right across from the stage door of the Royal Opera House, Bertorelli's inevitably hosts a high proportion of opera buffs and singers, so you should book far in advance for pre- and post-opera meals. The decor is chic and post-modern; the food is traditional Italian. Recommended are the hot mushroom and garlic salad and the saltimbocca alla romana (veal and ham in a butter and wine sauce). *44a Floral St., WC2, tel. 01/836–3969. Dress: casual smart. Reservations essential. AE, DC, MC, V. Closed Christmas.*

Inexpensive Mexican   **The Café Pacifico.** Reasonably priced Californian-Mexican or straight Mexican food is served in a young, lively, converted warehouse. The bar boasts a full range of tequilas (including frozen margueritas). If you go on a Sunday night you can enjoy live music as you devour your ceviche (marinated spiced fish, cold cooked in lime juice) or fajitas (marinated beef/chicken with onions, peppers, tortillas, cheese, and guacamole). *5 Langley St., WC2, tel. 01/379–7728. Dress: informal. Reservations not accepted for dinner. MC, V. Closed Christmas, Dec. 26, Jan. 1.*

Traditional English   **Porter's.** The place to choose for traditional—but filling!—English fare. Pies (lamb and apricot, or steak and mushroom, to name but two) are the specialty. Try the bread-and-butter pudding, or the potted Stilton cheese, if you still have room afterward. The dining room is large, with mirrors, wood carvings, and columns. *17 Henrietta St., WC2, tel. 01/836–6466. Dress: informal. Reservations not necessary. MC, V. Closed Christmas, Dec. 26.*

Vegetarian   **Food for Thought.** The simple basement restaurant (unli-
★   censed) seats only 50, and is extremely popular, so you'll almost always find a line of people up the stairs. The menu—stir-fries, casseroles, salads, and dessert—changes every day, and each dish is freshly made; there's no microwave. *31 Neal St., WC2, tel. 01/836–0239. Dress: informal. No reservations. No credit cards. Closed after 8 PM, 2 weeks at Christmas, public holidays.*

Bloomsbury

Expensive French   **Chez Gerard.** A superior steak-and-french-fries restaurant Chez Gerard offers a simple menu. Starters are light (tomato and basil salad, tuna with horseradish sauce), the main course is chargrilled steak or lamb, and dessert is chocolate mousse. *8 Charlotte St., W1, tel. 01/636–4975. Dress: informal. Reservations advised. AE, DC, MC, V. Closed Christmas.*

Greek   **The White Tower.** Barely changed since it began 49 years ago, the White Tower is the most upmarket Greek restaurant in London, with portraits on the walls (Lord Byron upstairs), glass partitions between the tables, and an entertainingly rhapsodic menu. Dishes range from the traditional—taramasalata—to the more creative—roast duckling stuffed with crushed wheat. *1 Percy St., W1, tel. 01/636–8141. Dress: formal. Reservations essential. AE, DC, MC, V. Closed Sat. and Sun., 3 weeks in Aug., 1 week Christmas, public holidays.*

Moderate
Traditional English

Auntie's. The place to find "authentic" English food ("the Colonel's curried egg mayonnaise," Barnsley lamb chop with plum and mint sauce, tipsy fruit trifle) in an Edwardian atmosphere —dark green walls hung with theater bills. It's rather small, so it can be more intimate than you might wish. *126 Cleveland St., W1, tel. 01/387–1548. Dress: casual smart. Reservations advised. AE, DC, MC, V. Closed Sat. lunch, Sun., 2 weeks mid-Aug., Christmas.*

Inexpensive
Dutch

My Old Dutch. Huge, 18-inch diameter Dutch pancakes are served with a choice of sweet or savory fillings. There are 67 varieties to choose from including spinach-and-ratatouille and "My Old Dutch"—chicken, ham, bacon, sweet corn, sweet peppers, and cheese. The setting is traditional Dutch. *131–132 High Holborn, WC1, tel. 01/242–5200. Dress: informal. Reservations for parties of 8 or more. AE, DC, MC, V.*

Indian

The Agra. Media folk are attracted to the great value and wide choice of curries, both meat and vegetarian, ranging from a mild chicken korma (cream and coconut sauce) to hot fish curry served here. Overhead fans, low lighting, and attentive waiters add a touch of class. *135–137 Whitfield St., W1, tel. 01/387–8833. Dress: informal. Reservations advised for dinner. AE, DC, MC, V. Closed Christmas.*

Mandeer. Buried in a basement, with tiled floors, brick walls, and real temple lamps, Mandeer features tofu curry and stuffed eggplant. Lunch is self-service and cheap. *21 Hanway Pl., W1, tel. 01/323–0660. Dress: anything goes. Reservations advised for Fri. and Sat. dinner. AE, DC, MC, V. Closed Sun., public holidays, 2 weeks over New Year.*

Seafood
★

The North Sea Fish Restaurant. This is a popular cabbie haunt, though you'll find a fair number of regular locals and tourists as well. Only freshly-caught fish is served—the seafood platter is recommended, and the Dover sole is superb, though it's the most expensive item on the menu. You can take out or eat in. *7–8 Leigh St., WC1, tel. 01/387–5892. Dress: anything from casual to bow tie. Reservations advised. AE, DC, MC, V. Closed Sun., public holidays, Christmas.*

The City

Very Expensive
International

Corney and Barrow. The outlandishly imaginative menu—wild boar and cognac pâté?—and daringly modern surroundings engage in a gripping struggle for supremacy. There's air-conditioning and inoffensive Baroque music. The location is convenient for the Barbican. *109 Old Broad St., EC2, tel. 01/638–9308. Dress: formal. Reservations advised. AE, DC, MC, V. Lunch only. Closed Sat., Sun., public holidays, Christmas.*

Expensive
French

Bubb's. Old Bailey lawyers, stockbrokers, and the diamond trade merchants flock here for lunch. The ambience is faintly-chaotic French-bistro (blood-red walls, white tablecloths, posters), and the food is as fresh as you'll find anywhere, and well prepared. Try the Barbary duck or the crème brulée. *329 Central Markets, Smithfield, EC1, tel. 01/236–2435. Dress: formal* *for lunch, informal for dinner. Reservations essential for lunch. No credit cards. Closed Sat., Sun., public holidays, 2 weeks Aug., 1 week Christmas.*

Coates' Café. This fashionable Art-Deco-style hangout of young City workers transforms from a cool, reserved lunch-spot, to a noisy but trendy cocktail-and-champagne venue (with pop videos) in the evening. The food (served only at lunch) is light, French, and surprisingly cheap. The menu, which changes we-ekly, might feature roast fillet of monkfish with broccoli mousse and red pepper sauce, or panfried lambs' kidneys with a dark port and a cream of thyme sauce. The wines, from owners Corney and Barrow, a long established wine broker, are excellent value. *45 London Wall, EC2, tel. 01/256–5148. Dress: casual smart (no jeans). Reservations essential. AE, DC, MC, V. Closed Sat., Sun., public holidays.*

Oscar's Brasserie. Located inside Temple Chambers, it's not surprising that Oscar's is full of hungry lawyers—though journalists also appreciate the French Provençal atmosphere and the cooking (mousseline of smoked trout, breast of pigeon in red wine on radicchio salad). The menu changes daily. *5 Temple Ave., Temple Chambers, EC4, tel. 01/353–6272. Dress: formal. Reservations essential for lunch. AE, DC, MC, V. Closed Sat., Sun., Aug., 10 days over Christmas, public holidays.*

★ **Le Poulbot.** One of the best fixed-price lunches in the City. It's part of the Roux brother's empire (*see* La Gavroche), and, like the other Roux restaurants, provides top-class, well-balanced food in an intimate red-plush setting. Poulbot specials include smoked salmon flan and lamb cutlets with crème of sweet pepper. *45 Cheapside, EC2, tel. 01/236–4379. Jacket and tie. Reservations 2–3 days in advance. AE, DC, MC, V. Lunch only. Closed Sat., Sun.*

International **Gallipoli.** Here's a different locale—a 200-year-old Turkish bathhouse, replete with gleaming mosaics and tiles, and a live band from 9 PM to 2:30 AM. A mix of City people and tourists frequent the place. The food has a strong Turkish slant—try the yogurt kebab or the fillet of duck with honey, lime, and orange. *8 Bishopsgate Churchyard, EC2, tel. 01/588–1922. Dress: formal. Reservations advised. AE, DC, MC, V. Closed Sun., Christmas, Dec. 26, public holidays.*

Seafood **Bill Bentley's.** You can see from the bare walls and the arched ceiling that this was once a wine merchant's vaults. There are two other branches in London, at Beauchamp Place, and at Baker Street, equally old-fashioned in feel, and both serving Bill Bentley's special oysters and seafood platters. *Swedeland Ct., 202 Bishopsgate, EC2, tel. 01/283–1763. Dress: formal. Reservations essential. DC, MC, V. Closed Sat., Sun., public holidays.*

Moderate **Ginnan.** A big favorite with Japanese businessmen, Ginnan's
Japanese premises, in a shopping precinct by St. Paul's, are small. Sushi (raw fish with rice) and tempura (deepfried vegetables and seafood) are specialties. *5 Cathedral Pl., EC4, tel. 01/236–4120. Dress: formal. Reservations advised. AE, DC, MC, V. Closed Sat. dinner, all day Sun., Christmas, Easter.*

Seafood **Rudland & Stubbs.** This informal oyster bar and fish restaurant is right beside the Smithfield meat market. The fish is fresh, brought daily—try the goujons of salmon with zucchini and salmon sauce, or the John Dory in dill sauce. *35–37 Greenhill*

Rents, EC1, tel. 01/253–0148. Dress: informal. Reservations advised. MC, V. Closed Sat. lunch, Sun., Easter, Christmas, public holidays.

Sweetings. City gents willingly stand in line to lunch at this tiny, basic, Victorian restaurant (a stone's throw from the Temple of Mithras). As you'd expect, the service is old-world courteous; the fish, cheese, and puddings comforting and well-prepared. *39 Queen Victoria St., EC4, tel. 01/248–3062. Dress: formal. Reservations not accepted. No credit cards. Lunch only. Closed Sat., Sun., Christmas, public holidays.*

Traditional English/ French **Rouxl Britannia** (the name is a Roux brothers pun!). This brasserie-style lunch place is decorated in no-nonsense black-and-white, with French café chairs. Try the roast wing of skate (a ray-like fish), or the potted tongue with horseradish sauce. *Triton Ct., 14 Finsbury Sq., London EC2, tel. 01/256–6997. Dress: casual smart. Reservations advised. AE, DC, MC, V. Lunch only. Closed Sat., Sun., public holidays.*

Pubs

Admiral Codrington. This friendly, upmarket Chelsea pub has a Victorian atmosphere, complete with gas lights, wood panels, antique mirrors, and a display of Toby jugs. There's a pleasant enclosed patio for summer drinking and barbecues, and a hanging grapevine that provides welcome shelter from the sun. On Sundays there's a traditional roast; on other days you can choose between a hot dish like shepherd's pie, or sandwiches and salad washed down with any of a wide selection of malt whiskies on offer. *17 Mossop St., SW3, tel. 01/589–4603.*

Black Friar. You can't miss it—it's the only wedge-shaped, or-nate building with a statue of a friar on the front as you step out of Blackfriars tube station! It dates back to the 17th century, though it was renovated by the Victorians who added the inlaid mother-of-pearl, the delicate wood-carving, the stained glass, and the bronze bas-reliefs of friars going about their daily business. In the "side chapel" you'll see red marble pillars and a magnificent mosaic ceiling, plus more friars, and devils, *and* fairies—all very Art Nouveau. There are about seven kinds of beer on tap. *174 Queen Victoria St., EC4, tel. 01/236–5650.*

Bunch of Grapes. This popular Victorian (1882) pub in the heart of Shepherd's Market, the village-within-Mayfair, just off Piccadilly, attracts a colorful crowd. In the upstairs dining room you pay a fixed price and fill up your plate as many times as you want. *Shepherd's Market, W1, tel. 01/629–4989.*

Cheshire Cheese (Ye Olde). The mood here is set by the low ceilings, wooden tables, sawdust floors, and the 14th-century crypt of Whitefriars' monastery under the cellar bar. It's one of London's best-loved, most historic pubs. (On Armistice day 1918, the pub parrot made the sound of a champagne cork popping 400 times, and then collapsed in a dead faint.) You can choose among three bars and three restaurants. The food is solid English traditional: Game puddings are the specialty. *145 Fleet St., EC4.*

Dirty Dick's. The namesake is a well-known dandy who went to pieces when his wife-to-be died the day before their marriage. He refused to clean himself and his house right up to his death. What was once the pub's decor—cobwebs, mummified cats, mouse skeletons, all fake—has now been put in a glass case downstairs. Nevertheless, the place still has great atmosphere. There's a fine spiral staircase leading to the wine bar upstairs. *202 Bishopsgate, EC2, tel. 01/283–5888.*

Freemason's Arms. This place is supposed to have the largest pub garden in London with two terraces, a summerhouse, country-style furniture, and roses everywhere. Why not try your hand at the 17th-century game of pell mell—a kind of croquet—in the special pell mell court, or at skittles in the indoor alley. It's a favorite Hampstead pub, and popular with well-known media people. *32 Downshire Hill, NW3, tel. 01/435–4498.*

George Inn. The inn sits in a courtyard where Shakespeare's plays were once performed. The present building dates from the late 17th century, and is London's last remaining galleried inn. Dickens was a regular—the inn is featured in *Little Dorrit*. Entertainments include Shakespeare performances, medieval jousts, and morris dancing. There's a choice between a real ale bar, a wine bar, and a regular restaurant. *77 Borough High St., SE1, tel. 01/407–2056.*

Jack Straw's Castle. Straw was Wat Tyler's comrade in the Peasants' Revolt of 1381, and was hanged outside. In Tudor times it was a favorite hangout for highwaymen, but by the 19th century it had become picturesque and respectable; artists painted charming views from it and Dickens (inevitably) stayed here. Sadly, it was blitzed during World War II, and rebuilt in the 1960s. You can admire the views over Hampstead Heath, drink (weather permitting) in the outside courtyard, snack in the bar, and dine in the Castle Carving Room. The cocktails are imaginative and fun. *North End Way, NW3, tel. 01/435–8374.*

The Lamb. Dickens lived close by and, yes, he was a regular here, too (he seems to have spent his life on a pub crawl). It's a jolly, cozy pub, with the original cut-glass Victorian screens. The food is home-cooked, and you can eat or drink outside on the patio. It's crowded in summer. *94 Lamb's Conduit St., WC1, tel. 01/405–0713.*

Lamb and Flag. This 17th-century pub, was once known as "The Bucket of Blood," owing to the fact that the upstairs room was used as an arena for barefist fighting. Now, it's a trendy, friendly, and entirely bloodless pub, serving food (at lunchtime only) and real ale. It's on the edge of Covent Garden, off Garrick Street. *33 Rose St., WC2, tel. 01/836–4108.*

Prospect of Whitby. This historic riverside tavern dates back to 1520, and was named after an old sailing ship. Once upon a time it was called "The Devil's Tavern," because of the numbers of low-life criminals—thieves and smugglers—who congregated here. It's ornamented with pewter-ware and nautical memorabilia. There's an excellent à la carte menu as well as good pub food. *57 Wapping Wall, E1, tel. 01/481–1095.*

Rose and Crown. One of the most haunted pubs in London. Condemned men, on their way to execution at Tyburn (now Marble Arch), once were locked up here for the night. Then, as ghosts, they returned and chose this as a congenial "haunt." It's not in the least spooky these days, surrounded by salubrious Mayfair houses, and it's extremely comfortable inside, with brown velour drapes and carpet. Hot and cold food is served at lunch and dinner, and real ales are on tap. *2 Old Park La., W1, tel. 01/499–1980.*

Sherlock Holmes. This pub used to be known as the Northumberland Arms, and Arthur Conan Doyle popped in regularly for a pint. It figures in *The Hound of the Baskervilles*, and you can see the hound's head and plaster casts of its monstrous paws, among other Holmes memorabilia (newspaper cuttings, etc.) in the bar. Upstairs there's a reconstruction of Holmes's study. Food is traditional English—try the "Sherlock Holmes Chicken." The fish is also good. The pub's situated just south of the Strand, at the Trafalgar Square end. *10 Northumberland St., WC2, tel. 01/930–2644.*

Spaniard's Inn. This is another historic pub on Hampstead Heath, with superb views of the city. It's so called because the Spanish ambassador to the court of James I lived here in the early 1600s. Dick Turpin, the highwayman, used to stay at the inn while on his robbing trips; you can see his pistols on display. Romantic poets—Shelley, Keats, Byron—hung out here, and so, of course, did Dickens. It's extremely popular, especially on Sundays when Londoners take to the Heath in search of fresh air. The attractive exterior is weatherboarded; the bars inside have old wooden beams. The rose garden, perfect for a drink on a sunny day, was the scene of the tea party in Dickens' *Pickwick Papers. Spaniards Rd., NW3, tel. 01/455–3276.*

Wine Bars

Archduke. One of the few congenial nightspots in the South Bank, and convenient for a post-theater or concert dinner. It's built into the railway arches under Hungerford Bridge beside the Festival Hall, and if you arrive before the jazz strikes up (8 PM) you drink to the sound of rumbling trains. You can sit on different levels among the plants and bright red pipes. The food is standard (quiches, apple pies), but upstairs there's a restaurant serving more interesting (and pricey) dishes, with international sausage specialties. *153 Concert Hall Approach, SE1, tel. 01/928–9370.*

Balls Brothers. A good place for a bite and a quaff in between City sightseeing. Fortify yourself in the cozy, wood-paneled bar with a grilled steak in French bread, or with some freshly made soup and cheese. Aim to arrive fairly early, because it tends to fill up fast. There are several other Balls Brothers bars, mostly in the City, each with the same list of over 60 wines. *2 Old Change Ct., St. Paul's Churchyard, EC4, tel. 01/248–8697.*

Le Beaujolais. Old school ties hang from the ceiling in this busy little French-style wine bar by Leicester Square tube. The staff and decor are both French; the food is a mixture of English (black pudding and apple sauce) and French (charcuterie and delicious creamy bries and camemberts). *25 Litchfield St., WC2, tel. 01/836–2277.*

Bleeding Heart. This is the yard that featured large in Dickens's *Little Dorrit,* though it's changed a lot since his day. The house the wine bar is in dates from the 14th century, though the present structure is Victorian—dark, low-ceilinged, and sober. It contains lots of Dickens memorabilia, including first editions, and there's an inviting piano room lined with wine bottles. The brasserie is particularly good value, with a fine selection of champagnes. The yard is said to be haunted by the ghost of Lady Hatton (Hatton Garden, the fabled jewelers' street, is a minute away). Eat at an outside table if you dare. *Bleeding Heart Yard, Greville St., EC1, tel. 01/242–8238.*

Bentley's. Seafood—oysters in particular—is the specialty here. Upstairs there's a restaurant, but the wine bar with its splendid marble counter and tables tucked away in alcoves is more attractive as well as being slightly cheaper. Recommended are the clam bisque and the baked fish pie. It's a two-minute walk from Piccadilly Circus. *11 Swallow St., W1, tel. 01/734–0401*.

Brahms and Liszt. (The odd name is Cockney rhyming slang for . . . well, drunk.) A convenient stopping-off place during a Covent Garden shopping spree, or after a visit to the Theatre Museum. The piped music can be loud, but the service is friendly, the atmosphere cordial, and the food good value. A vegetarian dish is available daily. *19 Russell St., WC2, tel. 01/240–3661*.

Bubbles. You can choose between charcoal grills in the ground-floor wine bar, or something more haute in the bistro downstairs. The wines are well chosen, and include some champagnes. The music (jazz) is played reassuringly low, and the decor consists of innocuous French posters. Go and walk off your pavlova in nearby Green Park. *41 N. Audley St., W1, tel. 01/499–0600*.

Criterion Brasserie. Located by the statue of Eros in Piccadilly Circus. Since it opened in the early 1980s, the Criterion, with its stunning decor (original Art Nouveau gold mosaic ceiling, marbled walls, long mirrors, potted palms) has become ever more popular with trendy West End workers for an after-work drink. A pianist serenades you as you snack on a salad or pâté. The food in the restaurant at the back is nothing to write home about. *222 Piccadilly, W1, tel. 01/839–7133*.

Crusting Pipe. Port is the specialty in this maze of converted wine vaults in the piazza, but there's an excellent selection of other wines by the glass or bottle. There are tables outside, and the food ranges over pâtés, cheeses, game pie, roast beef, and salads, to something from the grill room. *27 The Market, Covent Garden, WC2, tel. 01/836–1415*.

Ebury Wine Bar. This was one of the first wine bars to open in this country, in the 1960s, and it's still drawing in the crowds. In fact, it can get distinctly cramped at peak hours. The food is well worth it, however: Try a spring chicken with lemon and tarragon cream, and maybe a baked plum cheesecake to follow. You can have port or sherry from the wood (i.e. barrel), and choose from a list of around 60 wines. There's a minimum charge of £5 per head. It's located between Victoria Station and Sloane Square. *139 Ebury St., SW1, tel. 01/730–5447*.

Gordon's. The original "Watergate" is outside—in good weather you can drink by it and think sobering thoughts about politics and the way of the world. This 300-year-old cellar bar is somewhat reminiscent of a catacomb, slightly damp, with curved stone walls and creaky chairs. It's popular all the same, perhaps because of the generous portions of well-prepared dishes such as squid stew (hot dishes in winter only). The ports and Madeiras are excellent. *47 Villers St., WC2. Tel. 01/930 – 1408*.

Grape Street. Two minutes walk from the British Museum, this is a friendly, unpretentious basement wine bar (watch the top step, it's a different size from the rest!), decorated a restful, warm pink. There's a comprehensive wine list with some out-of-the-ordinary wines (such as the exquisite Portuguese João Peres), and excellent hot and cold dishes. The salmon kulebiak melts in the mouth. *2 Grape St., WC2, tel. 01/240–0686*.

Sloane's Wine Bar. Located next to the Royal Court Theatre. You can get coffee and snacks here outside licensing hours, as well as wine and home-cooked food, reasonably-priced, at lunchtime and in the evenings, when a pianist plays. The ambience is candle-lit, with large wooden tables set reassuringly far apart. Your fellow drinkers will be the upmarket Sloane set. *51 Sloane Sq., SW1, tel. 01/730–4275.*

Shampers. The wines here are from all over the world, from Chile to New Zealand, even England—200 by the bottle, 20 by the glass. The food, too, is better than the average wine bar's: Try the pork olives in mushroom and pepper sauce, and a magnificent chocolate cheesecake for dessert. The music is unobtrusive jazz. It's situated in a small road between Regent Street and once-trendy Carnaby Street. *4 Kingly St., W1, tel. 01/437–1692.*

Solange's. You'll find Solange's in a little alleyway near Leicester Square tube station, very handy for theaters, cinemas, or the bookshops on Charing Cross Road. There are tables outside for summer drinking. It's a two-story, French-style brasserie, invariably crowded, with interesting black-and-white photos on the walls, offering good food and wines. The service can be rather eccentric. *11 St. Martin's Ct., WC2, tel. 01/240–0245.*

Whittington's Wine Bar. This is a vaulted City cellar reputed to have been owned by Dick Whittington (Thrice Mayor of London). Dishes are imaginative (deep-fried artichokes in hollandaise sauce, prawn mousse) and you can choose from a wide selection of Australian, Austrian, Portuguese, French, and German wines. It's only open until 7 PM. *21 College Hill, EC4, tel. 01/248–5855.*

7 Lodging

Introduction

London hotels are among the most expensive in Europe in all grades, and the situation shows no sign of changing in the near future. We have noticed a distinct tendency on the part of our readers to feel that many London hotels simply do not give value for their rather inflated prices—especially when compared to their counterparts elsewhere in Europe. We should emphasize that our grading system is based simply on price, and does not itself indicate the quality of the hotel, although we have been at pains to select ones whose caliber is tried and tested. Our gradings are based on the average room cost, and you should note that in some establishments, especially those in the Very Expensive category, you could pay considerably more—close to the £200 mark in some cases. In common with those of most other European countries, British hotels are obliged by law to display a tariff at the reception desk. If you have not prebooked, you are strongly advised to study this carefully.

The general custom these days in all but the bottom end of the scale is for rates to be quoted for the room alone; breakfast, whether Continental or "Full English," comes as an extra. VAT is usually included, and service, too, in nearly all cases. All the hotels listed here are graded according to their summer 1988 rates, so check for the latest figures, remembering, of course, that there can be a significant difference off-season.

Be sure to book in advance as seasonal events, trade shows, or royal occasions can fill hotel rooms for sudden, brief periods. However, if you arrive in the capital without a room, the following organizations will be able to lend you a hand: Room Centre (U.K.) Ltd. (Kingsgate House, Kingsgate Pl., NW6, tel. 01/328–1790); Hotel Reservation Centre (by Platform 8 at Victoria Station, SW1, tel. 01/828–1849); and The London Tourist Board (also at Victoria Station, SW1; no telephone bookings).

A word of warning: you should be aware that one of the main complaints of late from visitors to London concerns the exorbitant rates exacted by certain accommodations agencies for their "services." Wherever possible, book directly with the hotel.

The most highly recommended hotels are indicated by a star ★.

Category	Cost*
Very Expensive	over £120
Expensive	£90—£120
Moderate	£45—£90
Inexpensive	under £45

cost of a double room; VAT included; add service

Credit Cards The following credit card abbreviations are used: AE, American Express; DC, Diners Club; MC, MasterCard; V, Visa.

Mayfair

Very Expensive **Athenaeum.** The Athenaeum occupies a superb position overlooking Green Park—jogging maps are provided for fitness

Lodging in Kensington, Knightsbridge, Chelsea, and Belgravia

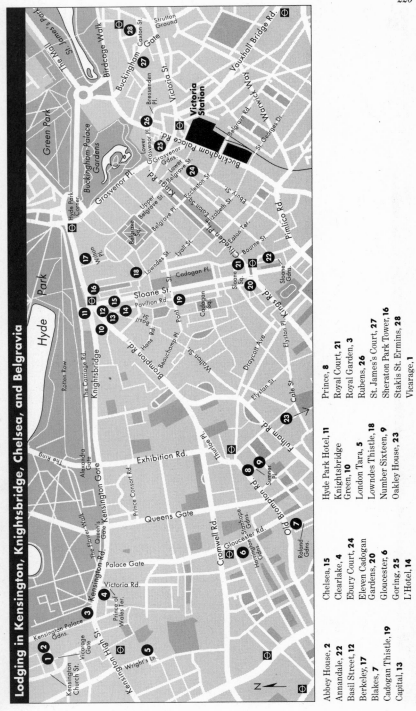

Abbey House, **2**
Annandale, **22**
Basil Street, **12**
Berkeley, **17**
Blakes, **7**
Cadogan Thistle, **19**
Capital, **13**

Chelsea, **15**
Clearlake, **4**
Ebury Court, **24**
Eleven Cadogan Gardens, **20**
Gloucester, **6**
Goring, **25**
L'Hotel, **14**

Hyde Park Hotel, **11**
Knightsbridge Green, **10**
London Tara, **5**
Lowndes Thistle, **18**
Number Sixteen, **9**
Oakley House, **23**

Prince, **8**
Royal Court, **21**
Royal Garden, **3**
Rubens, **26**
St. James's Court, **27**
Sheraton Park Tower, **16**
Stakis St. Ermins, **28**
Vicarage, **1**

Lodging in Mayfair, St. James's, Soho, and Covent Garden

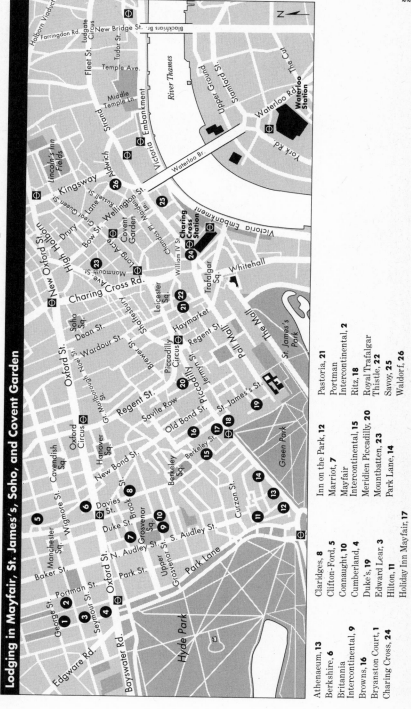

Athenaeum, **13**
Berkshire, **6**
Britannia
Intercontinental, **9**
Browns, **16**
Bryanston Court, **1**
Charing Cross, **24**

Claridges, **8**
Clifton-Ford, **5**
Connaught, **10**
Cumberland, **4**
Duke's, **19**
Edward Lear, **3**
Hilton, **11**
Holiday Inn Mayfair, **17**

Inn on the Park, **12**
Marriot, **7**
Mayfair
Intercontinental, **15**
Meridien Piccadilly, **20**
Mountbatten, **23**
Park Lane, **14**

Pastoria, **21**
Portman
Intercontinental, **2**
Ritz, **18**
Royal Trafalgar
Thistle, **22**
Savoy, **25**
Waldorf, **26**

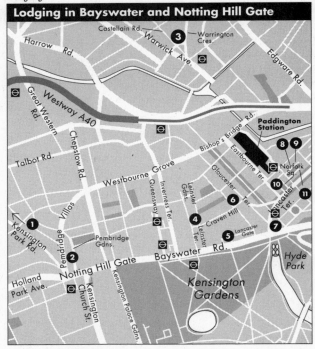

Lodging in Bayswater and Notting Hill Gate

enthusiasts. The hotel is in a modern building, which has recently been stylishly re-decorated with soft color schemes, leather-topped mahogany and yew furniture in the bedrooms, and luxurious marble-tiled bathrooms in the suites. It's the flagship of the Rank chain. *116 Piccadilly, W1V OBJ, tel. 01/ 499–3464, 112 rooms, all with bath. Facilities: double glazing, lounge, cocktail bar, restaurant, free in-house films, pianist in restaurant and lounge. AE, DC, MC, V.*

Berkshire. Ideally sited for Oxford Street shopping, and for the tube, with the Wallace Collection nearby. The unusual flatiron building was totally renovated in 1987/8, and the decor has Chinese accents throughout: There are exquisite oriental vases and lampshades in nearly all the rooms. You'll be more than comfortable in your room richly decorated with cream walls and ceilings, red or blue carpets, and tasteful landscape and nature paintings. In the drawing room you can feel free to doze peacefully in front of the open fire to the soothing strains of a harp, browse among the bookshelves, or simply sit back in an armchair and enjoy afternoon tea with a tempting cream cake. *350 Oxford St., W1N OBY, tel. 01/629–7474, 147 rooms, all with bath. Facilities: air-conditioning, double-glazing, CNN, free in-house videos, restaurant. AE, DC, MC, V.*

Britannia Intercontinental. Behind the imposing, cream-columned facade (across Grosvenor Square from the U.S. Embassy) are spacious and comfortable public rooms (with striking modern chandeliers), and well-appointed bedrooms, with fine, walnut-veneered furniture. You'll find the row of bow-fronted shops a charming and useful addition to the hotel. On top of this, the service is invariably helpful and friendly.

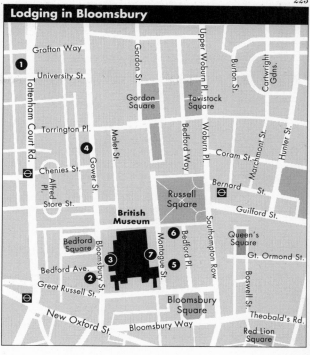

Lodging in Bloomsbury

Grosvenor Sq., W1A 3AN, tel. 01/629–9400. 354 rooms, all with bath. Facilities: laundry service, hairdressing, shopping center, free in-house movies, 3 restaurants. AE, DC, MC, V.

★ **Brown's.** Brown's still offers a country hotel atmosphere—wood paneling, grandfather clocks, large fireplaces, plenty of chintz upholstery. It is a discreet hotel, founded by Lord Byron's butler in 1837. The bedrooms vary in size—some are quite small, but all are elegantly furnished with matching olive carpets, velour armchairs, sweeping drapes, brass chandeliers, and light wallpapers. It's close to Bond Street where the high fashion stores and the private art galleries are. *34 Albemarle St., W1A 4SW, tel. 01/493–6020. 125 rooms, all with bath. Facilities: restaurant, lounge, writing room, cocktail bar. AE, DC, MC, V.*

★ **Claridges.** A living hotel legend, with one of the world's classiest guest lists. The liveried staff is friendly and not in the least condescending, while the rooms are never less than luxurious. It was founded in 1812, but present decor is 1930s Art Deco. Have a drink in the lounge (24 hours a day) and be entertained by the orchestra, or retreat to the reading room for perfect quiet, interrupted only by the sound of pages turning. The bedrooms are spacious and old-fashioned in style—the grand staircase and magnificent elevator impressive features. *Brook St., W1A 2JQ, tel. 01/629–8860. 205 rooms, all with bath. Facilities: lounge (with orchestra), hairdressing, valeting. AE, DC, MC, V.*

★ **Connaught.** Book well in advance for this *very* exclusive, small, elegant hotel, just off Grosvenor Square. The bar and lounges have the air of an ambassadorial residence, an impression rein-

forced by the imposing oak staircase and dignified elevator.
Each bedroom has a foyer and antique furniture, with fresh
flowers for that touch of the country. The Connaught is one of
the best bases for touring the capital: luxury and impeccable
service from top to bottom. *Carlos Pl., W1Y 6AL, tel. 01/
499–7070. 90 rooms, all with bath. Facilities: restaurant,
lounge, cocktail bar, air-conditioning, disabled access in some
rooms. MC.*

Dorchester. This hotel will be closed during 1989 for refurbishment.

Holiday Inn Mayfair. The Holiday Inn Mayfair is right by
Green Park tube and ideally located for walking, shopping, visiting theaters, or visiting the Royal Academy. It was converted
in the 1970s from an office block, and has changed hands a couple of times before settling down in its present incarnation. The
bedrooms are rather boringly furnished in international style,
the bathrooms on the small side. The main thing to recommend
this Holiday Inn is its location. *3 Berkeley St., W1X 6NE, tel.
01/493–8282. 186 rooms, all with bath. Facilities: laundry
service, lounge bar, restaurant, air-conditioning, AE, DC,
MC, V.*

Inn on the Park. Inn on the Park rejoices in an opulent interior,
an eminent situation near Hyde Park, and overall high standards. It was once one of Howard Hughes' hideaways. The bedrooms are exquisitely furnished and extremely comfortable:
the beds are gigantic, the bathrooms straight from Hollywood, with plenty of extras, such as bathrobes. The entrance
hall is a wonder of marble and crystal. *Hamilton Pl., Park
Lane, W1A 1AZ, tel. 01/499–0888. 228 rooms, all with bath.
Facilities: air-conditioning, shopping arcade, free inhouse
movies, valeting, garden, restaurant. AE, DC, MC, V.*

London Hilton. Though not up to the standard of some others in
the Hilton group, this high-rise hotel—refurbished in 1988—
does offer fine views over Hyde Park, plus some good bars and
restaurants, and an impressive array of facilities. The rooms
are pleasantly decorated in chintzy pastels, with Georgian-style furniture. The lounge, bar, and cocktail lounge have recently been revamped, and are now splendidly plush. The 13th
floor is for nonsmokers only. *22 Park Lane, W1A 2HH, tel.
01/493–8000. 446 rooms, all with bath. Facilities: restaurant,
hairdressing, free in-house movies, laundry, shopping arcade,
doctor, CNN, florist, health complex (inc. sauna/solarium/
massage), theater ticket desk, baby-sitting, airline reservations. AE, DC, MC, V.*

★ **London Marriott.** The Marriott overlooks Grosvenor Square,
round the corner from the U.S. embassy. A hyper-modern, efficiently computerized hotel (though its facade is 19th century).
Access to your room is by a coded key card (rare in Britain, although common enough in the States). Enormous closets, thick
carpets, marble bathrooms, and attractive furniture, make this
a good luxury choice. The foyer has splendid floral displays.
The porters are especially good with visitors' requests, and the
coffee shop is open 24 hours a day. *Duke St., W1A 4AW, tel. 01/
493–1232. 228 rooms, all with bath. Facilities: valeting, coffee
shop, lounge, 2 restaurants. AE, DC, MC, V.*

Mayfair Intercontinental. Photos of the actors who have performed at the hotel's theater adorn the silk-papered bedroom
walls. It's a stylish, relaxed hotel, decorated in a combination
of styles—English (dark wood, heavy leather) and French
(pale pastels and floral designs). You can choose between patro-

nizing the hotel restaurant, the **Château,** or walking a few yards to Langan's *(see* Dining) on the same street. *Stratton St., W1A 2AN, tel. 01/629–7777. Facilities: coffee shop, restaurant, free in-house movies, laundry. AE, DC, MC, V.*

Meridien Piccadilly. A massive, elegant, turn-of-the-century building, reopened in 1986 after a £16-million facelift and now the last word in luxury, mid-1980s style—though every effort has been made to maintain the original, clubby Edwardian atmosphere, especially in the ornate, Venetian-chandeliered Oak Room. Designer upholstery and drapes make the bedrooms extra-stylish—though they're mostly on the small side. The health club is probably the most luxurious and exclusive in London, and boasts squash courts, saunas, billiard tables, as well as a swimming pool. You can't be more central than here. *Piccadilly, W1V 0BH, tel. 01/734–8000. 284 rooms, all with bath. Facilities: 3 restaurants, bar, health club, library. AE, DC, MC, V.*

Park Lane. The Park Lane was built 60 years ago, and retains many of the original, elegant Art Deco features. Some of the rooms have distressing color schemes and discordant patterns, but the overall effect is one of space and comfort. Tea is served in the comfortable Palm Court Lounge, which has a fine raised ceiling with stained-glass panels. The bedrooms have double-glazed windows, and some have whirlpool baths. The hotel restaurant—**Bracewell's**—serves mouth-watering French cuisine. *Piccadilly, W1Y 8BX, tel. 01/499–6321. 325 rooms, all with bath. Facilities: lounge bar, health center, 2 restaurants, hairdressing, coffee shop, valeting, double-glazing, AE, DC, MC, V.*

Portman Intercontinental. A club-style hotel with rich mahogany finishings, heavy chesterfields, velour in the lobby and restaurants, light and airy bedrooms, and unusually spacious bathrooms. Since it was built in 1971 it has become a favorite with both tourists and businesspeople. Its location makes it handy for Oxford Street shopping and—if you're a classical music fan—a recital at the Wigmore Hall. *22 Portman Sq., W1H 9FL, tel. 01/486–5844. 275 rooms, all with bath. Facilities: bar, air-conditioning, double-glazing, 2 restaurants, valeting, laundry, free in-house movies. AE, DC, MC, V.*

Expensive **Clifton-Ford.** This is one of the most peaceful central London hotels, located in a quiet Georgian street, close to Oxford Street, and a short walk from Regent's Park. It dates from 1965, but has been extensively updated since then. Bedrooms are decorated in standard international-modes, but with all the latest accessories. In the evening, a pianist plays soothing music in the comfortable lounge-foyer. *47 Welbeck St., W1M 8DN, tel. 01/486–6600. 240 rooms, all with bath. Facilities: laundry, valeting, free in-house movies, lounge (with pianist), bar, restaurant, AE, DC, MC, V.*

Cumberland. This huge, busy hotel (built in 1933, with some Art Deco features on the facade and in the public areas) is double-glazed to counter the traffic noise of Oxford Street, and boasts every modern convenience. The bedrooms are comfortable and well-fitted, with adequate bathrooms. The hotel's restaurants—a carvery, a café, a Japanese restaurant, and a fourth, **Austen's**—serve enterprising food. Although there are no fitness facilities in the hotel, there's a pool and a health club nearby. A high proportion of the guests are business people. *Marble Arch, W1A 4RF, tel. 01/262–1234. 894 rooms, all with* *bath. Facilities: 4 restaurants, lounge, 3 bars, double-glazing, hairdressing, coffee shop. AE, DC, MC, V.*

Moderate **Bryanston Court.** Three Georgian houses converted into a ho-
★ tel, in a historic conservation area, a couple of blocks north of Hyde Park and Park Lane. The style is traditional English— open fireplaces, comfortable leather armchairs, oil portraits— though the bedrooms are more contemporary. It's family-run, and excellent value for the area. *56–60 Great Cumberland Pl., W1H 7FD, tel. 01/262–3141. 56 rooms, all with bath. Facilities: bar, lounge, restaurant. AE, DC, MC, V.*

Edward Lear. One-time home of writer/artist Edward Lear (famous for his nonsense verse), this good-value hotel has an imposing entranceway leading to a black-and-white tiled hall. Rooms on the street can be noisy, so ask for a room at the back. The breakfast room has huge French windows, and the management proudly uses the same butcher as the Queen. *28–30 Seymour St., W1H 5WD, tel. 01/402–5401. 30 rooms, 15 with bath. V.*

St. James's

Very Expensive **Duke's.** An exclusive, small, Edwardian hotel, its entrance lit
★ by gaslight, situated in a quiet cul-de-sac in the heart of St. James's. Portraits of dukes hang on the walls—just one of the touches that help to preserve its old-world, aristocratic character. The bedrooms aim at country-house comfort, while the snappy, modern bathrooms are equipped with imperial-size towels. Ask for a top-floor bedroom; they're the most spacious. *5 St. James's Pl., SW1A 1NY, tel. 01/491–4840. 36 rooms, all with bath. Facilities: restaurant, valeting, private dining. AE, DC, MC, V.*

The Ritz. Sumptuous Louis XVI decor, near-faultless service, and lively with it. Book in advance for tea in the famous Palm Court (dark pink velvet chairs, gilt statues, fluted columns, cascades of greenery), for which you will be expected to dress appropriately. The Long Gallery leads to the opulent dining-room, where you'll eat like a king under a frescoed ceiling—and be able to watch your fellow guests surreptitiously in the long mirrors. From the tall windows you can see a flowery terrace, and a small garden beyond it. The bedrooms are—as you'd expect—ritzy: antique furniture and mirrors, heavy brocades, and linen embroidered with a regal "R." *Piccadilly, W1V 9DG, tel. 01/493–8181. 128 rooms, all with bath. Facilities: restaurant, cocktail bar, valeting, laundry, baby-sitting. AE, DC, MC, V.*

Kensington

Very Expensive **Blakes.** One of the most exotically designed hotels in town. The
★ exterior is Victorian, but the interior is 1980s ultra-chic, with an arty mix of Biedermeyer, bamboo furniture, rich fabrics, leather, four-poster beds, and oriental screens. As you enter you'll see a dramatic square umbrella over the stairs that lead down to the mirror-lined restaurant, and a mountainous pile of Victorian-type luggage with a caged parakeet on top. There's an amusingly realistic model of Marlene Dietrich in the bar. The rooms have individual designs, varying from swathes of black moire silk to a more severe plain gray. (*See* Dining.) Your fellow guests are likely to be big names from the music and film worlds. *33 Roland Gdns., SW7 3PF, tel. 01/370–6701. 50*

rooms, all with bath. Facilities: restaurant, satellite TV, laundry. AE, DC, MC, V.

Royal Garden. A favorite with visiting diplomats, whose embassies are nearby. It's a substantial modern block, handy for Kensington shopping and museum visiting. Bedrooms and suites are furnished in neutral greens and browns, with floral fabrics and reproduction tables and chairs. Some rooms offer a spectacular view over Kensington Gardens, as does the **Royal Roof Restaurant** on the 11th floor. Enjoy a silver tankard of champagne sitting on a winged armchair in the club-like Gallery Bar. *Kensington High St., W8 4PT, tel. 01/937–8000. 384 rooms, all with bath. Facilities: hairdressing, coffee shop, valeting, laundry restaurant. AE, DC, MC, V.*

Expensive   **Gloucester.** A huge 1970s hotel, very popular with businesspeople, offering every modern convenience. The accommodations, in a variety of color schemes, are roomy, comfortable, and cleverly lit. If you take a room on the stylish Reserve Club floor you'll have the use of two extra luxurious lounges, *and* butler service. Beer enthusiasts will enjoy the "real ale" bar. *4 Harrington Gdns., SW7 4LH, tel. 01/373–6030. 531 rooms, all with bath. Facilities: coffee shop, car rental desk, gift shop, wine bar, real ale bar, health club, double-glazing, restaurant (with harpist). AE, DC, MC, V.*

★ **Number Sixteen.** A luxury bed-and-breakfast in a white-painted, porticoed series of Victorian houses, now united in one. It lies between peaceful, green Onslow Square, and busy Old Brompton Road, not far from the South Kensington tube. Each room has a different character, while the public areas are happily busy with a fascinating mix of antiques, prints, and curios. The hotel has an informal, civilized atmosphere, welcoming and relaxing at the same time. There's a charming garden. *16 Sumner Pl., SW7 3EG, tel. 01/589–5232. 32 rooms, all with bath. Facilities: bar, garden, laundry. AE, DC, MC, V.*

Moderate   **London Tara.** The London Tara is an international-style modern (1972) hotel, but the atmosphere is cordial, and the rooms are light and colorful. You can eat in any of the three restaurants—**Poacher's** (fish and game), the **Brasserie** (with carousel decor), or **Chevaliers,** in the nightclub, and relax in the piano lounge. There are 10 rooms available for disabled people. *Scarsdale Pl., Kensington W8 5SR, tel. 01/937–7211. 831 rooms, all with bath. Facilities: 3 restaurants, lounge, bar, laundry. AE, MC, V.*

★ **Prince.** Unashamedly upmarket, the Prince offers amazingly reasonable rates for what you get. Furnishings are all to a very high standard, and the bathrooms were fitted in such a way that the lovely cornices were preserved. The halls are papered in a mint-green Regency stripe, and the garden/conservatory is straight out of *World of Interiors. 6 Sumner Pl., SW7 3AB, tel. 01/589–6488. 20 rooms, 14 with bath. Facilities: lounge, laundry. AE, MC, V.*

Inexpensive   **Abbey House.** Close to Kensington Palace and the gardens, the Abbey House is in a fine residential block; standards are high, with unusually spacious and high-ceilinged rooms. *11 Vicarage Gate, W8 4AG, tel. 01/727–2594. 15 rooms, none with bath. Facilities: orthopedic beds. No credit cards.*

Clearlake. An attractive, self-catering hotel; the rooms are cozy, with refrigerators, ample storage space, and huge windows. Several of the studios and family apartments have full-kitchen facilities. *19 Prince of Wales Terr., W8 5PQ, tel. 01/ 937–3274. 20 rooms, all with bath. Facilities: baby-sitting, laundry, dry cleaning, bar. AE, DC, MC, V.*

★ **Vicarage.** Family-owned and -run for nearly 30 years, the Vicarage feels like a real home. It's beautifully decorated, in a quiet location overlooking a magnificent garden square and close to the Kensington shops. *10 Vicarage Gate, W8 4AG, tel. 01/229–4030. 19 rooms, none with bath. Facilities: lounge. No credit cards.*

Knightsbridge, Chelsea, and Belgravia

Very Expensive **Berkeley.** The Berkeley is a remarkably successful mixture of ★ the old and the new. It is a luxurious, air-conditioned, double-glazed modern building with a splendid penthouse swimming pool that opens to the sky when the weather's good. The bedrooms are decorated in a variety of enchanting styles (such as powder blue with glass tables and Wedgwood moldings) and each one has an anteroom and a palatial bathroom. Some of the antique furniture comes from the old Berkeley, in Mayfair. This is a very special hotel. You can choose between French cuisine in the restaurant and Mediterranean food in the **Buttery.** It's conveniently placed for Knightsbridge shopping. *Wilton Pl., SW1X 7RL, tel. 01/235–6000. 133 rooms, all with bath. Facilities: rooftop heated indoor and outdoor pool, gymnasium, massage, sauna, hairdressing, cinema, florist, 2 restaurants. AE, DC, MC, V.*

Capital. Book well ahead if you want a room here—the same goes for a table in their superb restaurant (*see* Dining). Small and elegant, in a quiet street by the side of Harrods, the Capital is highly recommended for the excellent, welcoming service it gives. Try for one of the 10 individually designed rooms in the Edwardian wing, which used to be Squires Hotel, fashionable in the 1920s, with a grand carved staircase. The whole hotel is beautifully decorated, with attractive fabrics, harmonious color schemes, and pleanty of plants and flowers. *22–24 Basil St., SW3 1AT, tel. 01/589–5171. 54 rooms, all with bath. Facilities: double-glazing, air-conditioning, bar, lounge, laundry. AE, DC, MC, V.*

Goring. Useful if you have to drop in at Buckingham Palace, just around the corner. In fact, visiting VIPs use it regularly as a conveniently close, and suitably dignified, base for royal occasions. Flowering windowboxes decorate the facade, but the lobby has been recently repainted in a very unfortunate shade of pink. The hotel was built by Mr. Goring in 1910, and is now run by third-generation Gorings. The atmosphere remains Edwardian: Bathrooms are marble-fitted and some of the bedrooms have brass bedsteads and the original fitted closets; many have been opulently redecorated. The bar/lounge looks onto a well-tended garden. *Beeston Pl., Grosvenor Gdns. SW1W 0JW, tel. 01/834–8211. 87 rooms, all with bath. Facilities: bar, restaurant, lounge. AE, DC, MC, V.*

★ **Hyde Park Hotel.** Opened in 1908, and in the 1920s the favored accommodations of sultans and maharajahs who would occupy whole floors with their accompanying livestock. It's now owned by Trusthouse Forte. The decor is distinctly High Victorian, with sky-high ceilings, sumptuous marble, gold-topped columns, potted palms, and sparkling chandeliers. Dine in the vast Park Room, with its curved balustrade and panoramic outlook onto the park. The bedrooms are furnished in the best possible taste, in golds, olives, creams, and beiges, with solid Edwardian dark wood furniture and pretty fresh flower arrangements. It's well-placed both for shopping in Knightsbridge and for strolling in Hyde Park, over which some rooms have good views. *66 Knightsbridge, SW1Y 7LA, tel. 01/235–2000. 186 rooms, all with bath. Facilities: lounge, hairdressing, bar, 2 restaurants (with pianist and singer). AE, DC, MC, V.*

Lowndes Thistle. On a quiet residential street between aristocratic Belgrave Square and Knightsbridge, the Lowndes Thistle enjoys a high reputation for its standards of comfort and service. The building is basically modern, but striving for an old-world effect, with reproduction furniture, chintzy fabrics, an Adam-style restaurant, and a Chinoiserie-style bar. The bedrooms are bright and spacious, with all the up-to-date accessories; bathrooms are marble-clad and carpeted. *21 Lowndes St., SW1X 9ES, tel. 01/235–6020. 80 rooms, all with bath. Facilities: bar, lounge, free in-house movies, restaurant. AE, DC, MC, V.*

Sheraton Park Tower. A circular 1970s tower block, two minutes from Harrods and Hyde Park, with stunning views from the penthouses on the 18th floor. The decor is sophisticated and luxurious: the lounge areas, and some of the bedrooms, are elegantly furnished in period style. Exercise bikes are available for those rainy days when you can't do your usual three-mile jog round the park. *101 Knightsbridge, SW1X 7RN, tel. 01/235–8050. 296 rooms, all with bath. Facilities: bar, coffee shop, restaurant. AE, DC, MC, V.*

St. James Court. An elegant, turn-of-the-century apartment block, which has been turned into a stylish hotel at vast expense. The grand reception area is furnished in marble and wood with lots of greenery, and the bedrooms (with glamorous bathrooms) are appealingly decorated in different color schemes. There's a stately courtyard with fountain, and a carved brick frieze portraying scenes from Shakespeare. One restaurant serves French cuisine, and the other, Chinese. *Buckingham Gate, SW1E 6AF, tel. 01/834–6655. 390 rooms, all with bath. Facilities: coffee shop, fitness center with sauna, spa, pools, 2 restaurants. AE, DC, MC, V.*

Expensive
★

Basil Street. Automatic membership for female guests at the ladies' club here—the **Parrot Club.** The Basil Street is a gracious, old-world, Edwardian hotel, on a quiet street, and family-run for three quarters of a century. The upstairs lounge is a peaceful spot for coffee, drinks, or afternoon tea. All the bedrooms are different, filled with antiques, and amazingly quiet. You can write letters home in the peaceful gallery, which has polished wooden floors and fine Turkish carpets. This is a very popular hotel choice for Americans with a taste for period charm. (*See* Dining). *Basil St., SW3 1AH, tel. 01/581–3311. 101 rooms, 90 with bath. Facilities: wine bar, lounge, ladies' club, restaurant. AE, DC, MC, V.*

Cadogan Thistle. The front part of this hotel used to be the London home of Lily Langtry, the famous actress and mistress of Edward VII when he was still the Prince of Wales. It's a turreted Edwardian building with teak furniture, and pretty, coordinated fabrics in the bedrooms. The bathrooms are boldly colored, with striking, hand-painted tiles. Don't miss the collection of Edwardian photos in the cocktail bar. *75 Sloane St., SW1X 9SG, tel. 01/235–7141. 69 rooms, all with bath. Facilities: bar, lounge, restaurant. AE, DC, MC, V.*

Chelsea. Within easy walking distance of Harrods and the Knightsbridge shops. The hotel dates from 1969. The glittering glass atrium immediately creates a striking effect, while the lounge, with its paintings, wine-red upholstery, and traditional furniture, is more old-fashioned and relaxing. Your room will have a large bed, brass light switches, plenty of space for writing, and contemporary dark wood fitted units—ask for a room with a view. A pianist or harpist plays in the cocktail bar. *17–25 Sloane St., SW1X 9NU, tel. 01/235–4377. 228 rooms, all with bath. Facilities: cocktail bar, air-conditioning, double-glazing, restaurant, lounge. AE, DC, MC, V.*

★ **Eleven Cadogan Gardens.** This aristocratic, late-Victorian, gabled town house is very popular with people who work in the international antiques trade. Fine period furniture, books, and magazines on the tables, landscape paintings and portraits, and captivating Victorian touches throughout, help to create the ambience of a family house of taste and character. The 1980s have left barely a trace here. Take the elevator, or walk up the fine oak staircase to your room, which will have mahogany furniture, restful color schemes, and pretty bedspreads and drapes. The best rooms are at the back. There's a private garden for use in warm weather. *11 Cadogan Gdns., Sloane Sq., SW3 2RJ, tel. 01/730–3426. 60 rooms, all with bath. Facilities: garden, laundry, chauffeur-driven car. No credit cards.*

★ **L'Hotel.** An upmarket bed-and-breakfast run by the Levins who also own the Capital next door. Unusual for a London hotel, the style is rustic/Laura Ashley; the entrance hall is matted, with stencilled patterns on the walls, just like the country house of yuppies with taste. The decor in the bedrooms is simple but elegant (white wrought-iron bedsteads, neutral colors, and patterns enlivened perhaps by a ruby-red stripe around the ceiling and in each corner). The excellent light breakfast served in **Le Metro** cellar bar is included in the price of your room. Book ahead—it's very popular. *28 Basil St., SW3 1AT, tel. 01/589–6286. 12 rooms, all with bath. Facilities: wine bar, restaurant. AE, V.*

Royal Court. This hotel is situated in fashionable Sloane Square, across from the Royal Court Theatre. A striking reception hall with chandeliers—one of which originally hung in the Vatican in Rome—welcomes you. The interior is light and elegant, retaining the original Victorian cornices, while offering up-to-date amenities in the bedrooms and bathrooms. **Court's** coffee bar is a popular rendezvous (open 10:30 AM to 11 PM) and the quaintly named **Old Poodle Dog** restaurant, with its wicker chairs and hanging baskets of ferns, provides relaxed surroundings for a meal. *Sloane Sq., SW1W 8EG, tel. 01/730–9191. 102 rooms, all with bath. Facilities: pub, café/bar, restaurant. AE, DC, MC, V.*

Rubens. The closest hotel to Buckingham Palace, opposite the Royal Mews, and handy both for Victoria Station and walks in St. James's Park. Decor is eclectic, with a rather pompous lobby, and a peaceful book-lined lounge downstairs. The bedrooms are decorated in pastel colors and tend to be rather noisy on the road side—but they include useful accessories like hair dryers. One of the restaurants has an à la carte menu, the other's a brasserie. *39–41 Buckingham Palace Rd., SW1W 0PS, tel. 01/834–6600. 191 rooms, all with bath. Facilities: bar, 2 restaurants, lounge, free in-house movies, laundry. AE, DC, MC, V.*

Stakis St. Ermins. Located close to Parliament Square and St. James's Park, this Victorian hotel has plenty of old-fashioned atmosphere, which plasterwork ceilings and dark woodwork help to accentuate. The bedrooms are roomy, with so-so bathrooms. If you're after something higher up the comfort scale, try for a suite or one of the club rooms. This is a favorite place for the business community. If you decide to eat in, there's a carvery, or a grill serving à la carte meals. *Caxton St., SW1H 0QU, tel. 01/222–7888. 300 rooms, all with bath. Facilities: coffee lounge, 2 restaurants. AE, DC, MC, V.*

Moderate **Ebury Court.** Five 19th-century houses converted into an old-fashioned, family-run country-house hotel, close to Victoria Station. The rooms are smallish and chintzy, with antique furniture to give them extra character—including a grandfather clock and a Hepplewhite four-poster bed. You have to pay to become a temporary member of the club and use its bar and lounge. The restaurant is intimate, and excellent value. *26 Ebury St., SW1W 0LU, tel. 01/730–8147. 38 rooms, 15 with bath. Facilities: club (with bar and lounge), restaurant. MC, V.*

Knightsbridge Green. There are more suites than bedrooms at this recently refurbished Georgian hotel, two minutes' walk from Harrods. One floor is French-style with white furniture; another English, in beech. Breakfast is served in your room—there's no restaurant in the hotel for lunch or dinner, but there are plenty in the area, and even more a little further afield, in Chelsea and Kensington. *159 Knightsbridge, SW1X 7PD, tel. 01/584–6274. 22 rooms/suites, all with bath. Facilities: club room. AE, MC, V. Closed 5 days over Christmas.*

Inexpensive **Annandale.** The Annandale, efficiently run by the affable Mr. ★ and Mrs. Morris, is excellent value for the money, and the many repeat visitors attest to the hotel's popularity. Breakfast is a tasty choice of kippers, Welsh rarebit, crumpets, cereals, and authentic Scottish porridge. *39 Sloane Gdns., SW1 8DG, tel. 01/730–5051. 12 rooms, 10 with bath. No credit cards.*

Oakley House. Impeccably Victorian outside, and a bit dark inside—though not at all dreary. The manager is bright and personable, and the rooms, while small, have attractive moldings and colorful Indian print bedspreads. The public showers are clean and absolutely gigantic. Self-service breakfasts. No tubes nearby. *71–72 Oakley St., SW3 5HF, tel. 01/352–9362. 24 rooms, 1 with bath. No credit cards.*

Bayswater and Notting Hill Gate

Very Expensive **Royal Lancaster.** A 1960s 18-story towerblock, with wonderful views over Lancaster Gate's Italian gardens. (The hotel can arrange for you to go horseback-riding in the park.) The cool decor of the bedrooms is stylish as well as relaxing, and everything's brand new. One restaurant serves French cuisine and has a fixed-price menu; the other is a conservatory-style brasserie. *Lancaster Terrace, W2 2TY, tel. 01/262–6737. 418 rooms, all with bath. Facilities: carpark, 3 bars, shops, beauty salon, double-glazing, air-conditioning, 2 restaurants, disabled facilities. AE, DC, MC, V.*

Whites. A cream-facaded Victorian "country-mansion" with a delightful white wrought-iron portico and a view of Kensington Gardens. Thick carpets, gilded glass, marble balustrades, swagged silk drapes, and Louis XV-style furniture all make this the most luxurious hotel in the area. Some of the bedrooms have balconies—one also has a four-poster bed—and the colors

are muted: powder blue, old rose, and lemon yellow, and prettiest when softly illuminated by the crystal wall-lights. The
bathrooms are splendid. *Lancaster Gate, W2 3NR, tel. 01/262–
2711. 55 rooms, all with bath. Facilities: lounge, laundry, free
in-house movies, air-conditioning, restaurant. AE, DC, MC,
V.*

Expensive **Abbey Court.** You enter this 1850 building through a stately,
★ double-fronted portico. (The owner is the director of the Historic House Hotels.) Each room is individually designed, and
some of the bedrooms have four-poster beds. It's a luxury bed-
and-breakfast, charmingly decorated with Empire furniture,
Venetian mirrors, and oil portraits. Only a short walk and
you're in delightful Kensington Gardens. *20 Pembridge Gdns.,
W2 4DU, tel. 01/221–7518. 22 rooms, all with bath. Facilities:
Jacuzzis, drawing room. AE, DC, MC, V.*

Moderate **Camelot.** Top marks to this affordable hotel, with its beautiful-
★ ly decorated rooms; even the public bathrooms are attractive.
The breakfast room has an exposed brick wall, a large open
fireplace, wooden trestle tables, and a highly polished wood
floor. *45–47 Norfolk Sq., W2 1RX, tel. 01/723–9118. 34 rooms,
28 with bath. Facilities: free in-house videos, lounge. MC, V.*

★ **Colonnade.** An attractive, family-run hotel in a Georgian building. The decor is homey (some of the wallpaper designs leave a
lot to be desired), but the service is friendly. Some rooms have
pleasant reproduction furniture (including the occasional four-
poster bed), others are slightly more high-tech. Orthopedic
bed boards are available on request. *2 Warrington Cres., W9
1ER, tel. 01/289–2167. 53 rooms, 45 with bath. Facilities:
bar, restaurant (breakfast and dinner only), orthopedic bed
boards, writing room. AE, DC, MC, V.*

Leinster Towers. This is a modest but comfortable hotel with
modern fittings (including tea-makers in the bedrooms), large
windows, and pleasant light color schemes (you step into an
airy, sea-green foyer). There's a cordial hotel bar, the **Duke of
Leinster,** with a medieval theme. At the end of the road is Kensington Gardens. *Leinster Gdns., W2 3AU, tel. 01/262–4591.
165 rooms, all with bath. Facilities: bar, restaurant, laundry.
AE, DC, MC, V.*

★ **Portobello.** Within walking distance of the Portobello antiques
market, and overlooking a delightful private garden. It's a tiny,
Victorian, terraced hotel (with some *very* tiny rooms!), but it
has a faithful core of visitors who go back again and again for its
relaxed informality. (There's no room service.) The suites have
sitting rooms attached, and there's a bright, congenial bar in
the basement. *22 Stanley Gdns., W11 2NG, tel. 01/727–2777. 25
rooms, all with bath. Facilities: bar, restaurant, laundry. AE,
DC, MC, V. Closed 10 days over Christmas.*

Prince William. A handsome, mid-19th-century building, not
far from Paddington Station, and handy for an overnight stay
on the way to the west of England. Most rooms have the original high ceilings, while those on the second floor have balconies
on which to soak up the elusive London sun. There's a cozy dining room. *42–44 Gloucester Ter., W2 3DA, tel. 01/724–7414. 42
rooms, all with bath. Facilities: bar, restaurant. AE, DC, MC,
V.*

Inexpensive **Ashley.** These three handsome Italianate terraced houses are
now run as a single unit overlooking slightly shabby Norfolk
Square. Though many of the rooms are small and somewhat

sparsely furnished, the unusually friendly and conscientious management (two brothers) make this a decidedly good choice. *15 Norfolk Sq., W2 1RU, tel. 01/723–3375. 52 rooms, 18 with bath. Facilities: lounge. No credit cards. Closed over Christmas.*

Kingsway. Rooms overlooking the square are the best bet, although all are clean and neat. Many have high ceilings and French windows. *27 Norfolk Sq., W2 1RX, tel. 01/723–7784. 32 rooms, 15 with bath. MC, V.*

Norfolk Court. A modest, pleasant, and small Regency hotel, less than a minute from Paddington tube. Some second floor rooms have French windows and balconies overlooking the square, and admirers of Art Deco will enjoy the touches in the landing windows and in the breakfast room. *20 Norfolk Sq., W2 1RS, tel. 01/723–4963. 28 rooms, none with bath. No credit cards.*

Bloomsbury

Very Expensive **Marlborough Crest.** The Marlborough Crest is useful for the British Museum and Oxford Street. House plants, gleaming brass, and attractive furnishings set the tone in this elegant Edwardian hotel. The bedrooms are of a satisfactory size, and have floral fabrics and reproduction furniture. You could dine in the chic **Brasserie Saint Martin,** and retire afterward to the more pubby **Duke's Head,** with its unusual mosaic-sided counter, for coffee or a drink. *Bloomsbury St., WC1B 3QD, tel. 01/636–5601. 169 rooms, all with bath. Facilities: brasserie, air-conditioning, double-glazing, lounge, laundry. AE, DC, MC, V.*

Expensive **Grafton Hotel.** This is a hotel of character and style, above all in the public areas. The drawing room still feels Edwardian with its red plush armchairs, Ionic columns, and open fireplace, and there are stained glass windows on every landing. The bedrooms are more modern in style, having recently been given a complete facelift. It's a good bet if you're planning to travel on to the north of England or Scotland, from nearby Euston or King's Cross stations. *130 Tottenham Court Rd., W1P 9HP, tel. 01/388–4131. 236 rooms, all with bath. Facilities: bar, lounge, restaurant, laundry, free in-house movies. AE, DC, MC, V.*

Moderate **White Hall.** An imposing entrance promises good things, which the interior more than lives up to. There's an elegant lobby with arched windows, and a garden bar leading onto a patio and not-too-manicured garden. A fine dining room offers both Continental and English breakfast. *2–5 Montague St., WC1B 5BU, tel. 01/580–5871. 80 rooms, 20 with bath. Facilities: bar, restaurant. AE, DC, MC, V.*

Inexpensive **Morgan.** A Georgian terrace hotel, family-run with charm and panache. Rooms are small and functionally furnished, yet friendly and cheerful overall. The tiny paneled breakfast room is straight out of a doll's house. The back rooms overlook the British Museum. *24 Bloomsbury St., WC1B 3QU, tel. 01/636–3735. 17 rooms, 9 with bath. No credit cards.*

★ **Ridgemount.** The kindly owners, Mr. and Mrs. Rees, keep their hotel clean and neat. The public areas, especially the family-style breakfast room, have a friendly, cluttered Victorian feel. Some rooms overlook a leafy garden. *65 Gower St., WC1E 6HJ,* *tel. 01/636–1141. 15 rooms, none with bath. Facilities: lounge. No credit cards.*

Ruskin. Immediately opposite the British Museum, the family-owned Ruskin is both pleasant and quiet—all front windows are double-glazed. Bedrooms are clean, though nondescript; back ones overlook a pretty garden. Note the bucolic mural (c. 1808) in the public sitting room. Well-run and very popular. *23–24 Montague St., WC1B 5BN, tel. 01/636–7388. 35 rooms, 7 with shower. Facilities: lounge. AE, DC, MC, V.*

St. Margaret's. On a tree-lined Georgian street, with an air of elegance just slightly gone to seed. You'll find spacious rooms and towering ceilings, with the added benefit of a wonderful location close to Russell Square. *26 Bedford Pl., WC1B 5JL, tel. 01/636–4277. 64 rooms, 45 with bath. Facilities: 2 lounges. No credit cards.*

Soho and Covent Garden

Very Expensive **Mountbatten.** Thirty years old, and now named after the late Lord Mountbatten, favorite uncle of Prince Charles. The decor gimmick consists of reminders of Mountbatten's life—photos of the estate where he lived, Indian furnishings, silks, inlaid tables, and screens. The bedrooms are moderately opulent, the bathrooms all tiled in fine Italian marble. Sample one of the eight Viceregal cocktails in the bar while listening to the pianist who plays—and sings—for you each evening. A few minutes' walk finds you at the Royal Opera House, or among the market stalls in the Covent Garden Piazza. *Seven Dials, Covent Gdn. WC2H 9HD, tel. 01/836–4300. 127 rooms, all with bath. Facilities: cocktail bar (with pianist), lounge (with harpist), CNN, free in-house videos, restaurant. AE, DC, MC, V.*

★ **The Savoy.** This historic, grand, late-Victorian hotel has long been a byword for old-fashioned luxury. Whistler painted the Thames from his balcony here, and it has always been a favorite address for American filmstars visiting London; some of them take up semi-permanent residence. The best rooms (with antiques, and magnificent cream plasterwork) overlook the river and cost £210; other rooms are in 1920s style, and still have their original bathroom fittings, with showerheads the size of sunflowers. Service is generally excellent, though reports of less-than-perfect treatment of women business travelers have recently hit the national press. The world's first Martini is supposed to have been mixed in the American bar here. *Strand, WC2R 0EU, tel. 01/836–4343. 200 rooms, all with bath. Facilities: hairdressing, florist, theater ticket desk, restaurant, grill room, valeting, free in-house movies, laundry. AE, DC, MC, V.*

Waldorf. An anachronistic hotel, close to the Aldwych theaters and Covent Garden. The public areas are very splendid: chandeliers and marble in the lobby, and fine wood paneling in the bar. Bedrooms are well-appointed and decorated in a variety of styles, though not all recently. Ask for a room away from the noisy street. A turn-of-the-century tea dance in the Palm Court Lounge is a must if you're staying here; even if you don't want to join in yourself, it's still fun to watch the dancers swirl round in their off-the-shoulder gowns. *Aldwych, WC2B 4DD, tel. 01/ 836–2400. 210 rooms, all with bath. Facilities: brasserie, lounge, hairdressing, valeting, restaurant, AE, DC, MC, V.*

Expensive **Pastoria.** The Pastoria is very handily sited, just off Leicester Square, on a quiet street. The building is about 70 years old, though the decor is modern and has recently been refurbished: limed oak bedrooms with light pink walls, navy blue carpets. There's a brasserie-style restaurant to dine in. Alternatively, Soho's Chinese and Italian (as well as just about every nationality under the sun!) restaurants are only a few hundred yards away. *3–6 St. Martin's St., WC2H 7HL, tel. 01/930–8641. 58 rooms, all with bath. Facilities: air-conditioning, restaurant, bar. AE, DC, MC, V.*

Royal Trafalgar Thistle. This one lies right beside the National Gallery, and is handy for the West End in general. It is a modern hotel, occupying the 5th to 7th floors. The decor embraces attractive brass fittings, light wood finishes, blue carpets and curtains. The practical bedrooms have every amenity, including tea- and coffee-making equipment, hair dryers, trouser presses, and color TVs. You can eat at the French-style brasserie, and drink in the hotel pub, which takes its cue from Nelson's navy. *Whitcomb St., Trafalgar Sq., WC2H 7HG, tel. 01/930–4477. 108 rooms, all with bath. Facilities: pub, brasserie, lounge. AE, DC, MC, V. Closed 6 days over Christmas.*

Moderate **Charing Cross.** Right over the railway station, this hotel is pure Victorian, as you can see from the high ceilings and the decor in the lounge and restaurant. Bedrooms have standard decor, but they're large and bright, and were due for refurbishment in late 1988. There's secondary glazing on the noisier Strand side, and rooms on the other side at the time of going to press commanded a good view of the Thames and the South Bank, though a building then under construction may have put a stop to that. A full gymnasium was also going to be installed in 1988. Centrally located and very convenient. *Strand, WC2N 5HX, tel. 01/839–7282. 218 rooms, all with bath. Facilities: coffee shop, lounge, 4 bars, wine bar, restaurant, sauna/sunbed/Jacuzzi in basement. AE, DC, MC, V.*

8 Arts and Nightlife

The Arts

For a list of events in the London arts scene, consult *Time Out*, *What's On*, or *City Limits;* the latter is better for fringe events. The evening papers, the *Standard* in particular, also carry listings, as do the major Sunday papers, the daily *Independent*, *The Guardian*, and the Friday edition of *The Times*.

Theater Most theaters have a matinee twice a week (Wednesday or Thursday and Saturday) and evening performances that begin at 7:30 or 8; performances on Sunday are rare. Prices vary, but you should expect to pay from £5–£6 for a seat in the upper balcony to £18.50 for a good one in the stalls or dress circle (mezzanine). Tickets may be booked at the individual theater box offices, over the phone by credit card (some box offices or agents have special numbers for these marked "cc" in the phone book), or through ticket agents such as **Keith Prowse** (tel. 01/ 741–9999, or look under *Keith* in the phone book for the nearest office). If you're coming from the States and wish to book seats in advance, Keith Prowse has a New York office (234 W. 44th St., Suite 902, New York, NY 10036, tel. 212/398–1430 or 1–800/ 223–4446). Alternatively, the ticket booth in Leicester Square (across from the Swiss Centre) sells half-price tickets on the day of the performance for approximately 45 theaters (subject to availability). Open Monday–Saturday 12–2 for matinees and from 2:30–6:30 for evening performances. There is an 80p service charge. For fringe theater, you can save yourself a trip to the outskirts by buying your tickets from the **Fringe Box Office,** located at the Duke of York's Theatre (St. Martin's Lane, WC2E 7NA, tel. 01/379–6002). Open Monday–Saturday 10–6; 50p service charge. Of course, all the larger hotels offer theater bookings, but as they tack on a hefty service charge, you would do better visiting the box offices yourself. **Warning:** Be *very* careful of scalpers outside theaters; they have been known to charge £200 or more for a sought-after ticket. Not only is the practice one to be discouraged, but you could easily end up with a forged ticket. In recent years, there has been another problem: unscrupulous ticket agents, who sell tickets at four or five times their price from the ticket box offices. While a booking charge is legitimate, this type of scalping certainly isn't.

Theater Box Office Information

Adelphi, Strand, WC2E 7NA, tel. 01/836–7611

Albery, St. Martin's Lane, WC2N 4AH, tel. 01/836–3878

Aldwych, Aldwych, WC2B 4DF, tel. 01/836–6404

Ambassadors, West St., WC2H 9ND, tel. 01/836–1171

Apollo, Shaftesbury Ave., W1V 7HD, tel. 01/437–2663

Apollo Victoria, Wilton Rd., SW1V ILL, tel. 01/828–8665

Astoria, Charing Cross Rd., WC2H 0EN, tel. 01/734–4287

Barbican, Barbican, EC2Y 8DS, tel. 01/638–8891

Comedy, Panton St., SW1Y 4DN, tel. 01/930–2578

Criterion, Piccadilly, W1V 9LB, tel. 01/930–3216

Drury Lane (Theatre Royal), Catherine St., WC2B 5JS, tel. 01/836–8108

Duchess, Catherine St., WC2B 5LA, tel. 01/836–8243

Duke of York's, St. Martin's Lane, WC2N 4BG, tel. 01/836–5122

Fortune, Russell St., WC2 B 5HH, tel. 01/836–2238

Garrick, Charing Cross Rd., WC2H 0HH, tel. 01/379–6107

Globe, Shaftesbury Ave., W1V 8AR, tel. 01/437–3667

Theaters and Concert Halls

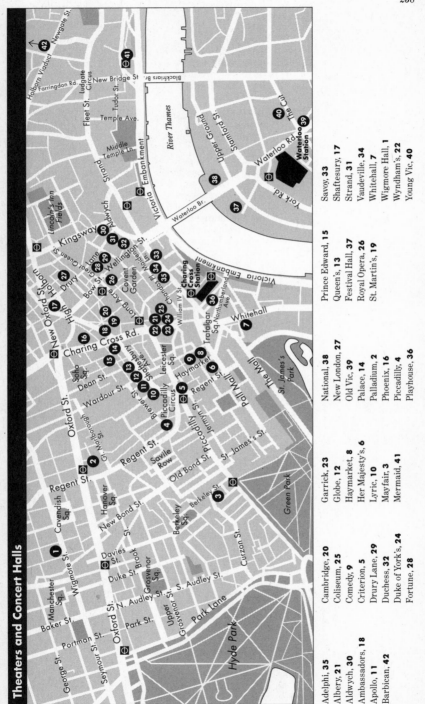

Adelphi, **35**
Albery, **25**
Aldwych, **30**
Ambassadors, **18**
Apollo, **11**
Barbican, **42**

Cambridge, **20**
Coliseum, **25**
Comedy, **9**
Criterion, **5**
Drury Lane, **29**
Duchess, **32**
Duke of York's, **24**
Fortune, **28**

Garrick, **23**
Globe, **12**
Haymarket, **8**
Her Majesty's, **6**
Lyric, **10**
Mayfair, **3**
Mermaid, **41**

National, **38**
New London, **27**
Old Vic, **39**
Palace, **14**
Palladium, **2**
Phoenix, **16**
Piccadilly, **4**
Playhouse, **36**

Prince Edward, **15**
Queen's, **13**
Festival Hall, **37**
Royal Opera, **26**
St. Martin's, **19**

Savoy, **33**
Shaftesury, **17**
Strand, **31**
Vaudeville, **34**
Whitehall, **7**
Wigmore Hall, **1**
Wyndham's, **22**
Young Vic, **40**

Haymarket, Haymarket, SW1Y 4HT, tel. 01/930–9832
Her Majesty's, Haymarket, SW1Y 4QL, tel. 01/839–2244
Lyric, Shaftesbury Ave., W1V 7HA, tel. 01/437–3686
Lyric Hammersmith, King St., W6 0QL, tel. 01/741–3211
Mayfair, Stratton St., W1X 5FD, tel. 01/629–3036
Mermaid, Puddle Dock, EC4 3DB, tel. 01/236–5568
The National Theatre (Cottesloe, Lyttelton, and Olivier),
South Bank Arts Complex, SE1 9PX, tel. 01/928–2252
New London, Drury Lane, WC2B 5PW, tel. 01/405–0072
Old Vic, Waterloo Rd., SE1 8NB, tel. 01/928–7616
Palace, Shaftesbury Ave., W1V 8AY, tel. 01/434–0909
Palladium, 8 Argyll St., W1A 3AB, tel. 01/437–7373
Phoenix, Charing Cross Rd., WC2H 0JP, tel. 01/836–2294
or 01/836–8611
Piccadilly, Denman St., W1V 8DY, tel. 01/437–4506
Playhouse, Embankment Pl., WC2N 6NN, tel. 01/930–4594
Prince Edward, Old Compton St., W1V 6HS, tel.
01/734–8951
Prince of Wales, 31 Coventry St., W1V 8AS, tel.
01/839–5989
Queens, 51 Shaftesbury Ave., W1V 8BA, tel. 01/734–1166
Regent's Park (open air), Inner Circle, Regent's Park, NW1
4NP, tel. 01/486–2431
Royal Court, Sloane Sq., SW1W 8AS, tel. 01/730–1745 *(see
also* Theatre Upstairs)
Royalty, Portugal St., WC2A 2HT, tel. 01/831–0660
St. Martin's, West St., WC2H 9NH, tel. 01/836–1443
Savoy, Strand, WC2R 0ET, tel. 01/836–8888
Shaftesbury, Shaftesbury Ave., WC2H 8DP, tel.
01/379–5399
Strand, Aldwych, WC2B 5LD, tel. 01/836–2660
Theatre Royal, Stratford, E15 1BN, tel. 01/534–0310
Vaudeville, Strand, WC2R 0NH, tel. 01/836–9987
Victoria Palace, Victoria St., SW1E 5EA, tel. 01/834–1317
Westminster, 12 Palace St., SW1E 5JA, tel. 01/834–0283
Whitehall, 14 Whitehall, SW1A 2DY, tel. 01/930–7765
Wyndham's, Charing Cross Rd., WC2H 0DA, tel.
01/836–3028

Fringe Theater Box **Almeida,** Almeida St., N1 1AT, tel. 01/359–4404
Office Information **Arts Theatre,** 6–7 Great Newport St., WC2H 7JB, tel.
01/836–2132
Bush, Shepherds Bush Green, W12 8QD, tel. 01/743–3388
Donmar Warehouse, 41 Earlham St., WC2H 9LD, tel.
01/379–6565
Half Moon, 213 Mile End Rd., E1 4AA, tel. 01/790–4000
Hampstead, Swiss Cottage, NW3 3EX, tel. 01/722–9301
ICA Theatre, The Mall, SW1Y 5AH, tel. 01/930–3647
Kings Head, 115 Upper St., N1 1QN, tel. 01/226–1916
Latchmere, 503 Battersea Park Rd., SW11 3BW, tel.
01/228–2620
Riverside Studios, Crisp Rd., W6 9RL, tel. 01/748–3354
Theatre Upstairs, Royal Court, Sloane Sq., SW1W 8AS, tel.
01/730–2254
Young Vic, 66 The Cut, SE1 8LZ, tel. 01/928–6363

Concerts The ticket prices to symphony-size orchestral concerts are
fortunately still relatively moderate, ranging from £2.50
to £12. Visiting celebrities, however, will command high-

er prices, and you should book well in advance for such performances. If you can't book in advance, then arrive at the hall a half hour before the performance for a chance at returns.

The London Symphony Orchestra is in residence at the **Barbican Arts Centre** although other top orchestras—including the Philharmonia and the Royal Philharmonic—also perform here. The **South Bank Arts Complex,** which includes the **Royal Festival Hall** and the **Queen Elizabeth Hall,** and the small Purcell Room, forms another major venue; the Royal Festival Hall is one of the finest concert halls in Europe. Between the Barbican and South Bank, there are concert performances almost every night of the year. The Barbican also features chamber music concerts, with such celebrated orchestras as the City of London Sinfonia.

For less expensive concert going, as well as taking part in a great British tradition, try the **Royal Albert Hall** during the Promenade Concert season: eight weeks lasting from July to September. Special "promenade" (standing) tickets usually cost half the price of normal tickets and are available at the hall on the night of the concert. Another summer pleasure is the outdoor concert series by the lake at **Kenwood** (Hampstead Heath) or at **Holland Park.** Check the listings or call the **English Heritage Concert Line** (01/734–1877) for details.

You should also look for the lunchtime concerts that take place all over the city in smaller concert halls and churches; they usually cost about £1 (some are free) and often feature string quartets, singers, jazz ensembles, or gospel choirs. **St. John's** and **St. Martin-in-the-Fields** are just two of the more popular locations. Performances usually begin about 1 PM and last an hour.

Concert Hall Box   **Barbican,** Barbican, EC2Y 8DS, tel. 01/628–8795
Office Information **Royal Albert Hall,** Kensington Gore, SW7 2AP, tel. 01/589–8212
St. John's, Smith Sq., SW1P 3HA, tel. 01/222–1061
St. Martin's-in-the-Fields, Trafalgar Sq., WC2N 4JJ, tel. 01/839–1930
South Bank Arts Complex, South Bank, SE1 8XX, tel. 01/928–3191
Wigmore Hall, 36 Wigmore St., W1H 9DF, tel. 01/935–2141

Opera   The main venue for opera in London is the **Royal Opera House** (Covent Garden), which ranks right alongside the New York Met—particularly where expense is concerned. Prices range from £2 in the upper slips (whether the stage is visible is anyone's guess) to £220 for a box in the Grand Tier. Bookings for a particular performance are subject to a period date and may be made at the box office.

English-language opera productions are staged at the **Coliseum** in St. Martin's Lane, home of the English National Opera Company. Prices here are generally lower than at the Royal Opera House, starting around £4, and productions are often a great deal more exciting.

Ballet   The Royal Opera House is also the home of the world famous **Royal Ballet.** Prices are slightly more reasonable for the ballet than they are for the opera, but bookings should be made well in advance, as it tends to be much more popular than opera. The **London Festival Ballet** and visiting international royal companies perform at the Coliseum from time to time. **Sadler's Wells Theatre** hosts various ballet companies—including the Royal and the Rambert—as well as regional ballet and international modern dance troupes. As may be expected, prices here are much cheaper than at Covent Garden.

Opera and Ballet   **Coliseum,** St. Martin's Lane, WC2N 4ES, tel. 01/836–3161
Box Office   **Royal Opera House,** Covent Garden, WC2E 9DD, tel. 01/240–
Information   1066
  Sadler's Wells, Rosebery Ave., EC1R 4TN, tel. 01/278–8916

Film   Despite the video invasion, West End cinemas continue to do good business. Most of the major houses (**Odeon, Cannon,** etc.) congregate in the Leicester Square/Piccadilly Circus area, where tickets average £3:50 to £4—though depending on the film, prices can double. Mondays and matinees are better buys at £2 to £2.50, when there are also fewer crowds. Prices are lower in the suburbs, but, unless you're staying there, any savings could be eaten up by transportation costs.

Cinema clubs screen a wider range of films: classics, Continental, and underground, as well as rare or underestimated masterpieces. Most charge a membership fee of around £1, though sometimes the membership card must be bought a half hour before the screening. Of the clubs, one of the best for value is the **National Film Theatre** (part of the South Bank Arts Complex), which is associated with the British Film Institute. The annual London Film Festival is held here in the fall; there are also lectures and presentations with visiting celebrities. Temporary weekly membership costs around 80p.

The **Institute of Contemporary Arts** (the Mall) often presents films on various aspects of the arts, while relevant films are shown at the **Commonwealth Institute** (Holland Park, W.11). Films are also shown at many of the national museums and galleries.

Nightlife

Jazz   **Bas Clef.** Owned by the delightful Peter Ind (himself a jazz bass player) in the basement of an old warehouse, it offers not only some of the best live jazz in London but the Anglo-French menu would satisfy any gourmand. Although it is difficult to see the stage from the tables, except from closed circuit screens, there is no problem with the acoustics. *35 Coronet St., N1, tel. 01/729 –2440/2476. Admission £3.50–£6 depending on the band. Open Tues.–Sun. noon–3 PM and 7:30 PM–2 AM. AE, DC, MC, V.*
  Dover Street Wine Bar and Restaurant. In a basement just off Piccadilly, this is a place where good jazz and fine food go hand in hand. Since the recruitment of a new chef it has become one of the hottest spots in the West End. *8–9 Dover St., W1, tel. 01/629–9813 or 01/491–7509. Admission: Mon.–Wed. £2–£3; Thurs. £3–£4; Fri.–Sat. £3–£5. Open Mon.–Fri. noon–3 PM (no music); Mon.–Sat. 6:30 PM–3 AM (music from 10 PM). Reservations advised. AE, DC, MC, V.*
  Palookaville. Though named after the American boxer, Joe Palooka, don't be deterred, this is a place for any jazz enthusiast. Whether eating (French and vegetarian menus) or simply

drinking you can sit in comfort and watch the band from your table or from strategically placed video screens. *13A James St., WC2, tel. 01/240–5857. Open noon–3 PM (no music); 5:30 PM–1:30 AM (music from 9 PM). Reservations advised Thurs.– Sat. AE, DC, MC, V.*

Pizza Express. One of London's principal jazz venues, with music every night except Monday in the basement restaurant. The subterranean interior is darkly lit and the menu, predictably, offers a range of traditional and vegetarian pizzas from £3. *10 Dean St., W1, tel. 01/437–9595 or 01/439–8722. Admission £5–£8 depending on band. Open from noon for food; music from 9:30 PM to 1 AM. Reservations advised on weekends. AE, DC, MC, V.*

Pizza on the Park. Situated in the heart of Knightsbridge, this popular pizza house reopened a year ago with the return of modern and traditional jazz played in the downstairs restaurant. Clean, fast service with a menu that includes the inevitable selection of pizzas, from £3. *11–13 Knightsbridge, SW1, tel. 01/235–5550. Admission £3–£8 depending on the band. Open daily; jazz Tues–Sat. 8 PM–1 AM. Reservations advised. AE, DC, MC, V.*

Ronnie Scott's. The legendary Soho jazz club which, since its opening in the early 60s, has attracted such names as George Melly, Courtney Pine, and a host of American players. With a successful blend of good food, live music, and subtle lighting, it still lives up to its reputation as the best jazz club in London. *47 Frith St., W1, tel. 01/439–0747. Admission £8–£10. Open Mon. –Sat. 8:30 PM–3 AM. Reservations advised.* AE, DC, MC, V.

Weekly music gigs in London are listed in full in either *Time Out* or *City Limits*, both available from most newstands.

Nightclubs **Barbarella Restaurant.** No membership is needed and no admission fee is charged at either address, but it is expected that you will eat. The service is friendly and cheerful and the dimly lit interior gives it a romantic air. Italian cuisine—à la carte— from about £15 a head. This is one of the few places in London where you can eat and talk in comfort without feeling jostled. Suitable for all ages. *428 Fulham Rd., SW6, tel. 01/385–9434 and **Barbarella 2 Restaurant,** 43 Thurloe St., SW7, tel. 01/584– 2000/8383. Open Mon.–Sat. 7:30 PM–3 AM (last orders 1 AM). Dress: smart. Reservations advised on weekends. AE, DC, MC, V.*

Legends. Revamped and reopened under ownership of Kate Richards two years ago, with an impressive high-tech interior designed by Eva Jiricna, this modern restaurant is particularly good at lunchtime. There's a large choice of cocktails served in the upstairs bar. Downstairs is a large, cool dance floor with a central bar. *29–30 Old Burlington St., W1, tel. 01/437–9933. Admission: Mon.–Thurs. £6 after 10 PM; Fri.–Sat. £8 after 10 PM. Open Mon.–Thurs. 5:30 PM–2 AM; Fri. 5:30 PM–3 AM; Sat. 9 PM–3 AM. Dress: stylish. AE, DC, MC, V.*

Stringfellows. Peter Stringfellow's first London nightclub opened nine years ago and is celebrity packed. Art deco motifs decorate the upstairs restaurant, with prices from £30. Mirrored walls and a heady light show set the tempo on the downstairs dance floor. *16–19 Upper St. Martin's La., WC2, tel. 01/240–5534. Admission: Mon.–Thurs. £6; Fri. £10; Sat. £12.50. Open Mon.–Sat. 8 PM–3:30 AM. Dress: high fashion/ smart. AE, DC, MC, V.*

Disco **Café de Paris.** Wednesday nights at the Café de Paris have made it one of London's hottest *boîtes de nuit*, attracting the likes of Mickey Rourke, Emily Lloyd, and Jasper Conran. Run by photographer Sterling, with Albert from Le Balajo in Paris, who flies across the Channel every Wednesday. Dinner is served on the balcony overlooking the dance floor, where you can people-watch in comfort. Alternatively, for those who would prefer to avoid the crush on Wednesday, there is a disco/dance for the more mellow on Friday and Saturday. *3 Coventry St., W1, tel. 01/437–2036. Admission £6 Wed., £4–£5 Fri., £5– £6 Sat. Open Wed. 10:30 PM–3 AM, Fri.–Sat. 7:30 PM–3 AM. Dress: stylish casual.*

Camden Palace. The jeunesse crowd is attracted by the famous theme nights, the fast-food-style restaurant and the renowned cocktail bar where you can order anything from Between The Sheets to a Slow Comfortable Screw. The large central disco features never-ending laser and light shows. *1A Camden Rd., NW1, tel. 01/387–0428. Admission: £1–£5. Open Tues.–Sat. 9 PM–3 AM. Dress: smart casual.*

Hippodrome. A huge neon figure of a horseman marks the entrance to Peter Stringfellow's newest and most lavish nightspot. The black-and-silver futuristic decor is complemented by the best light show in London, complete with laser beams and swirling mists. There are six bars and a balcony restaurant. *Hippodrome Corner, WC2, tel. 01/437–4311. Admission £6; or six-week membership (Black Card) £50 which allows member plus one guest free entrance. Open Mon.–Sat. 9 PM–3:30 AM. Dress: smart casual/stylish. AE, DC, MC, V.*

Le Palais. Originally known as the Hammersmith Palais, this club reopened, after extensive refurbishment, in 1986. The centerpiece of the modern high-tech interior is the large central disco. Italian food is served in balcony restaurants overlooking the dance floor. Five bars. *242 Shepherds Bush Rd., Hammersmith, W6, tel. 01/748–2812. Admission: Wed. £1–£3, Thurs.–Sat. £5–£6. Open Wed. 9 PM–2 AM, Thurs.–Sat. 9 PM–3 AM. Dress: smart casual.*

Xenon. The vast basement disco is home to three top international acts every night (dance, juggling, mime, magic). The modern black-and-silver interior with heady light show attracts a young, fashionable crowd. Upstairs piano bar (with live music) serves light snacks. *196 Piccadilly, W1, tel. 01/734–9344. Admission Mon.–Thurs. £5; Fri.–Sat. £8. Open Mon.–Sat. 9:30 PM–3:30 AM. Dress: smart casual. AE, DC, MC, V.*

Casinos The 1968 Gaming Act states that any person wishing to gamble *must* make a declaration of intent to gamble at the gaming house in question and *must* apply for membership in person. Membership usually takes about two days. In many cases, clubs prefer for the applicant's membership to be proposed by an existing member. Personal guests of existing members are, however, allowed to participate.

Charlie Chester Casino. The drawing cards here are an international restaurant and a modern casino with blackjack, roulette, and Punto Banco. *12 Archer St., W1, tel. 01/734–0255. Membership £5 for life. Open daily 2 PM–4 AM. Dress: jacket and tie.*

Crockford's. This is a civilized club, established 150 years ago, with none of the usual scrabble for tables that mars many of the flashier clubs. Attracts large international clientele since its move from St. James's to Mayfair. Offers American roulette,

Punto Banco, blackjack. *30 Curzon St., W1, tel. 01/493–7771. Membership £150 a year. Open daily 2 PM–4 AM. Dress: jacket and tie.*

The Golden Nugget. This large casino just off Piccadilly has blackjack, roulette, and Punto Banco. *22 Shaftesbury Ave., W1, tel. 01/439–0099. Yearly membership £1.15. Open daily 2 PM–4 AM. Dress: jacket (tie optional).*

Palm Beach Casino. Situated in what used to be the old ballroom of the Mayfair Hotel, this is a fast moving and exciting club attracting a large international membership. Smart red-and-gold interior with plush restaurant and bar. Club has American roulette, blackjack, Punto Banco. *30 Berkeley St., W1, tel. 01/493–6585. Membership £10. Open daily 2 PM–4 AM. Dress: jacket and tie.*

Sportsman Club. One of the only gaming houses in London to have a dice table as well as Punto Banco, American roulette, blackjack. *3 Tottenham Court Rd., W1, tel. 01/637–5464. Membership £3.45. Open daily 2 PM–4 AM. Dress: jacket and tie.*

Rock **100 Club.** Originally renowned as a place for traditional jazz (still played on Wednesday and Saturday) it has in more recent years produced some of the best rock gigs in London. Fast food available on Wednesday, Friday, and Saturday. *100 Oxford St., W1, tel. 01/636–0933. Admission £3–£5 depending on band. Open Mon.–Thurs. 7:30 PM–midnight, Fri.–Sat. 7:30 PM–1 AM, Sun. 7:30 PM–11 PM.*

The Rock Garden. Famous for the setting and for encouraging young talent to move on to bigger and better things. Talking Heads, U2, and The Smiths are just a few who made their singing debuts here. Music is in the basement where there is standing room only so it is advisable to eat first in the comfort of the American restaurant upstairs. There is also an advantage in eating first in that it earns you a reduction in admission to the music. *6–7 The Piazza, Covent Gdn., WC2, tel. 01/ 240–3961. Admission £4–£6 depending on band. Open Mon.–Sat. 7:30 PM–3 AM; Sun. 7:30 PM–12:30 AM. AE, DC, MC, V.*

Weekly events are listed in *Time Out* and *City Limits* or in one of the rock magazines such as *New Musical Express, Melody Maker,* or *Sounds* available every Thursday.

Cabaret **Bunjies.** Situated in a small, white-walled cellar just around the corner from the theater showing *The Mousetrap* is London's smallest (no more than 50 people) and liveliest cabaret venue. Busy, bustling atmosphere. Vegetarian food served in the restaurant, which is open every day. BYOB. *27 Litchfield St., WC2, tel. 01/240–1796. Admission £3. Open Mon.–Thurs. 9 PM –11 PM. Dress: casual.*

Comedy Store. From this small, crowded basement in Leicester Square comes probably the best comedy in London. Their famous improvised show called "Comedy To Go" takes place on Sundays. No advance booking and no admittance to anyone under 18. Each show lasts two hours. Buffet-type food (kebabs, moussaka, chili) is served from the counter. *28A Leicester Sq., WC2, tel. 01/839–6665. Admission £5; £6 midnight on Sat. Open Fri.–Sat. 7 PM–11 PM, Sun. 8:30 PM. Dress: casual.*

Singles **The Limelight.** Home away from home for most Americans. Owned by New York Limelighter, Peter Gatien, and situated in an old church. Lots of one-nighter shows and special events. One of London's most popular nightspots. *136 Shaftesbury Ave., WC2, tel. 01/434–1761. Admission: Mon.–Thurs. £5, Fri. £7, Sat. £10. Open Mon.–Sat. 9:30 PM–3 AM. Dress: casual.*

9 Excursions from London

Introduction

Here are five ideas for day visits to some of Britain's major sights outside London. Even the most patriotic Londoner will admit—eventually—that, however absorbing the capital is to get to know in detail, life does go on outside. Indeed, regional Britain has its own definite characteristics and values, often sharply contrasted with those of London.

All the places listed in this chapter can be reached in a relatively short journey from London, usually either by train or by coach. Note, however, that Stratford has no direct train connections with London, and the journey involves at least one change. It would be wise to check all train and coach times before the day of travel; weekend timetables vary, and journey times are often longer on weekends.

Bath

Getting There **By train** from Paddington station to Bath Spa: journey time 1 hour 20 minutes: trains about once an hour. **By National Express coach** from Victoria Coach Station: journey time 3 hours: coaches about every 3 hours.

Tourist Information **Bath Tourist Information Centre** is in the Abbey Churchyard, tel. 0225/62831.

Bath is a perfect 18th-century city—perhaps the most perfect in all Britain. It is a compact place, easy to explore on foot: The museums, elegant shops, and terraces of magnificent town houses are all close to each other. Far from being merely a museum piece, Bath today is a lively and vibrant area, with unrivaled galleries and eating places, and a thriving cultural life.

It was the Romans who first took the waters at Bath, building a temple in honor of their goddess Minerva and a sophisticated series of baths to make full use of the curative hot springs. To this day these gush from the earth at a constant temperature of 46.5°C. In the **Roman Baths Museum**, underneath the 18th-century Pump Room, you can see the excavated remains of almost the entire baths complex. *Abbey Churchyard. Admission £2.50 adults, £1.25 children. Combined ticket with Museum of Costume £3 adults, £1.50 children. Open daily 10–5.*

Next to the Pump Room is the **Abbey,** built in the 15th century. There are superb fan-vaulted ceilings in the nave.

In the 18th century, Bath became the fashionable center for taking the waters. The architect John Wood (1704–54) created a harmonious city from the mellow local stone, building elegantly executed terraces, crescents, and villas. The heart of Georgian Bath is the perfectly proportioned **Circus** and the **Royal Crescent.** On the corner, **Number 1 Royal Crescent** is furnished as it might have been when Beau Nash, the master of ceremonies and arbiter of 18th-century Bath society, lived in Bath. *Royal Crescent. Admission £1.50 adults, 80p children and senior citizens. Open Mar.–Oct. Tues.–Sat. 10–5, Sun. 2–5.*

Also near the Circus are the **Assembly Rooms,** frequently mentioned by Jane Austen in her novels of early 19th-century life.

This classical villa now houses a **Museum of Costume,** where some of the fashions of Bath's heyday are featured. *Bennett St. Admission £1.50 adults, 95p children. Combined ticket with Roman Baths Museum £3 adults, £1.50 children. Open daily 10–5.*

The city's main shopping areas are in Stall Street and Union Street: Explore the numerous narrow alleyways and passages leading off, all full of fascinating shops. Take one of these—say, Northumberland Passage—and head toward **Pulteney Bridge,** an 18th-century bridge over the river Avon lined with little shops. Then walk along Upper Borough Walls to the **Theatre Royal,** one of the finest surviving Georgian theaters in England.

Time Out Bath has a good selection of coffee and lunch spots. Try the **Pump Room** (Abbey Churchyard) for morning coffee or afternoon tea in elegant surroundings, perhaps listening to the music of a string quartet. Or, in nearby North Parade Passage, try **Sally Lunns,** where the famous Sally Lunn bun is still baked. **The Theatre Vaults** in Sawclose is a good place for a pre- or post-theater drink or meal.

Cambridge

Getting There **By train** from Liverpool Street station; journey time 1 hour; trains hourly. **By National Express coach** from Victoria Coach Station; journey time 1 hour 50 minutes; coaches hourly.

Tourist Information **Cambridge Tourist Information Centre** is in Wheeler Street, an extension of Benet Street, off King's Parade, tel. 0223/322640.

Cambridge is one of the most beautiful cities in Britain, and the celebrated Cambridge University sits right at its heart. Students have been coming to Cambridge since the end of the 13th century, and even in a short visit you will see fine buildings from virtually every generation since then, often designed by the most distinguished architects of their day. The city center is lively and compact—one of the special pleasures of Cambridge is that in just a few yards one can pass from the bustle of the shopping streets to the cloistered seclusion of one of the colleges.

As at Oxford, the University is based on colleges, each of which is an autonomous institution with its own distinct character and traditions. Students join an individual college and receive their tuition from the dons attached to it, who are known as "fellows." Each college is built around a series of "courts," or quadrangles. As students and fellows live in these courts, access is often restricted (especially during examination weeks in early summer). Visitors are not normally allowed into college buildings other than chapels and halls (dining rooms).

King's College is possibly the best known of all the colleges. Its chapel is a masterpiece of late Gothic architecture (1446), with a great fan-vaulted roof supported only by a tracery of soaring side columns. Behind the altar hangs Rubens' painting of the *Adoration of the Magi.* Every Christmas Eve the college choir sings the Festival of Nine Lessons and Carols, which is broadcast all over the world.

Behind King's are the famous "Backs," the gardens that run down to the River Cam onto which many of the colleges back.

From King's, make your way along the river and through the narrow lanes past **Clare College** and **Trinity Hall** to **Trinity,** the largest college, straddling the river. It has a handsome 17th-century great Court and a library by Christopher Wren. The massive gatehouse houses "Great Tom," a large clock that strikes each hour with high and low notes. Prince Charles was an undergraduate here in the late 1960s. Beyond Trinity lies **St. John's,** the second largest college.

Going in the other direction along the Backs from King's, you come to **Queen's College,** where Isaac Newton's **Mathematical Bridge** crosses the river. This arched wooden structure was originally held together by gravitational force; when they took it apart to see how Newton did it, they could not reconstruct it without using nails. In from the river, on Trumpington Street, stands **Pembroke College,** with some 14th-century buildings and a chapel by Wren, and **Peterhouse,** the oldest college. Beyond this is the **Fitzwilliam Museum,** which contains outstanding collections of art (including paintings by Constable) and antiquities (especially from ancient Egypt). *Trumpington St., tel. 0223/332–9090. Admission free. Open Tues.–Sat., bank holidays 10–5, Sun. 2:15–5.*

If you've time, hire a punt at **Silver Street Bridge** or at **Mill Lane.** You can go along the Backs past St. John's or upstream to **Grantchester,** the pretty village made famous by the poet Rupert Brooke. On a sunny day, there's no better way of absorbing Cambridge's unique atmosphere—somehow you will seem to have all the time in the world.

Time Out There is a coffee shop in the **Fitzwilliam Museum;** it's an excellent place for a pastry or a light lunch, as is **Henry's** in Pembroke Street. **The Pickerel** on Bridge Street, beyond St. John's, is a pleasant pub with a small garden.

Oxford

Getting There **By train** from Paddington station; journey time 1 hour; trains run hourly. **By coach** from Victoria Coach Station (several companies operate services); journey time 1 hour 40 minutes; coaches at least once an hour.

Tourist Information **Oxford Information Centre** is in St. Aldate's, opposite the Town Hall, tel. 0865/726871.

Oxford is a place for strollers. The surest way of absorbing its unique blend of history and scholarliness is to wander around the tiny alleyways that link the honey-colored stone buildings topped by "dreaming" spires, exploring the colleges where the undergraduates live and work. Like Cambridge, Oxford University is not a single building but a collection of 35 independent colleges; most are open to visitors, including many magnificent chapels and dining halls, though the times, displayed at the entrance lodges, vary. **Magdalen College** is one of the most impressive, with 500-year-old cloisters and lawns leading down to the river Cherwell. **St. Edmund Hall** has one of the smallest and most picturesque quadrangles, with an old well in the center. **Christ Church** is the largest, known as Tom Quad; portraits of former pupils hang in the medieval dining hall, including John Wesley, William Penn, and no less than 14 prime ministers. The doors between the inner and outer quadrangles of **Balliol College** still bear the scorch marks from the flames that burnt Archbishop Cranmer and Bishops Latimer and Ridley at the stake in 1555 for their Protestant beliefs.

The **Oxford Story** is a brand-new multimedia presentation of the university's 800-year history, in which visitors travel through depictions of college life. *Broad St., tel. 0865/728822. Admission £3 adults, £1.50 children. Open Apr.–Oct. 9–7, Nov.–Mar. 9–5:30.*

Two other places not to be missed are the **Sheldonian Theatre** and the **Ashmolean.** The Sheldonian was Christopher Wren's first building, which he designed like a semi-circular Roman amphitheater; graduation ceremonies are held here. The Ashmolean, Britain's oldest public museum, holds priceless collections of Egyptian, Greek and Roman artifacts, Michelangelo drawings, and European silverware. *Sheldonian Theatre, Broad St., tel. 0865/241023. Small admission charge. Open Mon.–Sat. 10–12:45, 2–4:45; closes at 3:45 Dec.–Feb. Ashmolean, Beaumont St., tel. 0865/27800. Admission free. Open Tues.–Sat. 10–4, Sun. 2–4.*

For a relaxing walk, make for the banks of the Cherwell, either through the University Parks area or through Magdalen College to Addison's Walk, and watch the undergraduates idly punting a summer's afternoon away. Or hire a punt yourself—but be prepared, it's more difficult than it looks!

Time Out The **Queen's Lane Coffee House** on High Street prepares inexpensive snacks and is popular with undergraduates. The **Eagle and Child** pub is an historic pub in St. Giles; a group of writers called the Inklings, including C.S. Lewis and J.R.R. Tolkien, used to meet here after World War II.

Stratford-upon-Avon

Getting There The **train service** is poor, and involves at least one change, at Leamington Spa. There is one semi-fast train each morning; journey time 2 hours 20 minutes. **By National Express coach** from Victoria Coach Station; journey time 2 hours 20 minutes; coaches about every 2 hours.

Tourist Information **Stratford Tourist Information Centre** is in Judith Shakespeare's House, on the corner of High and Bridge streets, tel. 0789/293127 or 0789/67522.

It goes without saying that Stratford is a must for Shakespeare enthusiasts. But even without its most famous son, the town would be worth visiting. Its timbered buildings show how prosperous it was in the 16th century, when it was a thriving craft and trading center. There are also attractive 18th-century buildings.

There are four main Shakespearean places of interest. The **Shakespeare Centre** and **Shakespeare's Birthplace** in Henley Street contain the costumes used in the BBC's dramatization of the plays and an exhibition of his life and work. **Anne Hathaway's Cottage** is the early home of the playwright's wife, in Shottery, on the edge of town; and in **Holy Trinity Church** Shakespeare, his wife, and several of their family are buried. *Shakespeare's Birthplace, Henry St., tel. 0789/204016. Admission £1.80 adults, 70p children. Open Apr.–Sept. Mon.–Sat. 9–6, Sun. 10–6; Oct., Mon.–Sat. 9–5, Sun. 10–5; Nov.–Mar.*

Mon.–Sat. 9–4:30, Sun. 1:30–4:30. Anne Hathaway's Cottage, Shottery, tel. 0789/292100. Opening times and admission charges same as Shakespeare's Birthplace.

Two very different attractions reveal something of the times in which Shakespeare lived. **World of Shakespeare** is a lavish spectacle using modern multimedia techniques to describe Queen Elizabeth's royal progress from London to Kenilworth Castle in 1575. A complete contrast is **Hall's Croft**, a fine Tudor town house that was the home of Shakespeare's daughter Susanna and her doctor husband. It has contemporary furniture and the doctor's dispensary and consulting room can also be seen. *World of Shakespeare, 13 Waterside, tel. 0789/69190. Admission £2.50 adults, £2 children and senior citizens. Open daily 9:30–5:30. Hall's Croft, Old Town, tel. 0789/292107. Admission £1.40 adults, 50p children.*

The Royal Shakespeare Theatre occupies a perfect position on the banks of the Avon. Try to take in a performance if you can. The company (always referred to as the R.S.C.) gives five Shakespeare plays each season, between March and January. The R.S.C. has two other theaters in Stratford, the **Swan,** where plays by contemporaries of Shakespeare are staged, and **The Other Place,** where lesser-known Shakespeare plays are given in repertory with new studio plays and fringe productions. It's best to book well in advance, but "day of performance" tickets are always available, and it is also worth asking if there are any returns. Programs are available in February from the *Royal Shakespeare Theatre, Stratford-upon-Avon, Warwickshire CV37 6BB, tel. 0789/205301.*

Time Out | **Mistress Quickly** in Henley Street serves light refreshments and meals throughout the day; an unusual feature is the jigsaw tree sculpture. **The Black Swan**—better known locally as the Dirty Duck—is a riverside pub serving good ales and bar meals. The **Theatre Cafeteria** is open all day, and provides a good snack immediately after a performance. The **Vintner Wine Bar** on Sheep Street serves large portions of excellent hot dishes, washed down by a selection of wines.

Windsor

Getting There | **By train** either from Waterloo direct to Windsor and Eton Riverside or from Paddington to Windsor Central, changing at Slough. Journey time 30 to 40 minutes from Paddington, 45 minutes from Waterloo; 2 trains per hour on each route. **By Green Line bus** from Eccleston Bridge, behind Victoria train station, *not* from Victoria Coach Station. Make sure you catch the fast direct service which takes 50 minutes and runs half-hourly; the stopping services take up to 1 hour 25 minutes.

Tourist Information | The **Windsor Tourist Information Centre** is in Central Station, tel. 0753/852010.

Windsor has been a royal citadel since the days of William the Conqueror, who built a timber stockade on a mound overlooking the river Thames soon after his victory in 1066. In the 1100s and 1200s Henry II and III added stone towers, but it was Edward III in the 1300s who transformed the old castle, building the Norman gateway, the great round tower, and new apartments. Thereafter the castle gradually grew in complexity and grandeur, as subsequent monarchs added new buildings or improved existing ones according to their tastes and their finances. Charles II restored the State Apartments in the 1600s, and in the 1820s George IV, that most extravagant of kings with a mania for building, converted what was still essentially a medieval castle into the royal palace the visitor sees today.

Windsor remains a favorite spot of the Royal Family. The Queen and Prince Philip spend most weekends here, often joined by family and friends. The State Apartments are also used from time to time to entertain visiting heads of state. The entire castle is closed when the Queen is in residence, but a large part—though not of course the Royal Family's private apartments—is open the rest of the time.

These are some of the highlights of the Castle: **St. George's Chapel,** over 230 feet long with two tiers of great windows and hundreds of gargoyles, buttresses, and pinnacles, is one of the noblest buildings in England. Inside, above the choir stalls, hang the banners, swords, and helmets of the Knights of the Order of the Garter, the most senior Order of Chivalry. The many monarchs buried in the Chapel include Henry VIII and George VI, father of the present queen. The **State Apartments** indicate the magnificence of the Queen's art collection; here hang paintings by Rubens, Van Dyck, and Holbein; drawings by Da Vinci; and Gobelin tapestries, among many other treasures. There are magnificent views across to Windsor Great Park, the remains of a former royal hunting forest. Make time to view **Queen Mary's Dolls' House,** a charming residence with every detail complete, including electricity, running water, and miniature books on the library shelves. *Windsor Castle, tel. 0753/868286. Precincts open daily 10–4:15 (till 7:15 mid-May–Aug.). St. George's Chapel. Admission £1.50 adults, 60p children under 16 and senior citizens. Open Mon.–Sat. 10:45–3:45, Sun. 2–3:45. State Apartments. Admission £1.80 adults, 80p children under 16 and senior citizens. Open Mon.–Sat. 10:30–5 (till 3, Nov.–Apr.), Sun. 1:30–5. Queen Mary's Dolls' House. Admission 80p adults, 40p children under 16 and senior citizens. Open daily 10:30–5 (Oct.–Mar. until 3).*

After seeing the castle, stroll around the town enjoying the antiques shops. Opposite the castle, the **Royalty and Empire** exhibition in part of the Central Station recreates in waxworks the arrival at the station of Queen Victoria to celebrate her Diamond Jubilee in 1897; the scene is incredibly lifelike. *Thames St., tel. 0753/857837. Admission £2.85 adults, £2 children under 16, £2.30 senior citizens. Open daily 9:30– 5:30 (till 4:30 Nov.–Mar.).*

A short walk over the river brings you to **Eton,** Windsor's equally historic neighbor, and home of the famous public school. (In Britain, so-called "public" schools are private and charge fees.) Classes still take place in the distinctive red-brick Tudor-style buildings; the oldest buildings are grouped around a quadrangle called School Yard. The **Museum of Eton Life** has displays on the school's history, and a guided tour is also available. *Brewhouse Yard, tel. 0753/863593. Admission £1.80 adults, £1.20 children under 16. Open daily during term 2–5, 10:30–5 on school holidays. Guided tours daily at 2:15 and 3:15; charge £2.40 adults, £1.80 children under 16, including admission to museum.*

Index

Personal Itinerary

Departure *Date*

Time

Transportation

Arrival *Date*   *Time*

Departure *Date*   *Time*

Transportation

Accommodations

Arrival *Date*   *Time*

Departure *Date*   *Time*

Transportation

Accommodations

Arrival *Date*   *Time*

Departure *Date*   *Time*

Transportation

Accommodations

Personal Itinerary

Arrival *Date*   *Time*

Departure *Date*   *Time*

Transportation

Accommodations

Arrival *Date*   *Time*

Departure *Date*   *Time*

Transportation

Accommodations

Arrival *Date*   *Time*

Departure *Date*   *Time*

Transportation

Accommodations

Arrival *Date*   *Time*

Departure *Date*   *Time*

Transportation

Accommodations

Addresses

Name	*Name*
Address	*Address*
Telephone	*Telephone*
Name	*Name*
Address	*Address*
Telephone	*Telephone*
Name	*Name*
Address	*Address*
Telephone	*Telephone*
Name	*Name*
Address	*Address*
Telephone	*Telephone*
Name	*Name*
Address	*Address*
Telephone	*Telephone*
Name	*Name*
Address	*Address*
Telephone	*Telephone*
Name	*Name*
Address	*Address*
Telephone	*Telephone*
Name	*Name*
Address	*Address*
Telephone	*Telephone*

Fodor's Travel Guides

U.S. Guides

Alaska
American Cities
The American South
Arizona
Atlantic City & the
  New Jersey Shore
Boston
California
Cape Cod
Carolinas & the
  Georgia Coast
Chesapeake
Chicago
Colorado
Dallas & Fort Worth
Disney World & the
  Orlando Area

The Far West
Florida
Greater Miami,
  Fort Lauderdale,
  Palm Beach
Hawaii
Hawaii *(Great Travel
  Values)*
Houston & Galveston
I-10: California to
  Florida
I-55: Chicago to New
  Orleans
I-75: Michigan to
  Florida
I-80: San Francisco to
  New York

I-95: Maine to Miami
Las Vegas
Los Angeles, Orange
  County, Palm Springs
Maui
New England
New Mexico
New Orleans
New Orleans *(Pocket
  Guide)*
New York City
New York City *(Pocket
  Guide)*
New York State
Pacific North Coast
Philadelphia
Puerto Rico *(Fun in)*

Rockies
San Diego
San Francisco
San Francisco *(Pocket
  Guide)*
Texas
United States of
  America
Virgin Islands
  (U.S. & British)
Virginia
Waikiki
Washington, DC
Williamsburg,
  Jamestown &
  Yorktown

Foreign Guides

Acapulco
Amsterdam
Australia, New Zealand
  & the South Pacific
Austria
The Bahamas
The Bahamas *(Pocket
  Guide)*
Barbados *(Fun in)*
Beijing, Guangzhou &
  Shanghai
Belgium & Luxembourg
Bermuda
Brazil
Britain *(Great Travel
  Values)*
Canada
Canada *(Great Travel
  Values)*
Canada's Maritime
  Provinces
Cancún, Cozumel,
  Mérida, The
  Yucatán
Caribbean
Caribbean *(Great
  Travel Values)*

Central America
Copenhagen,
  Stockholm, Oslo,
  Helsinki, Reykjavik
Eastern Europe
Egypt
Europe
Europe *(Budget)*
Florence & Venice
France
France *(Great Travel
  Values)*
Germany
Germany *(Great Travel
  Values)*
Great Britain
Greece
Holland
Hong Kong & Macau
Hungary
India
Ireland
Israel
Italy
Italy *(Great Travel
  Values)*
Jamaica *(Fun in)*

Japan
Japan *(Great Travel
  Values)*
Jordan & the Holy Land
Kenya
Korea
Lisbon
Loire Valley
London
London *(Pocket Guide)*
London *(Great Travel
  Values)*
Madrid
Mexico
Mexico *(Great Travel
  Values)*
Mexico City & Acapulco
Mexico's Baja & Puerto
  Vallarta, Mazatlán,
  Manzanillo, Copper
  Canyon
Montreal
Munich
New Zealand
North Africa
Paris
Paris *(Pocket Guide)*

People's Republic of
  China
Portugal
Province of Quebec
Rio de Janeiro
The Riviera *(Fun on)*
Rome
St. Martin/St. Maarten
Scandinavia
Scotland
Singapore
South America
South Pacific
Southeast Asia
Soviet Union
Spain
Spain *(Great Travel
  Values)*
Sweden
Switzerland
Sydney
Tokyo
Toronto
Turkey
Vienna
Yugoslavia

Special-Interest Guides

Bed & Breakfast
  Guide: North America
1936...On the
  Continent

Royalty Watching
Selected Hotels of
  Europe

Selected Resorts
  and Hotels of the U.S.
Ski Resorts of North
  America

Views to Dine by
  around the World